STAR.SHIPS

Gordon White

STAR.SHIPS

A PREHISTORY OF THE SPIRITS

BIBLIOTHÈQUE ROUGE
MMXVI

Star.Ships: A Prehistory of the Spirits was published by Scarlet Imprint in 2016.
Copyright © Gordon White. Typography and cover designs by Alkistis Dimech.
Text set in Magma Pro, with titling in Anacharsis. Cover image: 'Rocky Shore And Sea
Against Sky At Night' by Rahmat Ahmadi / EyeEm. With thanks to Paul Holman for
copy editing. The standard hardback and paperback editions were printed and bound
by Gomer Press. The fine edition was bound by Ludlow Bookbinders.

ISBN 978-0-9931200-9-1

WWW.SCARLETIMPRINT.COM

CONTENTS

ILLUSTRATIONS

fig. 1   *The author's grandfather, John White, and HRH Prince Philip, Duke of Edinburgh, on Manus Island, New Guinea, during the 1956 Royal Visit*

THE MISSION AT THE END OF THE WORLD

The Sepik is the greatest river no one has ever heard of. Winding like a cosmic serpent down from the New Guinea highlands, it has the fifth largest annual flow on the planet. Lacking a delta for her mouth, she stains the ocean brown for miles. Such is her volume, it is said that the local boatmen can draw fresh water straight from the sea. People have been living and dying on her banks for more than 40,000 years. She has welcomed and bid depart to whole cultures. She is untroubled by Ice Ages. My aunt was born on the banks of the Sepik and my grandfather once ran the province so named for it.

It is a place of curious survivals, of forgotten things. Up in the highlands, claims of seeing living examples of *Homo floresiensis* – the famous 'Indonesian hobbit' believed to have died out ten millennia ago – persist into modern times. The day my aunt was born, four Japanese soldiers, who had been hiding among the natives of Dutch New Guinea for the ten years since the war, arrived in the province capital of Wewak. They boarded a ship, the *Taisei Maru*, which had come to collect the remains of the war dead and return them to Japan. My grandmother covered the story for the Australian Broadcasting Corporation and then went into labour that night.

Stories are perhaps the most curious of survivals. They can fall in and out of remembrance. Who is telling them often matters more than *how* they are stored. For probably tens of millennia it was the shamans and sorcerers who kept the stories of the tribes, who held the mirror of identity and meaning up to their people. Like so much in the West, this function has been outsourced from us with predictably disastrous local consequences. In the mid-twentieth century, academia became aware that our understanding of knowledge is always situational and always contingent on cultural institutions that create that knowledge. But by then it was too late. Our stories had passed from us. This was too much power to hand over. It was a bad deal.

Any given field makes 'truth statements' that form a network of relationships with themselves, governed by a worldview that establishes what is or is not knowledge within that field. Stories that fall outside this network first become untrue, and then they fade completely from reality. In the early years of the twenty first century, the empowered, informed shaman is presented with the opportunity to rescue these fading stories from the spirit world and restore them to the tribe. As with all journeys to the spirit world, dangers abound for the unprepared. Discretion, parsimony and evidence-based reasoning, now that they exist in the wider culture, belong here as much as they do in the hard sciences. These are the fetishes we must carry to extract truthful stories from the spirits.

Although not my own, one more Sepik story is illustrative of the prey we seek and the nature of its habitat. In his classic *Eden in the East*, Dr Oppenheimer, while on medical patrol in the early 1980s, was treating an American woman who was living, along with her husband, among a tribe that had only been 'first discovered' the previous year. These Americans were missionaries of a new kind. Instead of teaching English to the tribe so that they may read the Bible, the Americans were there to learn the local language so that they could return to the Midwest and have an indigenous Bible printed. It occurred to Dr Oppenheimer that once these missionaries had left, the tribe would be filled with foreign stories and legends – of Moses and the flight from Egypt, of Noah, of Jesus – with no archaeological or genetic evidence indicating how these tales arrived in the first place. They would just be there, a memory of an imprint. Israelites standing uncomfortably under a banana tree spirit, warily eyeing the ancestral death masks, like confused foreign guests at a wedding reception. The Sepik keeps these ghosts, and many similar, older ones besides.

Stories, then, can move in a way pottery or malarial adaptations cannot. All archaeological evidence of contact is accompanied by cultural evidence, but not all cultural evidence of contact is accompanied by archaeological evidence. Stories can echo and refract through and beside the scientific story of mankind. They are special artefacts that cry out for a unique method of analysis. They are challenging prey to hunt.

After a childhood of wide-ranging Pacific travel, it was studying documentary film-making and cross-cultural studies that first opened up whole new vistas of comparative mythology for me. While still a student, I bought a very expensive camera to take SCUBA diving for sunken cities in Micronesia. This adventure is my own personal BC/AD pivot point. Nothing would be quite the same afterward.

Built from millions of tonnes of prismatic basalt and stretching over eleven square miles of mangrove swamp, the necropolis of Nan Madol is the most enigmatic site in the entire Pacific. One of the great joys of my life was canoeing along its canals, exploring its tombs and platforms, and diving in the murky, shark-infested water beside it, looking for evidence of earlier occupation.

The place is so completely out of context with everything else around it for hundreds of miles that Nan Madol feels like it should be a truly archaic survival, a relic of a long-vanished race. It isn't. Almost the only thing we know with any confidence about Nan Madol is when construction began on the current site, around the twelfth century. There are older buildings in London!

How Nan Madol was built, why it was built, where the millions of tonnes of basalt came from, the reason for choosing its location ... these are examples of advanced cultural technology that have moved through time without corresponding archaeological evidence. *When* it was built is almost the least significant part of its story. The irreconcilability of Nan Madol's mythology and its physical presence has stayed with me since that expedition.

Such an extreme disconnect between the physical and non-physical evidence is familiar territory for magicians. In the performance of it, magic feels supremely ancient. Even its most modern iterations feel like they were old when the world was new. Intellectually we know this is not the case, but we also know somehow that it probably is.

FURTHER RIVER SPIRITS

This book was not written on the banks of the Sepik, though she does feature in its tale. It was written on the banks of the Thames, the Tiber, the Hudson and the Seine, but the story is always the same because river spirits are always the same: How long have we been here? Who came before? Where did they go? Who or what answered their night prayers, and at what cost? Civilisation is the tobacco of river spirits. They seem to crave it, to will it into being up and down their banks, even though the relationship appears damaging over the long term.

As to why it is a creature as ahistorical as a chaos magician finds himself chasing down geneticists, historians and astronomers, pursuing Very Old Things, the compulsion is, inevitably, best explained with a story about stories:

In a story told about Aristotle in Europe, and about an Indian philosopher in India, the philosopher meets a village carpenter who has a beautiful old knife and asks him, 'How long have you had this knife?' The carpenter answers, 'Oh, the knife has been in our family for generations. We have changed the handle a few times and the blade a few times, but it is the same knife.'

The secret of the knife may well be the secret to magic's supremely ancient 'mouth feel.' There is a recursion of motifs, of consciousness experiences, of lived realities that hides western magic's true antiquity.

To examine stories is always perilous. Similarity is self-evident on the first pass, absent on the second, and both on the final pass. As Patrick Harpur points out, we cannot 'explain' or 'decode' a myth. To look for the historic or scientific 'truth' of a myth is but to retell the myth, albeit in a less satisfying way. We render unto materialism the control of our most precious mythologies if we allow them to be 'scientifically explained' to us. A new language is required. New words.

Wendy Doniger, one of America's most celebrated Indologists and cultural theorists, famously gave a lecture in the 1990s called 'Microscopes and Telescopes,' in which she defended the use of comparison in mythology from the scorched earth assault of late postmodernism. Myths can be examined through a metaphoric microscope, which reveal the thousands of glittering, unique manifestations of a particular story in a particular culture, or they can be examined through a telescope, where the personalities, codes of dress and foodstuffs fade from view, to be replaced by a wider vision of unifying themes across humanity.

One optic device does not invalidate the other, both have their place in analysis and both of them carry the same, often-unacknowledged interpretive risk; the eye itself.

We are always in danger of drawing our own eye, for we depict our own vision of the world when we think we are depicting the world; often when we think we are studying an other we are really studying ourselves through the narrative of the other. Our choice of lens level is arbitrary, but not entirely so, for it is circumscribed by certain boundaries that we ignore to our peril. The choice is heuristic: we choose a specific level in order to make possible a specific task. Where we focus depends on the sorts of continuities we are looking for; in all instances, something is lost and something is gained.

In the study of history or mythology, the twin technologies of the microscope and the telescope are available to all but it is only rarely that the eye belongs to anyone outside our materialist monoculture, rarer still that it belongs to the magician. That needs to change.

Giordano Bruno, my unofficial patron saint, wrestled with these familiar imbalances between lived personal experience and available physical evidence in this very town. Precisely what Bruno was doing in Oxford in 1583 is a matter of endless academic discussion. But it clear he was preaching and debating his own hermetic infinitism. Having stepped beyond Ficino's Catholic veneer and returned to a fully pagan hermetic system, he believed his use of Egyptian symbols, talimans and visualisation had uncovered humanity's 'source religion' and our clearest insight into the nature of reality. What he found in the Hermetica was a fervent belief in mankind's stellar origins and immortal destiny among innumerable worlds. The knife Bruno held in his hand was Graeco-Egyptian, but he knew it was older than that.

Published the following year, Bruno's *The Expulsion of the Triumphant Beast* demonstrates that familiar, ancient aroma the practice of magic gives off: Hermetic magic feels old, and the oldest thing he knew was Ancient Egypt, so it must have originated there.

A similar logical error is the politest way of explaining, four centuries later, Kenneth Grant's largely-unsuccessful attempts to shoehorn all of Thelema and the Cthulhu Mythos into Sumeria. He was also looking to match the feeling to the data. By the mid-twentieth century, Sumeria was the oldest 'civilised' culture we knew of.

Today it is not.

Non-Random Mythologies

Today, not only have the origins of civilisation changed beyond all recognition, but even the very word has begun to dissolve under a less Eurocentric analysis. Developments in geology, genetics, astronomy, archaeology and linguistics strain to breaking the underlying premises and assumptions of scientific materialism.

The western esoteric tradition has the opportunity to (finally) do away with the High Victorian assumptions that constitute our understanding of the origins of magical culture and rebuild atop some much better data. The picture that emerges in doing so is stunning in its implications.

This is not history. This is not archaeology. This is not folklore. This is a new skill.

But it is also an old one. It is not the skill of organising data points into a sequential historical narrative. It is the skill of context. Of *recontextualising* the Western magical tradition as it has arrived in our hands here in the twenty first century, rather than seeking to replace it wholesale with each new development, as if it were last year's smartphone. The magicians of the Renaissance or the Natural Philosophers of Charles II's Britain gathered observations and findings from the cutting edge research of their day to build a coherent view of their Art and their world. Just as they were, we must be polyhistors.

Returning once again to the upper reaches of the Sepik and the mission at the end of the world, we come to the key that unlocks this entire book and possibly even the secrets of the stars. Listen closely.

When seeking to explain the similarities between different cosmologies spread right across the globe, a materialist – ignoring the inherent hypocrisy in his or her position – will attribute this to similarities in the human mind or brain. Brains are the same everywhere, so beliefs are the same everywhere. We are somehow 'wired' to worship the sun or associate Venus with love. It's part of how 'primitive' humans make sense of the world.

If that were true – and it might be true in some cases – then the distribution of these similar beliefs, by definition, must be random, just as variations in eyesight or spatial awareness skills are randomly distributed. You would be surprised just how few beliefs are randomly or universally distributed.

If a belief is non-randomly distributed across cultures then some other mechanism of action is in play. Colonial expeditions, wars, trading partnerships, the collective unconscious. We may not be able to detect these mechanisms, just as you would not be able to detect traces of the American missionaries once they had left, but their presence nevertheless non-randomly distributed a Midwestern Christian narrative.

What happens then, when we look at the distribution of some of the core beliefs of the western esoteric tradition? Adopting the consensus that what we broadly know of today as magic coalesced into its recognisable form in the first and second centuries in Alexandria and the Eastern Mediterranean, what happens when we use that as our end point and look at the distribution of its foundational principles backwards in time, calibrating them in the light of recent historical and scientific data?

We find a very old story, newly re-emerged. A story that says something very profound about mankind and our companion spirits.

A new scientific discovery does not triumph by convincing its opponents and making them see the light, but rather because its opponents eventually die, and a new generation grows up that is familiar with it.
Max Planck, *Scientific Autobiography and Other Papers*

I ONE FUNERAL AT A TIME

Scientific enquiry's cherished claims of impartial, objective truth have certainly seen better days. After more than two decades helming the august *New England Journal of Medicine*, outgoing editor-in-chief, Dr Marcia Angell, said in the January 2009 *New York Review of Books* that 'it is simply no longer possible to believe much of the clinical research that is published.' Science is now so riddled with corporate self-interest and falsified experiment data that *Nature* reported that retractions have increased tenfold in the last decade, the tip of the iceberg. The replicability of even the simplest of experimental results is at an all-time low and getting lower. Casting aside the enormous ontological implications of this we are nevertheless told, as we have been for more than a century, that the edges of the map are being filled in.

Corporeal power has always been the ice-cold hand inside science's latex glove, waiting for you at the airport customs desk. It has never been the objective, absolutely true descriptor of reality that science journalists and other people with severely limited understandings of science claim it to be. Like all metanarratives of power, it is an unreliable narrator of incomplete utility.

In an act curiously resonant of initiation into the Classical mystery traditions, it is in acknowledging science's inherent unreliability, its limitations, that we restore its true utility. This is nowhere more necessary than in history and the story of mankind.

DANGEROUS ROADS

The historical is supremely political, supremely personal. There is a reason the stories of a culture are always kept with its priests. To tell someone where they are from is to tell someone who they are. A slave, a weaker gender, a god-king's subject, a sinner, too brown-skinned to understand property ownership.

Whilst the casual observer may conclude the battle for historical authenticity is a post-imperial one, this is not wholly true. It was an imperial battle when Europe's empires spanned the globe, but only because that is how Power was organised in the era of mercantile expansion. Today, historical narratives – justification narratives – emerge from more modern sources of power. It is the same story, told by different storytellers. History may well be written by the victors, but victors change and if we do not unwrite history then the propaganda from the previous regime still stands.

Despite the weight of evidence supporting an origin for rice cultivation in Taiwan and Island Southeast Asia before its subsequent onshoring onto the mainland, there is fierce resistance to these *observable facts* inside China. It is politically and racially repugnant that such an important innovation emerged first among those funny-faced island savages. And so it is largely ignored.

Israel's well-funded archaeological programme expands in lock-step with the growth of her illegal settlements, providing subtextual legitimacy for the Likud party's aim of restoring her biblical borders. Take a closer look behind the confident archaeological headlines, however, and you often find evidence ranging from the tenuous to the spurious.

The subcontinent provides the most tragically complete examples of the inextricability of power and history. In seeking to restore Dravidian and early Tamil culture to its true scope and antiquity, it has become a lightning rod for separatist politicians. Partition had the effect of placing most of the important Harappan and Indus sites inside a new country with a cultural and political regime that exhibits considerable hostility to non-Muslim historical narratives, meaning both academic access to and even basic upkeep of probably the most important sites of early urbanisation on the planet have been woefully neglected.

As for India herself, we have the 'here again, gone again' story of the Aryan invasion. Based on the complete misidentification of a few skeletons in the upper layers of Mohenjo Daro and a European refusal to believe that a people so brown could have given the world the Rig Veda, a fictitious invasion of lighter-skinned, charioteering 'Aryans' around 1500 BCE was declared the source of Vedic culture. In the twentieth century, they were described as a hardy race who, like all good primitives, deified natural phenomena and called upon their aid in battles; the Vedas were their battle hymns. Because the 'Aryan invasion' theory is not only racist but completely wrong, it has been quietly abandoned by the majority of scholars. However, this has left Indologists with what we might call the Jenga Paradox: the foundational bricks of the theory have been removed, but no one wants to admit such actions bring down the entire tower. It is how we can end up with straight-faced analyses such as this one, from Ariel Glucklich, theology professor at Georgetown, writing in *The Strides of Vishnu* as late as 2008:

> The subjects of the Indo-Aryan controversy were energetic and rambunctious people who probably arrived gradually from central and western Asia. They have been called Aryans (from *arya*, 'hospitable one'), but this should not be taken as an ethnic term. 'Indo-Aryan' is the somewhat more precise linguistic category that most scholars today prefer to use. As noted, the majority of scholars today, largely on the basis of linguistic evidence (for example, the absence of South Asian linguistic characteristics such as retroflection west of India), do support the migration hypothesis. The arrival of the Indo-Aryans probably took several centuries and was mostly peaceful, and evidence indicates that a genuine cultural exchange took place as they encountered indigenous populations, including the late phases of the Harappa culture. Few archaeological remains attest to the material culture of the mobile population or to the events of those centuries ... Virtually everything we know about these extraordinary people derives from their prolific literary output – primarily the Rig Veda.

To recap, there are no historical remains for this large-scale migration and the only evidence to support it comes from the documents created by this evidence-free culture. You can see the circular logic. Further problematising the lack of archaeological evidence is the growing genetic evidence of internal cultural continuity between the Harappan and later cultures, and the singular lack of genetic evidence for a large-scale migration of a people from who-knows-where between 1750 BCE and 850 BCE.

As for any attempts to trace stories into or out of India (or anywhere else, for that matter), the Platonic form of nationalism is always there. Returning to Dr Doniger:

Tale-tracking has political implications. Tellers tend to regard their own culture as the source and other cultures as the borrowers and to deny that they themselves have borrowed from other cultures, for reasons of status and hierarchy: to be upstream, to be the giver rather than the receiver, is to be superior. (Recall the old Soviet claims that Russians invented the telephone, etc.) Outside the culture, British (and German) scholars may well have been inspired to trace stories back to India (and China: the colonies), in part as an outgrowth of the nineteenth-century craze for origins (the source of the Nile, the source of Language [itself an old search, as in Herodotus's experiment with the infant who said 'bread' in Phrygian]) but also as a way of feminizing these cultures, as David Henry Hwang reminded us in M. Butterfly: 'The East is feminine – weak, delicate, poor... but good at art and full of inscrutable wisdom – the feminine mystique.' They tell good stories, but they need us to run their country. This was also a way of privileging the past of India over its present, as Sanskrit and the ancient Vedas were valued over vernacular languages and contemporary, 'idolatrous,' Hinduism: the thinking becomes, they used to tell great stories, but they need us now to run their country.

The Indus question will be explored in considerable detail in later chapters. For now, it is important to be aware that into the post-imperial academic power vacuum created by the end of the Aryan Invasion Theory have poured great volumes of Indian nationalist sentiment, unbalancing the quest for historical authenticity in the opposite direction. And so we must navigate between 'the Vedas originated within the same cultural groups that gave us Harappa and the Indus cities' (probably more right than wrong) and 'India invented and exported everything' (definitely more wrong than right).

These are dangerous roads, then. Dangerous as the people who travel them professionally.

THE BUDDHAS' REVENGE

Following the Taliban's appalling destruction of the Bamiyan Buddha statues in 2001, the editors of the prominent archaeology journal Antiquity did something very rare in academic publishing. They called out other forms of archaeological iconoclasm. They drew attention to a disordered house. They named names. They pointed fingers.

The editorial begins by shaming the non-publication of fieldwork results – at the time more than 80% of Italian fieldwork remained unpublished and much of the two decades of findings from the American team at Abydos still remain unpublished.

Regarding the latter, I have my suspicions as to why, which we will come to in a later chapter.

It also highlights a refusal to allow other researchers access to sites or archived material, for fear that others will publish first. Mycenaean tomb excavation reports that sat unpublished for fifty years prevented half a century of additional research that could have been undertaken. And when other researchers are actually allowed access, supervisors often usurp the ideas of their junior team member. Then there is the 'ferocious and bullying reactions to the slightest criticism, aimed especially at intimidating young colleagues.'

The final and most alarming finger-pointing goes to an even more serious problem. Outright fraud. There is the case of the Italian superintendent who took Mycenaean pottery sherds out of a museum store, then re-buried them in Tuscany so he could dig them back up again. Or the deputy director of the Tohoku Palaeolithic Institute in Japan, Shinichi Fujimura, who was videotaped burying artefacts to 'discover' again. At the time, Fujimura had the nickname, 'God's Hands,' for his amazing ability to unearth rare and significant artefacts. He admitted to placing 61 of the 65 pieces he had discovered, as well as all 29 of the pieces he had discovered the previous year. God's hands, indeed.

In the late nineties, Dr Anton Misfud reported that a cave painting of a bison bull on the wall of Malta's Hypogeum was 'removed at the express directive of the director of museums.' The bison bull is, of course, an ice age inhabitant of Malta and its presence on the walls of the Hypogeum pushes its date of construction back from the Neolithic into the Palaeolithic. As would the cave paintings discovered *under* some fifteen thousand year old stalagmites in Ghar Hasan on Malta's south coast. These were also mysteriously destroyed and the cave was covered with a locked, metal gate 'to protect a colony of bats.'

Malta has some of the Mediterranean's most astounding examples of early human culture and, as a result, has more than a century of highly dubious academic behaviour; misrepresenting chemical dating, swapping out older remains for younger ones and so on. In 1910, Sir Temi Zammit excavated the partial remains of more than 6000 people in the Hypogeum. By 1971, J. D. Evans, future Director of the Institute of Archaeology, lamented the loss of all but eleven skulls from the excavation. When Graham Hancock visited in 2001, there were only six left.

When Michael Cremo visited Ukraine's Dnepropetrovsk Historical Museum, the head of the archaeology collection, Dr Larisa Churilova, showed him artefacts that indicated an early Stone Age belief in reincarnation. Her reason for not publishing her findings was that the editors of journals are uncomfortable with cultural interpretations. They just want to print things like 'a stone flake two centimetres long was found at a depth of one metre in the excavation.'

If only it were so that editors found discomfort in cultural interpretations! The true source of discomfort arises from interpretations that step out of academia's specific cultural lens. After Michael Cremo, as part of an NBC documentary, was refused access to anomalous artefacts found in California gold mines and held at UC Berkeley, department archaeologist Jere H. Lipps attempted to stop the programme from being broadcast. Allison R. Palmer of the Institute for Cambrian Studies petitioned the Federal Communications Commission to fine NBC over the documentary.

Over the last century, a new power narrative has emerged that warps archaeological data into a specific shape the way a magnet affects iron filings. It is the unspoken belief that humanity is on a journey from *worse* to *better*, from primitive to complex, uncivilised to civilised. Our civilisation of perpetual war, total surveillance, obesity, runaway mental illness, overmedication, environmental degradation, widespread unemployment and scientific materialism has nothing to learn from the past because it is better. Enjoy that smartphone made by suicidal Taiwanese slave labour. Continue shopping.

Ancient history has become the wartime propaganda for Darwinian scientism. Data that contradict Power's latest belief system are suppressed, destroyed, attacked or ignored.

Even if contemporary historians pay lip service to the notion that this is no longer always the case, in most instances this means they are simply unaware of their own scientism. Any attempts to consider our Palaeolithic ancestors as more advanced than previously thought still carries the patronising tone of a complete stranger complimenting the artwork of a handicapped child. 'Look at how clever our inferiors were,' we say, as we die, fat and unhappy, waving our iPhones around for signal.

The magnet is still in effect, at least in terms of popular discourse. Nobody has rearranged the iron filings into a more accurate map.

ARTIFICIAL HORIZONS

You may not know it, but your understanding of ancient history probably owes almost everything to one man, V. Gordon Childe. He is the man who, in the mid-twentieth century, gave us the three distinct phases of preindustrial society we all carry around in our heads. These are savagery, then barbarism, then civilisation.

Entirely artificial horizons were drawn based on what Childe considered to be the hallmarks of advancement from one stage to the next and then every single culture that is or ever was got dropped into them. V. Gordon Childe gave us the magnet.

Savages have very unpleasant and dangerous lives, foraging and killing exclusively wild foods. Today we use the more polite term, hunter-gatherer, but the subtextual unpleasantness – the sense that these are lesser cultures leading largely miserable lives – remains.

Savages progressed to the higher state of barbarism during a period Childe named the Neolithic Revolution. Barbarians domesticate animals and begin agriculture. This surplus of food allows for barbarian cultures to become more complex and diversify. Priests emerge; villages are created; megalithic sites are constructed; people own things. As for civilisation? That only happens with the birth of the city. Because it can get difficult to demarcate when a large town becomes a city, it is best if urbanisation occurs in conjunction with writing. Without writing, a culture is probably 'high barbarian' at best. Sorry Incas.

It is because of Childe that we unthinkingly consider the Sumerians to be the first civilisation on earth, with Egypt and the Indus cultures getting the joint silver medal. At the time of the publication of Childe's seminal 'The Urban Revolution' in 1950, Sumeria was the oldest known culture to have both cities and writing.

These, then, are our artificial horizons. Fall outside them and you are in danger of being erased at the 'express directive of the director of museums.' Anthropology professor Michael E. Smith writes in 2009 that scholars today rarely cite Childe anymore, or even acknowledge his influence on their models. 'Nevertheless, the archaeological study of ancient complex societies is still dominated by the themes of urbanism, agricultural intensification and surplus, craft specialisation, social inequality, and the nature of power and state, each of which was first applied to archaeological data in a systematic fashion by V. Gordon Childe.'

The secondary impact of Childe's artificial horizons is more noticeable to magicians than it is to fraudulent Japanese archaeologists, and is just as dangerous as the primary one. Childe's was the first 'explanation' of progress that allowed cultural expression to be described in *exclusively material terms*. Stone circles were not constructed because of ecstatic communion with the gods, temples were not physical expressions of a profound devotional mythology. No. The inner motivations for outward cultural expression became entirely irrelevant, entirely redundant. Grain was stored, women were pregnant … time to build a temple.

In the 1960s, functional explanations for urban development were popular. This held that as cultures became larger and more complex, leaders altruistically stepped forward to take on the task of organisation for the good of the group. It may be no surprise to see this mirrors the postwar expansion of the state and its building programmes; mass immunisation, free education, infrastructure investment and so on. By the 1980s, a more 'political' interpretation reigned. Here it was the whims of the self-serving elite which triggered the building projects of early states. Again, we can see Childe's functional explanation refracted through the worldview of the time: Margaret Thatcher and Gordon Gekko as rulers of trickle-down urbanisation. More recently, explanations rely on 'human-environmental' interactions, which is why you cannot move for graduating theses that suggest 'ancient climate change' was responsible for absolutely any cultural development or change that shows up anywhere in the archaeological record.

It is this ideological underpinning that Michael E. Smith is alluding to when he writes about V. Gordon Childe's invisible impact on anthropology. We now consider it 'scientific' or 'professional' to describe cultural artefacts – non-physical objects – in exclusively materialist terms. Only a functional analysis of the mythological process is allowed, which is like describing your grandmother's famous chicken soup solely by its molecular constituency.

According to Curtis White, Professor Emeritus of English at Illinois State, leaving these assumptions unexamined is dangerous. In the Spring 2014 issue of *Tricycle: The Buddhist Review*, Linda Heuman wrote in her article, 'The Science Delusion':

> In White's view, once scientism rewrites our story so that the things human beings care about – like love, wonder, presence, or play – are reduced to atoms, genes, or neurons, human lives become easy prey to corporate and political interests. We become 'mere functions within systems.' White wants us to wake up and recognize that this view is not scientific discovery, it is ideology. Mistaking one for the other has profound consequences, 'not just for knowledge but even more importantly for how we live.'

Cultural evolutionism suggests that man moves up to naturally higher stages of development. Some societies could thus be considered superior to others based on technological complexity. From an historical research perspective, it also means that the further back you go in time, then by definition, the *less* complex human culture becomes. Otherwise something was awry with Darwin's theories. Anthropology's timeline became fixed, unidirectional. Reducing the story of humanity to mechanics, the story of a human to brain reactions, is not science. It is ideology, the wolf dressed as the sheep.

Whilst it always had a home on the mental landscape of the magician, the notion that progress and civilisation are not the same thing has wider appeal today than at any time in the recent past. It is our sacred duty to lean forward into this change, to ensure it has every chance of success. Without resorting to hoary tropes of the noble savage, it is self-evident to today's magicians that our distant ancestors also recognised that true depth of meaning in a human life goes beyond the physical, beyond the material effects that can be carbon dated. The Lascaux cave paintings are the tiniest tip of the largest iceberg, the scant physical extension of a non-physical realm so huge it dwarfs the sun. A materialist researcher can but stand before Lascaux's open cosmic doorway and announce 'we have no way of knowing what is behind it.' Speak for yourself, mate.

Subsequent to the invention of Childe's artificial horizons, it emerged that the development of grain-based agriculture was an unmitigated disaster for human health and longevity. What Childe saw as an evolution is a *devolution*. Measuring the march of civilisation from this point, we see a succession of politico-economic systems that purported to improve human existence – culminating in today's modern, materialist age – that have most often had the complete opposite effect. Rather than getting ever closer, we have moved further away from genuine sources of meaning and purpose.

Instead of measuring a civilisation by its density of sprockets, what happens when we consider civilisation to be a collection of values, thoughts, mythologies? What happens when we count up the non-physical sprockets? The human journey ceases to look like a collection of trailers before the beginning of *The Internet: The Movie* and starts to wobble. We have been more civilised, we have been less civilised. Humanity looks like a toddler learning to walk, sometimes taking steps, sometimes falling down.

'HOLY LAND' SYNDROME

Discoverer of Göbekli Tepe and its chief excavator, Dr Klaus Schmidt, famously warned against what he called 'Holy Land Syndrome,' which is the propensity for archaeologists to head out into the field with a spade in one hand and a Bible in the other. Holy Land Syndrome precludes the finding of something you didn't already expect to find.

This is a problem stretching back centuries. Archaeology, emerging out of antiquarianism, itself emerging out of Grand Tour dilettantism, unfortunately predates geology and genetics. The belief that the stories told in the Bible are in some or any sense accurate forms the baseline mythology of the field. In the words of Robert Anton Wilson, 'what the thinker thinks, the prover proves.'

Our understanding of how global cultures formed and are expressed has yet to be rebalanced. We have the implicit assumption that all major technologies have their origin in the Fertile Crescent, which was the first and only place we looked for them.

Even now, any suggestion that the observed cultural technology we associate with civilisation emerged anywhere outside this area is automatically on the back foot.

The twenty first century offers us a new Holy Land Syndrome. There is still the spade in one hand, but the Bible has been replaced with a very selective reading of *On the Origin of Species*. Science does not consider itself an ideology, as it claims to only deal with what is real. This is, of course, what every ideology thinks of itself. The complete hijacking of all non-physical criteria of being human in favour of the unfounded belief that we are meat robots, lacking in free will, has enormous implications for what it is the archaeologist actually finds. As she thinks, so she proves.

Right across the academic spectrum, the growth of STEM subjects (Science Technology Engineering Mathematics) has the unfortunate impact of closing down all ways of understanding or approaching truth that cannot be ultimately reduced to scientism's belief that only the material exists.

When it comes to the history of non-physical subjects like mythology and belief, this is putting the inmates in charge of the asylum. As Dr Naydler writes, 'in advocating that we explain religious phenomena in the nonreligious terms of the social sciences or linguistic anthropology, what is specifically religious is lost to view.' Attempting to view the mythic 'objectively' instantly destroys the subject one wishes to understand in the first place. However, attempting to view a mythic subject non-objectively in the academic arena is a recipe for career suicide. And so the academic treatment of the spiritual component of human life reduces the subject entirely to social and cultural conditions. Most academics end up where Mircea Eliade said they would:

> If these consequences are not always evident, it is because the majority of historians of religion defend themselves against the messages with which their documents are filled. This caution is understandable. One does not live with impunity in intimacy with 'foreign' religious forms, which are sometimes extravagant and often terrible. But many historians end up by no longer taking seriously the spiritual worlds they study; they fall back on their personal religious faith, or they take refuge in a materialism or behaviorism impervious to every spiritual shock. Besides, excessive specialization allows a greater number of historians of religion to station themselves for the rest of their days in the sectors they have learned to frequent since their youth. And every 'specialization' ends by making the religious forms banal; in the last instance it effaces their meaning.

Alexandre Afonso, a political economy lecturer at King's College London, points out that academia is almost identical to how drug cartels are economically organised;

with an expanding mass of outsiders and a shrinking core of insiders. Junior academics are prepared to forgo decent wages, job security and quality of life for the decreasingly likely chance of ending up in one of the few remaining tenured, top jobs.

With university budgets under pressure and the huge growth in PhDs, the economics of academia compounds a lot of the problems already inherent in its faintly ludicrous medieval structure. The man or woman at the top gets to have all the ideas, and your growth through the ranks is largely dependent on his opinion of you, which makes challenging his ideas increasingly risky. The result is a narrowing of perspectives down to as few as possible and the flight to research areas that have little risk of upending the prevailing paradigm. Consider this view from Eleanor Parker, a junior Oxford academic in Anglo-Saxon, and writer of the excellent blog, *A Clerk of Oxford*.

[A]cademia is not always a happy place to work. I'm a very junior academic, and to people in my position a career in academia offers a daunting future: a life of short-term contracts and little security, with very limited ability to plan ahead. You can probably imagine the psychological effects of this, and the impact it can have on one's confidence and sense of self-worth … Most of my friends are also early career academics, in a similar position, and when I look at them I see talented young people consumed with anxiety and fear about the future, constantly doubting their value as scholars, and consequently as human beings. [..]

The precarious nature of academic jobs is an endemic problem, perhaps not something individuals can do much about, but academics often don't help this pervading mood of anxiety by just not being very nice to each other … Part of the fear of failure is feeling almost desperately dependent on the goodwill of more powerful people, without any control over the fate of your own work; reviewers and academic publishers, for instance, have a huge amount of power over my future, and I have no influence on them whatsoever. I have to get my work published if I ever want to get another job, so they're free to treat me however they want and I have to do as they ask, lest they decide to say 'actually, we won't publish this after all.' That's a frightening situation to be in.

This is how you end up with a field that buries artefacts pilfered from its own museums, or destroys ones that don't fit inside an exclusively materialist understanding of a facet of the human experience that can only be understood non-materially. This is how you get conservative incrementalism instead of bold publishing break-throughs, as the junior academics wonder where their next meal will come from. There is no history without historiography.

STORIES WRITTEN IN BLOOD AND STONE

How are we to proceed if we do not wish to leave the story of us in such frequently slippery hands? This comes back to recognising the limitations of what scientific enquiry does and does not offer. Science values open-minded research but more often than not fails to get out of its own shadow and see the validity in alternate ways of thinking about the world.

Science locates its authority in its privileged access to 'the way things are.' However, because it can occasionally generate repeatable data, it has assumed that its interpretations are equally Real, that everything comes out of the kitchen perfect and all carrots are always roasted and only served on Tuesdays. Further mutations of this error include the presumption that facts can be ignored if they fall outside the boundaries created through self-appointed expertise, as we have seen throughout this chapter. Particularly in historical research, interpretation has been elevated above hard facts in defining what does and does not exist. The medieval church egregore that birthed academia and still gives it its shape is never more visible than in these moments.

So we begin at this very point of failure; recognising the difference between facts and their interpretation. Unto the archaeologists and chemists do we render the generation of radio-carbon data. Unto no one do we render the interpretation of them, especially when it comes to subjects their reality maps do not permit to exist. In no way is this to suggest that we reject all but our own interpretation, it is indeed to suggest the opposite. We reject *all* monopolies of interpretation and invite a chorus of informed analysis.

The journey thus begins with an examination of the data themselves, data that are generated in systems that suffer the least from interpretive ideology. These are the ingredients that show up at the kitchen's back door, not just the ones that appear on scientism's à la carte lunch menu. You are now on a strict diet of fresh facts only.

Because there is a fundamental disconnect between the generation of facts and the generation of interpretations, these two concepts move at different speeds, regularly falling out of alignment with each other. A recalibration of interpretation on top of the latest accumulation of facts becomes episodically necessary.

These recalibrations have occurred numerous times in the history of western historical research, and are presumably a function of a healthy ideological ecosystem. One of the most effective methods of clearing the biblical Creationists out of the early days of the Academy was to invent and unilaterally declare a belief in gradualism. There could be no Flood because geological change happens very slowly, there could be no six days of Creation because evolution happens very slowly. In the medium term, this was probably a necessary move. However, it set geology back decades because it turns out geological and climatic changes often do happen quickly and there have certainly been repeated worldwide floods of biblical proportion. The biological sciences are sadly still struggling to get out from underneath gradualist beliefs to a large extent, but their success in doing so requires bringing down Darwin's entire house of cards, so it is still a way off in the distance.

A second recalibration happened with the rise of postmodernism. Accompanying Childe's belief in the march of civilisation was the academic notion of diffusionism; the suggestion that technologies and sophisticated concepts occur in one 'better' culture and spread to 'lesser' ones. The Aryan Invasion Theory is a prime example of diffusionism. It carries with it some very unseemly, racial suggestions of the superiority of some groups over others and contributed to the European habit of stacking cultures into a hierarchy based on alarming and pointless criteria such as cranial fluid capacity and eyelid shape.

Like a mother separating her arguing children, postmodernism declared that everyone invented everything independently. Again, this was probably a necessary step on the way to de-racialising cultural analysis but it turns out there were a lot of babies in that bathwater. The limitations of this approach were almost immediately apparent but, by then, much of the damage was done.

The damage is typified in the problem of infinite regress. Fixating on individual contexts becomes smaller and smaller: one cannot make comparisons between cultures, one then cannot make comparisons between different locations within the culture, one then cannot make comparisons between different age groups within these locations, one cannot compare old women and young women, and so on. The result is to deny any shared basis between members of the same culture, to say nothing of humanity at large. Secondly, the atomisation of shared cultural experience led to the rise of a scientific materialist view of what might be shared between humans: you cannot make comparisons between Chinese and Malaysians, but 'rational thought' is universal. For once, the hijack was accidental, but no less dangerous for being so.

As Doniger says, 'comparison defamiliarizes what we take for granted.' Assumed universals such as rational thought or the experiences of gay men are quickly relativised. Indeed, any attempts to avoid comparison in cultural analysis fall into the logic trap of comparing the observer's culture to the one under examination. This is how one accidentally paints one's own eye instead of the subject under the microscope.

Besides, with the rise of globalisation and digital technology we can see first hand that ideas and technology certainly do spread between cultures in all directions, even ones with the same eyelid shape.

Indeed, the overall quest of this book is to fulfil the Sepik Revelation. To show that stories and non-physical technology do indeed move between cultures and down through time. Perhaps a lot of time. To accomplish this while giving the widest possible berth to the skeletons hidden in diffusionism's closet requires more data and less interpretation. Hard data. It is very difficult for a silt layer or an erosion pattern to be racist. Base pair deletions on your DNA are not especially bothered with how good a Muslim you really are. And the stars? Well, the stars do not stop turning for anyone.

The incorporation of scientific data into metaphysical worldviews is a trackway not unknown to magic. Consider the words of Alan Moore in his essay, 'Fossil Angels':

> This role, that of an all-inclusive 'natural philosophy,' obtained throughout the rise of classical civilization and could still be seen, albeit in more furtive fashion, as late as the 16th century, when the occult and mundane sciences were not yet so distinguishable as they are today. It would be surprising, for example, if John Dee did not allow his knowledge of astrology to colour his invaluable contributions to the art of navigation, or vice-versa. Not until the Age of Reason gradually prevented our belief in and thus contact with the gods that had sustained our predecessors did our fledgling sense of rationality identify the supernatural as a mere vestigial organ in the human corpus, obsolete and possibly diseased, best excised quickly.

There is even more recent precedent worth considering. Whatever else you think of the Golden Dawn, Theosophy, the Society for Psychical Research and its individual adherents, these groups formed during an imperial knowledge explosion. They each reaccumulated the data of the observable facts and launched their interpretations from them. It is easy to forget that the first translations, the first appearances of foreign or ancient knowledge in western esoteric discourse, happened due to the diligence of individual occultists. Sometimes it is even easier to forget that these underlying facts require episodic updating, and we have not been very good at it, beyond a half-hearted nod at an interpretation of quantum physics that is itself seventy years old.

It is the very definition of the Western esoteric tradition to search for the wider philosophical implications of the latest dispatches from the front of the Real. Science excels at generating facts, but magic has been generating meaning for perhaps fifty thousand years. We have been lax.

To abandon interpretation to scientism is to shirk natural philosophy's most sacred duty. Your tribe deserves better. And if you feel some residual squeamishness over who has legitimacy of interpretation in our culture, consider this. We are wholly justified in turning the question on its head and asking the scientists what it is they think they are doing swimming in our pool in the first place.

RESTORING MITHRAS: AN EXAMPLE

It continues to surprise those in the hard sciences just how much the unavoidable politics of the workplace extends into the actual subjects studied by their softer colleagues. Having encountered Dechend and Santillana's *Hamlet's Mill*, Italian physicist Giulio Magli endeavoured to write a more scientific paper looking for the possible prehistoric discovery of astronomical precession, rather than making the claim, as Santillana had, that all prehistoric cultures were aware of the phenomenon.

When he looked at the cult of Mithras for his 2004 article, 'On the Possible Discovery of Precessional Effects in Ancient Astronomy,' Magli noted that, 'the history of modern Mithraic studies is very instructive and almost unbelievable.' Overwhelmingly, Mithras is depicted as a young man, looking away from a bull while killing it with a sword. Under the bull, a scorpion strikes at its genitals. Depictions of a dog, serpent, crow, drinking vessel and a lion are extremely common. In the 1890s, a Belgian scholar by the name of Franz Cumont decided that Mithraism was an Iranian cult dedicated to a being known as Mithra. This is despite the almost complete lack of parallels between the two cults, including the presumably important bull sacrifice. To get around this, Cumont pulled the bull slaying from a separate Iranian myth involving Ahriman, in which Mithra is entirely absent.

It astounded Magli to note that the Cumont Doctrine persisted unchallenged up until 1970, even though the astronomical imagery in the Mithraic cult could not be more obvious if the god were depicted in a pointy hat with stars and crescent moons on it. The possibility of an astronomical interpretation was firmly quashed by the Belgian and remained a forbidden idea for more than seven decades.

Once the forbidden idea was readmitted, Mithraic studies grew in leaps and bounds. The mysteries of the cult were reflected in the star lore of the ancient night sky. The bull is Taurus, rising heliacally at the spring equinox in 2000 BC. The scorpion is Scorpio, rising in the same era at the autumnal equinox. The vessel is probably Aquarius. The celestial equator in 2000 BC crossed Taurus, Canis Major (a dog), Hydra (a serpent) and a scorpion. As for the lion, Leo was the summer solstice constellation at the same time. We thus have the tantalising possibility of a warrior god who is strong enough to fix and move the stars, a very compelling proposition for soldiers. Why lock in a date so long before the emerge of the cult? It was the end of the age in which Taurus rose in the east with the equinox sunrise. It was the death of the bull.

But whither the god himself? Mithras was probably not Orion as the asterism is seen from earth as being *under* Taurus, not above it as Mithras is in relation to his bull. In 1989, David Ulansey noticed that there is another asterism above Taurus, and that is Perseus. Perseus, depicted wearing a Phrygian cap. Just like Mithras.

Almost by definition, the archaeology of mystery cults suffers from a near-total absence of evidence. However it seems quite obvious that at least some aspects of star lore moved into and through this cult the way Bible stories moved in the upper reaches of the Sepik River.

Seventy five years may seem like a long time for an entire field of study to go off in the wrong direction, but it is actually only a few 'scholarly generations.' Cumont's best students – the ones who agree with him – become professors. Those professors have students and then begin to die off. Suddenly we see the tentative emergence of new interpretations, blinking in the sunlight. It is then only a scant few years before a new canon comes roaring to life, sweeping away the old. Returning to Max Planck's quote at the top of the chapter, this is how the eternal conflict between fact and interpretation plays out, this is how science advances ... one funeral at a time.

Book the hearse.

All our theories were wrong.
Ian Hodder, Stanford University

II THE CATHEDRAL PREDATE**ƨ** THE CITY

Before we knew how to farm, before we lived in villages, before we even knew how to make pots, we built a star temple on a hill. The simplicity of this statement belies its astounding implications. With one motion it demolishes Childe's materialist analysis of the human journey. We did not build Göbekli Tepe in Southeastern Turkey because a surplus of stored food allowed a priestly class to emerge and tell us make-believe stories. We did not monitor the movements of the stars because it told us when to plant crops, because we weren't planting crops.

We built Göbekli Tepe because it expressed something about ourselves and our place in the universe. The temple complex restores the quest for meaning to its preeminent place atop the goals of human life. Philosophy is rescued from being a mere nighttime hobby of farmers to being the defining human trait, that which we value most. This is what the site's discoverer, Dr Klaus Schmidt, means when he says that the cathedral predates the city. It may well have been the coming together for spiritual reasons that birthed settled cultures, rather than the other way around. We may literally state that mankind had civilising gods (for better or for worse!). Göbekli Tepe is probably the most important archaeological discovery of all time.

It is impossible to overestimate just how rare, just how precious such a find really is. There is barely any of Victorian London left a scant century of change later. Göbekli Tepe is *at least* twelve thousand years old. That is seven thousand years older than the Giza complex. The Great Pyramid is closer in time to us than it is to the creation of Göbekli Tepe. Writing in his *National Geographic* article, 'The Birth of Religion,' Charles C. Mann says that, 'Göbekli Tepe was like finding that someone had built a 747 in a basement with an X-Acto knife.'

Unlike other sources of pseudohistorical speculation – such as selective interpretations of Sumerian tablets or the wilful misreadings of Mayan carvings bearing a squinting resemblance to 1960s space suits – Göbekli Tepe, once seen, cannot be unseen. Its existence is a fact rather than an interpretation. A fact that has been easier to ignore than engage with over the last twenty years. Writing in 'Turkey: Archaeological Dig Reshaping Human History,' an article for *Newsweek*, Patrick Symmes observes, 'the real reason the ruins at Göbekli remain almost unknown, not yet incorporated in textbooks, is that the evidence is too strong, not too weak. "The problem with this discovery," as Schwartz of Johns Hopkins puts it, "is that it is unique."'

Uniqueness. The career academic's least favourite thing.

AN UNCOMMON DISCOVERY

For Göbekli Tepe to even exist today requires a string of low-probability events so remarkable that you would be forgiven for calling it fate.

Firstly, the entire site was deliberately and delicately buried in 8200 BC after thousands of years of continual use. In terms of scale, this burial was a community project equal to or greater than Göbekli Tepe's original construction, with some 300 cubic metres per enclosure, so there must have been a very important reason behind it. In and of itself, the burial is highly unusual. You only need to drive past an abandoned church to see that changing belief systems result in the abandonment of places of worship or, only slightly less commonly, in iconoclasm. And while there is some suggestion of scattered iconoclasm at Göbekli Tepe and Karahan Tepe, one does not see old churches wrapped in bubble wrap.

The second event that spared Göbekli Tepe is the sheer weight of time. Although the region was probably continuously occupied, it would be more than four thousand years before the early Mesopotamian civilisations began large scale sacred building anywhere near there. To paraphrase Tolkien, history became legend, legend became myth, and for ten thousand years the rings of stone passed out of all knowledge. It is just possible that there remains a cultural echo of this history/legend/myth continuum. Atop the mound of Göbekli Tepe is a *ziyaret*, a place of pilgrimage within the folk magic of the local cultures. In this case it is a single tree in an otherwise barren landscape, where locals will come to ask favours and leave small ribbons or offerings.

The final event that kept the site safe until its discovery by Dr Schmidt in October of 1994 was its misidentification as a graveyard, possibly a Byzantine or Muslim one, in 1963. Due to religious law, it is not permitted to disturb the remains of deceased Muslims. In that year, the site was first identified as Stone Age by American archaeologist, Peter Benedict. He missed that the entire hill he was standing on was man-made, referenced a graveyard but did not specify if it was modern or Byzantine, and then walked down off and away from the greatest archaeological discovery he would never make.

For three decades, Göbekli Tepe was relegated to a largely uninteresting entry in an aging site survey, until, in 1994, Dr Schmidt committed himself to visiting all known Stone Age sites in the area around Nevali Çori, a previously discovered Neolithic settlement nearby. He recognised what Benedict missed and has been excavating the site ever since.

LOCATING GÖBEKLI TEPE IN TIME AND SPACE

From the perspective of previous academic theories about the development of civilisation, we have seen that Göbekli Tepe should probably not exist. And from the perspective of the sheer volume of elapsed time between its creation and our modern age, we have seen that it should not have survived. This makes the site exceedingly rare.

With rarity comes the danger of overinflating the significance of a discovery, as if only the most important sites could have survived into the modern day. This may not always be the case. Someone has to win the lottery, after all, and winning does not confer retroactive significance on the lucky ticket holder. There may have been hundreds of sites like Göbekli Tepe stretching right across the Levant and Central Asia. Indeed, there are smaller temple sites in the same area, such as Karahan Tepe, which indicate that whatever cosmology expressed in the site design was at least locally distributed.

That being said, while the cosmology itself appears to have been widely dispersed, there is good evidence that Göbekli Tepe itself had higher status as a holy place within this belief system than any nearby sites, and so should be looked at most closely. This evidence comes principally from analysis on 130 obsidian samples from Göbekli Tepe by Tristan Carter of McMaster University.

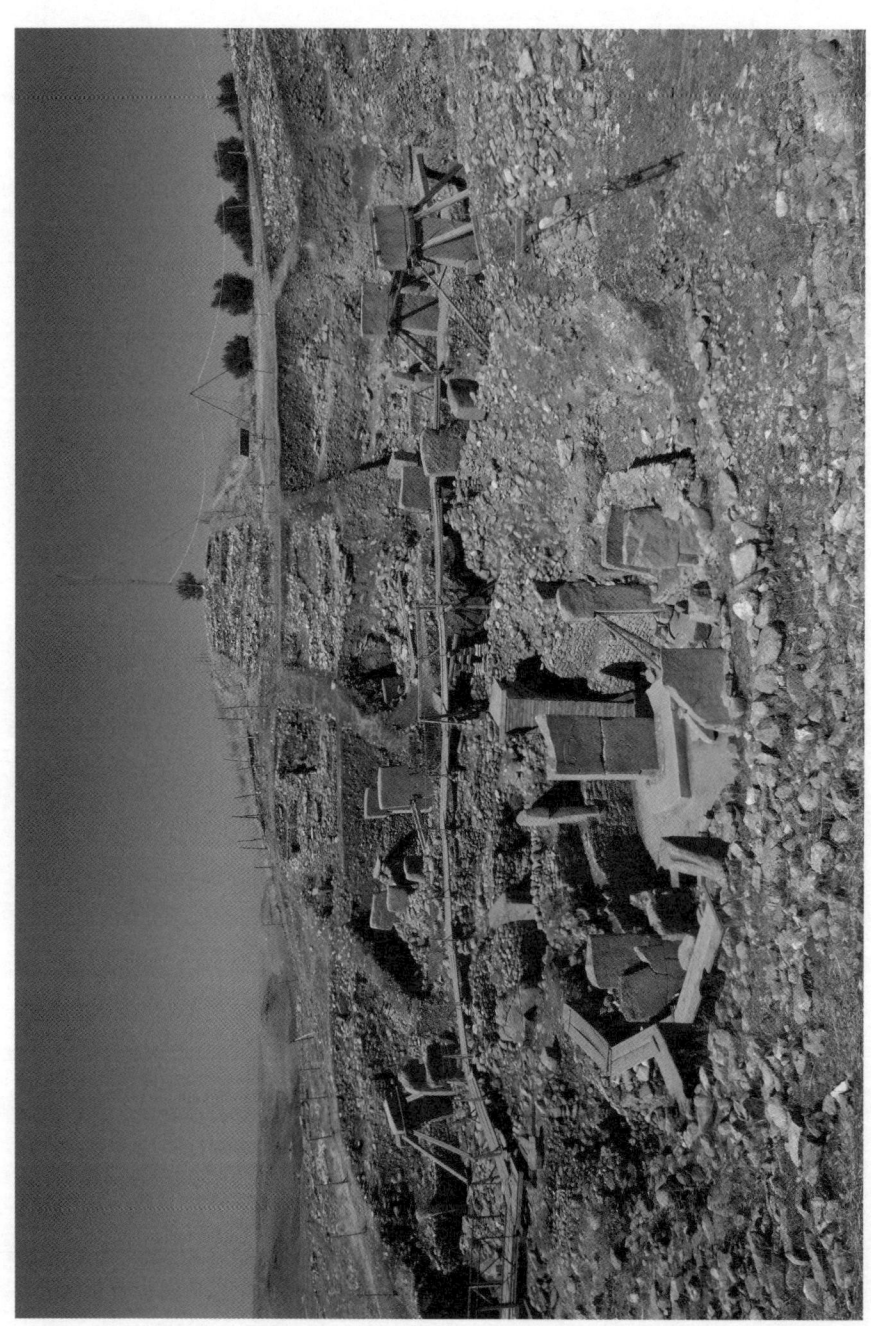

fig. 2   *Göbekli Tepe*

Obsidian found in situ originated in multiple locations from up to 300 miles away, and is stylistically similar to objects found in Iraq and Iran. Whilst there is no way of knowing whether the artefacts were taken directly to Göbekli Tepe or form a fingerprint of a long-vanished trading network it is largely irrelevant in determining the status of the site. Either way the site was a hub, known throughout the land. And so we are placed in the situation of estimating the footprint of something non-physical, a belief system, by mapping it to the footprint of something physical; in this case an obsidian trading network. It is a supposition, to be sure, but a sound one. In any case, in an era that predates the written word by more than five thousand years, supposition – *interpretation* – is the best we are going to get.

Göbekli Tepe is located in the upper arc of what we now call the Fertile Crescent. To the north are forested mountains, to the east is the biblical plain of Harran and stretching away to the south are the storied lands of Mesopotamia. On a clear day you can see into modern Syria from its summit. About fifty kilometres to the south east is another temple complex of T-shaped pillars arranged in ovoid layouts called Karahan Tepe, which is three times smaller and, at last dating, several centuries younger than its more famous sibling.

A similar distance to the north is the settlement of Nevali Çori, which is almost a thousand years younger than the earliest layers of Göbekli Tepe and was flooded in 1992 during the building of the Ataturk Dam. It was not a temple but one of the world's oldest permanent settlements.

So Göbekli Tepe was in use before the beginnings of settled life and agriculture, and remained in use after Childe's 'Neolithic Revolution' began in earnest. Here we come to a very important, 'blink and you missed it' swapping out of fact and interpretation, the understanding of which is crucial for a magical analysis of the site. According to the preliminary excavation report for the 2013 season, calibrated dating on charcoal residue in some of the ring walls gives a date for their construction early in the tenth millennium BC. Given that only a minority of the site has been excavated, and shaped bedrock was discovered underneath one of the enclosures in the same season, Dr Schmidt will be the first to tell you that *the earliest evidence of usage is not evidence of first usage*. He has said on numerous occasions that he expects the date of first use to be pushed back even farther.

But even with the dating where it is, the earliest use of the site predates settled agriculture by centuries. Thus, any attempts to *interpret* the complex as 'a temple showing the transition from hunter-gathering to settled agriculture' need to be seen for what they are: an academic attempt to claw Göbekli Tepe back inside their old model where savages cannot build and barbarians can. It softens the blow on their belief system somewhat, because it moves the large-scale monument building into an era when people were already constructing things anyway, rather than having to face the evidence that humans clearly built things that were important to them long before the emergence of the agricultural economics typically used to 'explain' such behaviour.

From a distance of twelve millennia out, five or more centuries does not look like a huge amount of time, so few people bat an eye when academics describe something as astonishing as Göbekli Tepe as belonging to a culture transitioning to settled, agricultural life. But this is like saying that the Gutenberg Press was created as part of our transition into the European Union. It is a nonsensical attempt to cling to the old interpretation despite the discovery of new, unambiguous facts.

No one is arguing that the latest stages of the complex do not post-date the adoption of agriculture, but this observation is being used to mask the fact that the earliest stages very much do not. The earliest stages of Göbekli Tepe – the largest and most sophisticated stages – are not the *beginning* of 'barbarism,' they are *the very end of* 'savagery.' Returning to the *Newsweek* article, we read, '[t]he temples thus offer unexpected proof that mankind emerged from the 140,000 year reign of hunter-gatherers with a ready vocabulary of spiritual imagery, and capable of huge logistical, economic and political efforts.'

Before anyone thinks of calling the by-now-ironically-named History Channel, the technical complexity of the site, whilst hugely impressive, is not in any way mysterious. In fact, that is one of the main points. In theory, humanity had the technical skill to construct the temple for tens of millennia before Göbekli Tepe was built, and this is but a very rare survival of it. You build Göbekli Tepe by hitting rocks with other rocks, then standing them up. No aliens required.

The anomaly is non-physical rather than physical: it is what this impressive complex reveals about the majesty and sophistication of the hunter-gatherer's inner landscape. As Johns Hopkins archaeologist Glenn Schwartz points out, this is the first time we see humans express the notion that they resemble gods. That has huge cosmological implications for how we view our distant past.

If V. Gordon Childe gave us some artificial horizons we should largely ignore, there are some very real physical ones we cannot. We often mistake a dearth of evidence for the cultural landscape of our hunter-gatherers for the belief that they probably did not have much of one. Large-scale ochre mining took place in Africa's Middle Stone Age over 100,000 years ago, and evidence of its use is still occasionally found dating before even that. However as professors Miranda and Stephen Aldhouse-Green, both of the University of Wales, Newport, point out in *The Quest for the Shaman*, art, once painted on cave walls older than 30,000 years generally now survives only as collapsed fragments. We face an immovable temporal barrier beyond which it is largely impossible to see with the spectacles of archaeology.

Fortunately, there are other spectacles in the dedicated folklorist's toolkit which we shall come to in subsequent chapters. In the meantime, it is important to realise that we really have few ways of knowing just when this high complexity of non-physical technology began, given fully modern humans existed for at least 200,000 years before the 'Palaeolithic Consciousness Revolution' we see beginning at Lascaux and culminating on a flint mound in South East Turkey. From a physical evidence perspective, we have a clearly defined palaeontological window.

In the satirical newspaper, *The Onion*, there is a popular article from more than a decade ago titled 'Archaeologist tired of unearthing unspeakable, ancient evil.' While this is a comment on Hollywood depictions of the field, it has a curious real world analogue. Great archaeological discoveries often trigger western esoteric revolutions as their ontological implications disseminate into the wider culture. Samuel and Moina Mathers first met in the Egyptian Gallery of the British Museum, for instance, and it is unlikely the sixties counterculture would have looked the way it did without the mid-twentieth century anthropological research into American Indian beliefs. Göbekli Tepe falls into the trigger category. In many ways the site is a new Rosetta Stone. It sits right at the very edge of a way of life we have at least some frame of reference for: settled agriculture; and overlaps another way of life for which we have none: hunter-gathering. Thus, written in both a language we can understand and one that we cannot, it offers our first and best opportunity to unlock the mysteries of mankind's earliest and longest-lived culture. It is a key made of stone and starlight.

SITE SURVEY

Göbekli Tepe is quite large, covering some nine hectares. Geophysical surveys suggest its total size may be more than thirty hectares. Prior to the construction of the temples, it was very likely a flint quarry used for the creation of spear and possibly arrow tips. This may be relevant in determining the nature of the gods and spirits that were eventually venerated there.

The site is characterised by two main layers. Layer II, the younger, reveals rectangular buildings and iconography that indicate that it belongs to the same culture as the nearby settlement of Nevali Çori. Whilst the story of mankind's first known settled towns is endlessly fascinating in and of itself, we shall not dwell on it for too long. Civilisation, such as it is, had begun in earnest by this point. It is what came before Layer II that I consider to be one of the most important battlegrounds in modern philosophy.

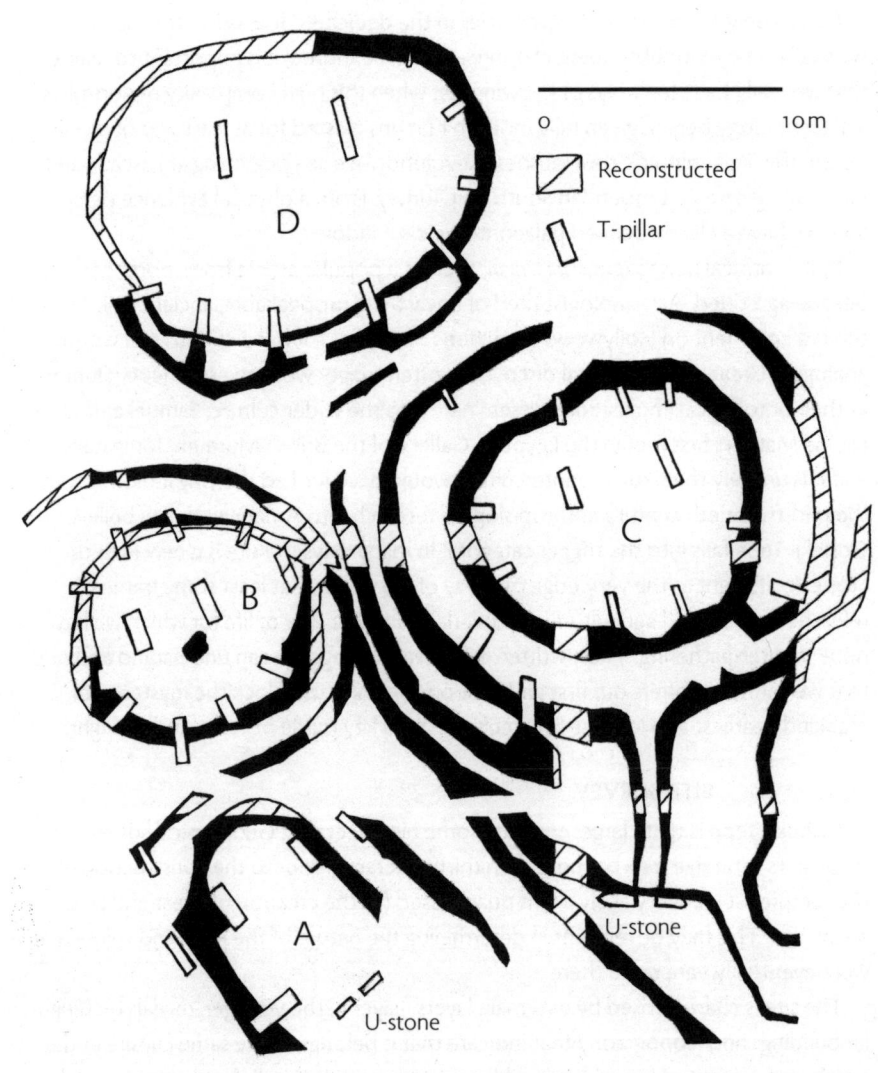

o ————————— 10m

▨ Reconstructed

▯ T-pillar

D

B

C

A

U-stone

U-stone

fig. 3   *Level III Structures A – D at Göbekli Tepe (after Schmidt)*

The older, Layer III, includes all the circular and ovoid temples with large, T-shaped humanoid pillars facing into the middle where two larger T-shaped humanoid pillars appear. The central pillars face south to south east. Some of the pillars are set directly into the bedrock, others into a terrazzo-like floor. They are often very tall and thin, and thus quite unstable, perhaps another indication of their ritual significance and use which will be explored below. Layer III is definitively preagricultural, although the large number of sickles found at the site demonstrates that wild grains, probably for the brewing of beer, formed part of the culture's diet.

As only a minority of the hill has been excavated so far, it seems likely that there are around twenty of these early circular enclosures covering the top and southern face of Göbekli Tepe. Later circles are less than half the size of the earlier ones which has been interpreted as indicating that the culture was in decline in later years.

Each of the enclosures is named in the order of its discovery: Enclosure A, Enclosure B, and so on. The pillars are often carved in both high and low relief and some imagery is more common in one enclosure compared to the next. For instance, Enclosure A has more snake imagery than Enclosure B, which has more fox imagery.

The largest is Enclosure D. It has two very large central pillars and 12 smaller ones surrounding it. The central pillars are the best examples of the compelling T-shaped humanoid figures that characterise many of the pillars on the site. In this case they have long thin arms reaching around to the belly area, some form of neck adornment and belts with what is probably a fox skin covering the groin. The belts themselves have a curious buckle or symbol that looks like our capital H. The central pillars face south. They do not appear to have a discernable gender. According to the preliminary excavation report for the 2013 season, large volumes of charred botanical remains were found, offering the exciting possibility of further calibrating the date of use.

Just to the southeast is Enclosure C. It has several concentric, interwoven walls containing smaller T-pillars around the two large central ones, at least one of which was probably deliberately toppled in antiquity. The diameter of the entire enclosure is approximately 30 metres. Enclosure C's floor is of cut, smoothed bedrock, out of which were also carved the 30 cm pedestals for the two large T-pillars. Described in the same preliminary report is the discovery that Enclosure C was changed substantially during its use. A south-facing entrance passage consisting of two narrowly-set walls entering into the larger, outer circle via what is described as a portal stone. At some point, this passageway was deliberately *walled up*. In 2012, a carved stairway was discovered at the entry-point of the passageway. Although the passage points almost due south, Enclosure C's central pillars point slightly more south-southeast, offering the suggestion that the temple's principal sacred axis has changed over time.

IMAGERY ANALYSIS

It is not just the conspicuous absence of any farmed animals in the large volumes of bones and detritus used as fill for the enclosures that tells us this is a hunters' temple, it is also the imagery.

Around half of the pillars so far excavated feature some astonishing relief carvings. The majority of the imagery depicted in Layer III relates to prey, alpha predators or otherwise dangerous animals, such as scorpions and snakes. You would not leave your children with any of the animals found on this hill. From the outset, we can see that Göbekli Tepe is not an example of 'primitive sympathetic magic,' designed to ensure a successful hunt. (I would argue that such an exclusive interpretation is largely incorrect anywhere in the Palaeolithic, but that is a separate issue.) Sources of food such as the aurochs, wild ass, gazelle and boar – in some instances depicted upside down – can certainly be found. But there are also many foxes, lions, leopards, cranes, storks, ibises, vultures and what may well be a crocodile, a culinary delicacy for which Southeast Turkey is not exactly famous. More on that later.

Different imagery tends to predominate in different enclosures. For instance, foxes and snakes are most common in Enclosure D. Enclosure C has no snakes but a lot more boars. It is not unreasonable to suggest that each enclosure had a presiding animal spirit, perhaps even the totemic spirit of the family group who may have 'sponsored' its construction. What has been described as a totem pole, carved with snakes and topped with birds, has been found in the northeast corner of a room in Layer II, so the interpretation may have merit.

The majority of the site's imagery is carved in low relief, although there are some exceptional examples of high relief carvings that Dr Schmidt has interpreted as 'temple guardians.' So far, all high relief depictions have been of 'ferocious' animals rather than game, lending credence to the hypothesis. In both cases, it is important to emphasise that the imagery is created by taking a larger stone and *carving off everything around the depiction*. With the pillars that include high relief sculptures, this means starting with a considerably larger piece of rock. Make a mistake and start again. These were not the idle scratchings of superstitious minds, they were planned inclusions from the very outset, and so were clearly weighty with meaning.

The high relief carvings tell us something else important, and that is that the eerie, quasi-human feel of the central T-pillars was a deliberate stylistic choice. They were not the crude attempts of a culture struggling with accurate depictions of their kings or chiefs. Some frankly very beautiful examples of stylistic naturalism can be found at Göbekli Tepe, even down to the individual carving of teeth and tusks. Those giant, faceless, thin-armed humanoids with jointed fingers, wearing fox-pelt over their belts with H-shaped buckles and strange neck charms, hovering in the centre of the sacred space are *supposed* to look like that. It almost makes you want to sleep with the light on.

It is worth considering the preponderance of snake depictions at some length. In at least once instance, the snakes are interwoven into a grid or mat, which is highly suggestive of the ectopic phenomena first seen when an entheogen begins to take effect. Indeed, ayahuasca, for instance, is often depicted as a female snake spirit. Geometric patterns coalesce into snakeskin, which coalesces into a giant snake and then the rest of the journey begins in earnest. Other single snakes are depicted crawling up the back or the side of the T-pillars. In Nevali Çori – which is a later settlement than Layer III – fully anthropoid statues were found with a snake climbing up the spine, over the top of the human head, with the snake's head ending in the centre of the forehead. The extremely high degree of similarity between this statue and both the Ancient Egyptian Uraeus and the Kundalini cannot be ignored.

In fact, in light of Nevali Çori's twentieth century discovery, it is worth bearing in mind that the land surrounding it during its occupation, with verdant grasslands, pistachio trees, einkorn wheat, oak, elm, wild sheep, pigs and cattle is an exact match for descriptions found in India's oldest religious texts, the Rig Veda. It is descriptions such as these that definitely rule out an exclusively Indian origin for Vedic culture – to which we will return in later chapters – but is presented here to demonstrate the strong circumstantial evidence of a continuity of cosmologies.

The possibility that Göbekli Tepe was a site of ritualised drug use is one that Dr Schmidt thinks is highly likely. Rectangular pits that were likely used for the brewing of beer – discussed below – have already been found on site and similar locations. Mandrake beer is known in Ancient Egypt from the legend of Sekhmet, where her consumption of it – as a proxy for human blood, no less – transformed her into the benevolent Hathor, 'the giver of life' after a drug-induced sleep. (The Old Arabic term for mandrake is *Abu' l-ruh*, 'master of the life breath.') It was also added to wine in Bacchic rites. In both instances we have much later echoes of the securing of immortality or transformation via an entheogen-induced shamanic journey.

None of this rules out the possibility that other, more traditional, shamanic allies were used. Along the top of the western side of the famous Pillar 43 in Enclosure D – the largest enclosure – are a sequence of images that look like three modern padlocks in profile. Graham Hancock refers to these as, 'the shaman's manbags.' But it is the carvings below these manbags that lend the interpretation credence.

Immediately below the manbags and at the base of the pillar are depictions of several cranes. The crane, like the ibis, is the shamanic animal *par excellence*, because it occupies the three worlds of land, water and air, moving seamlessly between them

fig. 4   *Pillar 43, Göbekli Tepe*

at will. Thoth, appearing fully-formed at the very beginning of Dynastic Egypt, is probably one example of the civilisational development of this intermediary, wisdom-imparting being. In other enclosures, dozens of smaller cranes are carved around the edges of the bases in which the central T-pillars stand. This animal is in some way involved in the comings and goings of presiding spirits of these temples, and quite possibly the humans who use it as well.

To the right of the large crane at the base of Pillar 43, although damaged, is a carving of a headless human with an erect penis. In between the small human at the base of the statue and the cranes and manbags at the top is a large scorpion and – in what is the largest carving yet found at the site – a large vulture or vulture/human therianthrope carrying a circular shape in its wing. Although some interpretations suggest this could be the sun, it is quite small and there is a headless human at the base of the pillar, so it is probably better understood as a head. Esoterically, it could be both, of course.

The combination of the bird – most often the vulture – and the head is repeated several times throughout the entire site. During the 2012 season, a larger-than-lifesize, realistic human head in the talons of a large bird was discovered in a deep sounding trench in the main excavation area. This is an image that is well-known from Nevali Çori and is thus highly suggestive of the continuation of 'headlessness' and the special significance of the head from the deep Palaeolithic into the post-agricultural era. Other carved heads have been discovered in the fill of various enclosures, and are curiously evocative of some comparatively nearby cultic practices in Jericho, 'Ain Ghazal and Tell Aswad, where human skulls were removed from corpses and given new faces made from gypsum plaster before being installed in ancestral shrines. As far back as 26,000 years ago (doubling the distance between Göbekli Tepe and us), graves where the skulls have been painted with red ochre are found. From the same era, the Gravettian graves – found across Europe – often contain headless skeletons or sometimes just skulls.

Let us not forget that the central pillars are themselves headless in a sense. In place of a skull and face, the deliberate stylistic decision was made to carve a narrow rectangular prism. Whatever these beings are, they are human*ish*, but decidedly not human in scale or appearance despite the artistic capacity to depict both being found at the site. They display neither gender nor race. And separating your head from your body seems to please them.

Returning to the possibility that Göbekli Tepe may function as a Rosetta Stone, the metaphor of the mangrove swamp is useful. The mangrove swamp is where the unknown ocean of the Deep Palaeolithic *overlaps* with the recognisable land of settled agricultural life. It is both places and neither. The twenty thousand years of enthe-ogenic, ritualised shamanism between the Lascaux Caves and Göbekli Tepe – the longest-running psychological experiment in the history of mankind – are evidenced in the spiritual practices found on this flint hill in modern Turkey.

Quite what it was these practices made contact with may also be in evidence. 'Twenty years ago everyone believed civilization was driven by ecological forces,' Schmidt told *National Geographic*. 'I think what we are learning is that civilization is a product of the human mind.'

ASTROTHEOLOGY

Dr Schmidt has referred to the T-pillars as 'a gathering of heavenly beings.' Despite some of them weighing in at over five tonnes, the extremely narrow 'feet' of the central T-pillars, resting in very shallow bases of only a few inches, give the curious impression of beings just barely landing on the ground.

Invisible from below, many of the tops of the T-pillars have 'cup marks' facing up to the sky, like those found in much later Neolithic sites across Britain, as well as in Southern India, Sulawesia, Korea and Japan. K. P. Rao of the University of Hyderabad has correlated some of the Southern Indian cup marks with constellations such as Orion and Ursa Major. In the case of Göbekli Tepe, I suspect these may have been filled with a liquid that could reflect and catch the starlight as in a mirror but that is my *interpretation* of the *fact* of their existence. (In later eras, it was quite common to 'catch' starlight in liquid.) Combined with the fundamental structural unsoundness of tall, narrow, heavy pillars resting precariously on carved bases, the existence of the cup marks suggests the enclosures were open to the night sky. Nothing resembling roofing has yet been found in the fill, but this may change as excavations continue.

The smaller, surrounding pillars facing into the central ones most commonly number twelve, but sometimes only ten. The number twelve, combined with images of the scorpion, the lion, the aurochs, some kind of reptile/dragon, the vulture and so on make it hugely tempting to leap to a zodiacal explanation for the enclosure's arrangement.

Perhaps this is so, but it is certainly more prudent to refer to Göbekli Tepe as a 'proto-zodiac.' Evidence of star lore and even, according to one NASA study, solar plasma events such as the Northern Lights, are indicated in Palaeolithic cave paint-ings in Europe and Australia. Star lore is extremely old, astrology significantly less so. Göbekli Tepe is probably our earliest evidence (so far) of attempting to cohere many pieces of star lore into a unifying cosmology, but you still cannot determine your natal chart with it. We see star lore with Dr Doniger's telescope, we see astrology with her microscope. It is a recipe for madness to confuse the two, one that is not helped by the fact that it is a Greek word with no Egyptian or Babylonian cognates. Precisely when star lore becomes astrology is largely a matter of opinion.

There is a common misconception that the Ice Age was wet, cold and snowy. Certainly, it would have been cold in Northern Europe but, at the time, a huge amount of the planet's water was locked up in glaciers and polar ice caps, so it was actually quite dry for much of the earth. Twenty thousand years of coming up on mushrooms under a canopy of stars undimmed by light pollution, industry or high atmospheric moisture can only have generated a profound and complex cosmology. It was the only show in town, after all, and you and I will never see it performed the way our ancestors did. We have mistaken the absence of evidence for the evidence of absence of Palaeolithic star lore and Göbekli Tepe appears, on the last page of a very long book, to correct that mistake.

As to the suggestion of solar influences at Göbekli Tepe, this interpretation is vanishingly weak. Firstly, why would non-agriculturalists care about the sun? Secondly, the enclosures are not circular, they are ovoid or womb-shaped. But perhaps most importantly, it is the north/south axis – with a particular emphasis on the south – that predominates over the east/west axis found in solar-aligned complexes. The pre-eminence of the sun in our earliest spiritual beliefs has been grossly over-inflated thanks largely to nineteenth century antiquarianism and the assumption that our ancestors were stupid enough to fear and misunderstand this bright object in the sky. Göbekli Tepe restores the star goddess and her children to their thrones.

Now we come to the potential alignments themselves. All the Layer III enclosure entrances and central T-pillars face south to southeast. It is reasonable to suggest that we should look in that corner of the night sky for the principal asterism. This does not preclude the presence of asterisms in other corners of the sky being represented, of course. Indeed, if this is a stellar temple it stands to reason that they probably were. Completely covered by a northeast wall of a rectangular room from the later Layer II, a totem pole reminiscent of those found in North America was discovered with what is probably a bear at its top. The northeast corner of the night sky contains Ursa Major, or the Bear. So it is possible that the association between this particular site and the stars was long-lived.

Returning to Layer III, the fact remains that the earliest enclosures all point to a highly resonant corner of the sky, so it is there that we shall look. There is also the fact that the oldest temples are on top of the tell ('hill') and the younger ones move further down the south face. We would not expect this from a site whose principal direction was anything other than 'southish.'

The entry 'portals' to the central ellipses do not all point in the same direction, but rather drift from a general southerly one with the earliest temple, to a more southest direction for the later ones. It needs to be borne in mind that each enclosure was deliberately buried before the next one was constructed (or thereabouts). It occurred to Boston University geologist Dr Robert Schoch that the directional change may have been caused by the results of precession. Reconstructing the night sky during the time the enclosures were in use, he noted that:

> On the morning of the vernal equinox circa 10,000 BCE, before the sun rose due east at Göbekli Tepe, the Pleiades, Taurus, and the top of Orion were in view in the direction indicated by the central stones of Enclosure D ... with Orion's Belt not far above the horizon as dawn broke (as seen from the best vantage points in the area). A similar scenario played out for the orientation of the central stones of Enclosure C in circa 9500 BCE and for Enclosure B in circa 9000 BCE. Enclosure A is oriented toward the Pleiades, Taurus and Orion on the morning of the Vernal Equinox circa 8500 BCE, but due to precessional changes, the entire belt of Orion no longer rose above the horizon before dawn broke. By about 8150 BCE the belt of Orion remained below the horizon at dawn on the vernal equinox. These dates fit well the time frame established for Göbekli Tepe on the basis of radiocarbon dating. Furthermore, Orion the constellation can be viewed as literally a torso in the sky with arms (but not legs), a headless hunter, similar to the iconography of the headless hunters represented by the central pillars of Enclosure D.

Dr Giulio Magli, who we met in the last chapter via his analysis of the astronomical components to the Mithras story, has also performed an archaeoastronomic survey of Göbekli Tepe and reached a different conclusion. Although his contention is that an Orion correlation would lead to too high a date for the structure, this is a premature analysis given that only a minority of the site has been excavated, and Dr Schmidt fully expects the evidence for first use to be pushed further back – his matching of the night sky to the date of Enclosure D as revealed in the preliminary report for the 2013 excavation season is closer than Dr Schoch's: 9300 BC. This is within one hundred years of the latest carbon dates and given there is an unavoidable fuzziness in both radiocarbon dating and reconstructions of the ancient sky, it is effectively a bull's eye.

At the latitude of Göbekli Tepe in 9300 BC, the night sky welcomed back a visitor that had not been seen for more than five thousand years. Sirius. The hunter's companion had returned.

As Sirius is a negative magnitude star, it is in principle visible just above the horizon; I will however allow in what follows as altitude of 1/2° (actually the horizon at the site estimated via satellite images looks flat towards the south-east). Then, it can be seen that the above azimuths match the rising azimuths of Sirius in the following approximate dates:

Structure D	172°	9100 BCE
Structure C	165°	8750 BCE
Structure B	159°	8300 BCE

The arc of sky covering Sirius/Canis Minor, Orion and then the Pleiades/Taurus has been a cultural focus for humans for tens of thousands of years. You can find them in Lascaux, you can also (possibly) see Orion in a 32,500 year old mammoth ivory carving found in Germany. Given the obvious symbolic parallels between Orion, the 'armed but headless' T-pillars and the status of Göbekli Tepe as a hunters' temple – as testified by the fact that the feasting remains are exclusively wild taxa and the tell itself was used to mine flint – it is reasonable to suggest that Dr Schmidt's 'heavenly being' is represented by the asterism we call Orion.

How are we to square the better symbolic parallels with Orion with the more accurate (so far) astronomic parallels with Sirius? For magicians, this is almost self evident. The hunter had acquired a companion, the brightest star in the sky at that latitude, no less. This is a cosmological event worth memorialising, worth celebrating.

We have no way of knowing whether our ancestors saw Sirius as a female companion – or even really if they saw Orion as male – we only know that they are companions, two stellar beings appearing to chase Taurus across the sky just as the herds migrate across the planes below, and just as there are two pillars in the centre of each enclosure, an otherwise uncommon temple arrangement.

It is not yet a solid, but the plot has certainly thickened.

RITUAL, FEASTING AND DEATH AT GÖBEKLI TEPE

The role of food and drink on this particular tell needs to be explored at some length, as it attests to both the status and function of the site.

Firstly, there is no water source nearby capable of sustaining a permanent settlement and no evidence of food preparation or waste has been found to suggest that Göbekli Tepe was occupied year-round. It was a site of supreme importance, but not one that was built to live in. That being said, Dr Schmidt has recently conceded the temple may have had a guardian who had food and water delivered to him/her/them by passing tribes, but evidence for this has yet to be uncovered.

This is not to say there is no evidence of food consumption at Göbekli Tepe. Rather, there is too much of it. Large volumes of animal bones, smashed to get at the marrow, have been found in the backfill of the enclosures, in amounts exceeding everything known from other sites at the time. Here is a very strong indication that the tell was a place of regular pilgrimage for surrounding tribes and family groups.

The health of the animal bones also speaks to the sacred function of the site. In one of the more flimsy attempts to pull Göbekli Tepe back into line with the outdated paradigm, Karl W. Luckert of Missouri State suggests that the temple's grandeur and uniqueness was a sign of desperation; appealing to the gods of the hunt in the face of a changing climate and the disappearance of the herds. (He also suggests the T-pillars are upside down phalluses, penetrating the earth mother. The book is not recommended.)

However, in the introduction to Luckert's own book, Dr Schmidt – wasting only one sentence before announcing his complete disagreement with the theory presented therein – mentions that the end of the Ice Age was a period of superabundance for this particular corner of Asia Minor. Rainfall increased, grasslands spread, herds grew. We see this reflected in the health of the feasting bones. The ritual attendees at Göbekli Tepe were not a hungry people.

We see a similar attempt to pull the earliest stages of the site back into a paradigm that allows anthropologists who have been teaching the wrong thing for forty years to continue doing so, in the suggestion that the site was a roofed, domestic dwelling. Such analysis ignores the complete absence of domestic waste found at the site, the fundamental instability of the central pillars for housing, the absence of roofing, the lack of water and the ritualistic burial and replacement of each enclosure. Also, contemporaneous dwellings are rectangular rather than elliptical, as we see at Nevali Çori – a site that also contains separate sacred and domestic structures. The interpretation relies solely on the straw man suggestion that hunter gatherers did not recognise a difference between the physical and the sacred, so these were houses in which they also maybe conducted rituals. The non-separation between the physical and the spiritual may be so, but you will also not find a single hunter gatherer society lacking in taboo areas, that is, spaces demarcated as belonging to the spirits rather than the tribe. It is imperative that a domestic reading of Göbekli Tepe be recognised for the academic gerrymandering that it is, and banished with laughter.

Risky though it is, a comparison with a much more recent hunter gatherer culture may be illuminating. The Boorong of Southeast Australia waited for Otchocut, the giant fish, to set with the sun. They then moved north to the Mille river, upon the banks of which their cousins dwelled.

Otchocut's sunset alignment coincided with the cod returning to the river to spawn. Travelling at night, ancestral and totemic spirit constellations would pass overhead, from east to west. Like many sophisticated hunter gatherer cultures, Boorong law required exogamy, or marrying outside the tribe. And so, on the banks of the Mille, families would reunite, celebrate, compete at spear-throwing, feast and arrange weddings. In the evenings, the young warriors would attempt to out-dance each other. As Alex Cherney and John Morieson point out in their paper at the 2010 conference of the La Société Européenne pour l'Astronomie dans la Culture:

> The Boorong might stay for several weeks especially if there was ceremony to take place, such as first initiation for boys or girls. By now the full heat of summer was upon them so on their journey home to proceed at night was the only option. If the northern sky was a progression from east to west, the southern sky was a re-volving scene where all the named ancestral heroes were visible for all the time, but sometimes hidden in the treetops. Bunya the possum was very evident at the top of the Southern Cross and every woman's totem, Yerredetkurrk, the owlet nightjar, is directly opposite in what we call Achernar. Halfway between the two is south so all the Boorong had to do was to keep in line with the halfway point and in three to four days they would be home.

It is unlikely the family groups of Asia Minor arrived at Göbekli Tepe expecting cod. What we have with the Boorong is a proof of concept that star lore can be used to guide disparate populations to a specific site for a multitude of spiritual and practical reasons. Certainly, there would have been the same need for exogamy, as we were not even living in villages at the time, so inbreeding would have been a constant risk.

There is even the indication for dancing, or at least music, being important at Göbekli Tepe. Firstly, and most astonishingly, the central T-pillars hum. If you slap some of them with the palm of your hand, they vibrate like a tuning fork, thus probably uncovering the reason for their extremely shallow bases and otherwise flimsy height and width. Considered in conjunction with the stone walls that form the ellipses of smaller pillars, the mind moves inevitably to an amphitheatrical effect of chanting, drumming and dancing, both people and 'heavenly beings' vibrating togeth-er with the sacred sound. Throw in the night sky, firelight casting dancing shadows of animal totems, the smell of roasted game and the suggestion of ritual intoxication and the whole place starts to sound ... well ... really quite fun.

Uncovered at nearby Nevali Çori and dating to a few centuries later are fragments of a limestone bowl depicting two persons with raised arms. Between them, a therianthropic turtle joins in the dance, as Oliver Dietrich suggests, 'maybe reflecting the altered state of consciousness of the dancers.' Turtles, like crocodiles, are not exactly endemic in Southeast Turkey.

The sonic qualities of Neolithic temples have been gaining wider awareness these past few years. The bluestones of Stonehenge 'sing' when hit with rocks. In Western European tombs and mounds, resonances tend to cluster around the 110–122 Hertz range, the same as a baritone voice. Maltese temples – currently considered Neolithic though very likely Palaeolithic in origin – provide similar results. Like astronomy, a scientific understanding of sound has typically fallen outside the more humanities-focused interpretations of ancient history. The implications of these Palaeolithic capacities are astounding and cry out to be explored, both personally and academically.

In the last few years, fragments of human bone have been found in niches behind some of the smaller, surrounding pillars. This opens up the intriguing possibility that Göbekli Tepe was used as a platform for excarnation. (I also suspect these surrounding pillars may represent individual tribal or family groups that convened at the site; Palaeolithic heraldry, if you will.) The preponderance of vulture imagery adds further weight to an excarnatory function. Excarnation is a post-mortem practice that has been used across Central Asia since the Neolithic and even survives to the modern day in the form of Tibetan 'sky burials.' I depart from Dr Schmidt's analysis that the presence of human bones means Göbekli Tepe was the site of a death cult. Funerals are held in churches, but churches have other functions. If the enclosures were portals to another world, principally one located *above* the earth, they would be excellent locations in which to dispose of highborn members of family groups or tribes – having the aviary ambassadors of the spirit realm carry the departed back up into the sky – but it seems to me a death cult would be associated with a lot more human remains than the fragments so far discovered. That being said, it is entirely reasonable to suggest one of Göbekli Tepe's primary magical functions related to crossing the mortem/post-mortem threshold. Deliberately smashed T-pillars are found buried, entire enclosures are also buried. Such ritual activity has an exact parallel in Sumeria, five thousand years later. The Mosaic Temple in Uruk – itself built over an earlier Ubaid temple – was demolished and ritually buried in the nearby *Riemchengebäude*.

Despite such a lengthy gap, there are other architectural parallels. At Nevali Çori and Cayönü, just as in Sumerian Mesopotamia, sacred structures were located at the edge of settlements, with later additions being built on top of earlier ones. As Dr Hauptmann points out, 'strikingly throughout the long course of Mesopotamian prehistory that covers a period between 6000 BC and 4500 BC from Hassuna to Halaf, it has not been possible to identify a definite ritual structure.' What this means is that, although the time gap is quite large, there are no immediately obvious intervening layers. We suggest that if Dr Hauptmann wishes to find them, he should both dig deeper at existing sites and rent some SCUBA gear.

BEER AND NETWORK EFFECTS

The complete absence of domesticated foodstuffs at Göbekli Tepe takes on a new dimension when you realise that large scale cereal production was taking place just over the modern day border with Syria at a place called Jerf el Ahmar in the tenth millennium BC. Given that such a date precedes the currently-known development of agriculture in the region, the suggestion is the site was used for the large-scale preparation of wild, foraged grain such as rye and einkorn. No storage structures have been found at the earliest stages, which may indicate the facilities were used as a sort of 'inter-tribal cooperative.' As Willcox and Stordeur point out, Jerf el Ahmar 'leave[s] no doubt that this was a community dedicated to the systematic production of food from wild cereals. Given the plausible suggestion that barley was being cultivated, the site opens a window onto a long period of pre-domestic agriculture. Rye was also harvested, its chaff used to temper mud walls.'

Moving on to something much more interesting than communally baked rye bread, it appears mankind's relationship with alcohol is a lot older than we expected. It used to be that historians assumed wine was first created with the domestication of grapes, but following discoveries in Iran or wine residue in stone bowls at the Neolithic burial site of Körtik Tepe – also in Southeast Turkey – we can now see that winemaking predates agriculture. From Dietrich: 'It can now be safely stated that people's first interest in wild grapes in western Asia was for alcohol production, evidence for domestication only following in the fourth millennium BC.' Dionysus: born wild on the hills and plains that are home to the ruins of a Palaeolithic star cult.

Very large capacity limestone vessels, up to 160 litres, have been found at all levels of Göbekli Tepe. Oxalate residue – which develops during the steeping, mashing and fermentation of cereals – has been found on some of them. A complete scapula was found in one of them, which is reminiscent of finds in similar bowls in the Syrian site of Tell 'Abr 3. The bones may well have been used for stirring and scraping the surface of the liquid. (Bone beer, anyone?) As no signs of habitation have been found at Göbekli Tepe, Dietrich suggests that the grains used in beer production may have been malted at nearby settlements and brought to the complex on special occasions, an hypothesis that aligns perfectly with the interpretation that it was an episodic gathering place for nearby (and possibly quite distant) tribes sharing the same cosmology.

As we saw with the Boorong people, such regular gatherings provide for some interesting network effects. Firstly, there are genetic ones in the form of arranged exogamy. Then there are the cultural and economic ones in the form of exchanges of information and practices. And finally, there may be technological ones, which is where Göbekli Tepe's story may become significant for the rest of human history.

Communal sites are vectors for the transmission of technology. We have already seen that the brewing of beer most likely predates the use of grain as a food staple, which only really took off following the development of agriculture. Once the domestication of wild grain had happened, it would have been at sites such as Göbekli Tepe that those who had worked this process out shared it with tribal groups who had yet to do so. Dietrich remarks, '[i]t is an intriguing thought that brewing and the domestication of wheat might be interrelated.'

Even more intriguing for the thesis of this book is a story told in the Sumerian 'Debate between Sheep and Grain.' It describes the creation of domesticated livestock and plants and their delivery to mankind on a high place where the god of wild animals was still in residence.

> When, upon the hill of heaven and earth, An created the Annunaki, since he neither spawned nor created Grain with them, and since in the Land he neither fashioned the yarn of Uttu (the goddess of weaving) nor pegged out the loom for Uttu – with no Sheep appearing, there were no numerous lambs, and with no goats, there were no numerous kids, the sheep did not give birth to her twin lambs, and the goat did not give birth to her triplet kids;

> Upon the pure place known as Duku, Cattle and Grain were created. Before this moment, not even the Annunaki knew what they were, or had words for them.

> [T]he Annunaki, the great gods, did not even know the names Grain or Sheep. There was no grain of thirty days; there was no grain of forty days; there was no grain of fifty days; there was no small grain, grain from the mountains or grain from the holy habitations. There was no cloth to wear; Uttu had not been born – no royal turban was worn; lord Niĝir-si, the precious lord, had not been born;

> The god of the wild animals was still in residence, he had not been banished. At such a time, people had not clothing or houses and ate wild vegetation like sheep.

> The god of wild animals had not gone out into the barren lands. The people of those days did not know about eating bread. They did not know about wearing

clothes; they went about with naked limbs in the Land. Like sheep they ate grass with their mouths and drank water from the ditches.

From the Holy Mound, domestication is sent down to mankind. At that time, at the place of the gods' formation, in their own home, on the Holy Mound, they created Sheep and Grain. Having gathered them in the divine banqueting chamber, the Anunnaki of the Holy Mound partook of the bounty of Sheep and Grain but were not sated; the Anunnaki of the Holy Mound partook of the sweet milk of their holy sheepfold but were not sated. For their own well-being in the holy sheepfold, they gave them to mankind as sustenance.

At that time Enki spoke to Enlil: 'Father Enlil, now Sheep and Grain have been created on the Holy Mound, let us send them down from the Holy Mound.' Enki and Enlil, having spoken their holy word, sent Sheep and Grain down from the Holy Mound.

Mythology is not history, but sometimes it is the vehicle in which history travels. Mythology is the wallpaper and history is the wall. A culture as decidedly pro-urban as Sumeria will necessarily have a negative view of preagricultural societies but it is extremely hard to argue that this story is anything but a cultural memory of humanity's transition to permanent settlements.

Where it becomes extremely compelling is that the transmission of grain-based agriculture happened at a holy mound upon which were resident sky beings and from which the god of the wild animals had not yet been banished. Beginning at this holy mound agricultural technology was disseminated across the world.

The ancient einkorn wheat, found in the hills surrounding Göbekli Tepe, just happens to be the single genetic ancestor of every strain of wheat grown and eaten across the earth. People gathering at a temple on a hill to worship 'heavenly beings' were like passengers in an airport during a pandemic. Wheat, and what to do with it, spread to every corner of the land. Mankind had civilising gods who were themselves anything but civilised.

THE CULT OF THE ANGELS
Fundamental to the exploration of this book is the question of what and how much may have survived across tens of millennia. If we see resonances between the spiritual practices of the tribes that convened at Göbekli Tepe but struggle to find intervening evidence, how are we to deal with this?

Returning to the concept of random versus non-random distribution of stories as described by Dr Oppenheimer, it is difficult to get any less random than the same stories told in the same place. The mechanism for transmission thus becomes psychic or unconscious – anathema for scientific materialism – or it becomes a matter of continuous cultural memory. It may therefore be extremely significant that there *is* an example of continuous cultural memory overlaid in the same locations that gave us star temples on a hill, heavenly visitors and the dissemination of 'civilisational' technology such as agriculture. And that is Yezidism.

According to former Harvard lecturer and world authority on the Kurds, Merhdad Izady, large amounts of Yezidi cosmology are actually Neolithic survivals.

Although the number of modern adherents is vanishingly small, such a long-lived religion has been in existence for enough time to have splintered into sufficient subsections that making macro statements is about as accurate as making macro statements about Christianity.

It can only really be said that three branches have survived from ancient times: Yezidism, Alevism and Yârsânism. All of them, however, past and present, share a fundamental belief in the existence of luminous angelic beings, numbering seven, that protect the universe from an equal number of dark beings who are the lords of matter. Similar to Hinduism, the cult is quite adaptive and universal, hybridising beings and philosophies encountered through either trade or migration, such as the transmigration of souls, emanatory creationism, Gnostic dual-*ish*-m and a cosmology that allows for the appearance on earth of world teachers such as Buddha, Jesus or Mohammed. The Yezidi branch even still retains vestiges of Mithraism, which is most noticeable in its festival calendar and corresponding rituals to do with perambulating bulls and communal feasting. Izady writes, '[t]he Cult is fundamentally a non-Semitic religion, with an Aryan superstructure overlaying a religious foundation indigenous to the Zagros.'

Mentioned by Herodotus, some Syrian and Turkish adherents of Alevism still maintain the rite of worshipping a deity represented by a sword stuck in the ground (which, to my eyes, looks rather like a T-pillar).

But it is the central Yezidi belief in Lucifer, Malak Tawus, as the world teacher and creator that is most suggestive of a very long-lived antiquity. Firstly, long before it was even a twinkle in History Channel's eye, we have a belief in celestial civilising beings. Secondly, the 'peacock angel' is commonly represented as a bird sitting atop a totem pole. Sometimes it is a rooster. Both species are genetically south Asian and this is something we will return to in later chapters. We return to Izady:

> The reverence of the Yezidis for divine manifestations in the form of a bird, the Peacock Angel, and the sacredness of roosters are just two better known examples. What is fascinating, but less well known, is that within 30 miles of the shrines of

Lâlish are the Shanidar-Zawi Chami archaeological sites of central Kurdistan, where the archaeologist Solecki has unearthed the remains of shrines and large bird wings, particularly those of the great bustards, dated to 10,800 ± 300 years ago. The remains are indicative of a religious ritual that involved birds and employed their wings, possibly as part of the priestly costume.

The representation of bird wings on gods was later to become common in Mesopotamian art ... The evidence of sacrificial rites practiced at ancient Zawi Chami may substantiate an indigenous precursor to modern Yezidi practice ... In light of the discoveries at Zawi Chami, the great bustard is a much more likely bird of the Yezidi icon.

Izady's book, *The Kurds: A Concise History* was published several years before Dr Schmidt's discovery of Göbekli Tepe. As such, he was not to know that within the range of the great bustard – the male of which is the earth's largest flying animal – the precise same imagery of totem poles with birds, the verticality of sacred origin and even the therianthropic half-bird/half-man imagery was to be found stretching back another two thousand years. Izady could only pull the beginnings of Yezidism into the Neolithic because that was all that was known at the time. However, here is Dr Schmidt describing the deceptive horizon between the Palaeolithic and the Neolithic:

I assume that since the late Palaeolithic at the latest, maybe even earlier, humans had religion. In my opinion, this is essentially indicated by evidence of burials, as after all providing a dead person with a grave, even with burial gifts, would hardly make sense without the spiritual background of the idea of an afterlife. A religion is not necessarily connected to the idea of a netherworld, but the existence of such an idea implicates the existence of a religion ...

Thus, early Neolithic religion at about 10,000 BC, no matter its nature, is rather a product of a very ancient development and not a new creation. We may assume that since the days of old there were handed down myths or mythological motifs, even if we will hardly be able to provide any real evidence for their existence in preliterate societies, not to mention their contents.

In much the same way that nearly one in two Americans believe that the world was created less than ten thousand years ago by an angry cloud man, while tweeting about these same beliefs on a slave-built device connected to hundreds of satellites orbiting the earth, it is a grievous interpretive error to assume technological change impacts belief systems at the same rate.

So, if parts of Yezidism are a Neolithic survival, then parts of it are actually a Palae-olithic survival, regardless of the subsequent appearance of towns and agriculture.

For the magician, the discovery of Göbekli Tepe at what was once believed to be the beginning of the human cultural story opens up vast new vistas on an era previously considered the domain of legend, with the tantalising possibility of exploring which parts of modern practice may be relics from this bygone age. For more than two thousand years, this era has been considered the home of true wisdom, *first* wisdom, the time before the Flood.

III   ET IN LAURASIA EGO

The last 140 years of the Western occult revival owe a great deal to the academic field of mythology and the antiquarian field of folklore. Consider for a moment the impact of Charles Godfrey Leland's *Aradia: Gospel of the Witches*, Robert Graves's *The White Goddess* or any of the works of Joseph Campbell. For better or worse, these fields provide a psychological and ideological framework in which magicians locate the context, origins and meanings of particular practices.

Magicians should at least shoulder some of the blame for the falling away of this relationship over the last thirty years but, as we saw in a preceding chapter, most of it must land on the moribund shoulders of academia as it struggled through post-structuralism and out the other end. At the level of group discourse, occultism's response to mythology's period in the wilderness has been to ossify around older, long-abandoned mythological frameworks. The time has come to recalibrate the relationship.

THE RETURN OF THE HOLLYWOOD EPIC

It is possible that the age of disjointed, milquetoast mythological interpretations has reached an inflection point. Long-abandoned as dubious preoccupations of Empires, the 'grand mythological narrative' is returning, this time (hopefully) in a far less political form.

Enter *The Origins of the World's Mythologies*, written by Harvard Indologist E. J. Michael Witzel and described by Wendy Doniger – she of the microscopes and telescopes – as an 'astonishing book.' And it is. Returning to Doniger's metaphor, Dr Witzel offers us one heck of a telescope. He has undertaken a comparative analysis of worldwide mythologies and mapped this comparison to archaeological and genetic data pertaining to the spread of humans out of Africa and around the globe. The results are hugely significant and, crucially, *provisional*. To his credit, Witzel admits that his very long book is only the first step toward an interdisciplinary approach to mythology, not the last. New data are guaranteed to appear that will move his proposed timelines, or suggest earlier connections between cultural groups, or place mankind in a specific part of the world at a previously-unknown date.

Witzel's theory is big, ambitious and new. Bold steps, taken with humility, are to be celebrated. They are the only way to break through the conservative incrementalism that has trapped academia in its death spiral down toward intellectual and monetary penury. They also say something profound about the origins of magic and the spirits. Occulture, like academic mythology, has a preference for looking *within* a system for connections – such as those between Hathor and Isis – rather than looking at the comparison between such systems. Here is Witzel describing his comparative approach:

> The next step in the comparison is the evaluation of the actual content of the texts. In comparative linguistics this would correspond to the studies going beyond single sentences to the investigation of texts, in other words, the structure (and interpretation) of the texts concerned. In mythology this would amount to the description of quasi-syntactical features, such as Propp's theory of the 30-odd constituents of Russian folk tales. However, comparisons of whole mythologies, corresponding in linguistics to that of, say, the Latin, Greek, Sanskrit, and beyond, the Egyptian, Sumerian and Nostratic languages and so on, are missing even now. In other words, we lack truly comparative and historical mythology, whose parallel in linguistics has existed since the early 19th century.

Given that languages contain whole cosmologies, Dr Witzel's comparative approach to mythology shines a brand new light on the interrelation of the gods and spirits of the western tradition. And such a light banishes the shadows of some persistent errors in magical reasoning.

Two such errors – actually both ends of the spectrum of the same error – are an over-reliance on archaeology's limited ability to tell us things about the non-physical world; and conversely the complete dismissal of archaeological evidence in either the creation of or the failure to update a magical worldview. Witzel empowers comparative mythology, linguistics, genetics and archaeological evidence to work in concert, using insights from one field to plug holes in another, while favouring none.

Independent local emergence of transcontinental and transoceanic motifs, and in the case of Laurasian mythology, of the complex Laurasian storyline, cannot be posited just because *current* archaeology does not yet indicate their existence. *Absence of evidence is not the evidence of absence*. Instead, the very existence of Laurasian myths in the Americas is proof of a pre-Mesolithic mythological tradition. The limitations of a purely archaeological model for the interpretation of the spiritual world of *any* early culture are conspicuous.

This interdisciplinary approach results in a global mythological scheme that has a time depth western esotericism is simply not used to dealing with. Whilst technically beginning prior to mankind's departure from Africa, the scheme pivots on that first colonial expedition. And so it is there that we begin.

THE PEOPLING OF THE EARTH

Mythology is crying out to be re-examined in the wake of what we now know about the peopling of the earth. When constructing grand narratives, insights derived from genetic research are our best defence against falling into the bad habits of either 'stacking' cultures in order of preference – the imperial error – or lazily relying on psychological explanations for similarities across place and time, which lacks evidence and fails to account for non-random distribution.

Given that the cells in your arms and legs are genetically identical, it is reasonable to suggest humanity has not quite got its collective head around precisely what our DNA is for. This does not mean we have not found it useful in other areas of research, particularly in the tracing of ancient population movements.

One of the purposes of my visit to Oxford mentioned in the prologue was to speak with researchers involved in the 'out of Africa' genetic study. What I needed reconciling was the very good genetic evidence that every human alive today is descended from the one African mother living between 200,000 and 100,000 years ago with the abundance of archaeological evidence that falls outside these dates, such as firepits in Israel and the UK that are twice as old again, and so on.

There are two main ways of calibrating these data:

1 If an earlier group of colonists left Africa and subsequently completely died out then, by definition, their existence would not show up in the blood of people still alive today as their genetic material has not been passed down. As a result, we also lack the DNA of the colonists to match against existing samples in the database, making it all but impossible to find the presumably-much-earlier Mitochondrial Eve in Africa.
2 With each passing year, it is becoming more obvious that we were not the only hominid game in town. Just in the space of the last decade, Neanderthals have progressed from being stupid, violent, language-free apes to a species capable of artistic abstraction in ochre painting found in Spain, pan-Mediterranean sailors, and a larger chunk of our own family tree than most of us realise.

The second point will take on increasing relevance as the book progresses, but for now it is important to realise that when we talk about how long a part of the world has been inhabited, we are really telling the story of our own bloodline, rather than the story of the place. In the coming decades, we may expect a continuous realignment of very early archaeological evidence with the migration of other hominids such as *Homo erectus* and the Denisovans, fleshing out the story of an Ice Age world of mysterious, sometimes competing, sometimes allying hominid species. As this book contends, just because we currently cannot – or will not – see it, the early human story is a lot longer and a lot more exciting than anybody expected. The whole situation calls to mind worldwide legends of mysterious companion races that we pushed to the margins of our habitats before losing sight of them completely. It is my contention that encounters with other hominids and/or their cultural remains may in some part be reflected in mythology. (The Oxford scientists would not be drawn on this hypothesis, obviously.)

Returning to the story of our bloodline, it appears our ancestors left Africa, turned right and hugged the coast all the way down through South Asia and into Australia. According to research by the Bradshaw Foundation, evidence of modern humans is found just across the mouth of the Red Sea from the Horn of Africa 90,000 to 85,000 years ago. By 75,000 years ago at the latest, modern humans had already made it right around the south coast of India and Sri Lanka to western Indonesia and up into what is now modern day Japan. A few thousand years later, humans had made it into Australia and what is now western Oceania. This is a surprisingly rapid trip. Perhaps beach jogging was our first leisure activity?

Based on studies of bottlenecks in the gene pool, those first migrants numbered very few, somewhere between 10,000 and 2,000 people. They would have brought with them an early African language and, crucially, a mythology. At present, there is no evidence of modern humans along the presumed coastal route of South Asia between Africa and the appearance of fully modern human remains in Australia by 50,000 BCE. Any such evidence is likely now under the ocean as a result of today's significantly higher sea levels. The Negritos (including the Malayan Semang, Philippino Negritos and the Andamanese) are suspected as being remnants of this first exodus. Whilst they all show genetic and linguistic intermixing with neighbouring groups, the Andamanese show the least intermixing. Dr Witzel considers this significant for his suggestions regarding the mythology of these explorers as there are large overlaps between Andamanese cosmology and that of indigenous African groups.

Secondary migrations subsequently occurred up into Eurasia and Europe from Southern and Southeast Asia at the end of an earlier ice age, between 52,000 and 45,000 BCE. Colonisation of the Americas first happened up the west coast of the Pacific and then back down its east coast into South America at the range of 30,000 – 20,000 years ago. (Assuming there was no trans-oceanic migration, that is. I suspect there may have been.) Successive Amerindian migrations from central Eurasia happened much later.

It may seem counterintuitive at first but similarities between mythologies separated in both time and space – such as the Andamanese and African pygmies – are methodologically important in building a global scheme. Witzel again:

> Just as in the spread of languages, certain motifs that are seen in individual myths and in ... mythology in general have been preserved at distant, diverse ends of the world; frequently it is not the immediate neighbors that are most closely linked, whether in myth or in language ... [I]solated, 'bizzare' features found in two distant areas usually are a sure hint at something old, an older, now lost structure, myth or mytheme.

Witzel describes the great civilisations of the ancient world as 'secondary centres of mythological innovation.' Mythology did not originate in these centres but was dramatically transformed by them. Rather than starting in locations such as Egypt, the

Indus and Mesopotamia, places of interest to a western view of itself and more easily interrogated by archaeology, we should chart the footsteps of our ancestors and see what is to be found there.

GONDWANA, LAURASIA AND PAN-GAEA

Witzel categorises the planet's mythologies into two macro-groups; examples of both still exist today; and one underlying group – mankind's earliest mythology – which is reconstructed from an examination of the overlaps between the two existent groups in much the same way as ancient languages are reconstructed. All three are discussed below.

1   GONDWANA MYTHOLOGY: 65,000 years old. This is the cosmology our ancestors took with them when they left Africa. These are described as 'a forest of stories,' which is a collection of discrete tales pertaining to the origin of individual creatures, how mankind first appeared, and taboos around tribal morality. Gondwana mythologies display little interest in the creation or destruction of the universe; indeed, probably the defining characteristic of a Gondwana mythology is that the creation/destruction story is absent and the universe has always existed and will always exist. Modern examples of Gondwana mythologies are found in Sub-Saharan Africa, Australia, New Guinea and parts of the western Pacific, all places of long-term isolation from other cultures and in the case of the latter two, where we very quickly arrived at on our out-of-Africa mission.

2   LAURASIAN MYTHOLOGY: 40,000 years old. Sometime around this date, somewhere in Asia or Eurasia, mankind developed what Witzel calls 'our first novel.' Laurasian mythologies begin with the creation of the world/universe and end with its destruction. In the intervening time we find the separation of heaven and earth, Creation existing through repeated epochs, the killing of a dragon or monster, a Golden Age and a Flood as punishment for mankind. Examples include Indo-Aryan mythology (and thus Sumerian, Babylonian and Vedic), Eurasian and European shamanism (and subsequently archaic Greek and Celtic), North Amerindian shamanism and North African belief (thus including Ancient Egypt).

3   PAN-GAEAN MYTHOLOGY: Between 150,000 and 65,000 years old. This is Witzel's reconstruction of mankind's first mythology, emerging some time in Africa after the appearance of modern humans. It contains a distant High God who may or may not have created the world but is uninvolved with it, a Trickster who teaches/ creates mankind, a spirit world viewed as a well of souls and probably a giant snake whose movements across the earth create the landscape.

This is a noble and ambitious exercise in examining non-random distribution. Witzel explains his methodology:

In actual procedure, when carrying out the Laurasian project, we have to start by stating obvious similarities between myths, sets of myths and whole mythologies. As a matter of principle and procedure, one needs two or three identical or similar items, best those distant from each other in space and time, to establish a common ancestral element. Comparisons of items found only in adjacent cultures are discouraged as they may be due to borrowing, but widely distant, remote mythologies (for example, those of Polynesia and ancient Israel, Scandinavia, or Greece or those of the Maya and Greeks) are especially useful. Pursuing these investigations, the Laurasian mythological model will gradually emerge and take shape.

We shall unpack the scheme in reverse-chronological order, beginning with Laurasia, and then address some of its shortcomings.

LAURASIAN MYTHOLOGY

The implication of mythic similarity points to a common pool of motifs that must have existed at a sufficient time depth to appear across such disparate corners of the world. Given that both Amerindian and Eurasian mythologies share the same Laurasian shape, this puts its appearance somewhere between 40,000 BCE and 20,000 BCE, 'somewhere in Asia.' Pinpointing the best case for precisely where in Asia requires the use of data points that Dr Witzel studiously avoids, which we will come to in later chapters. As we examine the components of Laurasian mythology, the most obvious examples that occur to you will likely be Judeo-Christian ones. This is to be expected as the Western world's dominant mythology is currently a Near Eastern one. However, as we saw from the examination of the history of archaeology and folklore, this does not point to a Near Eastern origin for the Laurasian story. Cultural prominence should not be mistaken for a point of origin. The Near Eastern variant of Laurasian mythology emerged at the comparatively late date of 3,000 BCE and thus could not have influenced the rise of the same 'mythological novel' we find in the Americas.

Laurasian mythology also exists in a variety of climates, putting paid to the idea that mythology exclusively arises as a product of human interaction with the local biosphere. (Though a coconut tree quickly becomes an oak tree as people move north, the tree remains.) Before examining the scheme in detail, I will mention that, working to Dr Witzel's timelines, Göbekli Tepe falls squarely into Laurasian time and space. This affords us an opportunity to analyse and counter-check its ritual function.

The World Egg

This is more properly considered the primordial waters/chaos/non-being-emerging-into-an-egg/hill mytheme, but that makes for an awkward subheading. Examples of this mytheme are found in Ancient Egyptian, Maori and Pacific beliefs, as well as Indo-Aryan, Eurasian shamanic, Hindu and Greek cosmologies.

Typically it entails the universe emerging from primordial waters as an egg, with half forming the sky and half forming the ground. Variants include the First Mound found in Ancient Egypt. The egg component is still evident there, however, where the waters of Nun are described as having no surfaces or edges and are compared to an egg.

In many of its variants, the world is created from the breaking of the egg in some form, and thus overlaps with the creation of the universe from the corpse of a defeated giant/dragon/monster. Sometimes it is the universe emerging from the egg but the physical realm is built of monster parts. Ymir, Pangu and Purusha are examples of this.

Father Heaven, Mother Earth, and their separation

The most obvious example of this mytheme is the Egyptian Geb and Nut – where the genders are reversed for reasons discussed later in the book – separated by their children, thus letting in light and air. An identical motif is found in New Zealand, across Polynesia, in Japan and Greece.

Variants include the Bible in which the Spirit of God 'moved upon the waters' and subsequently created/let in Light. A close match is also found in the Popol Vuh.

Typically, it is the children of this paring who are responsible for the separation of their parents and this act ushers in the next phase in Creation as well as commonly 'timestamping' the children to an era before the ascendant gods of that particular culture. As seen below.

Descending generations of deities and epochs

In a Laurasian scheme, the gods involved in Creation are 'under-worshipped' in their host cultures. Even worse, they are regularly depicted as monsters that need to be slain, such as the characterisation by the upstart Olympian gods of the Titans or some of the Hindu devas in Vedic and post-Vedic cosmology.

The classic example of this is the Sumerian depiction of Tiamat, her children and their confusing family tree of murder and intermarriage stretching over four generations. Most commonly we find associated with the story of killing the leader of the previous gods the notion that there are four specific ages, each increasingly degenerate. (We are now in the Kali Yuga, for instance.)

An exception to the degeneration of successive ages is found with the Pueblo and Mesoamericans, suggesting a change in the 'opinion' of aeonics among Laurasian cultures from positive to negative sometime between 20,000 BCE – when the Americas were presumably first colonised – and 4,000 BCE – when we first spy the aeonic model again in the archaeological record. A change in politics or climate, such as a worldwide flood, may have contributed to this. Witzel on the Maya system:

> The present (fifth) phase of the universe began when the dawn of the fifth sun appeared, after the previous Four Suns had failed. In these 'trial creations' the gods had unsuccessfully tried to create the world, light and human beings. The Four Suns correspond, sometimes even in name, to the Four Ages or four generations of the Indian, Near Eastern and Greek mythologies. The Navajo name their eras with the same colors as the western Eurasians: the Greek gold, silver, bronze and iron ages become their gold, silver, red and black ages. The myth is also found in South America, with the Incas.

The original 'positive' view of Laurasian aeonics is discerned by the progressive improvement of 'world governance' in most of its mythologies: the universe is in chaos, then it is run by monsters, then it is run by local cultural heroes (who nevertheless had dramatic or tragic lives), then it is run by humans. The notion of 'falling away' from a perfect state is presumably a later addition and probably arose in conjunction with mythemes pertaining to royal bloodlines and a Golden Age; both highly effective forms of local political propaganda.

The Trickster/Demiurge who brings civilisation

It has long been proposed that tricksters or demiurges represent 'leftover gods' from a previous cultural regime. If there is any accuracy to Dr Witzel's tripartite scheme then this may be simultaneously true and false. There is good evidence that the 'civilising trickster' is found in our earliest, Pan-Gaean level. Nevertheless, the insertion of a Demiurge into 'our first novel' suggests this new way of describing reality, the shamanic/chieftain description, had to solve the problem of what to do with all these leftover creators and creatrixes – the serpent, especially – contained within the underlying Gondwana stories. It is my strong suspicion that our changing opinion of the serpent over the last few tens of thousands of years is down to such a 'demiurgification.' Prometheus was a Titan, predating the Olympians, and the Serpent in Eden is a patently archaic mytheme. Look how it turned out for them.

Killing the Dragon

One of the cornerstone mythemes of the Laurasian storyline is the killing of a dragon or other enormous monster by a culture hero. Often it parallels or interrelates with the 'World Egg' mytheme in instances where the corpse of the dragon is used to construct the physical universe. Given that the dragon or giant snake is evidenced at much earlier levels than the emergence of Laurasian mythology, it is tempting to draw the conclusion that these stories represent the rewriting of cultural origins by a new power elite: the shaman, the chieftain, etc.

Examples of this mytheme include Marduk's destruction of Tiamat, a deity several generations older than himself; Leviathan, a more modern iteration of the same Near Eastern dragon story; and Indra's destruction of Vritra, 'firstborn of the serpents,' which releases all the world's water. The flood/water motif more often than not accompanies the dragon mytheme. Egypt, Greece, Northern Europe, China, Polynesia and South America – completing the Laurasian 'footprint' – all contain examples of this same story type.

A Golden Age

The inevitable next chapter in a 'novel' containing progressive aeons is a Golden Age where the gods lived with mankind, which is then followed by the withdrawal of the gods and the stewardship of the earth by half-human, half-divine beings. The majority of these mythemes are associated with the origins of noble or royal bloodlines and likely emerged during a time of social stratification. One does not need to look too hard for examples. Egypt, Sumeria, Vedic civilisation, China, Greece, Mesoamerica and South America. A lot of 'alternative history' involves zeroing in on one example, the Book of Enoch for instance, taking it literally and then making ambitious claims about the extraterrestrial origin of specific modern families or cultural groups.

Technically, nothing prevents a researcher from following the hypothesis that this civilising event literally happened and was caused by physical beings. However, such an hypothesis must be bound by the same rules of evidence as any other. It also, by definition, must examine the *original* telling of the story of our *first* civilising period, rather than arbitrarily selecting much later ones. Given that the homeland of Laurasian mythology still eludes us, such hypotheses are currently very tenuous.

A stronger, 'placeholder' hypothesis would be that this mytheme is a cultural memory of a moment of increased societal complexity involving the emergence of a new class of rulers taking their authority from the stories of an equally-new shamanic/priestly class, who may have been intermediaries for a new class of spirits or gods appearing some time around 40,000 years ago.

The Flood

If Dr Witzel's timelines are even slightly accurate, then Laurasian cultures had a story of a worldwide flood, typically interpreted as divine punishment for man's hubris, for tens of thousands of years before experiencing a worldwide flood at the end of the last Ice Age. Witzel's suggestion that these two events are entirely unrelated will be challenged below and explored in much greater detail in subsequent chapters. Even if the suggestion is accurate, and worldwide flood stories predate the end of the Ice Age, then going through just such an event would have been seen by the cultures who experienced it as typologically familiar. Put another way, having a very old story about a worldwide flood does not preclude the subsequent experience of just such a flood from surviving in your stories.

The Apocalypse

The Laurasian novel ends with one heck of a boss fight. In contrast to the 'eternalism' more commonly found in Gondwana mythologies, Laurasian mythologies not only have a beginning but will also someday end with the catastrophic destruction of the world.

GONDWANA MYTHOLOGY

Complex religion must have existed and been brought to Australia by 50,000 BCE at the very latest. The independent creation of Australian and African motifs can be excluded on the basis of the huge overlap between the two groups. The first Australian arrived with at least a few concepts they brought with them from home. Clearly some of the overlapping mythemes give us our starting point for constructing Gondwana mythology at this time depth.

What is important to remember is that Witzel's categorisation is not an evolutionary one. Gondwana stories are *older* than Laurasian ones but they still continue to this day in worldviews found in Sub-Saharan Africa, Australia and parts of Papua New Guinea, among other places. Cultures do not graduate from one collection of stories to another like cabin classes on an airplane.

From a magical perspective, the defining difference between Laurasia and Gondwana is that the former has a strong emphasis on the power of the word as opposed to the latter's stress on physical objects such as fetishes. This correlates to differing ontological emphases. Laurasian mythology seeks to explain the origin of a thing, as the knowledge of something's origin or name confers power over it. It is word and action that gives the Laurasian sorcerer his or her power. The role of a mediating object, such as a poppet, is less important. The prominence of power objects in Gondwanan magic reflects the lack of distinction between the profane and the spiritual. All of human existence is integrated into myth. Quoting Maurice Leenhardt's description of the Melanesian approach to myth, Witzel writes, '[t]he Melanesian projects himself into this world. He does not distinguish between reality and his own psychic life, between his self and the world. He plays a quasi-cosmic role.' Less care is given to the wording of an enchantment than is given to the quality of the power object used.

Once again, it is tempting to see the emergence of a new political class in this change of magical emphasis. To shift cosmic power from control of sacred objects to the naming and describing of things shifts power from the magical-asset rich to the lexicographers.

The most common components of Gondwana's 'forest of stories,' as opposed to Laurasia's 'novel' include the following.

1 CONTINUOUS CREATION. Gondwana mythologies contain numerous discrete stories of the origins of things, animals and most especially humans. However these most commonly take place on a canvas of a pre-existing, eternal universe. There is also no final destruction of the world. Gondwana's principal ontological concern is the shaping of the earth in such a way that makes human life possible. Typically this is seen in the activities of the trickster.
2 TOTEMIC ORIGINS OF MANKIND. In most Gondwana mythologies, mankind has its origin in a tree. Variants include a tree stump or split bamboo. Less commonly this is a rock or clay. (Both motifs, and particularly the tree, continued into Laurasian mythology. They can be found in the Bible, the Eddas, etc. Continuity of 'tree burial' is also seen in the Osiris myth.)
3 A DISTANT HIGH GOD. If some form of creation happened, it was instigated by a distant high god who has subsequently removed himself from heaven and is no longer worshipped, nor does he respond to worship.
4 FULLY DEVELOPED POLYTHEISM. The deities that do receive worship are local, nature spirits as well as ancestors.
5 A CIVILISING TRICKSTER. Occasionally the trickster is the same as the distant high god. More commonly it is his son or emissary who descends and teaches cultural technology to mankind. Often, mankind displays hubris and is punished by a flood.
6 THE (RAINBOW) SERPENT. Sometimes the high god takes the form of a giant serpent and creates the earth by the movements of his body, such as in Melanesia. Other times the serpent is a separate being. The most famous example of this is the Australian Aboriginal Rainbow Serpent, a concept also found in Southern Africa, Iran, India, Burma and South America. In Arnhem Land, the Rainbow Serpent is the

supreme creatrix. She is represented as the Milky Way in the night sky and carries the ancestors of the Aborigines in her belly. However it is clearly stated that the sky and earth already existed.

On that last point, it is interesting that the oldest archaeological evidence of ritual ever found on earth was discovered in Botswana by University of Oslo researchers. Offerings of arrow tips and similar objects, dedicated to a giant python whose body movements shaped the land have been found at a time depth of 70,000 years ago. This strikes me as something of a smoking gun for the Gondwana hypothesis.

PAN-GAEAN MYTHOLOGY

Pan-Gaean mythology is Witzel's tentative reconstruction of what mankind's first cosmology may have been. Obviously there are no extant examples of these beliefs or languages. However the methodology is sound and the insights are useful in the potential repositioning of western magic. The reconstruction is less arbitrary than it might initially appear. Just as Laurasian mythologies retain a certain amount of Gondwana motifs, a similar overlapping approach can be used to posit Pan-Gaea.

Most widespread among the earliest cosmologies is the notion of a high god departing a pre-existing earth for the heavens. At some stage he (most often he rather than she) sends down a trickster emissary to teach culture and hunting to mankind. There is typically some story of humans violating a taboo and triggering punishment. A 'well of souls' where humans come from and return to appears in evidence. I also suspect based on the Botswana research and the widespread appearance of the Rainbow Serpent that a large snake either was the high god or is in some way associated with him. Local spirits and the worship of stones and unusual features in the terrain that are occupied by said spirits also appear likely.

Sacrifice is prominent in hunter gatherer society and the necessity of killing is probably reflected in the destruction of the dragon/monster and the carving up of its corpse to create the world: without this act of violence there is nothing. Dr Witzel suggests that this belief may be the ultimate origin for the much later desire to build in stone. Regardless of their astronomical alignments, stone circles are in some sense a map of a world. To build one may well be a replaying of the carving up of a primordial monster. Given the prevalence of stone worship at a very early age, this is hugely intriguing.

SHORTCOMINGS IN THE THESIS

Being the first to say something is very often more trouble than it is worth. To Dr Witzel's credit, he admits his thesis will certainly be subject to modification and elaboration as more information comes to light. For the purposes of our research there are some notable shortcomings.

1 An underemphasis on star lore and navigation which are found in abundance in the Gondwana mythologies of Australia. The persistence of specific asterisms through history is one of the through lines of this book and broadly supports Witzel's thesis.

2 Staying firmly within the canon of what are acceptable data in mainstream academia. For instance there is no mention of complex megalithic sites that fall outside the broad Gondwana/Laurasia grouping, such as Gunung Padang in Indonesia. A professional Indologist is expected to say 'we don't know where the Laurasian homeland is but it's in the Nostratic area' without evidence.

3 'That's a story for another time' is invoked when the evidence points in a direction that would make mainstream academia uncomfortable. An example would be the appearance of Gondwana motifs in South America much earlier than the dates currently accepted for the population of the continent. (These are motifs that could only have got there via trans-Pacific navigation.)

4 Witzel refers to flood myths as 'incidental' and spread in a 'quasi-universal' way, which is an academic way of sidestepping the very likely situation that *some* myths may encode *some* real events. This dismissal is glaring because detractors could similarly refer to the appearance of his own Laurasian 'story line' as 'quasi-universal' or 'incidental.' We will examine in detail the distribution of flood motifs around the world. They appear with the highest density in areas that were subject to the greatest amount of land loss at the end of the Ice Age and the lowest density in areas that lost the least land. That non-random distribution requires explanation.

5 Witzel won't be drawn on whether some of the flood myths may relate to an actual event but is happy to suggest that the concept of a primordial ocean surrounding the land is a likely cosmology to emerge as colonists left Africa and spent a few thousand years walking along the coast of South Asia into Australia. This isn't to suggest his hypothesis of the primordial ocean is not keenly observed. It is. Half the entire universe for our ancestral colonists would have been ocean; a source of food, wonder, and a direction from which they could be sure they would not be subject to predation, unlike the grasslands and thick jungle on the other side of the sand. Witzel appears to choose the motifs that may have at least some literal origin based on personal preference.

6 The perhaps understandable inability to interpret the simultaneous development of artistic and spiritual concepts at 40,000 BCE all around the world without recourse to a spirit model or even a consciousness one. Witzel's overlay of the mythological motifs of the world with the archaeological evidence of this great cultural flowering highlights its strangeness in a way that is hard to ignore. So we will not.

7 The suggestion that Gondwana mythologies aren't interested in the creation of the world needs to be challenged in some scenarios. For instance, the Melanesian gods created the islands they settled rather than the whole universe. But the Melanesians did arrive there after the Flood. This means not only is the story literally true in some sense, it hints at the possibility that the act of Creation happened elsewhere. I suspect Laurasian mythology emerged in Island Southeast Asia, as we shall see, so the creation of the islands should be seen as a separate event to the creation of the universe. It is important to note that challenging this 'hard line' does not invalidate the Laurasia/Gondwana grouping and could conceivably be used to locate the Gondwana 'origins' for mankind's first concern with the beginnings of the universe.

For all of these shortcomings I forgive him entirely. Firstly, because the theory is delivered with rigour and humility. Secondly, the broad strokes appear not only correct but hugely, hugely useful to the further investigations of the origins of western magic.

SHAMANISM THROUGH TIME

As so many others have pointed out, shamanism, like linguistics (discussed in the next chapter), struggles under an historiographic challenge. The first region to be studied, Central Eurasia, has been used as the template by which others are measured. When working to timescales that cover tens of millennia and across the geography of the whole planet, this can be misleading.

Due in large part to the work of Mircea Eliade, we think of 'shamanism' as originating or templating in the area of the world that gave us the term. While history has been kind to Eliade's analysis of Siberian shamanism, his work on African and Australian traditions has not held up quite so well, and is even racially problematic. He considered the Australian versions to be 'debased,' for instance.

Based on the genetic and linguistic evidence that has subsequently come to light, we must reverse Eliade's directionality. Shamanism, in the academic sense, refers to indigenous spirit traditions tied to particular cultures and places. The overlapping beliefs and practices – of which there are many – moved out of Africa and into South Asia and Australia before human migration took them north into Eurasia. Thus we can see the retention of some Gondwana layers – such as cave initiation and shamanic dancing – but also the development of some specifically Laurasian techniques that came later – such as the use of drumming in association with the shamanic dancing.

Indeed, Witzel suggests that Laurasia's 'novelistic form' may have been a shamanic performative device to encourage memory retention of a culture's 'forest of stories.' A linear plot line is easier to recall and, crucially, retransmit with minimal change, than a non-linear one. The precision alignment of stone circles found right across the Laurasian footprint may represent underexamined evidence of this 'secret knowledge' that accompanied the rise of these new, novelising shamans. The process of incorporating disparate Gondwana star lore into a coherent system that could be predicted, measured and controlled by a new social class at the same time that an identical process was happening to the 'forest of stories' is too compelling to ignore.

Perhaps most interestingly, overlaying shamanic studies on a Laurasia/Gondwana framework provides insight into which magical techniques may be the longest lived. Extant shamanic traditions, such as those of the San, that occur in the parts of Africa that probably gave rise to the first modern humans, have techniques for moving 'heat'/energy up the spine and out through the head. This flow is symbolised as a serpent, within a culture that also has a rainbow serpent that aids shamans with shamanic flight. The same motif recurs obviously in India and Australia. You will recall it is also evident in the statues found near Göbekli Tepe and in the uraeus headdress of the Pharaohs, among many other examples. Here we likely see a supremely ancient process of manipulating energy upward and out, then the subsequent journeying thanks to the assistance of an animal spirit such as a snake or a bird. By the time this practice reaches Siberia the snake has become the world tree (the combination of both echoes through Genesis and into Kabbalah) but the directionality is the same.

Examining these similarities in light of the archaeological evidence of mankind's earliest ritual being devoted to a giant snake should have us all looking at the contents of our grimoires and magical cosmologies in a new light.

THE SPIRIT INTERPRETATION

This could almost belong as another shortcoming in the thesis were it not a near universal and entirely expected blind spot found across the modern academic spectrum. Witzel notes that the emergence of the Laurasian storyline broadly coincides with the so-called 'Palaeolithic Renaissance' in both time and space. While it is tempting to completely conflate the two, the fact remains that the Renaissance also occurred in Gondwana cultures, particularly those of Northern and Eastern Australia, home to some of the most vivid and compelling cave art on the planet.

The simultaneous, dramatic changes in symbolic thinking in differing cultures and local biospheres are difficult to reconcile in models that exclusively rely on materialist explanations. Dietary changes or environmental pressure cannot be posited as the Renaissance occurred across diverse climates. A specialist readership such as this one requires an additional interpretation, if not explanation.

Based on eminent mycologist Gastón Guzmán's analysis of the worldwide distribution of psilocybe mushrooms, it is interesting to note that their tropical and subtropical distribution overlays with South East Asia, New Guinea, Northern and Eastern Australia, New Zealand as well as Central America, the northern parts of South America and Central Europe. (The New Guinea/East Australia/New Zealand variants are very closely related to the Mexican ones, I note in passing.) Crucially for any attempt to fold entheogenic theory into the Pan-Gaea/Gondwana/Laurasia paradigm, the fungus is almost entirely absent from the parts of Africa believed to first give rise to modern humans but is found in high concentrations in the areas our colonising ancestors quickly moved to, in the case of South East Asia/New Guinea/Australia, and neatly overlays with examples of the Palaeolithic Renaissance, both in Gondwana and Laurasia cultures. Thus while the origin or 'reason' for the first emergence of mankind's spiritual impulse, the African Pan-Gaea cosmology, continues to elude us, it may be that we are seeing here the evidence for an encounter with a new class of spirits or consciousness effects, triggered by the colonists' encounters with the psilocybin molecule, resulting in similar spiritual and artistic responses within different cultures.

Given that we are talking about fungi and cultures with perishable artefacts at a time depth of 40,000 years, it is not clear what archaeological evidence we would ever expect to prove or disprove this hypothesis, although there are numerous depictions of mushrooms or humans with mushroom hands, etc. in later cave art, and indeed at Göbekli Tepe. It may be that mushroom encounter rates rose with the development of forest burn off as a strategy for growing the numbers of prey animals. This form of animal population management was still being practiced by the Australian Aborigines as late as last century. More animals, more dung, more mushrooms. (Certain geologists suggest that all grasslands are manmade. But for our purposes, there is no way to distinguish manmade burn offs from fires caused by lightning strikes.)

Western magic's 'immortality tech' is almost entirely Laurasian: the use of words and ritual, the ascent or reascent into heaven, the mythological context of a prior age of wisdom teachers who have passed the techniques down to us, the tree of life and an eschatological milieu. While Laurasia may be the 'containing narrative' for Western magic, many of its spirits are at least Gondwanan and potentially Pan-Gaean. You can even make the case – and I do – that 'true' Western magic, devoid of its much, much later onboarding of Neoplatonism, is a practical application of a Pan-Gaean worldview: God may exist but its existence is materially irrelevant; the Trickster/Devil is the gatekeeper and lord of culture; and it is recourse to local spirits and the dead by way of sacrifice that is the most commonly performed action.

The witch is a very old woman and she has been on a long, long walk.

DIGGING IN THE WRONG PLACE

This book tells the story of at least one advanced culture that existed prior to the end of the Ice Age, and the survival of some of its cultural practices and spirits down into the practice of western magic in the twenty first century, albeit in dramatically different outerwear. So it is an 'alternate history' book, which puts it in, shall we say, mixed company?

One of the great gifts of the Laurasian model is that it provides a countercheck of linguistic, genetic and archaeological evidence to some of the bolder claims of alternate history. It is worth highlighting some of these claims so you can see how wheat is separated from chaff.

1 *Looking for Noah's Ark.* Noah is a recent example of a much older flood myth, inherited by Near Eastern cultures. Why then, would we expect to find a 3,000 year old boat on a hill when the original story is at least 10,000 years old? (The construction of ritual boats, on the other hand, is attested to all across the Laurasian footprint.)

2 *Plato's Atlantis.* A variant of the above error, with the addition of mistaking technological complexity for cultural complexity because that is what we value in the west. Atlantis is an example of a retained memory of earlier cultures, to be sure, and very possibly a retained memory of the first Laurasian culture.

3 *The location of the Garden of Eden.* Eden is a Near Eastern variant of Laurasia's 'Golden Age' motif. The tree, snake and immortality fruit make that pretty clear. Again we face the problem of using as a map the literal description of a tumbled down, 20,000 year old story that was first told a long way from Judea.

4 *The Nephilim and the Book of Enoch.* Another example of a retelling of the much older Laurasian concept of the descent of spirit beings and an age of half-human, half-divine rulers and culture heroes. If it happened in any physical way, it happened tens of millennia prior to the story of Enoch.

5 *Similarities between Mesoamerica and Egypt.* There are certainly many similarities between these two regions. Typically this is expressed as 'how could this be when they are separated by so much time and distance? Ergo aliens.' The similarities are entirely predicted in the Laurasian model, whereby it was Laurasian cultures who colonised both areas between 30,000 and 10,000 years ago, and retained variants

of the same motifs. Dynastic Egypt and Mesoamerica (may have) had no contact, but wind the clock back far enough and the transmission vector becomes clear.

6 *Literal interpretations of Moses.* These are typically accompanied by a confused description of the Amarna Period of Ancient Egypt, with Akhenaten inventing monotheism (sometimes because of aliens), and then something to do with swamps, chariots, king tides and a volcano. But Moses is a lawgiver type, along with Manu, Menes, etc and the 'baby in the reeds' storyline is attested in Laurasian mythology as part of either the Culture Hero, Flood or Golden Age motifs. (It may actually be Gondwanan when you consider the Milky Way as the divine river/mother as found in Australia.) In any case, Akhenaten did not invent monotheism. He was not even a monotheist.

7 *OOPARTs.* Out Of Place Artefacts, such as those collected by Klaus Dona and Michael Cremo. A lot of these actually fall within my scheme of significantly more complex cultures existing before the end of the Ice Age. Over the next few years, these OOPARTs may revert to being ARTs. Some of the artefacts, particularly those in the Americas, with dates of 150,000 – 200,000 years or more can be interpreted as evidence of the complexity of other hominins, or evidence of earlier, ultimately unsuccessful, colonists, both of which are predicted in my thesis. (And some of them, frankly, may be evidence of full-blown extradimensional visitation more than a million years ago. Much of their evidence is hugely intriguing.)

8 *The Annunaki.* This topic will be dealt with at length later in the book but it is sufficient to say that, rather than aliens arriving in nuclear powered rocket ships to create mankind to mine gold to save the atmosphere of their home planet, a more satisfying interpretation is that the Sumerians had the most vivid example of the Golden Age/Era of Demi-Gods motif out of anywhere in the Laurasian footprint. Else you have to explain why these are dozens of similar motifs around the world that resemble an extraterrestrial event that 'really happened' in one specific part of it.

9 *Egyptians in America, Australia, etc.* Sure, why not? Nothing but an improved understanding of ancient maritime technology and the loosening bonds of academic timidity prevent the suggestion that trans-oceanic trade or exploration was undertaken by Dynastic Egypt. However the commencement of Dynastic Egypt is fairly well corroborated around 3,500 BCE, which is vastly too late to have caused a cultural transfer to or from the Americas/Australasia. (Ancient Egyptian culture extends much further back than Dynastic Egypt, of course.)

DIGGING IN THE RIGHT PLACE?

From a magical perspective, one of Dr Witzel's more useful classifications is what he calls 'grandfather stories' and 'grandmother stories.' Grandfather stories are the 'official' cosmologies that emerged with the rise of the Laurasian shaman/priestly class. It is the formation of the sanctioned belief system with its kingly stamp of approval. Grandmother stories are the survival of earlier, Gondwanan motifs in the form of folklore, fairy tales and children's bedtime stories. This is similar to Professor Tolkien's description of fairy tales as 'the furniture in the nursery': The furniture begins its life in the dining room or the bedroom, then it gets old and is replaced with something newer. The old furniture is relegated to the nursery, given to children to batter, and is ignored or forgotten by the 'official' world of the adults. But it was once official, sanctioned, even prominent.

Witzel uses as an example of a grandmother tale the widely told children's story that babies are delivered by a stork. In Germany, the stork story begins with the bird picking the baby up from what is effectively a 'well of souls.' This exact same motif in found in African Gondwana cultures and is likely Pan-Gaean in origin.

When looking for magical survivals through grandmother tales it is worth observing that folk magic or 'women's magic' retains the emphasis on fetishes and physical objects over the emphasis on correct words as found in grandfather tales. The pivot of this book's content away from an examination of Palaeolithic star lore to an examination of the continuity of spirits and magical practices in the west emerged from a discussion with Jake Stratton-Kent, author of *Geosophia* and *The Testament of Cyprian the Mage*. Given the presumed female origins of goetia in Archaic Greece, and its emphasis on trafficking with the dead, then the 'grandmother tale' interpretation posits the intriguing possibility that, far from reaching the end of the 'goetic hallway' in Archaic Greece and being unable to go any further, we have instead found a doorway, opened it and spied a much, much longer corridor beyond. The practical implications of such a possibility are profound.

Somewhere in between Africa and South America, taking the long way around, mankind's spirituality transformed from a 'forest of stories' to our 'first novel' and the key components of the western magical tradition began. This happened at a time after the first colonisation of Australia and in a place necessarily north of it.

Perhaps not too far north?

IV ISLAND OF DRAGONS

The further back in time we travel, the fewer the archaeological data points and the greater the desire to connect what little of them remain into parent-child relationships. It is quite clear that the gods of both Egypt and Sumeria are present at Göbekli Tepe, albeit in atavistic form. However, it does not necessarily follow that those tribes who buried the last enclosure immediately wandered south and founded two of the three great civilisations of antiquity. Mistaking resonance for *direct connection* has trapped many a magician in the garden maze of Choronzon's summer palace. The Laurasian model described in the previous chapter is our best interpretive framework for exploring these correlations.

When dealing specifically with physical evidence, it is essential to recognise just how rare these data points are and to realise that they hint at a much larger world of which we only have a fragment, then seek to build out a new, evidence-based world from this knowledge. Otherwise, you are a farmer who discovers a Roman coin in a field in Somerset and declares that the empire began right here by your apple trees.

More than any other error – and there are so very many to choose from – this is the mistake that has led most Atlantologists into madness and ridicule. The last century has shown that mankind indeed survived through a worldwide cataclysm when an area the size of Europe and China combined sank beneath the ocean. But at the moment there seem to be more lost continents than there are Starbucks. The cause of this error is understandable. As Dr Oppenheimer writes in *Eden in the East*:

> When breakthroughs like cereal farming, pottery and bronze making occur at the same time in widely separate regions, the usual explanation is that these discoveries were independent. This may seem a weak argument but for academics it is much safer to say this, rather than risk ridicule by having to prove how the inventions were transmitted over great distances. Theoretically, both points of view have an obligation of proof. The alternative hypothesis for the Neolithic Revolution – and one which seems more plausible than the independent origins implied by the archaeological record – is that farming technology was invented in one cultural region over a long period; knowledge of the innovation then spread to other continents by sea and land routes.

So much for mainstream academia. The current state of affairs in independent or alternative research, populated with ridicule and shysters, is just as bad, if not worse.

This bifurcation into 'aliens' in the alternative camp and 'nothing happened, move along' in the mainstream camp was not always so. In fact, for the vast majority of western history, it was taken as fact that civilisation predated a worldwide sea-flood and was probably restarted by its few survivors. As the historicity of this state of affairs reemerges into the light, we learn that this notion – in all likelihood a cultural memory – was one of the babies thrown out with the bathwater of biblical Creationism. In one of the scientific method's first clashes with the incumbent priestly class, the notion of a worldwide flood, Noah's Flood, was dismissed as unscientific and so any civilisation destroyed by said flood must also be balderdash. This was a necessary casualty on the way to dethroning Creationism. It may have taken a hundred years, but geology is finally recovering from its combat wounds.

Along with geology's recovery has come the emergence of genetics as a means of tracking ancient population movements, and advances in linguistics as a means of tracking their complexity. After two millennia of mistaking mythology for history and following echoes of echoes of echoes of stories to points all over the planet, hoping that X marks the spot, we have never been in a better position to generate facts upon which we can overlay interpretations.

A perfect storm of prejudices and personal predilections has trapped the story of the Flood, and who it affected, for a long time. Atlantis is not Thera. Atlantis is not the marshlands near Valencia. Atlantis is not the Bimini Road. Atlantis is not the submerged harbour of Alexandria. Atlantis is a flood story, one of many. And flood stories turn out to have a decidedly nonrandom distribution.

The continent with the least flood stories is Africa, which just so happens to be the continent that suffered the least land loss at the end of the Ice Age. The area of the world with the most flood stories is Island Southeast Asia, home to more than half of all flood legends, which just so happens to be the part of the world that suffered the most land loss at the end of the Ice Age.

As to the assumption that islanders have more experience with sea floods and are thus bound to have more stories about them, this explanation is unsatisfactory and frankly racist. It assumes a fisherman in the Bismarck Archipelago cannot distinguish between a global cataclysm and the Easter tides. But just as with the Hawaiians and their words for rain, or the Eskimos and their words for snow, a Chuukese villager will forget more about the ocean after a night out on *sakau* than you or I will ever know in our lifetime. The human mind cannot see colours it does not have words for. There may be considerable accuracy in such a volume of flood stories, if we have the words to see them.

AND DID THOSE FEET?

We will return to flood stories in the next chapter. In order to determine whether any of them constitute cultural memories, we must first examine what actually happened, and to whom.

There are some very specific reasons as to why the history of Island Southeast Asia and the nations of the Pacific are so little known. Firstly, these places are a long way from London and Amsterdam, two of the main trading centres that reincorporated these areas back into a global economy. Secondly, by the time it came to examining their stories, much of the singular narrative of 'world history' was already written and so the evidence was shoehorned into a structure it simply did not fit, like a wicked stepsister's foot squeezing into a glass slipper. That is how we have ended up with the situation of tenured academics saying that the largest humans on earth – the Polynesians – descended from the probably the smallest – the Taiwanese – in a matter of a few centuries.

To suggest that this may have been wrong was to suggest that the story of East Asia was wrong, which was to suggest that the story of Western Asia and Europe and Africa was wrong. Picking up a different metaphor, the jigsaw of history was complete but for one piece, the Pacific, which did not fit in the last remaining place. Better to smash it in and hope nobody noticed than admit the whole puzzle needs starting over.

Thus, the safest way forward is to layer data from the hard sciences on top of each other and look for where they pile the highest, and only then invite interpretations of our unusual jigsaw piece from the Humanities end of the spectrum.

GEOLOGY

The area of the earth that lost the most amount of land following the three separate sea level rises at the end of the Ice Age was Island South East Asia. Geologically, this entire region is now known as the Sunda Shelf, a formation of comparatively shallow seas off the Malay Peninsula and around Sumatra, Java and Borneo, making up part of the Asian continental shelf.

Looking east from Sundaland, there was a small, island-strewn ocean, housing Sulawesi, Timor and others, before the giant, connected continent of Australia and New Guinea, called the Sahul Shelf.

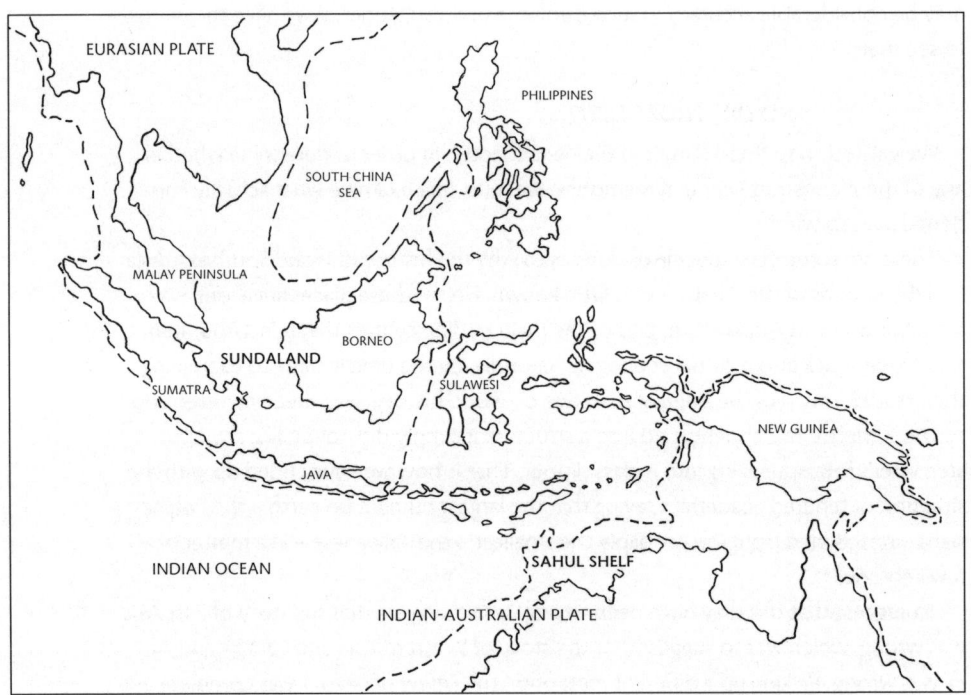

fig. 5   *Sundaland and the Sahul Shelf*

Between the last glacial maximum and the end of the Ice Age, it lost more than half its total land, an area greater than modern day India. Before then, it would have been a rather idyllic place, consisting largely of flat, grassy plains, sheltered river valleys and numerous pine forests. We think of the area now as warm, humid and tropical but it was only the northern half of Borneo that was 'everwet.'

Perhaps significantly for any hypothetical development of an Ice Age culture, there were no large land predators – such as sabre-tooth tigers – for the early humans to contend with.

The sea between Sundaland and the Sahul Shelf was by no means a barrier. It may well have been something of a Palaeolithic Aegean. Evidence of fishing and aqua-culture dating back thirty thousand years has been found as far out as the Bismarck Archipelago. On Timor, one of the islands in this sea, a beautiful, 35,000 year old carved bone spear point was found. Sue O'Connor, of the Australian National University, noted that its notches are almost identical to 90,000 year old spear points found in Africa, perhaps giving us an even earlier date for the beginnings of the Gondwana mythological scheme (or at least some cultural continuity forward from Pan-Gaea into Gondwana). Decorated spear points are a little like Turkish star temples, their rarity is not an indication of their uniqueness. Both require a culture in which to evolve.

GENETIC8

The length of time modern humans have existed in a temperate, largely preda-tor-free environment that is now mostly lost beneath the ocean is highly significant in determining when and where Ice Age cultures may have developed complexity. Overlaying these two data instantly removes most of the more ambitious suggestions for the location of a so-called lost continent. But the insights afforded us by genetics do not stop with the peopling of the earth we saw in the last chapter. Far from it.

Returning to the metaphor of modern humans not being the only game in town, Sundaland was a veritable casino of different games. Out of anywhere on Earth, Island South East Asia is emerging as the place with the highest density and greatest variety of hominins. Most famously, we have *Homo floresiensis*, the 'Indonesian hobbit' with whom we shared the landscape for at least thirty thousand years. Its origins are ultimately unknown, but it is currently suggested that it evolved from an even earlier colonial expedition from Africa and our shared ancestor may be more than two mil-lion years old. Perhaps every ex-Africa group turns right and keeps the ocean on their right until they run out of land?

A more recently discovered hominin, the Denisovan – so named for the Siberian cave in which the first finger bone of the species, 50,000 years old, was discovered –

was also a contemporaneous inhabitant of Sundaland with Homo sapiens. In fact, the highest levels of Denisovan genetic admixture have been found in blood samples in Island South East Asia and Oceania, demonstrating that we not only lived in the same vanished continental area, but also had sexual contact.

According to Mark Stoneking, professor at the Department of Evolutionary Genetics at the Max Planck Institute for Evolutionary Anthropology, 'the fact that Denisovan DNA can be detected in some but not other original inhabitant populations living in Southeast Asia today shows that numerous populations with and without Denisovan DNA existed over 44,000 years ago. The simplest explanation for the presence of Denisovan genetic material in some but not all groups is that Denisova people themselves lived in Southeast Asia.'

Finding the 50,000 year old finger bone of an Oceanian hominin in a cave in Siberia is another one of those facts that leap out to tell us the story of our distant past was a lot more complex and a lot more global than it initially appeared.

A Taiwanese fisherman, 25 kilometres offshore, recently hauled up the jawbone, called Penghu 1, of what is probably another entirely new hominin species. It dates to between 130,000 and 190,000 years ago or 10,000 to 30,000 years ago. If those dates look strange, that's because they are. Being dredged from the ocean floor did not allow for it to be studied in stratigraphic context, all the collagen had leached out, which prevented radiocarbon dating, and U-series dating was unreliable due to a uranium overprint in the sea water. Nevertheless, that more recent date range puts Penghu 1 in the same location as modern humans at a time when we were there.

The potential for Sundaland and Sahul sexy times do not end here, either. Neanderthal admixture is often higher in East and Southeast Asian populations than with Europeans. It is also emerging that large amounts of genetic material responsible for our modern immune system – perhaps up to 70% – are the result of introgressions from these archaic near-human species, and that this transfer occurred after we left Africa. In a literal sense, it was 'laying with the daughters of Man' that may have led to the survival of the little colonial project we call modern humanity.

A BRIEF MYTHOLOGICAL INTERLUDE

I am aware that the suggestion that 'laying with the daughters of Man' has some historical corollary is often highly dubious. It has a tendency to lead very quickly to claims that conehead aliens are our overlords and their descendants still run the world. This arises from a persistent confusion of mythology with history. But as Karen Armstrong points out in A Short History of Myth:

[I]n the pre-modern world, when people wrote about the past they were more concerned with what the event had meant. A myth was an event which, in some sense, happened once, but which also happened all the time. Because of our strictly chronological view of history, we have no word for such an occurrence, but mythology is an art form that points beyond history to what is timeless in human existence.

Mythology allows for the retention of meaning within a culture, meaning that may have arisen as a result of historical events in the far distant past. It is our failure to recognise the conflation of timelines into contemporaneous religious expression.

The Nephilim are not Denisovans who lived in Sundaland. However, there was a scientifically observable sexual transfer of genetic material between males who weren't *Homo sapiens* and females who were in the distant past, which would have presumably been reflected in the mythology of the time. It may well be that this Palaeolithic mythology had some influence on the Eurasian stories that ultimately became the Babylonian and Hebrew Nephilim stories. These encounters may well be survivals of 'Gondwana history' into 'Laurasian mythology.' Interpreting any of these 'story layers' literally or in isolation will lead you astray.

A RETURN TO GENETIC8

Because of the high frequency of their occurrence, mutations or adaptations forming as a response to disease or environmental conditions are frequently used to track ancient population movements. From the Spice Islands, which were mountains at the time, we have a 30,000 year old genetic adaptation to cold weather. A very similar adaptation is found in contemporaneous samples from northern Europe. As mentioned in the opening of this chapter, Sundaland had a temperate climate and was – and is – considerably warmer than northern Europe. The only environmental factor that might lead to this adaptation would be open ocean travel, where it can get very cold and wet at night. This adaptation is found in Polynesian samples right across the Pacific.

Perhaps the most famous population marker is the Polynesian Motif. It is actually three separate malarial adaptations, from oldest to youngest, and the story of its distribution is the story of Sundaland.

1 The oldest of these 9 base-pair deletions, called by Dr Oppenheimer 'the Asian grandmother,' is 60,000 years old and originates on the mainland. This aligns well with the current understanding of when Sundaland was originally inhabited and

from where. It also shows up in American samples but whether this is because the mutation happened before the populations separated and went north into America or whether it was spread at a later date through the Pacific is not known. It is probably both, as we have evidence from a study published in *PLOS Genetics* in April 2013 of trans-Pacific contact in Ainu blood samples dating back at least 6,000 years and possibly up to 10,000, based on cultural similarities between the Ainu and the Jōmon of Japan. If you are looking for the smoking gun for global sea travel right at the end of the Ice Age, then this may turn out to be it.

2 Returning to the Polynesian Motif, the second substitution is called 'the Southeast Asian mother' and is most likely to have originated, as you might expect, in Southeast Asia or Island Southeast Asia. It is the most widely distributed of the three markers, reaching right out into Oceania and Polynesia, as well as back into India and even up into Tibet. The birth of the Southeast Asian Mother from the Asian Grandmother happened 30,000 years ago.

3 The final substitution, the 'true' Polynesian Motif, originates in eastern Indonesia 17,000 years ago – long before the end of the Ice Age – and spreads eastward into Melanesia perhaps around 6,000 years ago and then out into the Pacific with successive waves of colonisers over the next five millennia. This 'first stage followed by many stages' aligns precisely with the hypothetical migrations of the refugees of a dramatic sea level rise and their descendants.

It is useful to consider the specific genetic links between this corner of the world and subsequent areas of examination. The map shows where else on the planet you can find genetic evidence tying back to the Austronesian-speaking domain of Island Southeast Asia. It is highly suggestive of a shared origin for some physical and non-physical technologies.

Most significantly, there is penetration of the Southeast Asian Mother into India, particularly in the north, as well as a sharp north/south divide that aligns well with current archaeological interpretations of pre-Vedic and Dravidic divides. (Although I expect a further blurring of this archaeological divide in coming years.) South India and Sri Lanka actually show more diversity in these 9 base-pair deletions from Southeast Asia, however they trace back to everywhere except the Malay Peninsula, where the Southeast Asian Mother originated. This diversity likely indicates sustained east-to-west contact at an earlier date. (Increasing diversity is associated with longer periods in which mutations can form and be passed down.) Returning to Dr Oppenheimer:

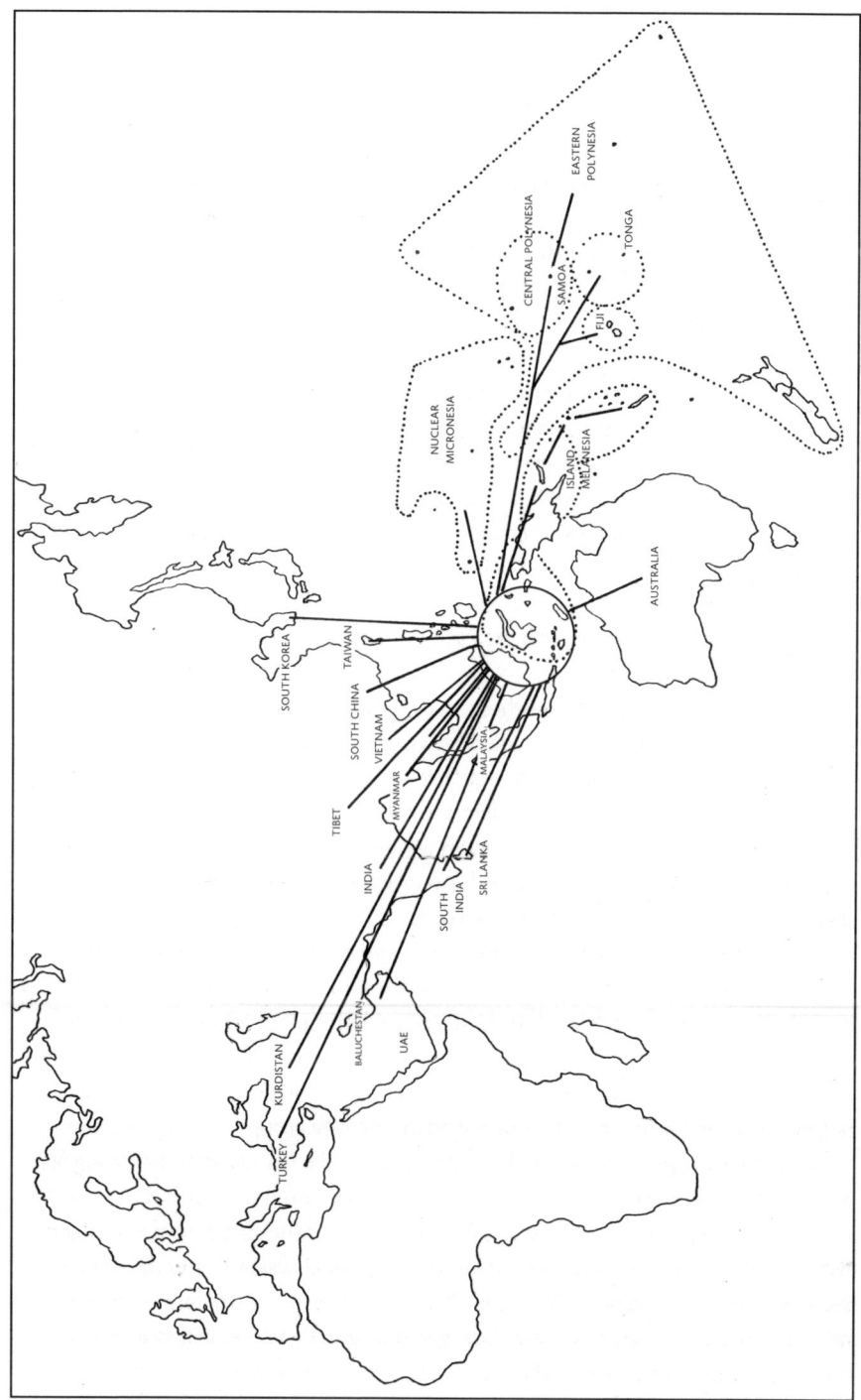

The final prediction of the southern Austro-Asiatic homeland hypothesis is that the migration of Austro-Asiatic speakers to India went through the Straits of Malacca shortly after the rising sea opened it over 8,000 years ago ... A recent analysis of Indian mtDNA types reveals not only multiple East Asian intrusions into the Indian subcontinent, but a clear north-south division as well. Another conclusion from this latter study is that the antiquity of East Asian mtDNA markers suggests a very ancient migration west.

Asian mtDNA markers also show up very early in parts of Scandinavia, particularly in Finland. It is interesting to note that the Saami, whose *Kalevala* has Asian and Pacific echoes, may be genetically the closest to those first Asian arrivals. Layering in thalassemia data on top of mtDNA results, a picture of contact from Southeast Asia, to India and the Bay of Bengal, stretching up into the Middle East and Kurdistan also begins to form. Dr Oppenheimer concludes that genetic trees constructed for Asian populations all have Southeast Asia placed in their oldest branches. It is these same markers that were carried out into the Pacific, north along the Chinese coast and even across to the Middle East.

Searching for the counter-hypothesis to the Southeast Asian influence on Eurasian cultures and mythologies, the so-called 'pincer model' suggests there was a second exodus out of Africa around 40,000 BCE that went eastward into Eurasia and the Levant. If this were so, such an expedition would have left a genetic fingerprint that would allow us to easily identify the resulting Central Asian group. There is no such evidence and so far no Central or North Asian lineages have been found that are not ultimately derived from Southeast Asian ones.

On the other side of the Pacific, more and more genetic data find themselves in alignment with the broad strokes of early human population movements as described in both the Laurasian model and the linguistic analysis described below. Brazilian geneticist Sérgio Pena has found mtDNA markers in the skulls of the indigenous Botocudo people that also show up in Polynesians and as far afield as Madagascar, which is largely the same footprint as the Austronesian language group.

So we have the geology of a sunken land, we have the genetic data indicating first arrival and contact with other archaic humans and we also have blood markers indicating the spread of these people toward the corners of the globe most associated with the emergence of V. Gordon Childe's concept of civilisation after the last great sea level rise at the end of the Ice Age. What is so crucial to understand – and so often misunderstood – is that these data show genetic contact with *existing local populations*, not the peopling of otherwise unoccupied lands from an origin in Southeast Asia.

Such a situation has mythological parallels in the flood stories of each of the areas with evidence of contact: the arrival of wisdom teachers from a sunken land across the sea. It is the contention of this book that some of these flood stories are tumbled down cultural memories of just such incidents.

In the last chapter we were introduced to Dr Witzel's Laurasian scheme, which he admits is currently lacking a homeland. Indologist to the last, it seems his refusal to consider Sahul or Sundaland as the first place to give rise to the Laurasian storyline is down to personal preference. In earlier versions of his thesis, Dr Witzel maintained that the rise of Laurasia was associated with the hypothetical 'second exodus' out of Africa into Central Eurasia, where the Laurasian theme developed, before realising it has zero genetic evidence to support it. Rather than reconsider the growing evidence of cultural and genetic complexity in Sahul/Sundaland, he relies on yet another hypothesis: 'we will have to account for the spread of Laurasian mythologies into Southeast and East Asia with a different scenario – for example, a purely hypothetical second wave of migration via India to Southeast Asia or a post-Ice Age reflux into Southeast Asia from what is now China by speakers of Tibeto-Burmese and Austric languages, whose ancestors had arrived there at c. 40 kya.' Once again, we mention the obligation of proof.

Dr Witzel does, however, make the very good point that chickens and pigs, both native to Southeast Asia, are almost absent in other Laurasian mythologies. The expectation appears to be that this would not be the case if the Laurasian storyline emerged there. They may not be evident in mythologies, but they are certainly evident in spiritual taboos and dietary prohibitions. By his own scheme, the rise of the Laurasian novel long predates the domestication of the pig or chicken so I am not sure what kind of visibility he expects them to have in mythological motifs.

Ultimately, the question then becomes whether we have data indicating the rise of cultural complexity in Sundaland so very long ago. And the answer is yes.

LINGUISTICS

Historically, the study of ancient languages suffered from its own challenges to do with both artificial and real horizons. Because the field of linguistics first arose within Indo-European languages, it began by tracing its own family tree backwards, noting loan words and comparisons, effectively building a family tree back to a presumed root language. (Which, incidentally, arose in eastern Cappadocia, not overly far from Göbekli Tepe, around the time the temple was still in use.)

Such analyses are fine, however they have a horizon of utility of about 7,000 years ago, beyond which most competent linguists will tell you there simply aren't enough words available for meaningful comparison. Dr Johanna Nichols, linguist at UC Berkley, makes this observation in her *Linguistic Diversity in Space and Time*:

[T]here has been a strong tendency to approach all historical problems as problems in the structure and description of family trees, as well as a tendency to assume that the great majority of languages in any continent naturally go back to a single ancestor just as the great majority of languages in western Eurasia do. In fact, however, a number of historical problems ... are better approached as population-typological or geographical issues. Such an approach has the advantage that it can take us farther back in time than the comparative method can and see graspable facts and patterns where the comparative-historical method has nothing at all to work with ... The fate of Indo-European, or more generally the fate of a group of typologically similar language families from post-Neolithic inner Asia, has not only distorted theory and method but skewed nature and reality as well.

About 7,000 years ago is where our particular story ends rather than begins. To get beyond this, Dr Nichols pioneered a methodology that, in terms of its usefulness and implications, is on par with the discovery of archaeological stratigraphy.

Briefly, she classified much of the world's languages into yes/no categories based on their grammatical structure. Do they have a 'subject-object-verb' word order, for instance. The resulting data lend themselves to a fascinating statistical analysis of linguistic diversity.

To take just one example of the effects that can be observed, reductions in linguistic diversity are often associated with rises in cultural complexity. On the surface, this may appear counterintuitive but we know it from the historical period. The rise of empires led to the spread of Latin or Arabic or English or Spanish across previously diverse and discrete linguistic territories. This shows up as a reduction in grammatical complexity as indigenous languages are either obliterated or hybridised in order to facilitate economic and political communication across much larger land areas.

[T]his survey has uncovered no evidence that human language in general has changed since the earliest stages recoverable by the methods used here. There is simply diversity, distributed geographically. The only thing that has demonstrably changed since the first stage of humanity is the geographical distribution of diversity.

Collections of grammatical structures – either increasing or decreasing in complexity – can then be observed moving through the tongues of the world. What Dr Nichols discovered were three great stages in the peopling of the world.

The first stage began in Africa more than a hundred thousand years ago and was a time of great linguistic diversity. 'Societies would have been small, simple and autonomous, and the environment was of course tropical, conditions that foster diversity today.'

The second is called the stage of expansion, from about 60,000 years ago to 30,000 years ago. It is characterised by population movements that would have required knowledge of seafaring and adaptation to sometimes extreme climates. 'This stage too must have involved increasing diversity for that part of the linguistic population that participated in the expansion, but it may ultimately have led to the extinction of many lineages that did not, for the genetic density in Africa and tropical Eurasia is now very low.' The second stage aligns pleasingly with the location and timing of the Southeast Asian Mother's appearance in Sundaland.

The third and final stage provides the most significant linguistic evidence for the cultural impact of cataclysmic survivors on the development of culture elsewhere in the world. Beginning at the end of glaciation, Dr Nichols shows that it is 'circum-Pacific colonisation that has populated most of the world, given rise to most of the genetic lineages of human languages and colonised the New World.' The trip to the Americas was up from Sundaland rather than across from Siberia, following the sea level rise that accompanied the end of the Ice Age.

Narrowing back down to the dominant language family of the area, Austronesian, we find that it actually stretches all the way from Madagascar, along the coast, through Island Southeast Asia and out into the vast Pacific. It is unrelated to any mainland Asian language families and its homeland has not been definitively identified, although Wilhelm Solheim believes it is probably in eastern Indonesia. He calls the maritime culture that developed it the Nusantao. As Dr Oppenheimer notes, 'even non-linguists might think it surprising there is not a single mainland tongue to give firm Asian provenance for the Austronesian family. Asia is after all the nearest continent.'

Despite the complete lack of evidence, the spread of Austronesian into the region was historically tied to the spread of rice cultivation into South East Asia. There may well be something to this theory, however recent archaeological evidence suggests the spread went in the opposite direction, from the islands to the mainland.

AGRICULTURE

There is a very ethnocentric perceptual bias in how we conceive of farming. We tend to picture the classic amber waves of grain. This ignores the fact that for most of agriculture's history, most of the world's population actually ate rice.

The bias does not stop there. We also have a tendency to picture farming as the replacement of indigenous plant life with one or two imports that are tended and harvested on an annual basis. But if we widen our definition to include cultivation of local species – to giving Nature a helping hand in doing what she was already doing – then the story becomes quite different, and significantly older.

Yams, for instance, are absurdly easy to cultivate. You put a few of them in the ground and ignore them. When you come back, you have a lot more. Wild yam and taro cultivation was happening in Indonesia around 15,000 years ago. By about 7,000 BCE we begin to see evidence of barley cultivation in the Indus Valley. At this time, in the mountains of New Guinea, locals had been draining swamps for wild plant cultivation for millennia.

Further north, the Jōmon of Japan had developed pottery for fish storage by 13,000 BCE, indicating that the so-called 'Pre Pottery Neolithic' we see at Göbekli Tepe is not a universal term. It is the Jomon, incidentally, who have the strongest genetic links with the Americas. Stones for grinding wild cereals appear in the Solomon Islands 26,000 years ago, more than ten millennia earlier than in the Fertile Crescent. Returning to the growing evidence for rice cultivation before the flood, remains have been found in two caves on the Malay Peninsula; the Spirit Cave and the Sakai Cave, possibly going as far back as 10,000 BCE. This is significantly in advance of rice cultivation on the Asian mainland. Rice is a remarkable plant. From Sri Owen's *Rice Book*:

> Upland rices grow in forest clearings or unterraced hillsides, asking only for generous rainfall. Swamp or deepwater rices are happy in flood conditions near river mouths, able to grow 10–15 centimetres a day to keep pace with the rising water level ... Traditional rice varieties reach maturity in anything from 140–240 days; some modern ones mature in 90 days, allowing a quick-moving farmer to grow two, three, or even four crops in a year.
>
> That is another astonishing characteristic of irrigated rice. You can grow it in the same field, year after year, indefinitely – some rice fields are believed to have been continuously cropped for two thousand years or more.

If you are looking for the starch that would be the easiest to gradually cultivate over centuries of observation, and the one that would net the largest reward in doing so, then it is probably rice. We will never know if Sundaland's river mouths held cultivated rice fields but they were almost certainly home to the uncultivated grain.

It is interesting to note that the earliest evidence of rice growing in Northern India aligns with the timelines for genetic contact with Island Southeast Asia. It is similarly interesting to note that the latest evidence from the Zagros Mountains of Iran has led archaeologists to conclude that 'there was no single origin for agriculture' in the Fertile Crescent as they have not found one. This interpretation, as Dr Oppenheimer points out earlier in this chapter, has an obligation of proof.

Tracing the genetic origins of domesticated foods offers the alternate palaeological researcher a plethora of smoking guns. You are unlikely to find less scrupulous divisions between fact and interpretation. The sweet potato has been proven to have arrived in the western Pacific (Sundaland) from the Americas 'some time in prehistory' and then is ignored. The melon, an important foodstuff in China and Iran around 5,000 BCE, must have been domesticated in Africa (or Australia) before that. The cucumber originated in the Himalayas but was grown in huge quantities in Ancient Egypt. Chickens, also Southeast Asian, appear in Egypt by 2,000 BCE. Recent mitochondrial research into the earliest domestication of chickens demonstrates that this Southeast Asian bird, fully domesticated, was found in Northern China by 10,500 BCE.

The dog appears to have been domesticated from a local wolf population somewhere south of the Yangtze 16,500 years ago, with the genetic diversity getting higher the further into Southeast Asia the samples came from.

'Lemon' and 'cinnamon,' both Austronesian words referring to Southeast Asian plants, appear at the very beginning of the Indus culture. The Hindu words for cloves and camphor are also Austronesian imports, thus completing, in Dr Oppenheimer's words, 'a chain of Austronesian language contact stretching from Japan around the coast of Asia to the birthplace of Western civilisation.'

Further evidence of the high level of cultural complexity in what is now Island Southeast Asia can be found by looking in the opposite direction to the general Northwest path our story will follow. As we have seen, there is a high degree of overlap between Siberian shamanic and North American indigenous beliefs. This is to be expected given the evidence for migration around the 10,000–15,000 BCE mark, at which point these cultures were solidly Laurasian. However, there is significantly less overlap between the indigenous beliefs of South America and North America, with Southern cultures showing a much higher overlap with Melanesian and Australian beliefs. Given the much earlier date of arrival into South America – between 30,000 and 20,000 BCE at the latest – an opportunity to countercheck the cosmology of Sundaland presents itself. This will be explored in the next chapter.

A QUESTION OF STRUCTURES

Given that we have to replace harbour breakwaters every century or so due to the natural erosion of wave action, the expectation of finding the type of Palaeolithic remains that would satisfy a Hollywood set designer is, politely, ambitious. This would be the case even if the end of the Ice Age had been a gradual process, but it is becoming clear that, at least once in our history, human eyes witnessed mile-high superwaves hurtling back across the exposed ocean bed toward them. You only need to watch a few videos of the Japanese tsunami to see what can happen to even technologically advanced cultures following what was a tame sea incursion by historical standards.

However, it is possible there are indeed remains of physical, potentially megalithic structures on Sundaland. Close to the Indonesian capital of Jakarta is a site known as Gunung Padang, usually translated as 'Mount Meadow/Field' which does not make much sense. A secondary translation of 'Mount of Light' or 'Mountain of Enlightenment' seems more likely.

Gunung Padang is a large hill composed of overlapping, columnar basalt 'logs' that form a rough step pyramid shape. Tens of millions of years ago, as the andesite lava cooled and contracted, cracks propagated throughout the rock. This process resulted in the creation of surprisingly geometric hexagonal 'logs,' clumped together like a fistful of pencils. These columns form vertically but are comparatively easy to dislodge and use for building material, even with the means available twenty thousand years ago.

Many of the columns are arranged horizontally into walls and also roofs of interior chambers that have been detected inside the structure. It is currently composed of five terraces with a base that covers an area of 150 metres by 40 metres. These terraces are outlined with what appear to be both building foundations and pavements.

Gunung Padang is aligned just off North, but directly faces another 'holy mountain' in the same area, indicating that it may be part of a much large ritual complex. The hills surrounding Gunung Padang are currently used for growing tea but have a very long history of gold mining. Indeed, the area has long-lived mythological associations with gold. Old mines and tunnels are commonly found under the plantations. In light of the discovery of Gunung Padang's advanced age, it is worth considering whether some of these tunnels require redating.

Its summit today is about 3000 feet above sea level. During the Ice Age this would have been much higher as the sea level was much lower. In fact, from the top of Gunung Padang, you would have had a commanding view north across the plains and hills of Sundaland.

fig. 7   *Gunung Padang pyramid*

According to Dr Robert Schoch's analysis of the geological evidence, which encompasses ground penetrating radar, electrical resistivity, seismic readings and bore hole drilling, the earliest use of the site definitely dates to 14,700 BCE and potentially up to 22,000 BCE and beyond. At either end of this date range, we are still firmly in the Pleistocene and getting on towards Dr Witzel's 30,000 BCE date for the development of Laurasian mythology which, you will recall, counts the Mound of Creation among its mythemes.

Staying with that idea, Dr Schoch has identified human-shaped, internal lava tubes within the mound. The entrance to one of them, at Layer 3, dates to around 10,000 BCE which is right at the beginning of the end of the Ice Age. A major chamber with a length of around 15 metres is located about 30 metres under the summit. Given the subsequent genetic, mythological and linguistic connections to other pyramid or ziggurat-building cultures around the world, it is extremely tempting to consider the possibility that they could have represented not only the Mound of Creation, but potentially a human-altered volcano – even this specific volcano – with all the subsequent chthonic meanings that would imply.

Much has been made locally of the recent findings by Dr Danny Hilman Natawidjaja that his noninvasive geophysical studies have yielded a date of over 20,000 years old. It is no reflection of Dr Natawidjaja's scientific credentials – he received his PhD from Caltech – to suggest caution in interpreting the significance of these results. His was a government study and the idea that 'Indonesia is Atlantis' falls squarely into the politics of science discussed in an earlier chapter. In confidential discussions had during the research for this book, I have been made aware of the fact that there are a number of 'true believers,' so to speak, holding high office in the Indonesian government.

None of this invalidates Dr Natawidjaja's data but it certainly speaks of the need for additional caution before conclusions can be drawn. We already know Island South East Asia was a site of Ice Age cultural complexity. Sulawesi is home to some of the earliest cave art belonging to the Palaeolithic Renaissance, with an age of 40,000 years ago. This date will likely be revised down, given it was drawn from the mineral accretions on top of a painted handprint. In this exact corner of the world we have:

- Genetic evidence indicating mankind has been here for tens of millennia.
- Linguistic evidence indicating a rise in cultural complexity.
- Some of the earliest examples of the Palaeolithic Renaissance anywhere on earth.
- A climate that supported incidental contact with entheogens.
- Some of the earliest, if not the earliest, evidence for agriculture on earth.

- Subsequent genetic and linguistic links to the parts of the world we traditionally associate with the 'rise of civilisation.'
- And now we have a very large, artificial structure that is highly resonant with the beliefs and architecture of these later cultures.

If this is not the actual homeland of Laurasia, and thus much of the western magical tradition, then the culture or cultures of Sundaland certainly had a profound impact on wherever that place may turn out to be. It is certainly an extreme case of non-random distribution.

Where might we look to find evidence to validate this hypothesis?

∇   STAR LORE

Let us begin with a story of two brothers. One is industrious, the other is lazy and feckless. The feckless one killed his industrious brother and then tried to deny the act to their father. The father curses his murdering son and sends him into exile, along with all his descendants. A similar story is told in New Guinea. Dr Oppenheimer suggests these tales may be mythological memories of population changes associated with the peopling of the Pacific. There are numerous stories detailing family squabbles and brothers leaving with their families for distant islands so there is much to commend this suggestion.

Similarly, wherever the first variant of Cain and Abel was told, it seems pretty clear it a mythological memory of hunter gatherers and early farmers uneasily living in the same space. It may well be that the Tongan, New Guinean and Near Eastern variants are, in fact, localisations of the exact same incident. Even if they are not, the 'warring brothers' mytheme is a component of the Laurasian 'novel.' There are multiple examples of Laurasian mythology right across the Pacific. Essentially, every story in the first ten or so books of the Bible is found in the mythology of Melanesia and Polynesia. The parallels are so startling that the first missionaries to arrive thought they had discovered the lost tribe of Israel.

These glaring similarities have led to some confused hypotheses over the years, such as a South American or even Babylonian origin for the Pacific peoples. Today we have the Laurasian framework and genetic information pointing to an older, shared origin to understand why these parallels exist. The watery creation, the separation of sky and earth, the creation of man from earth and woman from his side, the duelling brothers, the flood. All are in evidence and all had to come from somewhere. Which brings us to geography.

It is not often evident when looking at a flat map, but the Pacific Ocean is a hemisphere. The colonisation of its tiny islands is a feat of exploration unmatched until the moon landing. Beginning in the Southwest Pacific, the first grouping of islands to the east of New Guinea is known as Melanesia, meaning 'middle islands.' Further east from them – including New Zealand, Hawaii and Easter Island – is Polynesia, meaning 'many islands.' To the north of New Guinea, the islands – including Guam, Pohnpei, Chuuk and Yap – are known as Micronesia, which you can probably guess means 'small islands.'

The origin of the Austronesian-speaking, agricultural, open-ocean-navigating Polynesians is finally undergoing a rare academic sea change (if you'll excuse the pun). Previously, it was stated that the Austronesian-speaking Polynesians emerged from mainland Asia via Taiwan, bringing with them a distinctive pottery style, known as Lapita, around 1500 BCE, sailed to Melanesia and then quickly – we are talking a scant few centuries – colonised the entirety of Polynesia, all the way to Easter Island. This is despite the fact there is no evidence for Lapita pottery in mainland Asia and, as we saw in the preceding chapter, no evidence for an Austronesian language homeland there, either.

When combined with the more recent genetic evidence, and even sites like Gunung Padang, frankly, it becomes clear that the continuity of culture in Eastern Melanesia is very long-lived indeed. We are dealing with cultural groups that have been occupying this area since before the end of the Ice Age. Lapita pottery is certainly excellent evidence of trade and migration around 800 BCE, but we need to consider the 'mystery' of the Polynesian homeland solved. It is under the sea, just where they have always said it was.

Whenever they first made it to Melanesia, these Ice Age 'climate refugees' existed in a state of near total isolation right up until the arrival of Europeans. As such, they

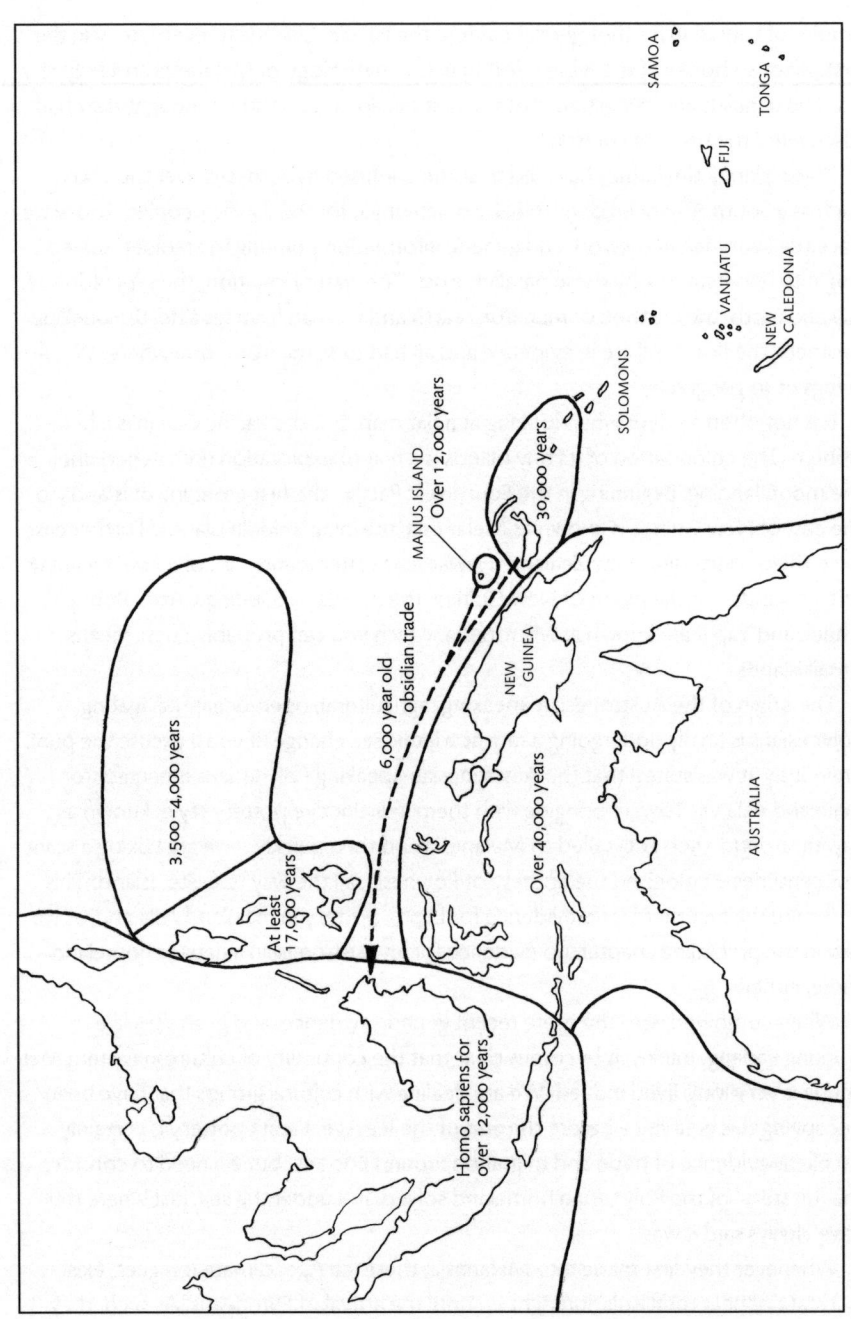

SAMOA

TONGA

FIJI

VANUATU

NEW CALEDONIA

SOLOMONS

MANUS ISLAND
Over 12,000 years

30,000 years

6,000 year old
obsidian trade

NEW GUINEA

3,500 – 4,000 years

At least
17,000 years

Over 40,000 years

AUSTRALIA

Homo sapiens for
over 12,000 years

84   *fig. 8*   *The earliest evidence of modern human habitation in different regions of Austasia and Oceania (after Oppenheimer)*

offer us the best example on earth of a 'control group' to ascertain which elements of the western magical tradition may be antediluvian survivals and specifically survivals from a sunken homeland. Hence the interest we must pay to their mythologies.

Comparative mythology works best when you have a control group. If we wish to ascertain which aspects of magical cosmology predate the end of the Ice Age, and where and in which order they developed, then we should try and find a place on earth which, since the sea levels rose, has had as little molestation as possible. This place is the Pacific in general and Polynesia in particular. Dr Oppenheimer once again:

> The Polynesians' spiritual life was rich with large pantheons. In all groups the Sun God was paramount and in some he was called Ra, as in Ancient Egypt. Almost without exception their myths recalled a lost earthly paradise to the west or the northwest, called variously Avaiki and Bolutu. A story similar to Adam and Eve is widespread, with most languages using ivi as the word for a bone. A story of two brothers of different cultures having a fight was prevalent. The ancestors of these people, and their Austro-Asiatic-speaking neighbours now on the Asian mainland, founded the first complex societies in Southeast Asia. While cereal agriculture was a mainland development, hierarchical societies, the concept of kingship, magic, religion and astronomy were features of the maritime coastal Austronesian peoples. What I suggest here is that these development preceded similar changes in western Asia, and that in their dispersals the Southeast Asian explorers fertilized the Neolithic cultures of China, India, Mesopotamia, Egypt and Crete.

One of my enduring memories of shooting a documentary in Pohnpei was just how over-governed the islands were. Layer after layer of kingship, conferred by blood and ultimately the stars. In almost every case across Micronesia and Polynesia, these tribal and governmental authorities originate in a sunken homeland. It is this mismatch between cultural complexity, its origin and the total amount of land 'under management,' so to speak, that has tripped up atlantologists for more than two centuries and led to them (and me at least once) launching diving expeditions off the coast of Pacific islands in search of sunken ruins.

The Pacific is one of the few places on earth where the archaeology, genetics and local mythologies are actually in alignment. Maori iwi can trace their descendants back a specific number of generations to the waka they arrived on. We can be reasonably confident regarding the dates of colonisation of Pacific islands. This is not to say they were not known of or even used before these dates, of course. In fact they very probably were, as we shall see. But the earliest dates for the *continuous occupation* of some of the farther flung islands by these specific cultures is not going to move much beyond the second half of the first millennium CE, thousands of years after the end of the Ice Age.

Magic does not warp very often. Ritual magic is inherently conservative. Laurasian magic in particular is entirely predicated on following the correct procedure. In the books of Jake Stratton-Kent you can observe this inherent conservation of form even as Mesopotamian and Greek gods and daimons become the spirits and demons of the grimoires. And so we must read the following myths with both an eye for overlapping cosmology and one for continuity of ritual function. The very best data points for such a counter check are twinkling above our heads.

GONDWANA STAR LORE

Let us briefly return to Sunda and Sahul land and the first arrival of our ancestors 50,000 years ago. What is so important to understand is that this area formed the ideal sailing nursery. Sundaland itself, when still above sea level, had an interior with dozens of rivers that would have required some form of vessels or logs to cross. The coastal landscape was one of repeated bays and islets. Also, winds across the Wallace Line, a species boundary line that separates Borneo and Sumatra (Sundaland) with New Guinea and Australia (Sahul land), reversed with the seasons. This meant that even if you got 'trapped' on landmasses east of home, you could always rely on a breeze to get you back eventually.

Similar seasonal effects to do with wind and current reversals are found right across Island Southeast Asia and the Western Pacific. The ocean could be read in a way that is entirely opaque to modern eyes. Water colouration, the appearance of certain birds, how the light refracts at the horizon, the arrival of bioluminescent plankton or fish at certain times of the year, these were the compasses and sextants of the Sundaland people. Over the horizon travel and deep water fishing were occurring by 30,000 BCE. Today, the Torres Strait Islanders – who we will meet below – use stellar scintillation, stars' twinkling effect, to determine levels of moisture and turbulence in the atmosphere, enabling them to predict weather patterns. Planets are of no use to them because they do not twinkle. I believe this behaviour may have been more widespread and could be significant in determining why stellar mythology predates planetary mythology.

Eclipsing the flawed 'mainland Asia' theory for the origins of the Polynesian argonauts is a model devised by Wilhelm Solheim known as the Nusantao Maritime Trading and Communication Network (NMTCN). Taking the name Nusantao from *nusa* meaning 'south' and *tao* meaning 'man/people,' Solheim posits a multidirectional expansion of an open-ocean trading network centred in what was then eastern Indonesia or possibly the Philippines. He suggests that the single-outrigger canoe was invented around 13,000 years ago, just before the end of the Ice Age, and that open ocean trading occurred principally in the Sunda and Sahul areas but also stretching north up to Japan and as far west as Madagascar by 5,000 BCE. His evidence is both archaeological: obsidian trading, etc; and linguistic: the footprint of the Austronesian language. Much like the earliest sailing nursery, the vast distances between Southeast Asia, Madagascar and probably all the way to Africa were reliably navigable thanks to the Monsoon winds. Over a 12 month period you could catch them one way and then catch them back home again. The NMTCN was the vector for the transmission of ideas, genes and artefacts across half the world and it is from these cultures that the Polynesian argonauts developed and went on to ultimately colonise the Pacific.

So even before the end of the Ice Age, you have an extant sailing nursery that develops over millennia from rafts to canoes to outrigger canoes that becomes a demi-global trading network once much of the land sinks beneath the ocean. And where you have a sailing nursery, you have what we can cheekily call a stellar nursery.

The University of New South Wales's Duane Hamacher is doing amazing work in the field of Indigenous Australian astronomy and astrotheology. Much of it involves investigating the oral survival of stories of ancient meteor impacts and volcanic eruptions and the like. It thus provides a useful counterpoint to Dr Witzel's dismissal of the possibility that mythology can encode memories of actual events because Hamacher has demonstrated that it clearly can. This information has been a long time coming. Most non-Australians are only dimly aware of just how raw the deal was that the First Australians received, even by colonial standards. They were not even included on the census as members of the Commonwealth until 1967 and, to this day, there is a widespread belief that no Aboriginal counting system went above the number four. Such were the racial headwinds preventing a thorough examining of Australia's indigenous astromythology.

In many ways, this is surprising. So much of indigenous life is defined by astronomy. The sun, moon and stars are used for time-keeping, hunting calendars, navigation over land and sea, as well as informing customs, taboos and social hierarchies. Knowledge of the night sky is transmitted through ritual, song, story, rock art, and the arrangement of sacred stones. The traditions associated with certain asterisms are used to describe the origins of man, animals and the landscape. Quite a number of these asterisms represent, to my mind, Gondwana-era spirits that have survived into the modern day, making them tens of thousands of years older than western esotericists commonly assume.

Some examples, then, beginning with my personal favourite, from the Arrernte people of the western Central Desert. During the Dreaming, a group of women/stars were dancing a *corroboree* (ceremony) beside the Milky Way. One of the star women put her baby down in its *coolamon* (basket) beside the Milky Way. Because they were dancing, the women did not notice that the baby and its coolamon fell to earth, driving the ground up where it landed. The coolamon fell on top of the baby and hid it from its distraught parents, who, to this day, search for it every night. They are the Morning Star and the Evening Star. The coolamon can still be seen in the night sky under the Milky Way, falling to earth. It is the Southern Cross.

Are we spying an early version of the 'Baby by the River' motif commonly found in the Near East? Perhaps. In the case of Orion and the Pleiades, however, I will put money on it. Hamacher points out that many Aboriginal cultures associate Orion with groups of young men, particularly hunters or fishermen. The asterism and its associated stories often form the basis of important male initiation rites. In the Yolngu language, Orion is called *Djulpan*. The three belt stars are three brothers sitting in a canoe, across its width. Betelgeuse is the front of the canoe and Rigel is the back. The brothers were blown into the sky for illegally capturing a kingfish – i.e. violating a taboo. The kingfish is what we would call Orion's sword.

Another story from the Central Desert has Orion, called *Nyeeruna*, chase the seven sisters of the Pleiades known as the *Yugarilya*. He is kept apart from them by the eldest sister, *Kambugudha*, who is the Hyades asterism. Kambugudha constantly counters Nyeeruna's fire magic and club with her own fire magic, while other astral bodies taunt him for his failures.

All in all, 90% of the collected Aboriginal stories associate Orion with a hunter or hunters and the Pleiades with a woman or a group of women. Noting the high degree of similarity between European and Indigenous Australian mythemes, Hamacher observes, 'This may indicate either cultural convergent evolution, reflecting the subjective masculine and feminine appearance of Orion and the Pleiades respectively, or else suggest a much earlier story common to both cultural roots.' The former suggestion is one of those pseudoscientific glosses common to academia when it is confronted by the latter suggestion and its implications.

Stories of the stars are also used for timekeeping and maintaining hunter gatherer calendars. Staying in the Central Desert, when the Pleiades rise with the morning sun, the Pitjantjatjara people know that the dingoes are pupping. Kambugudha placed dingo pups between Nyeeruna and her sisters in one telling of the Orion legend. In Victoria, the Wergaia traditions tell of a time when the people faced drought and starvation. A woman called Marpeankurric went out searching for food for her tribe.

Eventually she found a nest and dug up thousands of nutritious ant larvae that sustained her people through the drought. Upon her death, she ascended to the sky and became the star Arcturus. When Marpeankurric rises in the evening, the local people know it is the time of the year to harvest the ant larvae.

TORRES STRAIT ISLANDER STAR LORE

The Torres Strait Islands are located between Australia's northernmost tip and Papua New Guinea. There are 250 islands over 48,000 kilometres of shallow ocean water. Fourteen of the islands are inhabited.

Although Torres Strait Islanders are Indigenous Australians, they are not Aborigines but are, in fact, Melanesians. Their culture dates back 8,000 years when the islands were formed at the end of the Ice Age. As such, their highly sophisticated astromythology affords us one of the best attempts to recreate the cosmology of the sunken Sahul and Sunda areas at the time of their inundation. I believe it is here that we can see 'missing link species' between Gondwana and Laurasian mythology. It may be we are looking at the 'first draft' of Dr Witzel's novel.

As you would expect, Orion and the Pleiades feature, as Utimal and Usmal. Their rising in the November skies tells the islanders to plant their gardens in advance of the Kuki season, a time when strong winds and heavy rain blow from the northwest and the intervals between the storms feature no wind at all. This is not good sailing weather. Utimal and Usmal also mark the time when the turtles and dugong are breeding.

Appealing on a personal level, there is the stellar shark, Baidam, which is comprised of some of the stars of Ursa Major. When Baidam appears in the skies over New Guinea, the islanders know it is time to start planting sweet potato and banana. When Baidam's nose touches the horizon at sunset, it is tiger shark breeding season – very much not a time you want to be in or on the water.

Tagai

Tagai is the principal Torres Strait Islander creation deity in a very Gondwanan sense of the term: he is the culture hero from whom the laws and customs descend but he did not create the universe. He is a great fisherman whose form encompasses several asterisms in the southern sky: the Southern Cross is his left hand holding a spear, his right hand is the constellation Corvus and he stands in a canoe that is formed by the stars of Scorpius.

One day, Tagai descended from the stars to go fishing in his outrigger canoe with a crew of 12 *zugubals*, beings who take on human form when they descend to earth. Unable to catch anything, Tagai leaves the canoe to try spearfishing on a nearby reef.

He tells the crew not to drink his water while he is gone. The zugubals finish all their own water and, because it is a very hot day, they then drink Tagai's water – violating a taboo. Tagai returns and finds all his water gone. Furious, he kills them all, separates them into two groups of six and returns them to the sky, where they form the constellations of Usmal (Pleiades) and Utimal (Orion), thus providing another men/hunters/Orion connection. So angry is Tagai that he places the two groups of zugubals in the northern half of the sky and demands they never come near him, which is why Tagai stays in the southern half of the sky.

PER8I8TENCE AND DEVELOPMENT

It is clear that many Gondwana elements such as the Rainbow Serpent, the violation of taboo and the origin of humans and tribal technology have persisted in the night sky. The stars are a remarkable storage facility for cultural knowledge. It is my contention that the development of star lore from 'tribal library' to 'life cycle calendar' to ever more precise navigational systems is in some way associated with the rise of Laurasian mythology, and thus astrology and western magic. It is important to realise that 'development' in this context does not mean 'evolutionary improvement' but rather the additional layering of complexity into the continuation of earlier star lore. Consider that using spirit beings represented by asterisms such as Baidam or Tagai to navigate is to literally be guided by specific gods, and the ability to predict their arrival, timing and movements is to have either the power of, or power over, the gods. The stories associated with these beings and their asterisms remain. They have simply had an additional function layered onto them.

Eventually, continual improvements in the accuracy of prediction may have given rise to the 'magical immortality tech' of the Vedic, Harappan and Near Eastern civilisations, in particular, the rise to prominence of the planets over the constellations. Planets are almost useless to navigators, obviously, but they are very useful if you are in the business of creating and running a royal mythological calendar. Their movements are more rapid, more dramatic, and thus require the shamans and nascent priestly class to demonstrate ever more complex mathematical abilities. It is to that increasing complexity that we now turn.

8PLENDID I8OLATION

The Polynesians have an unmistakably Laurasian cosmology and are self-evidently the planet's best ancient navigators. As a control group they are very useful in calibrating the continuation of Palaeolithic forms – the spirits as asterisms – within the 'civilisational' context of the post-Ice Age era. When examining the following mythemes, it is useful to consider again the words that open this chapter: 'may have retained their original culture with least dilution.' It is very unlikely we are looking at the direct transfer of the cosmology of a sunken land. These are purely Polynesian myths. They are, however, the best pieces we have available to attempt any hypothetical reconstruction. For those unfamiliar with Polynesia, the many similarities to the western esoteric tradition are remarkable. By the time we reach Eastern Polynesia, you will feel right at home.

Tangaroa

The god of the ocean and most commonly the creator. Depending on the island, Tangaroa is also called *Tagaloa* (Tongan), *Ta'aroa* (Tahitian), *Kanaloa* (Maori), *Tangaloa* (Hawaiian). In the Marquesas, Tangaroa is called Tanaoa and is the god of the Primeval Darkness. In other islands he is known simply as *A'a*. (A'a is also a Hawaiian name for Sirius.) It is interesting to note the phonic similarities found in Polynesian mythology with Ra – sun god in the Pacific and Egypt – and the Sumerian Ea, nearly identical to A'a.

So huge is Tangaroa that he only breathes twice every two hours, which causes the low and high tides on the ocean. In the Tahitian story, *Ta'aroa* means 'Unique One,' which I interpret to mean 'First, Alone.' Before creation he lived in the Cosmic Egg, turning endlessly in infinite darkness. In some versions of the story, the eggshell is all that separates earth and sky. One day he cracked the egg and called out. The empty universe did not respond. He threw part of his shell into the air to create the heavens. He used the other part to create the rocks and the sand. Angry and horrified at his empty universe, he dismembered himself and built Creation. In the Tuamotu version of this act, he made the clouds out of his skin, the mountains from his spine, the fertile earth from his flesh, the trees from his feathers, the fish from his nails, the crustaceans and eels from his innards and he used his blood to dye the sky red. Only then did the first day dawn. Throughout this act of dismemberment, Ta'aroa remained Ta'aroa, and in his head he conjured into existence all the other gods. His shell, despite being broken, also remained as the principal point of creation, and everything became its own version of this shell: thus the earth is a complete shell, the human body is a complete shell, and so on. Everything is 'shell shaped,' reflecting its ultimate origin in the cosmic egg.

Here we find the expected mytheme of the universe being created from a dismembered giant. More interestingly we have a creation story that looks Brahmanic and a microcosm/macrocosm view of the universe as Mind of God that you would be forgiven for mistaking as Hermetic.

Tane

Staying with the Tuamotu, Tane was the second son of Atea, the Sky Father. They eventually fought for rulership like Zeus and Chronos.

In the Maori stories of Tane, he is the son of Rangi, the Sky Father and Papa, the Earth Mother. Tane separated the eternal embrace of his parents so that light could enter the world. He was constantly battling with his brother the storm god Tawhiri. There is not a single part of this story that is not found in Egypt.

Tane is also known as the Lord of the Forests, *Tane-Mahuta*. Tawhiri chased Tane's fish children from the forests into the ocean where they were ruled by Tangaroa. These are probably the *Taiparu* or 'Peerless Ones,' a Pacific version of faery beings, as Tane was their lord. There are repeated fish/star symbol crossovers in the Pacific and Southern India. It is interesting to note the fish symbolism of wisdom teachers in places such as Sumeria, probably noting their descent from particular gods/asterisms.

In an act with faintly biblical overtones, after separating his parents, Tane covered his father's nakedness with the God of Mists, *Kohu*, the Milky Way, called *Ika-Roa*, and their children, who were the stars.

When Tane's mother, Papa (confusing, I know), refused his sexual advances Tane created the first woman out of Hawaiian sands, *Hine-hau-one*, or 'Earth Girl.' Their daughter, *Hine-nui-te-po* also subsequently refused her father's advances and fled to the Underworld where she became the goddess of Death. Note the 'Nuit' in the name.

Maui

Maui could be the archetypal civilising trickster. In some variants of the 'separation of sky and earth,' this feat is accomplished by Maui, not Tane.

When he was born prematurely, Maui's mother threw him into the ocean, paralleling the numerous 'abandoned baby by the water' motifs. He lengthened the daylight hours so that humans had more time for work by slowing the sun using his dead grandmother's jawbone; a fairly transparent piece of astrotheology.

Maui also stole fire from the people of the underworld and gave it to mankind. In another adventure in the underworld, Maui attempted to achieve immortality by passing through the vagina of his grandmother Hine-nui-te-po, the goddess of Death, and out her mouth. He failed and was killed, triggering the permanent withdrawal of immortality as an option for humans and beginning the taboo against incest.

Stories of Maui also contain a dragon-slaying motif. The wife of a giant sea eel, *Te Tuna* ('The Penis') ran away and began a passionate affair with Maui. Eventually Te Tuna sought her out, triggering a tidal wave with his penis as he approached land. Maui deflected the wave by displaying his own penis. They fought and sexually entered each other before Maui was ultimately victorious, beheading Te Tuna and burying his head. From his head sprouted the first coconut tree, which gave mankind solid and liquid sustenance. The violent sexual encounter has echoes of the story of Set and Horus, among others. As is common with the Trickster motif, many of Maui's stories are sexually graphic, if not downright bawdy.

The Sacred Tree

Maui's is not the only motif associated with the coconut tree, as you might expect. Genetically American, the presence of the coconut across every piece of habitable land in Polynesia is physical evidence of sustained trans-oceanic adventures thousands and thousands of years ago. Given the shape of the coconut, many of the stories involve decapitation. I suspect, however, that this is a genus-specific version of a wider shamanic/tree spirit/dismemberment story.

From eastern Papua, one story involves a man who would always return at the end of each day with his basket full of fish. Jealous, the other men followed him to the beach one morning to discover his secret. On the beach, the man removed his head and stowed it under a bush before walking into the water. Once in the water, all the nearby fish swam into his gullet. Returning to land, he vomited them all up, restored his head to his shoulders, threw the small ones back into the ocean and placed the large ones in his basket. The next morning the other men took the fisherman's head and buried it. When he returned to the beach and found it gone, he fled back into the sea, turned into a fish and was never seen again. Where the head was buried sprouted a coconut tree. Interestingly, it was a woman who first tasted its magical flesh, just as in the Eden story.

The coconut origin story from the island of Djaul involves even more dismemberment. Two brothers were returning to land with their canoe laden with fish when the sea giant, Lumukaka, appeared. They threw the fish to him and fled but Lumukaka pursued them. The younger brother told his older brother to cut off his arm and throw it to the sea giant. This only slowed him a little so he told his brother to cut off his other arm. And then his two legs. By the time they reached land, the younger brother was just a torso and a head. The boys' grandfather said to bury the younger brother's head, which they did. The next day the older brother went to the burial site and found a puppy. His grandfather said to leave it alone because it will turn into a coconut tree that will provide food, drink and firewood, which it did.

The puppy element is interesting given the role of canines as gatekeepers between the human world and the otherworld. Beyond this, the dismemberment/sacred tree motif is seen (along with a canine) in the story of Osiris who is dismembered and trapped in cedar. Contained in the tree/immortality story we have the repeated refrains of the trickster and the hunter/fisherman. In the case of Osiris this gives us another overlap with the constellation of Orion.

Dr Oppenheimer suggests that the sacred tree/sustaining life motif may have had its origin in the earliest days of Sundaland with the indigenous banana tree; the coconut still millennia from appearing on Sunda beaches. In a very literal sense, the banana tree is the father of a tribe because of its abundance and caloric density allowing for population growth. It is also interesting to note in passing that the banana shares 50% of its DNA with mankind.

Atutuahi

Atutuahi is the star Canopus, hymned as 'the Mother of the Moon and Stars.' Sometimes male, Atutuahi is one of the primary stars used by the Polynesians for open ocean navigation, equivalent to the Northern Hemisphere's Pole Star. (There is no Pole Star in the Southern Hemisphere and there will not be one for around 2,000 years.)

Phil Coppens, in *The Canopus Revelation* mentions that the lack of awareness of the primacy of Canopus in Ancient Egypt is odd and may be due to the fact that the star is not visible in the skies of Western Europe; home to most of the world's Egyptologists. Though his underlying thesis that Canopus is the 'true' Osirian star lacks credible evidence, the association is nevertheless there in part (along with Khonsu) and could be due to a survival of the much earlier association of Orion and canoes/fishing, given its subsequent Greek association with ships and the Argo. Consider Coppens's characterisation of the status of Canopus in Hinduism; the star is known as *Agastya*, a Rishi (sage). It is the helmsman of Argha, son of Varuna, goddess of the waters.

The Serpent and the Tree

Returning to the tree, we have repeated serpent/tree symbolism that contains hybrid versions of the serpent/civilising trickster from Gondwana mythology and the more familiar serpent/tree/taboo symbolism from Laurasian stories.

On the North New Guinean island of Siar, there is a legend of a group of hunters catching a snake in a tree. They decide they will eat it the next day. That evening, all the women of the group had a dream where the snake told them, 'if you eat me, the whole tribe will be drowned.' Only one woman took the dream seriously and sailed away with her two children, a boy and a girl. The other tribesfolk ate the snake and the village sank beneath the ocean. The woman's two children are the ancestors of Siar and the nearby islands.

In Fiji, the giant serpent, *Degei*, who had always existed, lived in the sky with one other being, a she-hawk called *Turukawa*. One day, Turukawa laid two eggs, one containing a human boy and the other containing a human girl. Degei kept the eggs warm in his coils until they hatched. Degei then created the banana tree to feed them as children. When they were grown, he taught them to grow and harvest yams and taro. He also gave them fire and taught them speech. Later these two children went on to populate the earth.

Io

Io is a very common Polynesian name for the high creator god. Like 'Ra' and 'Ea,' which persist in Near Eastern and North African civilisations, I suspect this is an example of a very, very long-lived sacred syllable. Consider how close Ea, IAO, Yahweh and Io sound when said out loud. The word also means 'hawk' in Hawaiian. Linguist and Pacific scholar Jan Knappert believed the word may have been taboo, replaced with *Atua*, which means 'Old One.'

The most common story involves Io speaking light into being when there was only darkness upon the waters. He then contemplated light and called darkness back, creating the first day. It is also often Io that separates the sky from the land. In Maori mythology, Io is both god of the house and of knowledge. Some of his epithets were *Io-Te-Waiora*, 'Io, the Source of Life' and *Io-Matua-Te-Kore*, 'Io who has no parents.' The tale is told in a Maori hymn to Io:

Io dwelt within the breathing-space of immensity.
The Universe was in darkness, with water everywhere.
There was no glimmer of dawn, no clearness, no light.
And he began by saying these words,
That He might cease remaining inactive
'Darkness become a light-possessing darkness.'
And at once light appeared.

(He) then repeated those self-same words in this manner.
That He might cease remaining inactive:
Light, become a darkness-possessing light.
And again an intense darkness supervened.
Then a third time He spake saying:
'Let there be one darkness above,
Let there be one darkness below.

Let there be one light above,
Let there be one light below,
A dominion of light, a bright light.'
And now a great light prevailed.
(Io) then looked to the waters which compassed him about,
and spoke a fourth time, saying:
'Ye waters of Tai-kama, be ye separate. Heaven, be formed.'
Then the sky became suspended. *'Bring forth thou Tupua-horo-nuku.'*
And at once the moving earth lay stretched abroad.

This comes from the 1907 *Journal of the Polynesian Society*, translated by Hare Hongi, which relates that these words were 'transmitted down through the generations. Our priests joyously referred to them as being the ancient and original sayings.' The hymn was also used as an incantation to quicken barren wombs, to lift up depressive hearts and anywhere else that installation of a little Light may be useful.

Castor and Pollux

In Polynesia, the stars of Gemini are known as *Hui Tarara*. In a parallel to Indian star lore, they were originally human and fled to the sky, becoming stars, when they heard they were to be separated.

Another name for Pollux is *Rehua*. He is the star god, living in the highest heavens, a realm no human has ever reached. His son, *Kaitangata*, fell to earth, and the blood from his fall is the sunset. Maui is descended from Rehua, the star god.

The Moon

It is a common mistake to assume that traditional cultures saw the moon as female when it appears that a slim majority of them actually saw it as male. The suggestion for why this is so – which I find credible – is that in hunter-gatherer cultures, it was the men who 'went away' or 'journeyed' in hunting parties, just as the moon does. The sun is much more reliable and thus appears as female more often than you would expect. (Attending an Australian school, we used to sing an Aboriginal folk song called *sun-a-rise, she come every morning*.)

Thus is it unsurprising that the Polynesians saw the moon as male. Sort of. Yes, *Marama* is the moon god, but his wife *Ina* (or *Rona*) is the moon goddess. Think of them more as occupants of our satellite, rather than it being a manifestation of one or the other. Ina taught the women of the earth to weave baskets. In Hawaii, she is called *Hina* and is goddess of the fish. She taught Hawaiian women how to make barkcloth.

On the island of Aitutaki, Ina's husband was a human she took back up to the moon. When he showed signs of ageing, she created a rainbow bridge to send him back to earth so that he could die.

Night and the Morning Star

Venus is known as *Kopu* or *Malara*, and, according to Jan Knappert, 'she is much admired for her beauty.' As previously mentioned, the goddess of the night sky is called Hine-Nui-Te-Po, which I find highly suggestive of Nuit.

Kingship

Consider how many 'alternative history' books would have remained unwritten had we not confused *kings* descending from the stars with *kingship* descending from the stars! In Polynesia, a king, *ariki rahi*, became a divine being at the moment of his coronation. His kingship was ordained by and descended from the stars and his word became law.

I believe the increasing complexity in star lore over the millennia – and in particular that first jump toward precise measurement that is in some way associated with the rise of the Laurasian 'novel' – has much to do with the emergence of divinely ordained, absolute rulers. Priests are ever putting 'their man' on the throne. Correctly dating this concept throws a very unflattering light on some of the zanier origin theories for the Pharaohs and Sumerian kings.

Spider

In Micronesia, the creator god is known as Nareau. Before creation, he walked alone through the primeval matter of *Te-Po-ma-Te-Maki*, 'the Darkness of the Embrace.' Nareau used a giant eel to separate 'the embrace' of earth and sky. He fashioned the first man and woman from earth and water. These two humans gave birth to several of the gods, including the god of the Waves; *Na Kika*, the octopus; and *Ruki*, the sea serpent.

Aries

In Hawaii, the constellation of Aries is called *Kūkalaniʻehu*, 'Kū of the misty heavens.' He is the god (*akua*) of war on Kauaʻi and Oʻahu.

Pleiades

The rising of the seven star spirits of *Matariki*, 'little eyes' in the skies above New Zealand in late May or early June is considered Maori new year. Just as we saw in the Torres Strait, the cluster is a cornerstone of both agricultural and hunter-gatherer calendars across the Pacific.

Milky Way

Considered the property of the Night Goddess in parts of Polynesia, the Milky Way is known as *Ika-Roa*, 'The Long Fish, who Gave Birth to all the Stars.' Here the fish/star symbolism that I suspect we see in Sumeria is repeated. In some variants, Ika-Roa is simply the Mother of the Stars.

A Maori motif that has similarities to the Torres Strait Islander and Aboriginal myths sees Tane gathering up clumps of little stars in his canoe and this is what forms the Milky Way, a rather beautiful image.

Pyramids

It is not very widely known that pyramids and other stepped, sacred platforms were built on a very large scale across the Pacific. Most were razed by missionaries. They were called either *marae* or *morai*, which according to Jan Knappert meant they contained 'houses of god' within them. One such structure in Tahiti measured 267 feet in length. Given the recent dating of Gunung Padang in Indonesia, and the fact that it was a large hill shaped into a step pyramid, the case for a Sahul/Sunda origin for this particular type of sacred architecture is considerably strengthened.

RAPA NUIAN EXCEPTIONALISM

Rapa Nui, or Easter Island, has long fascinated historians and researchers of every stripe. It is probably the most isolated place on earth, being more than 2,000 kilometres away from the nearest inhabited island (Pitcairn, population: 67) and 3,700 kilometres off the Chilean coast. The enigmatic *moai* – statues with elongated heads, tiny hands and piercing eyes – stare out across the endless ocean with their mouths resolutely shut. If there is anywhere that absolutely breaks the mainstream model of Pacific history it is here. The accepted version of events does not stand up to even the slightest scrutiny. How could it? Officially, Rapa Nui was the last of the Pacific islands to be colonised, yet it has the most extreme examples of megalithic and astronomical culture found anywhere in the ocean.

The orthodox chronology is as follows:

- Rapa Nui is believed to have been first colonised between 700 AD and 1200 AD.
- The population peaked at 15,000 but a combination of disease and mismanagement of resources dropped it down to around 3,000 by the time of European

contact a few centuries later. This would make it fairly unique in the over-managed Polynesian world.
- The rulers had hundreds and hundreds of moai built 'to keep the farmers busy in the off season.'
- It was discovered by Dutch explorers on Easter Sunday, 1722, hence its name. By this point the local culture was in a degenerate state and very few of the Rapa Nui people could read their mysterious Rongorongo script.

Let us have a closer look at these 887 moai, through the eyes of a tenured geologist, Dr Robert Schoch. In his *Forgotten Civilisation: The Role of Solar Outbursts in Our Past and Future*, he records the following observations from his visits to Rapa Nui.

- The average weight for one of the moai is twelve tonnes. The largest is 75 tonnes and an unfinished moai, still in its quarry, is approximately 250 tonnes. Those farmers must have had a long off-season.
- There appear to different eras of moai building, with the earliest probably being carved from basalt. Dr Schoch observed some of these basalt moai had been repurposed into dwellings and sacred platforms, as well as showing signs of being recarved. (The moai in the British museum has later carving all down its back.) For a stone object to be repurposed it is, by definition, older than the structures it is incorporated into.
- Despite the island's small land area, the basalt quarries have yet to be located. Based on his understanding of volcanic stratigraphy, Dr Schoch suggests they would not be found where the other quarries are located – toward the top of the volcano – but lower down, perhaps under the current sea level.
- Probably the world's most famous scuba diver, Jacques Cousteau, observed large, rectangular cut-outs in underwater basalt that resemble the holes left in Rapa Nui-an quarries. It is very unlikely the Rapa Nui were undersea miners, which begs the question of when these rectangular quarry marks were above sea level.
- Just as with his observations of the water erosion on the Sphinx, Dr Schoch noticed varying levels of erosion on the moai, indicating dramatically different ages for some of them.
- Some of the moai have sedimentation built up around them to a depth of six metres. Based on an analysis of the difference in sedimentation between today and photos of the same moai from 130 years ago, Dr Schoch has calculated that some of the moai were installed at a vastly earlier date than is currently accepted by historians.

- The long-fingered, thin-armed carvings on the moai are highly reminiscent of the T-pillars at Göbekli Tepe, even down to the way the hands rest on the abdomen, almost in an asana pose.
- There are shaped lava tunnels on Rapa Nui. If it transpires that the tunnels inside Gunung Padang in Indonesia are also shaped by human hands, and all available evidence suggests that is the case, then it may be another cultural continuity.

All of these observations are in addition to the persistent challenge of how these multi-tonne objects were placed on their sacred platforms, called *ahu*. In many instances, the moai have been installed miles from where they were struck from the rock. Local legend says they were walked into place, or flew through the air by the use of mana. A similar story accounts for the appearance of the giant basalt logs that built Nan Madol on Pohnpei. They come from a promontory on the other side of a very mountainous island and the one modern attempt to move a smaller log by raft sank immediately in the harbour when the log was placed upon it.

As for the suggestion that the Rapa Nui people debased their own environment and were living in a state of near-total social collapse at the time of first European contact, this is one of those historical theories – like the Aryan Invasion Theory of India – that has been completely dismissed for a lack of evidence but not been replaced with anything else. In the journal *Energy and Environment* (2005 Vol. 15, Issue 3/4) Benny Peiser, a visiting fellow at the University of Buckingham, observes that 'there is no compelling archaeological evidence for any of the key claims of societal dissolution and breakdown before the 18th century.' Once again, we return to the obligation of proof. Without this, the claim that the moai were part of an ancestor cult that ended just prior to European contact as the Rapa Nui people descended into cannibalism to stave off starvation struggles to find legitimacy. There is no evidence of cannibalism and plenty of evidence of the continuity of the moai-building custom, such as the unfinished statues still in the quarry.

The population estimates of approximately 2,000 inhabitants at the time of European contact are derived from the best guess of the Dutch explorers during their Easter Sunday visit. What is important to bear in mind is that the Dutch were attempting to count a population they had just opened fire on, having shot dead about a dozen of them following a misunderstanding between the Rapa Nui and the sailors. Counting fleeing or hiding natives when they have the home ground advantage is bound to lead to significant under-reporting.

So that is no archaeological evidence of social collapse or cultural debasement and an under-reporting of a population at first contact that would then spend the next century dying of Western diseases and being abducted by Peruvian and European slave traders. By the time accurate records were made by the missionaries, Rapa Nui society really was in a state of collapse. The 'decline' hypothesis arose in the 1970s and 1980s when the likes of Jared Diamond were attempting to sell their racially problematic views of how cultures rise and fall. Shifting the blame from the colonists to Rapa Nui itself provided a neat, hermetic 'example' of the theory. Pity about the facts.

As you might expect, the indigenous origin story is significantly different. One of the founders of the culture, King Hotu-Matua, came from the island of Hiva, which was sinking. However, Rapa Nui was already inhabited in some accounts. There were two groups of people during the foundational days of the island: the *Hanua Eepe*, 'long-eared,' and the *Hanua Momoku*, 'short-eared.' According to Dr Schoch, some versions of these tales have the moai-building culture arriving with the Hanua Eepe, who also enslaved the Hanua Momoku until they one day rose up, cornered the 'long-eared' on one section of the island and killed them all.

What is commonly left out of a reliance on the population estimates of the Dutch explorers – and may have bearing on the suggestion there were two groups on the island – is that they also recounted seeing living giants. In the exact words of the explorer C. F. Behrens, '... with truth, I might say that these savages are all of more than gigantic size. The men are tall and broad in proportion, averaging 12 feet in height. Surprising as it may appear, the tallest men on board of our ship could pass between the legs of these children of Goliath without bending the head. The women can not compare in stature with the men, as they are commonly not above 10 feet high.' It is frustrating that mainstream historians can trust the accuracy of one part of their account while completely dismissing the other.

It does not come into the journey of this book but we should ourselves be slow to dismiss these accounts. The Mound Builder culture of North and South America appears to be anything but a hoax, although it certainly was a cover-up. Abraham Lincoln even mentioned them in speeches. Rapa Nui would be precisely the sort of place you would expect to find a relict survival, just as the diminutive *Homo floresiensis* – a hominin I find even less plausible than giants but nevertheless existed – was found on the other side of the Pacific. Interestingly, early European accounts of Indonesia speak of a living race of very small humans, so there may well have been another relict survival into the modern era within the western remains of the Sunda empire.

fig. 9   *Rapa Nui moai*

RAPA NUI STAR LORE

The official dating of the arrival of the first humans at Rapa Nui – between 700 CE and 1100 CE – is not based on any genetic data but exclusively on archaeological evidence. If Dr Schoch's analysis of the island is even slightly correct, it is also based on *selective* archaeological evidence, whilst ignoring the sedimentation around the moai and lack of granite quarries, as either of these would push the date back quite significantly. Another example of this selective evidence would be the reliance on a change from palm to grassland around 1200 CE – contiguous with the presumed first arrival of the Polynesians – whilst ignoring the same palm-to-grassland change that occurs at 450 BCE.

It may be the case that 100 CE was indeed when the first people arrived at Rapa Nui. The hypothesis that Polynesian cultures were the most likely to retain elements of the Sunda and Sahul cosmologies remains in play. It is, however, considerably strengthened if it transpires the islands have been, or were once, occupied significantly earlier. The reason for this is Rapa Nuian star lore is astoundingly similar to the emergence of star lore with the first 'civilisations' of the Near East and Indian subcontinent. It has the highest degree of ritual overlap out of anywhere in the Pacific which could be explained by using an earlier date of first settlement, contemporaneous with the proposed influence on points west, after which point in time the Rapa Nuians remained in the most splendid of isolations out of anywhere in Polynesia. We shall return to this suggestion following an analysis of their star lore.

Rapa Nui provides the best example in the Pacific of the use of astronomy and star lore for reasons other than navigation. It was home to a powerful priesthood who used their knowledge of observation of the stars to set a yearly calendar of ritual and domestic activities. Most of the information regarding the sacred astronomy of this priesthood was collected in the late nineteenth and early twentieth century, probably the very last time any of these practices remained in living memory, and sometimes only as remembrances of tales told by grandparents. In fact, a lot of the star lore lay forgotten in dusty boxes in the Royal Geographic Society until 1983, when the unpublished field notes of ethnographer Katherine Routledge's 1914–1919 studies were located. She managed to find two elderly inhabitants who could allegedly read some of the mysterious rongorongo script, although their description of the meanings differs markedly.

Carved onto wooden tablets and seemingly kept in the majority of Rapa Nui homes, this script was only first discovered by Europeans in the 1860s, at which point missionary zeal led to the fiery destruction of most of them. Now only a few dozen remain and many of these are scattered across western museum collections. These tablets are a couple of centuries old and likely copies of earlier tablets or carvings.

Currently undeciphered, the rongorongo glyphs repeat in a way that leads some researchers to suggest they are or were sacred chants. But, as we shall see, there is a good case to be made for suggesting these are depictions of stars and sky phenomena. One interpretation does not preclude the other, of course. Indeed, it seems likely they are sacred chants of star lore, which is not at all without precedent across Polynesia.

Some of the symbols are very similar to glyphs found on other Pacific islands, particularly in Hawaii and Micronesia. Quite suggestively, there is also a stylistic overlap with the also undeciphered Indus script. If these similarities are anything other than accidental, then they may well point to a shared origin, perhaps even a Sundaland one. Even more intriguingly, Dr Schoch sees similarities with both the Nazca Lines and carvings found at Göbekli Tepe. For all of these to have a common origin, we are indeed back in the early days of Southeast Asian colonisation, which is the last time the ancestors of all these cultures were in the one place.

Returning to Katherine Routledge, she was told there were several classes of astronomer priests, each trained to and then tasked with recording the movements of specific asterisms, principally Orion, the Pleiades and Sirius/Canis Major from certain *ahu*, or sacred platforms. Although the earliest interpretation of these ahu were that they were aligned to solstices and equinoxes (western antiquarians having a tendency to overemphasise the sun), it turns out that those that *do* have sky alignments are better matches for the rising of specific constellations. And it is those with stellar alignments that are the best constructed out of all the ahu. Caves and natural rocks were also used as observation points. One promontory on the Poike Peninsula is called *Papa ui hetu'u*, 'the rock for star-gazing.' Near to the promontory was a rock Routledge identified as having a cup hole 'star map' of the Pleiades. Cup holes are common in megalithic sites across Western Europe and also feature on the tops of the T-shaped pillars at Göbekli Tepe.

Like we find in Western Polynesia, the Eastern Polynesian year began with the rising of the Pleiades, called Matariki. However in the east, they are more explicit about what this entails. During Matariki, the gods descended from the skyworld, *ao*, to mingle with humans in the realm of the living, called *kainga*.

Matariki inaugurated the 'bountiful season,' called *Hora Nui*. Beginning at this point and proceeding through the year, the ritual marking of the annual cycle was called 'the Work of the Gods.' This calendar was lunar, rather than solar, which is another overlap with early Indian culture. In order of importance, the preeminent asterisms and constellations should be familiar by now.

Orion

Orion has three separate names in Rapanui star lore. They are *Tautoru*, the Three Handsome Ones, which are the belt stars; *E tui*, 'The Expelled,' which is the constellation itself; and *Tau ahu*, 'Beautiful Firebrand,' the name for Rigel and the wife of one of the belt stars. Along with the Pleiades, Orion's Belt was the most important asterism.

Immediately following the first lunar month of *Hora Nui*, marked by the Pleiades' arrival into the sky, was the lunar month of Ruti, where Orion's Belt was high in the sky and rituals were held to honour the chiefs and ancestors. The next three months deal principally with the location of the Pleiades and Orion's Belt in the sky and their relationship to Mars, Canopus and other important stellar objects. The month of Tara Hau, when the Pleiades disappeared beneath the horizon, signalled a time of calamity for man until the next Matariki festival in several months' time. Again, this is curiously redolent of Ancient Egypt.

Other Important Stars

Other stars, planets and constellations of significance recur. Chief among them are Sirius, *Te pou o te rangi*, the Post of the Sky; Canopus, *Po roroa*, the Great Darkness, used in conjunction with Orion's Belt to time the planting season; Mars, *Matamea*, Red Eye, observed from Routledge's observatory on Poike and probably considered a bad omen. Vega, Antares, Alpha Centauri, Beta Centauri, Venus and Aldebaran were all named, tracked and calendarised in the 'Work of the Gods.'

Other Ritual Activity

Turmeric, which is native to southeast India, was made into a body paint called *renga* during the Matariki festival. Offerings of turmeric were also made to the high chief. If this is not an historical development – which is unlikely – then we are left to wonder how a member of the Indian ginger family ended up on the most isolated island on earth, more than half a world away.

Rapa Nui's astronomer-priests were known as *tohunga*. The exact same word in Maori means expert or wise man, equivalent to the Hawaiian *kahuna*. In New Zealand there were tohunga specialising in navigation, medicine, stars, canoe building and so on. On Rapa Nui, it was the tohunga who read the sacred chants of the rongorongo script. According to what Katherine Routledge was told, these tohunga lived in circular stone towers called *tupa*. The majority of these tupa are clustered in the northern part of the island, where we also find 'the rock for star-gazing' and plenty of ahu. A 2010 Explorers Club Flag Expedition to Rapa Nui found that all but one of these tupa had entranceways that were oriented to a star or asterism in some way involved in the

'Work of the Gods.' It may be that measurements were taken when the stars appeared in the doorway or it may even have been a way of drawing down a particular asterism into its tower. Again we immediately think of Egypt.

GATHERING UP THE STARS

What are we to make of Rapa Nui, then? It is apparently the last island in Polynesia to have been colonised, as recently as only a thousand or fifteen hundred years ago. Yet it has geological, archaeological and potentially ritual evidence to suggest activity in much earlier times. Rapa Nui may have been an outpost of the Nusantao Maritime Trading Network that arose immediately after the end of the Ice Age. Or it may have even been a holy island that was not permanently occupied and used as a sacred or holy site, both before and after this point. Perhaps it was a combination of sacred site and sailing stop-off point, never permanently occupied and visited at intervals determined by the stars and the seasons, such as was the case with Göbekli Tepe. One of the names for the island means 'navel of the world,' hinting it may have had a ritual value far in excess of its comparatively meagre resource value.

If such a scenario is accurate, it provides a 'solve' for the otherwise incongruous data suggesting both very early and very late occupation: it was a site that was used and known during a time when the sea levels were much lower, then it was abandoned or the original inhabitants died out. Then it was recolonised by the descendants of these first occupiers in the first millennium CE and some of the remaining megalithic infrastructure, such as the basalt moai, were repurposed.

Whatever the scenario, the island is the most challenging and most rewarding place to look for where, in the words of Dr Oppenheimer that open this chapter, survivors of a sunken landmass may have 'retained their original culture with the least dilution.'

Right across Melanesia, Micronesia and Polynesia we have the demonstrable continuity of Gondwana star lore being developed into a highly sophisticated form of Laurasian astronomical knowledge used for navigation and the precise measurement of a ritual year. We find the Gondwana/Laurasia crossover of star lore in the same part of the world – Sunda and Sahul land – where linguistic evidence records the first rise in cultural complexity since we left Africa, which also seems to have stepped, pyramidal hills built before the end of the Ice Age. This part of the world also has genetic, archaeological and potentially linguistic links to the 'first cilivisations' of Harappa, Sumer and Egypt, as well as probably South America (although we are now heading in the opposite direction).

Over the last one hundred and fifty years, historians have looked for singular, linear answers: cities started *here*. The people next door learned from them and then built cities. Pyramids started *there* and then their neighbours copied the form. This linearity simply does not match what we now know about early human population movements or the 'overlap analysis' of world mythology that points to much, much older shared origins of specific gods and cosmologies. This book does not suggest that all culture and civilisation came from the scattered survivors of Sundaland, setting out in ships to become the world's wisdom teachers. It seems increasingly clear that early communities across Eurasia had hugely sophisticated cosmologies and even architectural capacities by the end of the Ice Age, the original elements of which they may have brought with them as human populations moved up into Eurasia and Europe from South Asia during a brief warm period as the mtDNA evidence suggests. Instead, this book suggests that survivors of the sinking of Sunda and Sahul brought technological and *magical* techniques with them to populations across central and western Asia that were already *in situ* and likely even had vaguely recognisable pantheons and practices. It is also fairly likely that the Sunda survivors knew of these scattered communities if the evidence for transoceanic and transcontinental trade is considered.

Moving from Wendy Doniger's microscope back to her telescope, we find in the star lore of the Pacific a concept of divine kingship descending from the night sky, the magic of immortality and human origin associated with particular asterisms and the belief that actions or architecture 'below' are in some way aligned with that which is 'above.'

Even more than that, we have specific asterisms such as Orion and even god names that recur in both description and magical function for the next five thousand years. We can now posit that creating a map or replica with specific points in the night sky, a concept we see executed throughout dynastic Egypt and continuing into the hermetic traditions of the Classical Age, seems to be a very long-lived one. The development of this star map with ever more precision is, I believe, the 'wisdom of the sages come down to us from a time before the Flood,' as it is commonly described. It grew in a highly specific incubator: the interactions with the spirit world conducted by a culture or cultures of highly proficient open ocean navigators for whom precision was a literal matter of life and death. And the proof of their supreme competence is the very fact of the existence of their descendants living on every piece of habitable land in the Pacific, an ocean which covers half our planet's surface.

It must have been quite an event to set these ancient Argonauts on such a journey.

Ah, Solon, Solon, you Greeks are ever children.

VI   HOW A WORLD ENDS

It is the evening of August 28th, 1859. The night sky over London fills with incandescent, swirling light. Too far south, too bright and the wrong time of year to be the Northern Lights, these displays are curiously humanoid, witnesses describe the display as looking like couples performing a waltz.

About forty hours earlier, an enormous coronal mass ejection (CME), accompanied by a solar proton event, erupted from the sun and tore through space in our direction. (Synchronicitists take note that it took seventeen hours to arrive.) When it reached the earth, this CME, in the form of a spiralling double helix, collapsed the magnetosphere, pushing our 'magnetic shielding' down to just seven thousand kilometres from its usual sixty five thousand. As the outpouring of plasma swirled around and past our planet, its magnetic field pivoted so that it was opposite the Earth's field, releasing enormous amounts of energy. It was this energy that generated the brilliant light show witnessed by Victorian Londoners.

This is known today as the Carrington Event and whilst it is the largest such CME of the previous few centuries, it is comparatively minor when viewed over a longer timeline of the last few hundred thousand years. The damage was limited mostly to the telegraph system of the day, which was a mere two hundred thousand kilometres of cabling. Some telegraph operators found that they could operate their equipment even when it was unplugged from its battery, other stations reported strange and gar-bled messages, yet more witnessed sparks flying from their machines. As a disquieting aside, a Carrington level event reaching the Earth today, for which we are overdue, would fry the nerve system of the entire planet. Replacing it would take over a year. The death toll would climb into the millions, higher in the developed world than the developing, as everything from modern farming techniques, food transportation and emergency services rely entirely on modern communication.

Researchers such as Paul LaViolette have noticed the startling similarity between descriptions of the Carrington Event and humanoid petroglyphs from the Neolithic. There is much to recommend the suggestion that aberrant space weather is recorded in some of the world's earliest art and mythology. Even NASA has noted that some of the depictions on the ceiling of the Rouffignac Cave in France probably represent auroras.

Given what we know about the antiquity of certain mythemes – many of which are significantly older than the end of the Ice Age – the question then becomes how we separate out the 'real' from the 'mythological' when examining a climate event that was positively biblical.

VAN DIEMEN'S LAND

A few decades before the Carrington Event and on the other side of the world, George Augustus Robinson is committing that sort of helpful genocide in which the empire specialised. It is 1831 and he is on the east coast of Tasmania, rounding up the few remaining Aborigines who have not fallen to disease or the settlers' guns so that they can be resettled into reservations on some islands in the Bass Strait.

The helpful Mr Robinson hears a story from the indigenous people. They tell him that Van Diemen's Land (Tasmania) was once connected to New Holland (the Australian mainland). Their ancestors had walked over and then the sea level had risen to where it is today. In Europe at the time, the closest thing the Academy had to an Ice Age theory was an explanation for the dispersal of rocks in the Alps that may have had something to do with glaciation. There was some speculation that perhaps the polar ice caps had extended further down to the bottom of the temperate zones. Regardless, these were certainly not the circles that George Robinson moved in. Originally from London, he had first attempted to seek his fortune in Nicaragua, however the colony he had selected turned out to be a fraudulent enterprise. (This was not uncommon.) Tasmania was his second choice of location in which to strike it rich, and he left a wife and five children behind in order to do so. Greedy and drearily religious, he was not the type to commence a speculative geological investigation under his own initiative, although his diaries certainly suggest he believed himself capable of doing so.

To his credit, Robinson went this far: 'For aught we know V.D.L. (Van Diemen's Land) might at an early period have been joined to N.H. (New Holland) in which case the tradition would be true.' Almost two centuries later, we know the tradition is indeed true. Tasmania became an island fourteen thousand years ago, tens of millennia after the first Aborigines arrived there, cut off from the mainland by 200 kilometres of unpredictable and extremely dangerous seas. If you are looking for evidence that the oral traditions of hunter gatherer societies can convey accurate historical information then this is it. The native Tasmanians' understanding of the geology of their homeland was significantly more advanced than that of their technologically superior neighbours. George Robinson's story is a very compelling proof of concept.

Recent research into Indigenous Australian folklore has found additional accounts of the end of the Ice Age among tribes near modern day Melbourne, Kangaroo Island, Rottnest Island, Fitzroy Island and the Tiwi Islands. Quoted in *Scientific American*, the University of New England's Nicholas Reid said, 'There are aspects of storytelling in Australia that involved kin-based responsibilities to tell the stories accurately. Cross-generational scaffolding can keep a story true.'

THE FLOOD

The modern world's chronological understanding of time aligns poorly with how cultures previously viewed past events, which was largely either place-based or part of a wider mythology of group identity.

This has led many an historian astray when he or she goes off looking for the 'real' Noah's Ark or some such thing. The error in this case is applying a modern literalism to the location and dating of that particular iteration of the story which can only ever be culture and location-specific. Consider the changing fashion styles of Jesus and Mary as they move across Europe over the centuries, getting whiter and whiter until Mary ends up with the flowing red hair of the Celts, dressed as a member of the French court. You are bound to be disappointed if you take this as your map and go looking for first century Christians in North Wales, but this is what seekers after Noah's Ark are doing.

Combining an understanding of geology with an awareness that mythology's primary purpose is cultural expression rather than scientific depiction, we can nevertheless construct, if not a map, then at least a key with which to interpret various maps.

More than any other tableau, the Flood requires the most rigorous distributional analysis. There is a veritable deluge of flimsy pseudopsychological 'explanations' for the prevalence of Flood myths around the planet, or in Witzel's case, outright dismissal because of a personal preference that in *this* particular case, mythology should not be capable of transmitting actual events. Other evidence-free suggestions range from metaphors for amniotic fluid and the birth process to the notion that the Flood represents the collective unconscious or the dream state. Again, such explanations require the stories to be randomly distributed, and they most certainly are not. The next most common dismissal, as mentioned in a preceding chapter, is that stories of global cataclysms are sometimes written off as a confused exaggeration of local weather events by unsophisticated tribespeople. The research into the stories of the First Australians does not bear this out.

With respect to the magical tradition and what may represent Palaeolithic survivals, the presence of non-randomly distributed flood stories – and who or what managed to survive them – offers us the opportunity for some careful calibration. Because in the western tradition, the story of the Flood is intimately tied up, for better or for worse, with the notion of 'lost wisdom.' None of this suggests that parts of the world that were impacted less by the end of the Ice Age fail to demonstrate Palaeolithic continuity, just that they may lack a definitive 'mythic calibrator' to determine what happened before the end of the Ice Age and what happened afterward. Africa is the best example of this. It is the continent that suffered the least amount of land loss at the end of the Ice Age and has probably the lowest number of indigenous flood myths relative to the number of local cultures. However, prior to the expansion of the Muslim and then northern European empires, African cultures, particularly in the south, were comparatively unmolested for hundreds of thousands of years. It seems very likely that many of the beliefs found here are Palaeolithic survivals. With fewer intervening 'calibrating cataclysms,' we have fewer opportunities to time stamp these myths.

THE END OF THE ICE AGE

Transitioning out of the Pleistocene was not a single event. Beginning around 12,000 BCE, the climate started to warm and much of the water locked up in glacial ice began to melt. There followed a short cold spell known as the Younger Dryas, then the planet rapidly warmed again and we moved out of the 'official' Ice Age. According to Greenland ice core data interpreted at the University of Copenhagen, this final warming could have happened in as short a time as three years.

If we include the inundation of the Arabian Gulf that occurred around 6,000 BCE, however, we are looking at three separate and sudden sea level rises. These were anything but gradual. The change in the pressure exerted on our squishy planet as ice sheets melted or slipped off the land and into the ocean like ice cubes into a drink caused dramatic earthquakes, volcanic eruptions and superwaves of up to a mile high.

Taking just one location as an example, the meltwater flowing from the Canadian ice sheet into the Arctic around 12,000 BCE is estimated by the University of Alberta's Professor John Shaw at being 10 million cubic metres per second. This rate would drain Lake Ontario in less than four days. Staying in the same area, the Laurentide ice sheet spent centuries forming a giant lake as it gradually melted, which was protected from the ocean by an enormous ice barrier. Around 6,000 BCE, this barrier melted and the lake poured through the Hudson Strait and into the ocean. The volume of water added to the world's oceans from this event lifted the sea level by about 20–40 centimetres instantly. In some parts of the world, once the resulting tsunamis were over, this event would have moved the shoreline dozens and dozens of kilometres inland.

The last two decades of geological research have yielded some very compelling insights as to what was happening with the planet's space weather while the sea levels were rising. Based on an analysis of Kilimanjaro ice cores, Dr Robert Schoch explains that during the period of 9,700 BCE to 6,000 BCE sunspot activity varied widely. It was initially extremely active, then plunged to levels of very low activity, then rose again. Although it is likely this solar activity had an impact on the dramatic climate events occurring on earth, the mechanism for how and by how much is not currently clear. We can be extremely confident, however, that whilst our ancestors were experiencing superwaves, earthquakes, volcanic eruptions and dramatic changes to their food supply, the sky would also periodically light up with the sort of dancing figures that were witnessed over London during the Carrington Event. It would be stranger if ancient mythologies didn't include references to the most dramatic climate upheavals hominins have ever experienced than if they did.

SUNDALAND

As for the impact of the end of the Ice Age in the corner of the world that provides us with the most compelling genetic and linguistic evidence for Pleistocene cultural complexity? It would have been extreme. The Sunda Shelf, as the name implies, is quite flat. According to Dr Oppenheimer, the maximum horizontal distance between 20 metre depth contours is almost 2,000 kilometres. When the sea came in, it went far, fast. Every ten centimetre sea level rise would push the water a kilometre inland, meaning the initial flood would have gone four kilometres inland in under two days. Here Dr Oppenheimer tactfully understates the drama of this catastrophe in *Eden in the East*:

> We can imagine that the sea would not have come in quietly. Further fluctuations would have resulted from rebound of the Earth's crust relieved of a heavy load.

The impact of these events on archaeological visibility is significant. Evidence of coastal or lowland settlement – where the majority of mankind has always lived – before 6,000 BCE is probably lost forever. In addition to this permanent horizon, there is a secondary one as the sea levels actually rose *above* their present levels with the final glacial melt and only settled back down in approximately 3,500 BCE. Hence the survivors of the first cataclysm who returned to the coast are under another silt level.

It is tremendously significant that the resettling of the sea back to its present level occurs at the same moment that twentieth century archaeologists considered the 'sudden beginnings of civilisation,' particularly in the next two parts of the globe we shall examine as they both also suffered significant land loss. Indeed, it is that very period between 6,000 BCE and 3,500 BCE that is the most confusing when it comes to the study of civilisational emergence. The implications of the geology of the final sea level rise is that the rise of 'civilisation' was anything but sudden and its antecedents should be sought under the silt. As for *their* antecedents, it is unlikely much of them will ever be found.

INDIA

The postcolonial toxicity that afflicts Indian history is probably nowhere more evident than in its marine archaeology. It is evident that the coastline holds numerous underwater settlements, both around the northern part of Sri Lanka and off the western coast of the mainland, where the Indus and Saraswati would once have drained into the sea. The next largest amount of land lost to the ocean is off the coast of Bangladesh in the Bay of Bengal, which remains prone to flooding today. During the Boxing Day tsunami when the ocean receded by almost a mile, numerous submerged remains were exposed to the air for the first time in thousands of years.

Unfortunately, the political desire to declare India as the sole source of all subsequent civilisations has led to some overly ambitious interpretations of the marine evidence. There are certainly manmade objects under the water, sometimes miles off the coast of India and Sri Lanka, which by definition makes them antediluvian. However, to immediately leap to the conclusion that these remains are Krishna's lost city of Dwarka or Kumari Kandam is to fall into the same trap as researchers looking for Noah's Ark or the 'real' Garden of Eden. By the time these stories are being told they are separated by millennia from the geological events they may be describing. We are talking about fuzzy memories rather than precision ones.

Discernment is once again required in separating the archaeological facts from their interpretation. Because the facts are quite clear. At its height, the Indus culture had at least six cities of more than 30,000 residents, kiln-fired bricks requiring temperatures of up to 1,700 degrees, and it appears with a fully formed script at the same time as the final geological silt layer. Off the coast of this civilisation there are submerged, manmade objects. From a purely physical level it is irrelevant which of these objects are 'Dravidic' and which of these objects are 'Harappan.' How these objects and climate events may have been refracted through mythology is the topic of the next chapter.

SUMERIA

The Ice Age experienced its final death rattle in the Arabian Gulf, right beside the mysterious culture we most closely associate, correctly or incorrectly, with the rise of civilisation. What role flooding has played in the story of the Sumerians, the people who gave the west the majority of our flood myths, has been a cause of considerable debate for more than a century.

Now known as the Flandrian Transgression, the sea level overshoot actually took the ocean about 180 kilometres inland from where the Tigris and Euphrates currently empty into the ocean. This transgression puts the shoreline right at the gate of the ancient city of Ur and within twenty five kilometres of the even older city of Eridu. It also made the settlements of the state of Lagash coastal. Just as is the case in Sundaland, we are presented with an initial flood more than ten thousand years ago that turned the idyllic Arabian valley into the Arabian Gulf, then a second marine incursion that moved the shoreline further up the two main rivers, then, several thousand years later, a final flood that initially moved the shore even further inland before pulling back almost a hundred kilometres to its present position.

Finding archaeological evidence above and below the resulting silt level has caused no small level of confusion. Returning to Dr Oppenheimer:

It was as if a curtain of water had been drawn across the remains of previous coastal settlements. Pots and implements that allow archaeologists to define prehistoric cultures were inaccessible; they lay under silt and under the sea, miles from the shoreline. But there was a window. Over the next few thousand years the sea level settled back by up to 5 metres, and the coastline emerged again, to a distance of over 100 kilometres. This partial drawing back of the curtain allowed Woolley to peer under the silt layer, at the few hundred years after the main force of the flood of Utnapishtim struck. Because marine inundation persisted from around 7500 to 5500 years ago on many of these sites, there was a big gap between the archaeological remains under the silt layer and those above it.

The Woolley he is referring to is Sir Leonard Woolley, the British Assyriologist and archaeologist known for his excavations at Ur, a man that history has been kind, then unkind and now slightly kind to once again. During his examination of the city of Ur, he encountered the silt layer that we now know was laid down by the Flandrian Transgression and declared two mostly wrong things. Firstly, that this was evidence of the Old Testament Flood, which is wrong simply because the Flandrian Transgression postdates the earliest iteration of the Flood story that ultimately came to be included in the Bible.

Secondly, he declared that the silt was laid down by a marine flood, not a riverine flood. At the time, with Ur so far from the shoreline and being situated on a river, he was widely mocked for his assertion. He even managed to calculate the height of the ocean at the time as being about four metres above its present level. In this instance, we now know that Woolley was correct and his public detractors were wrong. Not only that, but his calculation of the sea level was admirably close to what geology has demonstrated. He simply lacked a mechanism to explain precisely what the ocean was doing there that did not rely on Scripture.

A revised geological understanding has failed to disseminate publicly into wider Assyriology (although I have personally had some frank private discussions on the subject with academics). Much of this may be down to the persistent stink of churchiness associated with using the 'F' word. As such, 'Woolley's Flood' is still considered to be riverine. The source of the confusion seems to be a lack of understanding that a marine incursion up a river delta would lay down estuarine silt rather than marine silt anyway. Just think about how water would move upriver and form a 'wall' that would lead to the river depositing silt brought down from the mountains at the new shoreline.

Woolley was dismissed but he is the perfect example of 'the story' coming down to us out of sequence, a concept we will return to again. There were actually several floods, the first and second of which would have left the earliest sites underneath today's shoreline. The last of which took the ocean right up to Ur and Eridu, flooding at least one of them, in 3,500 BCE, exactly when Sumerian civilisation bursts fully formed onto the scene, and coinciding with the story of the seven fish sages arriving from the east with the skills of high civilisation. Incidentally, although it is deeply unfashionable now thanks to its origins in a very racist period of European exploration, evidence from the skulls of these first Sumerians demonstrates they were brachycephalic, suggesting an eastern origin.

The curious geography of Sumeria's earliest period fits with the notion of them as coastal seafarers. It also makes it a near certainty that Sumeria's 'sudden' appearance in the archaeological record is illusory and that its earliest layers lie both under and across at least one ocean. In all likelihood, Eridu is not the oldest city, merely the oldest coastal city not destroyed by the invading sea. In other words, it may be the last old city to be built at the post-glacial highwater point. Looking at the evidence for Eridu's earliest layers, Dr Oppenheimer observes that the Ubaid people who fashioned the oldest pottery found at Eridu also appear to have given both Eridu and Ur their names.' He suspects, probably correctly, that the Ubaid people built coastal settlements which are now on or under the seabed of the Arabian Gulf.'

Once the sea had rolled back and in the subsequent 1,500 years, the Sumerian and Babylonian civilisations climbed up the rivers of the Tigris and Euphrates, taking with them the stories of the floods of Utnapishtim, Gilgamesh and eventually Noah.

FIRE IN THE SKY

The cause or causes of Ice Ages are not even close to being fully understood. They certainly repeat, but they do so irregularly. This rules out some kind of solar 'supersea-son' as a singular 'cause.' And the volcanic explanation – that ash blocks out the sun for years at a time – would leave clearly discernable geological layers.

Currently, the Younger Dryas Impact Hypothesis, out of Harvard, is the frontrunning explanation for the snap cooling that preceded the end of the last Ice Age. Ice core data show a 100-fold increase in platinum concentrations 12,890 years ago, which align with oxygen isotope measurements indicating a sharp drop in temperature.

It is believed that a large meteor hit the North American ice sheet, which could have killed 75% of the continent's population, wiped out large mammals such as the mammoth and changed oceanic circulation. Such an event would certainly go a long way to explaining the extremely rapid melting of some of the ice sheet. Rock scoring found in Canada indicates large flows of liquid water rather than the movement of glaciers. A large, burning space rock may account for this.

More recently, however, David Meltzer of Southern Methodist University has re-examined the data from 29 American sites used to support the Impact Hypothesis and the date ranges stretch a lot further on either side of the supposed meteor event. This makes it unlikely that the abrupt climate change was caused by a single event – always the preferred explanation of the academic. Once again, the facts remain and the interpretation needs revising. And what the facts indicate is our ancestors lived through a few centuries of some fairly extreme space weather.

Around 9,500 BCE, the sun was extremely active, with a record number of sunspots. For the next 1,500 years, sunspot activity varied dramatically. Between 8,800 BCE and around 6,000 BCE, activity continued to fluctuate, only with diminishing highs. These fluctuations correlate, albeit imprecisely, with the climate changes associated with the Dryas periods. Clearly there is some correlation between solar activity, space debris and the end of the Ice Age.

It is possible that the absence of definitive evidence is itself a form of evidence. Emerging from the global interest in climate research accompanying our Anthropocene is a new appreciation for the impact of cosmic rays and solar activity in weather formation. Acidity spike data from the Cariaco Basin and dramatic increases in nitrate ion concentration in ice core data from several sites around the world point to some extreme coronal mass ejections around this time. Analysis of solar flare tracks on the glassy surface of the point suggest the same thing; that solar flare activity has varied by a factor of more than fifty between the end of the Ice Age and now.

Extreme space weather – perhaps caused by physical and electromagnetic debris travelling through the solar system – may even show up in more prosaic explanations. A large gravitational wave, which can currently only be detected indirectly, would trigger earthquakes and volcanoes on earth as it passed by and through the planet. Independent researcher Paul LaViolette points out that the day after the 2004 Boxing Day tsunami, the earth was hit by a major gamma ray burst from a neutron star located 50,000 light years away. The energy released by the flare from this distant star was greater than all the energy given off by the sun in the last hundred thousand years.

Geologist Dr Robert Schoch, in *Forgotten Civilisation*, explains how the impact of such extreme events may have been experienced by our ancestors.

LaViolette discusses some of the effects of a massive SPE and the attendant solar activity for the Earth. The ozone layer, our protection from deadly ultraviolet (UV) rays, would have been greatly depleted, with major ozone holes forming in some areas, that is, if the ozone layer had not been destroyed completely! Increased doses of damaging, and potentially lethal, UV radiation could have posed a major hazard for organisms on Earth, especially in high and middle latitudes. Besides the increased UV radiation, high-energy cosmic rays that are part of a major SPE would penetrate the atmosphere and raise radiation levels on the ground. According to LaViolette's calculations, unprotected organisms at sea level during the event of '12,837 cal yrs BP,' which is the focus of his paper, could have accumulated radiation doses of 3 to 6 Sieverts (a unit of radiation exposure, 1 Sievert = 100 rems [an older unit of radiation doses]) over a period of two or three days. Lethal radiation doses for humans are in the range of about 3.5 Sieverts, and for many large mammals in the 3- to 8-Sievert range. The best mode of protection at the time, both from the UV radiation and the cosmic ray radiation, may have been to seek safety in caves and other underground shelters (*Space Daily* 2011; LaViolette 2005). Interestingly, Austrian archaeologist and speleologist Heinrich Kusch and his wife Ingrid Kusch have documented hundreds upon hundreds of tunnel systems under Neolithic settlements found throughout Europe and Turkey, some dating back to around twelve thousand years ago (Kusch and Kusch 2011). According to Heinrich Kusch, based on the number of tunnels that have survived to the present day, the original extent of such tunnels must have been absolutely enormous! According to him, many of the tunnels 'are not much larger than big wormholes – just 70 cm wide – just wide enough for a person to wriggle along but nothing else. They are interspersed with nooks, at some places it's larger and there is seating, or storage chambers and rooms. Taken together it is a massive underground network' (Heinrich Kusch, quoted in *Austrian Times* 2011; see also *Daily Mail* 2011).

We are thus presented with the curious situation of having three sources of data – mythological, archaeological and geological – each on their own qualifying as circumstantial, but viewed collectively as something much more tantalising.

It is worth considering some of the Sumerian mythological descriptors, as they point to climate events beyond a 'mere' change in sea level. In the Atrahasis telling of the Flood, not only are the pasturelands covered in white salt – suggestive of a sea incursion – but the resulting famine where families turn to eating their children is accompanied by scabs appearing on the skin and mouths.

Significantly, Atrahasis's boat must be protected from the sun, and is thus fully sealed over. Enki even gives him a sand clock that lasts seven days so that he knows when to come back out. The Flood, when it came, was accompanied by an extremely loud noise, darkening skies and a raging wind from Adad. Anzu tears at the sky with his talons, breaking it and letting the flood in. Consider this excerpt:

The kasusu weapon went against the people like an army
No one could see anyone else,

They could not be recognised in the catastrophe.
The Flood roared like a bull,
Like a wild ass screaming the winds howled
The darkness was total, and there was no sun.

Not only do we have a description of a worldwide flood, but it also appears to have been accompanied by space weather so extreme that it has convinced more than a few people it is a description of the Sumerian space gods getting back in their ships and bombing the planet from orbit!

Given that the majority of the Earth's surface is covered by ocean, it is more likely than not that one or more large plasma events would have hit the sea. This would not show up anywhere in the geological record and would throw huge amounts of water up into the atmosphere, which would necessarily have to come back down in continuous heavy rainfall: forty days and forty nights of circumstantial evidence on a continuous feedback loop.

In his recent book, *The Ark Before Noah*, Dr Irving Finkel notes that all the animals on board the earliest version of the ark were predomesticated. They were part of a preagricultural culture's food supply. At his book launch in London, I had the occasion to ask him whether he thought that meant the Sumerian flood stories were a cultural memory of the end of the Ice Age, a time before agriculture. His eyes widened and he said that it was a huge issue that is probably worth us all thrashing out one day. Translating his response from the academic, that means *yes, but I am not going to be the first one to say it.*

ATLANTIS

Inevitably, any discussion of the veracity of flood stories brings us back to the jewel in the western tradition's flood crown: Atlantis itself. It has already been noted by various researchers over the last twenty years that the dates Solon was given for the true age of Egyptian civilisation line up not only with the geological age of the Sphinx (8,000 years old in the sixth century BCE) but also with the end of the Ice Age, and thus the most significant flood event we have experienced in twenty millennia.

In light of the increasingly archaeological and geological visibility of the Palaeolithic and the Pleistocene, it is worth looking in more detail at what the priests actually had to say about world-ending catastrophes.

And then one of the priests, a very old man, said, 'Ah, Solon, Solon, you Greeks are ever children. There isn't an old man among you.' On hearing this, Solon said,

'What? What do you mean?' 'You are young,' the old priest replied, 'young in soul, every one of you. Your souls are devoid of beliefs about antiquity handed down by ancient tradition. Your souls lack any learning made hoary by time. The reason for that is this: there have been, and there will continue to be, numerous disasters that have destroyed human life in many kinds of ways. The most serious of these involve fire and water, while the lesser ones have numerous other causes. And so also among your people the tale is told that Phaethon, child of the Sun, once harnessed his father's chariot, but was unable to drive it along his father's course. He ended up burning everything on the earth's surface and was destroyed himself when a lightning bolt struck him. This tale is told as a myth, but the truth behind it is that there is a deviation in the heavenly bodies that travel around the earth, which causes huge fires that destroy what is on the earth across vast stretches of time. When this happens all those people who live in mountains or in places that are high and dry are much more likely to perish than the ones who live next to rivers or by the sea. Our Nile, always our savior, is released and at such times, too, saves us from this disaster. On the other hand, whenever the gods send floods of water upon the earth to purge it, the herdsmen and shepherds in the mountains preserve their lives, while those who live in cities, in your region, are swept by the rivers into the sea. But here, in this place, water does not flow from on high onto our fields, either at such a time or any other. On the contrary, its nature is always to rise up from below. This, then, explains the fact that the antiquities preserved here are said to be the most ancient.

Here we have further descriptions of extreme space weather in the form of chariots of the gods, repeated destructions of mankind (in keeping with a dramatic several millennia), the burning up of humans on the earth and destruction with a thunderbolt.

We also see different mortality rates for different settlements, depending on what kind of calamity is afflicting mankind. In fact, the chilling image of bodies being carried downriver into the sea is also found in the Sumerian flood myths, where the womb goddess accuses Enlil of cruelty for the genocide of his children: 'Would a true father have given rise to the rolling sea, so that [their bodies] could clog the river like dragonflies?' Returning to the Egyptian priest's words to Solon in *Timaeus*:

The truth is that in all places where neither inordinate cold nor heat prevent it, the human race will continue to exist, sometimes in greater, sometimes in lesser numbers. Now of all the events reported to us, no matter where they've occurred – in your parts or in ours – if there are any that are noble or great or distinguished in some other way, they've all been inscribed here in our temples and preserved from antiquity on.

In your case, on the other hand, as in that of others, no sooner have you achieved literacy and all the other resources that cities require, than there again, after the usual number of years, comes the heavenly flood. It sweeps upon you like a plague, and leaves only your illiterate and uncultured people behind. You become infants all over again, as it were, completely unfamiliar with anything there was in ancient times, whether here or in your own region.

Again, I find the alignments with human population and distribution estimates with the description of 'summer and winter' highly suggestive. To me it speaks of parts of the earth opened and closed by ice and sea, as well as dramatic changes to grasslands that were quick enough to snap-freeze mammoth with their mouths still full of wild flowers.

As for what is preserved across cataclysms and *how*, we shall certainly return to that. You are invited to consider 'the heavenly flood ... like a plague' in light of the radiational impact of a presumed solar particle event.

And so, Solon, the account you just gave of your people's lineage is just like a nursery tale. First of all, you people remember only one flood, though in fact there had been a great many before. Second, you are unaware of the fact that the finest and best of all the races of humankind once lived in your region. This is the race from whom you yourself, your whole city, all that you and your countrymen have today, are sprung, thanks to the survival of a small portion of their stock. But this has escaped you, because for many generations the survivors passed on without leaving a written record.

Again, this description of the origin of the Greeks is significant because it is exactly correct. The last twenty years of genetic research have revealed a migration from the Levant and Anatolia out into the Mediterranean around 8,000 BCE, followed by another two millennia of 'sloshing around' from Greece to Malta to Menorca to Italy and back. It is likely these migrants were the 'Ur' culture for the Greeks and Etruscans, as well as being the people who would subsequently introduce more 'Eastern' ideas into the Celtic tribes.

The location and timing of this migration puts it exactly where and when the Göbekli Tepe culture was winding up. Thus it is both the origin of einkorn wheat agriculture, used by the Etruscans; and viticulture, used by everybody. (The presence of an ecstatic god of meat-eating, drug-taking and wine who hails from a foreign hilltop and is associated with the mystery of agricultural renewal should be ringing a few bells about now.)

Inevitably, it seems, the Atlantologists have missed a trick. We have all been looking for the physical location of a political metaphor – whose existence is the least interesting part of the story – rather than calibrating the parts of the legend we can actually fix to some observable facts. Because what is so compelling about the Atlantis story is that it appears to be an example of Ice Age stories surviving all the way up to the sixth century BCE with a reasonable degree of accuracy. The implications for what else may have survived long enough to be able to impact the formulation of the western magical tradition are wide-reaching.

THAT WHICH IS IMPERISHABLE

Out of the disasters associated with the end of the Ice Age came stories of giants, little people, angels and refugee wisdom teachers dedicated to rebuilding civilisation. The Flood is the pivotal event in the western mystery tradition, and I mean pivotal literally. Pinning it down finally provides us with a fixed location from which to view what came before and what came after.

The default 'alternative historical' explanation for how the various sites around the world appear to encode astronomical and mathematical information is that they are in some sense a 'warning' for future generations about what has happened and what will presumably happen again. These hypotheses strike me as quite weak. You will struggle to find instances in the historical record for times when mankind gave even the slightest shit about our children and grandchildren. Most of the time, we are either raping them ourselves or packing them off as sex slaves in politically expedient marriages to nearby warlords. Today we cannot even manage to keep the planet liveable for the next two generations.

It is a fundamental misreading of eschatology to assume we are concerned with the survival of humans rather than *wisdom*. Either given freely or torn from the hands of uncaring gods, it is the technology for immortality that must survive. That is a near-universal Laurasian refrain.

Thus it is more appropriate to consider these sacred sites as expressions of that which is imperishable, rather than the imperishable things themselves. In any case, it is frankly bad magic to think merely building a temple out of stone will enable it to survive cataclysms. You only need to spend an hour or so on YouTube looking at the impact of a recent tsunami on the world's most technologically advanced civilisation to see that it is a recipe for heartache. These 'expressions of the imperishable' would be what the Egyptian priest told Solon was the 'education' that needed to be rediscovered. Consider this quote from historian Graham Robb's *The Ancient Paths: Discovering the Lost Map of Celtic Europe*.

> A historian of the Iron Age is often left with nothing but a question mark, like a shepherd clutching his crook when the sheep have run away. Does the microscopic artistry of Celtic smiths imply an equivalent expertise on a larger scale, or was the artist's forge a lonely light in a small, dark world? If some grand measurement and ordering of the Continent was attempted, there must have been a coordinating body or at least an efficient sharing of scientific secrets, and there are few signs of this in the unpromising debris of hill forts and farmsteads ...
>
> If no means of determining longitude was devised before Hipparchos, how did Hannibal, for instance, manage to navigate his way along the Heraklean diagonal, and how was he able to rejoin the solar path after being forced to deviate from it? How could the pathways of the Celts have been anything but a wonderful mirage? A clue can be found, surprisingly, in Pliny the Elder's credulous encyclopaedia of wonders, *Historia Naturalis* (c.78 AD). In a chapter which is bizarre even by Pliny's standards, he describes two ancient 'experiments,' the purpose and result of which escaped him almost entirely. He knew only that they had something to do with the curvature of the earth, which 'discovers and hides some things to some, and others to others.' Someone had evidently tried to explain to Pliny the problem of longitude.

It seems that with each new season, the earliest dates for megalithic structures in Western Europe get pushed back another millennia or so. The vast majority of them are postdiluvian, but at least some of the sites now look to be antediluvian in the sense of first being used before the end of the Ice Age. (And there may well be more under the cold waters off Britain's northeast coast.)

Consider the fascinating story of what we now call the Megalithic Yard. In a fine example of relentlessness, an Oxford professor of engineering science, Alexander Thom, ruined nearly fifty of his wife and friends' summers by packing them off all over Brittany and the British Isles, measuring megalithic sites, year after year. By the end of his life, he had built a database of megalithic measurements that has yet to be surpassed today. He claimed to have discovered three units of ancient measurement that he called the Megalithic Yard (2.722 ft), the Megalithic Rod (2.5 MY) and a Megalithic Inch (one fortieth of a MY).

Obviously this did not go down well – and has not gone down well – with historians whose theories do not match the statistical facts found by an actual professor of engineering. How could a preliterate society create a unified system of measurement across so diverse a terrain?

Easily, it turns out. All you need is time, which our ancestors certainly had. You could ball up some dung on a horse hair, create a pendulum and end up with an accurate measurement for both the circumference of the earth and the moon. From Christopher Knight and Alan Butler's *Before the Pyramids*:

> We think it is fair to suggest that the first machine ever invented by man was the plumb-bob/pendulum. A small ball of clay on the end of a piece of twine or long strand of straight hair is a wonderful device that interacts with the Earth in a very predictable way. Held stationary, it will always point down to the centre of the planet, which allows the user to check verticals during construction of any sort. Verticals are also necessary for good observational astronomy. When the device is swung gently to and fro in the hand it becomes a timekeeper, like a modern metronome (which is only an inverted pendulum).
>
> But the real beauty about pendulums is that their frequency with which they swing is only determined by their length, so if you count a set number of beats for a given period of time (such as the period it takes a star to traverse a known gap), you will always end up with the same pendulum length.
>
> We found that half a Megalithic Yard pendulum was the origin of the whole measurement system rediscovered by Thom.

With a few bits of wood and twine, an ancient engineer could confidently calculate the circumference of the earth. He or she would face east and observe the rising of a star or planet and then observe where they descended over an artificial horizon like the top of a henge or part of an observational platform, counting pendulum swings between the rising and the setting of these astral bodies. When Christopher Knight ran his suggestions by a chartered civil engineer by the name of Jim Russell, this is the response he got:

> If I wanted to study the movement of the planets and stars without modern instruments, I would need a fixed point from which to make measurements. I would need middle distance reference points to check the star and planet movements against an artificial horizon. Ideally I would be within shouting distance of my assistant placing the reference points 360 (or 366) degrees around my reference point (right a bit, left a bit, SPOT ON).

These hypothetical descriptions are highly resonant with the mysterious 'Stretching of the Cord' ceremony that the Egyptian king and priestess of Seshat were required to perform in the laying out of pyramids, the astronomical alignments of which have boggled our minds for thousands of years. We are approaching a solution to the observable fact that the dimensions of the earth are encoded in the construction of the Great Pyramid without recourse to alien space ships. One final quote from Christopher Knight on that subject.

Neolithic sky-watchers would clearly have understood that there were two constantly repeating patterns taking place – the day and the year. It is almost impossible that they would have failed to realize that the daily pattern fitted into the yearly pattern 366 times. As far as they were concerned, the year was a great circle of 366 days in duration and so the origin of the degree of arc as 1/366th of a circle. By contrast, the modern convention of 360° in a circle is as primitive as the ancient Egyptian year of 360 days – it simply isn't correct. The two errors are entirely historically related, and though we now do at least use a year of 365 days, we never corrected the mistake regarding the number of degrees in a circle ...

The ancient system of geometry has greatness running right through it. It divided the Earth's polar circumference into 366° and then subdivided each degree into 60 minutes of an arc, with 6 seconds to each minute. And, amazingly, each second of the arc is exactly 366 MY in length.

To sum up, count 366 swings of a pendulum between the rising and setting of, say, Venus, between two artificial markers and the length of your pendulum is half a Megalithic Yard. 366 is the number of days in an ancient year and the number of degrees in an ancient circle. The unit of measurement you have created can also be used to calculate the circumference of the Earth, because 366 Megalithic Yards is exactly one second of its arc. This same number, 366 Megalithic Yards, is precisely equivalent to 1,000 Minoan Yards. As for the Egyptians, if you create a circle that has a circumference of one Megalithic Yard, then this circle has a diameter of one royal cubit. And the remen, an ancient Egyptian unit of measurement for land and roads, is the hypotenuse of a square around the Megalithic Yard circle.

Squaring the circle. Imagine that. If you are as confused as Pliny about now, do not worry. The point is that there is a universal unit of length found in Minoan Crete, the earliest architecture of Ancient Egypt and Northwest European megaliths that can deliver an accurate measurement of the earth using some clay, twine and a few magical friends. It is a mathematical impossibility that this exact unit of measurement was arrived at randomly by at least three separate cultures and that they also accidentally calculated the true circumference of the Earth.

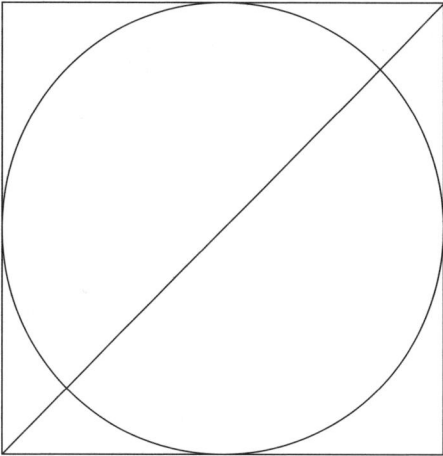

fig. 10   *The relationship between the Megalithic Yard and the Egyptian remen*

Christopher Knight's subsequent explanation for this, that colonists from the British Isles may have influenced the culture development of the Minoans and Egyptians lacks mythological or genetic support. Nevertheless, that is merely an interpretation. His mathematical facts are sound. Given the available genetic and cultural data, it seems more likely to me that we need to 'step up' the family tree and look for a common origin for these measurements.

The time-depth for a common origin of megalithic measurements puts us squarely back before the end of the Ice Age and is very likely a form of Laurasian 'high magical technology.' Appearing at the very latest just after the end of the Ice Age – and thus by definition having been developed during it – we perceive a way of viewing the universe that links the number of days in a year to the number of swings of a pendulum, to the layout of sacred sites, to the circumference of the earth and all tied back to the movements of the stars. We see the macrocosm of the night sky linked by skilled observers to the microcosm of our smallest moments, a map of both the inner and outer universe. We see the development of ancient navigational techniques into a precision magical system for use on land. We see proto-hermeticism writ large.

The past is not a natural growth but a cultural creation.
Jan Assmann, *Cultural Memory and Early Civilization*

VII   EXPULSION FROM EDEN

At this point in our story, with the exception of Antarctica, humans have occupied every continent on earth for tens of millennia. They have just undergone the most significant climate event since leaving Africa. However, postdiluvial migration – for which we have genetic, cultural and linguistic evidence – need not be a mass activity. To posit connections between Island Southeast Asia and the appearance of the Sumerian and Harappan civilisations is not to imply that the Sunda survivors loaded themselves onto fleets of ships and then set off for points west, populating the empty or unknown lands of the subcontinent and the Near East. Indeed, we saw that the majority of survivors largely stayed in Melanesia for the next few thousand years before permanently inhabiting the rest of the Pacific.

Cultures already existed in the lands that would become India, Pakistan and Arabia prior to the dramatic technological and cultural changes that we are told arose independently, simultaneously and within a few centuries of the post-Ice Age climate stabilisation. Indeed, if Dr Witzel's timelines are correct, these cultures may have already shared a broadly Laurasian cosmology of earlier common origin by this time. Nevertheless, when it comes to the sudden appearance of cultures or cultural technology with no local antecedents, undeciphered scripts and languages entirely unrelated to those around them (but with compelling connections to cultures further afield) at a broadly simultaneous time, we have more questions than we do answers. Those answers we do have run the gamut from the highly speculative to the downright racist.

THE SPACES BETWEEN

The creation of borders on maps throws geopolitical challenges at the future and identity political challenges at the past. It is an action that works backwards and forwards in time. The Act of Partition that created the modern states of Pakistan and India, a decision which had a widespread impact on global security, has also had a widespread impact on our understanding of the past. Today, the vast bulk of archaeological sites that comprised the Harappan and Kulli cultures are located in the nations of Pakistan, Afghanistan and parts of Southeast Iran. This means that over the last five decades or so, they have been managed by regimes with varying interest in pre-Muslim cultures and in some cases are outright hostile and destructive toward them.

On the other side of the border, Indian archaeology has occasionally been caught in the identity politics of both Nationalism and Independence. Indeed, the famous Harappan site of Lothal, in coastal Gujarat, was first discovered as part of a deliberate project to uncover an Indian equivalent to the ancient city of Mohenjo Daro, which fell on the Pakistani side of the border. Once again, we cannot understand history without historiography, and we cannot understand historiography without global geopolitics.

As is probably obvious, this state of affairs is not going to be resolved in a single chapter of an occult history book, nor will it likely be resolved in your lifetime. If you do not mind attracting a little NSA attention, it is well worth an hour or two of your time on Google Earth, looking at the various river valleys of Pakistan, western India and the shape of the coastline heading west into Iran and the wider Arabian region. You quickly become aware of just how interconnected this area would have been for cultures with even the slightest nautical competency. The same annual monsoon action that brought the Nusantao backwards and forwards from Southeast Asia enabled regular, sustained contact from India's southernmost tip to the Horn of Africa, up the Arabian Gulf and right along the coastlines in between.

Broadly speaking, we have the Dravidian/Tamil language and cultural groups in Southern India and Sri Lanka, who have genetic and linguistic connections to South-

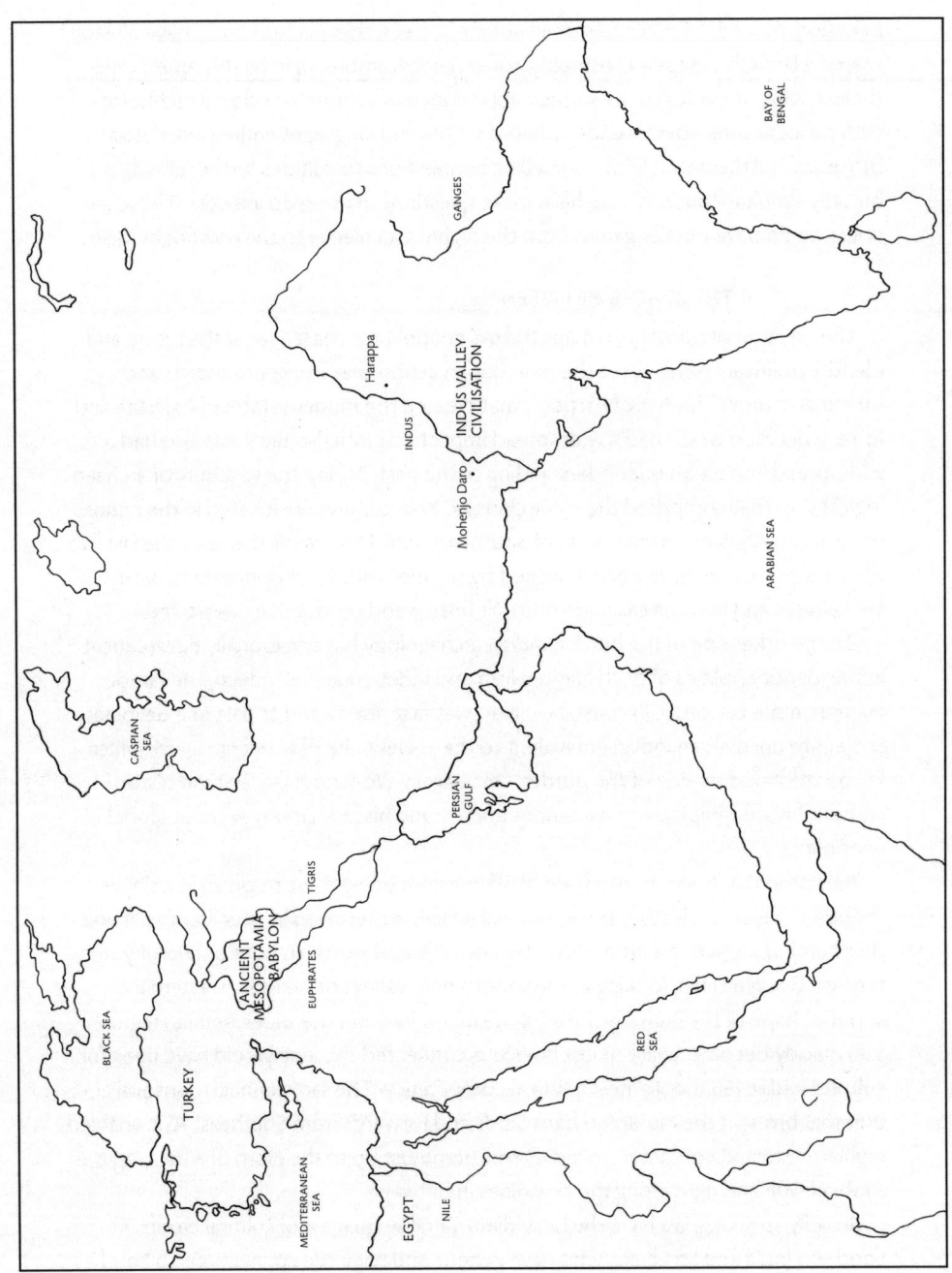

BAY OF
BENGAL

GANGES

Harappa

INDUS VALLEY
CIVILISATION

INDUS

Mohenjo Daro

ARABIAN SEA

CASPIAN
SEA

PERSIAN
GULF

TIGRIS

ANCIENT
MESOPOTAMIA
BABYLON

EUPHRATES

BLACK SEA

RED
SEA

TURKEY

MEDITERRANEAN
SEA

EGYPT

NILE

fig. 11   *The great rivers and the Indus Valley, Mesopotamian and Egyptian civilisations* east Asia on the eastern side and genetic and (reconstructed) linguistic relationships to the Horn of Africa and Southwestern Iran to the west. These groups have a low genetic correlation to the upper reaches of the Indus Valley, where we first see evidence of the Harappan civilisation. There is effectively zero genetic correlation between Dravidian groups and Central Asia at the time depth we are looking at, and only a small correlation between Central Asia and the proto-Harappans (sending the Aryan Invasion Theory packing). The Sumerians have morphological connections to both South India and Southeast Asia (as well as the expected Semitic and African morphologies) but possess a language that is entirely unrelated to anything nearby, with the exception of Elamo-Dravidian (from Southwest Iran). Elamo-Dravidian, however, is currently only a hypothetical, reconstructed language. Domestic varieties of sheep and goat were introduced to Northeast Africa (i.e. Egypt) from Southwest Asia (Southern Pakistan and India) by 6,000 BCE, and if this was an overland introduction then it had to occur through almost all the areas we have just discussed. Shell trading appears to have begun in earnest over the same geographic location but potentially up to a thousand years earlier.

What is apparent is that probably the most important period of intercultural contact in western history currently resembles nothing so much as Dresden after the war. Mercifully, we do not need to rebuild it. It is sufficient for our purposes that there are multiple hard scientific data demonstrating contact before and after the end of the Ice Age. This enables us to examine the star lore of these areas, whether they overlap and whether – as well as *when* – they demonstrate increasing complexity.

INDIA

When it comes to the origins of the 'Vedic civilisation' and whether it originated in India or somewhere else in Central Asia, I simply do not have a dog in that particular fight. Nor is it overly relevant to an examination of mythological vectors across cultures. Its age, rather than its provenance, is what is important here. It is nevertheless worth noting that every single event described in the Vedas happens inside India, which would be unusual choice of setting for an imported mythology. (Although not entirely without precedent.) Regardless, dating an oral tradition by simply guessing it is a thousand years older than the first appearance of it in written form – which neatly summarises the official position – is highly dubious, particularly when the oral tradition shares so much symbolism with a culture, the Harappan civilisation, that was apparently entirely separate and ended a scant few centuries before the oral tradition began; especially when this so-called Vedic civilisation is currently missing a homeland. (Dr Witzel puts it in Bactria. I ask for actual evidence of that.) The whole thing becomes even more dubious now that we have evidence of the longevity and fidelity of oral traditions stretching over millennia from Australia and Melanesia. It seems much more likely that it is an older, indigenous mythological tradition that arose in a culture that had a high level of foreign contact, which we know to be the case from the available genetic and cultural evidence.

When condensed into a single sentence, the official narrative looks rather flimsy, bordering on the absurd: some chariot-riding people we have never found, whose homeland is still missing, who are absent from the genetic record, created these hunting and fire worship hymns no earlier than 2,000 BCE and probably by 1,400 BCE somewhere in greater Punjab or a bit beyond. As mentioned, this puts its creation within a scant few centuries of the end of the Harappan civilisation to which it is apparently unrelated. But we also have no idea what language the Harappan culture spoke, nor have we deciphered their script, but it also definitely has nothing to do with the more northern Vedic language or the Dravidian language to the south.

The whole thing is a mess. A mess that tidies itself up considerably when you match the various motifs, flora and fauna mentioned in the hymns to the changing landscape of South Asia. The Vedas appear as the very end of a long oral tradition rather than the beginning of a written one.

The Gondwana/Laurasia model makes it clear that there was a sizeable overlap of cosmologies across vast land (and sea) areas. This reduces the Edwardian archaeological need to find the X on the map. Given the timeframes under discussion, it is only to be expected that the flora and fauna of the hymns would change. A picture of an oral, shamanic, Laurasian tradition changing over time emerges; changing both biospherically and linguistically.

EURASIA AFTER THE FLOOD

When the early Indologists declared that the flora and fauna in the Vedas – the lack of tigers in the earliest hymns, for instance – made it unlikely they were composed in India, they were largely unaware of the biospherical changes the humans living in Eurasia had already been through, especially considering that central and southern Eurasia had been occupied for 30,000 to 40,000 years. Viewed over such a long timeline, the changes to the local ecosystem resemble nothing quite so much as watching the film *Baraka* speeded up.

- DURING THE ICE AGE: Central Asia and Northwest India was a dry desert steppe, broadly similar to what we might find today in Mongolia.
- IMMEDIATELY AFTER THE ICE AGE: Between 9,000 BCE and 8,000 BCE, increased rainfall

and global temperatures brought dense birch forests to these regions, closely followed by oak (mentioned in the Rig Veda). Southern India did not experience much of a climate change, perhaps only 1 degree, so the same conditions for flora and fauna continued.

- 6,000 BCE – 3,000 BCE: The western coast of the Black Sea – where today there are forests – was steppe. The eastern coast – which is today steppe – was forest. The coasts switched to their 'modern' configuration by 3,000 BCE. In the Altai region (Kazakhstan, Mongolia), the steppe became dense conifer forest at 6,000 BCE. In northern India, willow, juniper and oak appeared on the Kachi plain. Lake levels rose early during this period and then gradually receded.

- 2,000 BCE: By this point, the forests had long left the northern steppe of Central Asia, the southern steppe had become dry, northwest India was slightly cooler than it was today but otherwise largely resembled today's climate, as did the entire Eurasian continent.

If Dr Witzel's timeline and geographic reach for Laurasian cosmologies are broadly accurate, that suggests that these climate changes were absorbed into an existing belief system, rather than being a crude reaction to local conditions. To put it another way, the same creator god was called upon in the dense conifer forests as was called upon out on the reappearing steppe.

Once again, recourse to hard scientific data sheds surprising new light on the development and transmission of mythology. In *The Origins of the World's Mythologies*, Witzel observes in passing – and misses the potential significance of – that, in between the Last Glacial Maximum and the end of the Ice Age, there was a grassland corridor running southeast to northwest across India up toward the Near East. To the east of this corridor there would have been marshy, predator-infested jungles and to the west there would have been impenetrable, snow-covered mountains. So there was an actual highway between our previous point of interest, Sundaland, and our current one, the top of the Indus.

CALIBRATING THE VEDAS

In the absence of any credible evidence that the Vedas were wholly foreign to India and first created at the very young date of 1500 BCE by a people for whom we have zero genetic evidence and who are currently missing a homeland, it seems that calibrating the hymns with what we know of the flora and fauna described in them may shed some light on their true age.

What is important to realise from the outset is that they were not all written down at the same time. First came the Rig Veda, then the Yajur Veda, then the Sama Veda and finally the Atharva Veda. The prevailing theory is that these four texts were all written down within a couple of centuries of each other. However, these timelines are in stark contrast to the dramatic changes in landscape, farming, clothing and technology described in the various hymns. If they were transcribed so close to each other, then not only are we missing their home culture, we should be looking for one that underwent the kind of changes the western world experienced over the last century. Quite simply, the numbers do not stack up.

Instead, we should consider that, as oral texts, the Vedas are a highly conservative form of cultural storage and are thus likely to have retained 'memories' of ancient climates and experiences, just as we saw with the Australian Aborigines.

The following examples of possible calibration owe a great deal to the work of Dr Premendra Priyadarshi, Fellow of the Royal College of Physicians of Edinburgh and – man after my own heart – an independent researcher with a mind for hard science. His excellent *In Quest of the Dates of the Vedas* is highly recommended for anyone with an interest in the origins of Indo-European mythology. We move from the oldest to the newest of the hymn collections.

Rig Veda

The earliest of the Vedas does not mention wheat, rice, lentils or date palms, which is surprising given that any hypothetical Aryan hymn singer would be familiar with all of them. It would be unsurprising if these hymns represent the oral tradition of preagricultural nomads such as one might find before or at the very end of the Ice Age. Cold climate trees such as the oak, long extinct by the proposed period of Aryan influence of 2,000 BCE to 1,500 BCE, do warrant a mention.

Somewhat famously, the Rig Veda does describe the mighty Saraswati River – extinct for four thousand years – in full flow. The Saraswati lost its connection to the Himalayan glaciers around 7,000 BCE and gradually declined to a trickle before finally dying around 2,000 BCE, before the accepted date for the codification of the hymns themselves. She is described as both a mighty river and a goddess in the Rig Veda, but by the time of the youngest hymn collection, the Atharva Veda, she is described 'only' as a goddess.

Staying with the liquid theme, water wheels are mentioned as being in use, suggesting that the water table in northwest India was significantly higher at the time, such as one would expect in a landscape of roaring glacial rivers. The beaver is not mentioned in the Rig Veda, but it is mentioned in the next-oldest collection, the Yajur Veda. Beavers cannot survive in fast-flowing rivers, nor are they particularly well disposed to grasslands. They would, and indeed did, prefer the post-5,000 BCE climate, when the landscape was covered in dense poplar forests, perfect for building dams on the slowing Saraswati. The beaver became extinct in this area by 2,000 BCE, again before the accepted date for the earliest Vedic text. The creature is not mentioned again after the Yajur Veda.

The Rig Veda mentions lions, wild horses, wild camels and leopards, all consistent with an open grassland environment. It does not mention the tiger, the rhinoceros, the tortoise or the crocodile, which would have been absent from such an environment.

Of particular interest is that, unlike later Vedas, the Rig Veda makes no mention of seals, writing, pens or styluses, statues or burnt brick, all of which are present in Harappan culture, which supposedly predates it. Had the Rig Veda been composed around 2,000 BCE – by whomever you wish to presume did so – this would have been thousands of years after the introduction of such technology right across Eurasia and would presumably have made it into at least one hymn. It makes more sense to propose, as Dr Priyadarshi does, that the Rig Veda come down to us from a time before any of these things.

There are other technological suggestions that this may be the case. The Rig Veda makes no mention of cotton. Cotton trees are mentioned in the Yajur Veda and the Harappans, again apparently older than Vedic civilisation, wore cotton clothing. It does, however, mention wool, a far more suitable material for clothing in a land of glacial rivers and mountain passes. Recall that the sheep, an Indian animal, was introduced to Northeast Africa by 6,000 BCE.

Interestingly, Dr Priyadarshi suggests the preeminence of the fire god, Agni, in the Rig Veda above the other Vedas, would be in keeping with a culture living in a cold climate rather than a warm one. That is certainly food for thought.

Yajur Veda

Dr Priyadarshi suggests that the Rig Veda was composed between 6,000 BCE to 5,500 BCE. After this time, the climate went from dry/cold to warm/wet which, inevitably, matches the second-oldest of the Vedas, the Yajur Veda. We see mentions of the monsoon as well as evidence for settled agriculture such as wheat, rice, lentil and date palm. This would be in keeping with the arrival of farming to northwest India in the early Holocene, a time of much higher rainfall. The rainfall was lower than today but the postglacial rivers were in full flow. Combined with the warmer climate, this is great farming weather. The era is known as either the Early Harappa or Mehrgarh Period II.

There are no burnt bricks in Mehrgarh Period I, just as there are no burnt bricks in the Rig Veda. By contrast, the Yajur Veda describes and also implies the extensive use of burnt bricks. Indeed, burnt bricks – mysteriously fired at temperatures so high archaeologists do not yet know how they accomplished it – is characteristic of High Harappan and Indus culture, beginning in earnest during Mehrgarh Period II. The Yajur Veda specifically pays homage to social classes such as sewer workers who tend drainage pipes, roads and other cultures constructed out of burnt brick. In point of fact, it is one of the most adored objects in the entire text. Combined with the climate data and the references to agriculture, the presence of burnt brick in the Yajur Veda suggests a composition date no earlier than 5,500 BCE and probably slightly after that.

Amulets, not mentioned in the Rig Veda, make their first appearance in the Yajur Veda and, as we know, Harappan civilisation was positively awash with the things. We also see the first mention of writing, another Harappan feature.

The water wheel is absent but the potter's wheel makes its first appearance here, too. The potter's wheel appears in the archaeological record of the region during the Mehrgarh Period II. You will not find anywhere in Eurasia where the potter's wheel is absent by 1,500 BCE, the currently accepted dating of the composition of the Vedas. So its absence from the Rig Veda, if it was composed at such a late date, is unusual to say the least.

Two agricultural products appear in the hymns for the first time that may be highly significant in correlating Harappa with both a Sunda influence and a Sumerian influence. Rice, which locates its genetic origin and first evidence of cultivation in island Southeast Asia, gets its first mention. That could suggest not only a change in climate making the cultivation of rice possible but also, given the broad timeline match, a diffusion of rice growing techniques from the southeast to the northwest. Mehrgargh Period II, with its burnt bricks and potters' wheels and so on, was a time of high cultural complexity which may be due in part to outside influence.

The second agricultural product worth noting that makes its first appearance in the Yajur Veda is sesame, both in wild and cultivated form. Not mentioned in the Rig Veda, sesame oil became an important component of Vedic rituals. The sesame plant is summer-flowering and requires warm weather, likely originating in southern India. In fact, the Dravidian word for sesame, *ellu*, was borrowed into the Sumerian and Akkadian, and became our word 'oil.' Burnt sesame seeds have been found in Indus sites dating back 3,500 BCE. Much like the appearance of the Austronesian words for 'cinnamon' and 'lemon' in ancient India, the use of the same word for the same substance stretching from the Dravidian region, through the Indus region and into Sumeria is compelling evidence for very early contact.

Sama Veda and Atharva Veda

Even working to Dr Priyadarshi's extended timeline for the first composition of the Vedas, by the time we get to the youngest two, we are firmly within the accepted era for Mid or Late Harappa. Fascinating though these texts are in their own right, they cannot tell us much regarding potential Palaeolithic survivals.

INDIAN STAR LORE

A curious thing happens when you map the early Vedas to the climate changes associated with the end of the Ice Age. You begin to see their star lore in a new light, but also a new context. For instance, the prominence of a lunar calendar rather than a solar one takes on additional context when you see the same calendrical system showing up among the Sunda survivors of Melanesia and Polynesia. Jake Stratton-Kent notes in his books that there is considerable academic debate as to whether the lunar calendar (and thus eventually the lunar mansions and decans) originated in either China or Babylon. Given that it also shows up in near identical form across Polynesia and, as we are about to see, is evident in the Vedas, we are forced to declare both sides wrong and posit an ultimate origin considerably earlier than 1,000 BCE. Otherwise this calendrical technology is unable to influence such geographically disparate cultures. They are looking for parents and actually finding siblings. The lunar calendar is clearly older, emerging from cultures that – being pre- or non-agricultural – had little use for the sun. It is also easier to visually track the movement of the moon through its mansions because you can actually look at it.

Luni-Solar Calendar

A substantial minority of scholars believe that India derived its astrological and calendrical system from Mesopotamia. Evidence marshalled for this position is the Babylonian Mul.Apin Text from around 1,000 BCE. Like the Rig Veda, Mul.Apin has 360 days/720 'day and night moments' as well as an intercalary thirteenth month every five years to reset the calendar.

The trouble is 1,000 BCE is much, much too late in the story if it turns out the Rig Veda describes an oral tradition going back to at least the end of the Ice Age. An identical calendar is found in Polynesia, China, Egypt and Sumeria, suggesting its origin in the original Proto-Laurasian culture of Sundaland. There is also the not insignificant observation that Mul.Apin is principally concerned with the movement of the planets (it is Babylonian, after all) and the planets are of passing importance in Vedic star lore, just as they are in Polynesia and among the Torres Strait Islanders. (Planetary astrology achieved its high importance during the Hindu era.) If the star lore of the western esoteric tradition derives from a Palaeolithic navigational culture, and I believe it does, then we can expect that the oldest versions of this astrological tech will place greater emphasis on the stars than the planets.

Two Rig Vedic hymns following on from each other describe the 'twelve fixed parts of the wheel' in context of the sun, followed by a description of the twelve places of the moon, with a mention of the intercalary 'hidden' month. Another hymn to the Ashvins – who some have interpreted as Mercury and Venus given their status as wandering sunrise/sunset horsemen – is probably the earliest description of the twelve zodiacal signs (particularly if the Rig Veda is as old as its floral and faunal descriptions suggest).

The system of lunar asterisms in Mul.Apin, clearly derived from the Sumerian 'three star lists,' is very similar to the nakshatra system referred to in the Rig Veda and described in much more detail in the Atharva Veda. There were presumably 24 nakshatras – one for each half month – but three of them were split again to align the mansions with lunar sidereal months, bringing the total number to 27. The nakshatra system is potentially highly illuminating when it comes to the origin and true antiquity of the western esoteric tradition. Each nakshatra had a presiding deity and formed a counter-balancing pair with the nakshatra found 180 degrees away in the opposite corner of the sky, much as we find in the decans. (Yes, 27 is an odd number. There is a 28th, or hidden nakshatra called Sati, who was not invited to Shiva's self-sacrifice by drinking celestial poison and thus returned to the 'normal' part of the night sky. Fudging the books is an ancient practice.)

Pleiades

Did you think we were done with the seven sisters? Perish the thought. Just as we find in Polynesia, the year begins with the heliacal rising of the Krittikas in the east. However, thanks to the impact of precession, it seems highly likely the Pleiades were spiritually significant long before taking up position in the eastern corner of the dawn sky, which would be in keeping with the proposed true age of the Rig Veda.

Dr B. G. Sidharth, an astronomer with some thirty years' experience and director of India's B. M. Birla Science Centre has matched mentions of the sky location of different asterisms in the Vedas to when they last occupied said locations and come up with a date of 7,300 BCE for the Vedic age. In his fascinating book, *The Celestial Key to the Vedas*, he avers these hymns describe a *continuous system of astronomical observation* going back to 7,300 BCE and beyond, rather than a system formed at such an early date that was subsequently passed down. His description of a corpus of star lore growing in sophistication is in almost perfect agreement with Dr Priyadarshi's mapping of the changing flora, fauna and technology found in the Rig Veda and the Yajur Veda.

Dr Sidharth draws our attention to a Rig Vedic hymn in which Prajapati, the year, begins with the nakshatra Rohini rising at the winter solstice at the same time Antares rose at the summer solstice and the nakshatra Purva Bhadrapada rose with the autumnal equinox. For all these conditions to be met, we are looking at 10,000 BCE, mid-point of Dr Witzel's Laurasian storyline and contemporaneous with the probably-astronomical temple of Göbekli Tepe. In the Mahabharata, composed much later than the Rig Veda, this same sky pattern is referenced again. Indra – the presiding ruler of the nakshatra Rohini – yields his place 'at the head of the gods' to Karttikeya, ruling deity of Krittikas. Due to precession, Aldebaran (Rohini) moved from its winter solstice position to be replaced by the Pleiades (Krittikas) at around 8,500 BCE. Further corroboration of these early dates comes from commentaries on the Rig Veda that describe the Krittikas as 'first of the divine stars,' i.e. rising at the winter solstice, and end with Vishakha (Libra) at the summer solstice.

Viewed with the eyes of a practical occultist, what is interesting is that the asterism as well as the directionality are equally important. Later Vedic texts describe the Krittikas as 'never swerving from the east,' which is very difficult to do over such a long timeline unless you start celebrating the heliacal rising of the Pleiades on a different quarter day. Indeed, the University of Helsinki's Asko Parpola has found a number of cultural references that tie the Pleiades to the autumnal equinox and potentially to Harappan ritual, bringing us to 3,000 BCE and landing us back in Dr Priyadarshi's timeline. This will be discussed below. Dr Sidharth sees meaning in a curious passage in the (much later) Mahabharata where the age of the Krittikas came to an end. The people wanted it to return and convinced the deity to do so. This may be a cultural expression of the Pleiades leaving one quarter day and then appearing on another, millennia later.

As expected, there is a Seven Sages/seven wives/banished to the sky motif in the Vedic descriptions of the Pleiades, just as we find in the Pacific. There is a component to this motif that is probably highly significant. After a confusing birth story involving Agni's wife impersonating six of the wives of the Seven Sages because her husband wanted to bed them, she is impregnated by Agni and gives birth to Karttikeya, who is then raised by the actual wives of the Seven Sages in the sky/in the Pleiades. Karttikeya rides a peacock, native to southern India, and the 'eyes' in its plumage probably represent the stars of Pleiades. (Recall that in the Pacific, 'Matariki' is known as 'little eyes.') Peacock and star motifs are prominent on pottery in some late Harappan burial sites. Moving into historical times, Karttikeya – known as Murugan – was and is immensely popular in Southern and Tamil regions, right across to Singapore. He is commander-in-chief of the army of the gods and 'precedes' them, just as the Pleiades appear first of all the constellations. That the Pleiades would be so popular in the southern parts of the subcontinent would be in keeping with any potential influence from Island Southeast Asia at an early date, especially if the 'little eyes' component is factored in.

And if your mind has already landed on peacock angels and various 'birds on sticks' survivals from further north in Eurasia, then you are already several chapters ahead.

Stellar Fish

Staying in areas of Tamil influence for the moment, we quote from Asko Parpola's 'Beginnings of Indian Astronomy with Reference to a Parallel Development in China':

> Native Dravidian names of stars, asterisms and planets preserved in Old Tamil texts can be read in the logo-syllabic Indus script, where the most common Dravidian word for 'star,' mīṉ, is expressed with the picture of its homonym mīṉ 'fish.'
>
> Among the Dravidian star names ending in mīṉ that are attested to in Old Tamil is vaṭa-mīṉ 'north star'; this compound has a counterpart in the Indus script, where a pictogram resembling the 'three-branched fig tree' motif of Harappan painted pottery occurs several times immediately before the plain 'fish' sign. A homonym of vaṭa 'north' is vaṭam 'banyan fig,' the mighty tree with rope-like air-roots from which it has got its name. This Dravidian homonymy explains two conceptions of Puranic cosmology, the banyan as the tree of the northern direction and the idea that stars and planets are tied to the pole star with invisible 'ropes of wind.' As early as in Ṛgveda 1,24, reference is made to stars being 'fixed above' and to a banyan tree held up in the sky by King Varuna.

Fig and fish combinations recur in seals and pottery right across the Harappan age. Found at Mohenjo-Daro, seal H-179 depicts a humanoid deity *inside* a fig tree, flanked by fish. This has echoes backwards into the Laurasian motif of tree burial/tree spirits, and forwards into the Osiris myth. The continuity of these motifs backwards from Old Tamil into both Harappan artefacts and the Rig Veda tells us several very important things. Firstly, it demonstrates that the Indus culture very likely spoke a form of Proto-Dravidian. Secondly, it is further evidence connecting the Rig Veda to Harappan culture. Thirdly, it demonstrates that these probably extremely ancient motifs have survived in recognisable form into the historical period (which is the whole point of this book, of course).

Finally – and I think most significantly – we have the explicit connection between stars and fish. Parpola believes the fish/star *min* derives from the Proto-Dravidian word for 'to flash, shine, glitter.' On my childhood trips to Fiji I would watch schools of juvenile barracuda from the edge of a jetty after supper. On a clear evening, it is not hard to see where the association comes from. It also recalls to mind the fishing/canoe motifs of the Pacific, the Milky Way as river (much as the celestial Ganges pours down on Shiva's head) and, crucially, provides an important solution to the 'Seven Sages dressed as fish-men' motif encountered in Sumeria. These aren't space-suits. The sages are the stars and, specifically, they are probably the Pleiades. The 'night sky as ocean with heavenly rivers and heavenly fish' also survives into the Babylonian phase.

Fish were a common pottery motif from the earliest Harappan periods and are among the most common signs in the Indus script. The Sumerian script had a pictogram for 'star' and so did not use 'fish' in its place. Sumerian depictions locate the star pictogram near the heads of divinities to denote their divine origin. If 'fish' and 'star' were interchangeable in Harappa and the Indus culture, then the exact same practice emerges. This would explain why the famous 'Master of the Animals' seal from Mohenjo Daro has two fishes next to his head. It also invites us to some very specific interpretations of many other seals. Consider seal H-9 below, referenced in the same article by Parpola.

fig. 12   *Seal H-9 from Harappa. (Image courtesy Archaeological Survey of India)*

It has the number seven, then fish. Interestingly, it also has a bull. The Pleiades, as you know, constitute part of the constellation of Taurus. But is there evidence for the existence of the Classical astrological constellations at this time depth?

Other Constellations

In the later Babylonian texts, the names used for recognisable constellations are all Sumerian, with the prefix *mul*, meaning star. For instance:

- Mul.Ur.Gu.La – Star lion
- Mul.Gir.Tab – Star scorpion
- Mul.Gu.An.Na – Bull of the sky/stars

These names suggest that at least some of the classical astrological system had been developed by the third millennium BCE at the latest. It is with this insight that we can look at some of the Harappan seals and iconography; specifically the Proto-Shiva seal M-304 from Mohenjo Daro. It depicts a horned figure sitting in a yogic pose with some undeciphered glyphs, including a fish, running along the top. Commonly described as having three faces, a better interpretation is that the Proto-Shiva has four faces, with the fourth facing away from the viewer.

fig. 13   *The four-faced 'Proto-Shiva' on seal M-304. (Image courtesy National Museum of India)*

Such an interpretation sheds new light on the four animals surrounding him, making them guardians of the four directions, expressed as constellations. This would align not only with Vedic and Harappan rituals – discussed below – that involve the king facing toward or marking the four directions, but would also bring the artefact into alignment with subsequent depictions of various Hindu gods.

The so-called 'mother goddess' seal found in the Northwest Indian site of Kaliban-gan depicts a decidedly unmatronly female – some might say virginal – seated atop a lion. The constellation Virgo appears above Leo. Possibly adding further emphasis to this analysis is the presence of a water carrier in the top left; the yoke across his shoulders looks decidedly well-balanced, like scales.

Very Large Numbers

Returning to Dr Sidharth's research, he describes some of the very elaborate mathematics found in the Vedas which, along with the fish/star symbolism, have implications for how we interpret – and have historically misinterpreted – the tremendous antiquity of the first Sumerian rulers, among others. They suggest a level of astronomical complexity far in advance of what is commonly expected and, conveniently for the thesis of this book, line up precisely with when we would expect to find the influence of sophisticated climate refugees arriving from points east. Read through this a couple of times.

- We know that a year is 360 days. A *divine* year is 360 earth years, scaling up from the human to the gods.
- There are 12,000 divine years in each yuga, or Great Age (we live in the Kali Yuga), which is divisible by the 12 stations/asterisms of the sun.
- Each yuga/Great Age is thus 4,320,000 *earth* years, and each one is divided into four eras whose ratio diminishes, 4:3:2:1. (The same number, 4,320,000 appears in Sumeria when describing the ages and lifetimes of antediluvian kings, suggesting a shared origin of high astronomical mathematics.)
- Each of these four 'sub eras' consists of a main section and two subsections, like dawn and twilight, that are both 10% of the total time. So the Krita Yuga is 4,000 divine years, with a 400 divine year period before and after it. The next Yuga is 3,000 divine years with two 300 divine year windows on either side, and so on.
- Dr Sidharth notes that this '10% on either side' feature actually matches real twilight on earth: sunrise and sunset are the periods when the sun is less than 18 degrees below the horizon, and it obviously makes a 180 degree journey through the sky each day.

- There is one final compelling numerical relationship to consider: A full day is 86,400 seconds, meaning a day and a night period are composed of 43,200 seconds each.

There is more, specifically to do with the Vedic awareness of the extremely long cycles of eclipses. From *The Celestial Key to the Vedas*:

In computing a Great Age, the Markandeya Purana invokes the factor '71 and a fraction thereof.' This is an interesting clue. In fact, because of precession, the vernal equinox moves along the ecliptic by one degree in a little over seventy-one years. When we take this into account and remember that Śiva causes a total solar eclipse in the lunar asterism Púshya, or Delta Cancri, at the end of the Great Age (as, in fact, is specifically mentioned, for example, in the Mahābhārata, Vána Parva), it is easy to see that after about 4,320,000 years a total solar eclipse recurs in the same lunar asterism when the Sun is at a fixed point in the ecliptic, say, the vernal equinox. This follows from the fact that 432,000 years are almost exactly divisible by the eclipse cycle of 6585.32 days (18 years and 11.33 days, the saros). Secondly, the period of 4,320,000 years is divisible by the precessional cycle of 25,867 years, corresponding to a precession of 50.1 arc seconds per year, a value close to today's accepted value of 50.26 arc seconds per year. It is interesting that this concept of Śiva shooting his arrow from the constellation of Púshya originates in the earliest piece of Hindu – indeed Indo-European – literature, namely the Ṛg Veda itself.

There is also an interesting numerical twist here: 86,400,000 equals the product of $1^1 \times 2^2 \times 3^3 \times 4^4 \times 5^5$! This kind of relationship is typical of the poetic and esoteric nature of ancient Hindu astronomy.

Astronomers make their own fun, eh? But the good doctor brings up an excellent point: the composers of the Rig Veda had a hugely sophisticated mathematical component to their star lore – at a date that straddles the end of the Ice Age – that suggests to those in the know that the movements of the macrocosm are reflected in the movements of the microcosm, that there is a fractal component to this sky/ground dualism. Additionally, it encodes some alarmingly precise measurements for cosmic phenomena that took mankind literal millennia to prove correct.

Ring any bells?

Harappan Structures

Armed with an awareness of the sophisticated astronomy evident in the earliest of the Vedic texts, any number of Harappan rituals and structures begin to actually make sense. This is yet further evidence for their contemporaneity, especially when their complexity moves along a spectrum from 'present, but nascent' – as found in the Rig Veda – to 'full blown sky/ground dualism' as evidenced in the Yajur Veda. And so we return to the humble burnt brick.

Returning to the 'no bricks in the Rig Veda' and 'many bricks in the Yajur Veda,' it is highly illustrative that, in the context of listing the various nakshatras, we find specific instructions on how to construct Vedic fire altars. 10,800 baked bricks are required, which is 360 (days in a year) x 30 (days in a month), over five levels. Most commonly, these fire altars are representations of the creator god, Prajapati, who also represents the entire year. Thus we have the construction of a calendrical, microcosmic cosmos. It was, of course, the Harappans who built towns with populations numbering in the tens of thousands out of millions and millions of baked bricks.

Other Indus seals depict seven priests tending a fire altar. The site of Kalibangan, home of the mother goddess seal, has seven fire altars. Given the role of the Pleiades and their association with Agni/Prajapati/the beginning of the year, it is difficult to draw any conclusion other than the suggestion that Harappa and the Vedas are intimately related, especially as the Pleiades rose on the vernal equinox during the Harappan era.

It seems likely that the Harappans made use of gnomons or 'sun sticks'; Once you have ensured a completely flat base, a stick perpendicular to the horizon can be used to determine solstices and equinoxes based on taking shadow measurements at midday. About a dozen 'pedestals' have been found at Mohenjo Daro whose use is currently unknown. They look like solid, inverted bowls with a carefully flattened base and an indentation in the top which could have held a wooden gnomon (or possibly a lingam). Adding credence to the gnomon interpretation is they are decorated with the trefoil pattern known to be associated with stars on the royal robes of Mesopotamia. The Vedas and their subsequent commentaries record multiple instructions for the building of gnomons.

Also worth noting is that several Harappan towns, including Rahman Dheri (3,000 BCE), were oriented to the cardinal directions. Streets and buildings in Mohenjo Daro diverge two degrees from the cardinal points which, as Parpola notes, would align perfectly with the setting of Aldebaran behind the Kirthar mountains in the west. Aldebaran is in between the Pleiades and Orion. It is a star in Taurus, the bull. At Mohenjo Daro's latitude, Aldebaran is also close enough to the ecliptic to be regularly occulted by the Moon, such as at times around the autumnal equinox.

Kingly Ritual

Just as in Polynesia and Sumeria and Egypt, the ritual actions of the king were crucial in aligning the heavenly and terrestrial realms. He was the cuckoo in the imperial clock, setting the royal calendar at regular intervals.

This notion of kingship *descending* from the stars, and the king *going up* to the stars to ensure immortality and the wellbeing of the tribe is highly likely to be the origin of the hermetic and Classical ritual magic we find in the grimoires, having come down to us via the dual routes of the Nile and the Fertile Crescent. If this stellar technology reaches back to the first emergence of the Laurasian storyline, as I believe it does, then we may, with a straight face, say western ritual magic is at least 30,000 years old. We may also, with a smiling face, send the Ancient Aliens crowd back to the library to check their numbers.

The earliest Vedas regularly mention the four or sometimes five directions of space. Returning to Asko Parpola's 'Beginnings of Indian Astronomy':

One ritual connected with the directions of space is crucially important for understanding their ideological significance. This is the 'mounting of the regions' (*digvy-āsthāpanam*), which is an essential part of the Vedic royal consecration. In this rite – also called Varuṇa-sava as it is connected with the God Varuna, the 'divine king' – the king at his consecration dons the *tārpya* garment ornamented with applicated figures of *dhiṣṇyas*, i.e. ritual fireplaces equated with the stars ... This royal robe of Varuna almost certainly goes back to the trefoil-ornamented 'sky garment' of the Harappan 'priest-king' modelled on Mesopotamian prototypes. Then the king makes a step in each of the five directions, therewith ascending the zenith: 'from the quarters he goes to the heaven'...; for 'heaven is the quarters of space (*diśo vai svargo lokah*).' The Śatapatha-Brāhmaṇa (5,4,1,8) explains: 'It is the seasons, the year, that he [the *adhvaryu* priest] thereby makes him [the king] ascend; and having ascended the seasons, the year, he is high, high above everything here.'

In the explicit use of directionality, we clearly see the shamanic origins of a ritual designed to both appropriate and set right the entire universe. Viewed with the eyes of an occultist rather than an academic, we can spy the exact same ritual form present in Old Kingdom Egypt and Sumeria; so we now require an origin date for this 'astronomical immortality tech' old enough to have influenced the very beginnings of all three cultures. We also require a location for this tech that reconciles with its presence in the Pacific and South America.

HOW MUCH HARAPPA?

There are few places where academia has so boxed itself into a corner as with the Indus Valley cultures. We are presented with an entire civilisation whose written language we cannot decipher ending just before a mysterious cultural group – without a homeland or genetic footprint – shows up with an apparently rapidly-assembled cosmology that not only describes the end of the Ice Age in Northwest India but is an exact match for many of the ritual items and structures found in Harappan cities.

Realigning the cosmology of the Vedas with the development of the Harappan civilisation paints a more complete picture: we see Laurasian pastoralists survive a climate event and then immediately develop in cultural and spiritual complexity; trading with, influencing and being influenced by their neighbours in all directions; all of whom underwent a simultaneous technological leap at this time that is so impressive we might cheekily refer to it as the first space race, given its intimate association with stellar ritual magic.

Refuseniks to the Ice Age/Harappa/Vedas realignment are, by definition, navigating with a dramatically incomplete map. At its height, it is estimated that the Indus Valley alone was home to a million people. The recently discovered Harappan city of Rakhigari is estimated to stretch over more than 224 hectares, of which only the tiniest minority have been excavated. The story of Harappa is not even close to being told in any complete fashion, and to confidently declare its total separation from the Eurasian oral cosmology known as the Vedas is foolishness in the extreme. Let no one tell you otherwise.

SUMERIA

There is no question that the Sumerians, and specifically their origin, are downright weird. None other than Carl Sagan himself said that if any ancient culture had had contact with extraterrestrials, it would have been the Sumerians.

Around 3,500 BCE they appear fully formed in the archaeological record, speaking a language entirely unrelated to those around it, building great cities and ziggurats, irrigating the desert and writing, writing, writing as if the entire civilisation had some form of OCD dementia.

Mainstream academia's refusal to close the Sumerian story's gaping holes has unfortunately led to a lot of people parking their flying saucers in them. In the otherwise excellent *The Ark Before Noah: Decoding the Story of The Flood*, Dr Irving Finkel moves straight from acknowledging we have no idea where Sumerian language came from to describing the language itself and how the reader may interpret Sumerian texts. We should expect better.

Returning to the evening of Dr Finkel's book launch, I asked him about the fact that the earliest version of the Flood myth, based on his own translation, has animals put into the ark that are all predomesticated, that is *wild* animals, from a time before farming. My question was whether he thought that meant the entire Flood myth had its origins in a cultural memory of the end of the Ice Age, i.e. a time prior to animal domestication. He described my question as 'huge' and probably warranted a whole separate conference to 'really thrash that out.' This is academic speak for 'yes, obviously, but I don't want to be the one to say it. (In his defence, I probably wouldn't risk a dream job at the British Museum, either.) In what has become the definitive undergraduate textbook on the subject, *A History of the Ancient Near East*, Marc Van De Mieroop writes:

> The rapid increase in settled populations at that time cannot be explained with certainty. It seems too fast to have been the result of indigenous population growth alone, even if new agricultural conditions promoted demographic expansion. There may have been an increased sedentarization of semi-nomadic people previously unrecognizable in the archaeological record, or outsiders may have entered the region because of climatic changes or other reasons.

Thus we can place the blame for the rapid growth in 'Annunaki bloodline' jibber jabber at the feet of academic timidity and groupthink, rather than at the feet of Sitchin and Von Daniken. The first step is, inevitably, admitting we have a problem. Like Harappa, we are operating off a tiny dataset compared to what is actually available. Only a minority of Sumerian tablets in public hands have ever been translated. Notorious financial forecaster and analyst Martin Armstrong, a former private collector of Sumerian tablets, estimates that the tablets in public hands are themselves a minority of the total excavated number, with a significant majority furnishing private collections around the world. The modern black market for Sumerian antiquities is now entering its second century.

It is not just tablets. We are also missing entire cities. Recently released images from Cold War satellites show dozens and dozens of cities and large towns that have clearly never been excavated. All of this before we even get to the fact that Sumeria appeared beside the high water mark of the end of the Ice Age, *at* the end of the Ice Age, with a worldwide Flood and stories of civilising sages as cornerstones of their cosmology. The gun could not possibly be emitting more smoke!

By now, the story of Mesopotamia's influence on western esotericism is a fairly well told one, so we will not dwell on it here. The goal of this book is to push the timelines back beyond it quite significantly and also demonstrate other, underappreciated vectors of influence in general. What we need to do here is demonstrate the earlier origins of and influences on the Sumerians to bring them into alignment with the geology, genetics and astrotheology of contemporaneous cultures, because it very likely says something profound about the journey of the Laurasian storyline in general and magic in particular.

This also serves to permanently banish the aliens back into the sky, and frees up modern esotericists to look anew at Sumerian star lore and what it might mean for contemporary practice. Much like Dynastic Egypt, the holes in Sumeria are all bunched up at the beginning. Once the culture actually gets started, the flying saucers have a tendency to vanish on their own and Bronze Age civilisation continues on its merry way. So like the Flandrian Transgression bringing the ocean up to the gates of Eridu, we bring our story to the door but we do not enter.

Sumerian Morphology

The reason for contemporary squeamishness about cranial and skeletal studies is not because the data are unsound, it is what the data have historically been used for. Late nineteenth century examinations of the cranial capacity of sub-Saharan Africans was used to demonstrate they were 'less intelligent' than Caucasians, for instance. This is obviously the most preposterous pseudoscientific conclusion but the actual data – that skull shapes differ between racial groups – are sound. A good example of using these data correctly would be the field of forensics, where human remains are gradually identified based on their morphology.

There is perhaps a secondary reason for modern historians to pretend these data do not exist. And that is because, in cases such as Sumeria and Egypt, we once again have hard scientific evidence that falls outside of their preferred story of what happened in the past. What came to be known as 'the Sumerian problem' in the last century was the realisation gleaned from skeletal and cranial evidence that the Sumerian cities were multi-ethnic. The story of attempting to solve the Sumerian problem mirrors the story of increasing racial awareness inside archaeology over the last 130 years. It begins with invading superior races, the 'real Sumerians,' dominating an indigenous Semitic tribe. The Sumerians came from Iran, the Sumerians came from the Caucasus, the Sumerians came from wherever.

At its core was the early twentieth century belief that race and civilisation were interrelated, probably the source of diffusionism's unpopularity today. As the realisation grew that race and civilisation were arbitrarily connected – and that both terms probably do not have much underlying reality, anyway – 'the Sumerian problem' stopped being a topic of discussion. 'New Archaeology' arose in conjunction with postmodernism, that described culture as exclusively the interaction of a population with its local environment.

Nevertheless there are still all those skulls and bones languishing in London's Natural History Museum and the Field Museum of Natural History in Chicago. A 1930s analysis of skulls from Kish revealed a small minority of Austric skulls, a smaller minority of Armenoid skulls and a large majority of skulls described as 'Eurafrican.' Somewhere near the centre of the Sumerian problem was the early twentieth century realisation that most of the Sumerian depictions were round-headed and most of the skulls uncovered were long-headed; only a minority matched the skulls as depicted, so 'clearly' these must have been an invading elite.

It has been almost a hundred years since these interpretations were taken seriously. Other options have emerged. Given that 'Eurafrican' skulls have the same features as Australoid – that is southern India/New Guinean/Australian – some have posited an influence from the Dravidian regions up into Sumeria at an early date. Others have countered by saying it is not that unusual for Africans to have been living in Kish or Eridu given their locations, which is certainly true, but the same can be said of India (which is my preferred interpretation of the skulls). In any case, there are multiple genetic links between East Africa and Dravidian India at an early date so I am not sure how useful the distinction really is. It appears that since probably before the end of the Ice Age these cultures were sailing up and down the coast and catching the Monsoon to and from the Horn of Africa.

That complexity is sort of the point. In the oldest extant Sumerian city, Eridu, cultural continuity in temple design and use has been demonstrated from the Ubaid period up into the Sumerian period. Looking at the change from the Ubaid period to the Uruk period, the archaeologist Henri Frankfort noted that the people associated with this cultural change were brachycephalic, a skull shape commonly associated with people from the east.

Eridu

Eridu is the oldest Sumerian city (above sea level). Given it exhibits continuity from the Ubaid period up, that means it dates to around 5,000 BCE at the latest. (Interestingly, this is the same time as Mehrgarh Period II, about when we see fired bricks and probably the increased astronomical complexity of the Yagur Veda.)

PERIOD	DATING (BCE)	COMMENTS
Hassuna /Samarra / Halaf	5500 – 4500	Neolithic/Chalcolithic archaeological cultures
Ubaid	5000 – 3600	rural settlements in southern Mesopotamia; introduction of artificial irrigation
Uruk	3600 – 3100	large-scale urbanisation; first pictographic script
Jemdet Nasr	3100 – 2900	development of the cuneiform script
Early Dynastic I/III	2900 – 2350	many Sumerian city states in southern Mesopotamia; Semitic states in the north
Akkadian/Gutean	2350 – 2100	unification of Mesopotamia by a Semitic dynasty; invasion of Guteans from Gutium
Ur III	2100 – 2000	reunification by a Sumerian dynasty

There certainly appears to be more continuity between the various periods, particularly at Eridu, than a neat little table may immediately imply. Crucially when tracking magical vectors or survival, these continuities appear to be cultural rather than technological. If Dr Oppenheimer is correct, which seems likely, that the earliest layers of the Ubaid period are at the bottom of the Arabian Gulf, then he suggests the civilising component of the story of Ea – a very Austronesian-sounding name – may well reflect an historical episode: Ea brought the seven amphibian sages from the East to teach mankind the skills of civilisation. Ubaid pottery continued in the same location, Eridu, as the later, and cruder, Uruk pottery style. From an archaeological perspective, this is further evidence for cultures with different levels of technological complexity occupying the same space.

It seems significant that temples, which were larger to begin with, became smaller than palaces or kings' residences over the course of Sumerian civilisation. Dr Oppenheimer suggests this could indicate the initial pre-eminence of a new priesthood – and I would say an astronomical priesthood – gradually declining as power centralised around the king. If this is indeed the case it may have coincided with the gradual rise to pre-eminence of the planets and the sun over the lunar/stellar calendar.

Repositioning the Flood

You will recall that the ancient Near East flooded at the end of the Ice Age in three distinct phases.

- 9,000 BCE: First, there was the flooding of what is now the Arabian Gulf but would have been a presumably quite lovely river valley at the time. (Great place to live!)
- 5,500 BCE: Further flooding of the gulf that brought the Tigris and Euphrates river mouths to approximately where they are today.
- 3,500 BCE: The Flandrian Transgression, that took the coastline a further 180 kilometres inland, very close to Eridu. The sea level gradually subsided to its present level over the next one and a half thousand years.

If you cast your eyes back up to that table of Sumerian periods, you will quickly see some highly suspicious alignments. Realising there were three distinct inundations also provides a neat solve for some of the absurdities associated with the earliest dynasties of Kish, Ur and Erech. The King Lists unambiguously state that 'the flood' happened before the first dynasties of these three cities. This is commonly assumed to be the Flandrian Transgression, but that only gives a few hundred years for the Early Dynastic Period to begin. The 'solve' for this, such as it is, is to state that Kish, Ur and Erech's dynasties ran concurrently *à propos* of any evidence pointing in this direction.

Of course, if 'the flood' refers to the 5,500 BCE inundation of the Arabian Gulf, then we have a lot more runway in which to allow these dynasties to take off. We also have an opportunity to look at the eight kings who reigned 'before the flood.'

On that last note, the king lists begin with kingship itself descending from heaven, just as it does in Polynesia and the Vedas. The extremely long reigns of these first kings – widely misinterpreted as proof of their alien status – are in the very literal sense astronomical numbers.

- The first king, Alulim, ruled for 28,800 years. This divides precisely into 4,320,000 150 times, or three times into 86,400.
- The next king, Alalngar, ruled for 36,000 years, which is half a precessional cycle of 72,000. (And 1/120th of 4,320,000.)
- En-men-lu-ana actually ruled for the Vedic number of 43,200 years.
- En-men-gal-ana was another 28,800 reign.
- Dumuzid, the Shepherd, ruled for 36,000 years. Incidentally, if 'the Shepherd' isn't Orion, I will eat my hat.
- En-sipad-zid-ana also had a 28,800 reign.

Interestingly, the remaining two kings' shorter reigns (of 21,000 years for En-men-dur-ana and Ubara-Tutu's brisk 18,600 years) cease dividing conveniently into the cosmic Vedic number and become divisible by 12, which is a more human/earth centric number; the twelve constellations.

The supposedly 'human' first kings of the First Dynasty of Kish which follows on from these large numbers, after the Flood, are also divisible by 12. 'After the flood had swept over, and the kingship had descended from heaven, the kingship was in Kish.' Jushur ruled for 1200 years, Kullassina-bel for 960 years, and so on. Not all of the First Dynasty kings are neatly divisible by 12, but a majority of them are, which indicates the same progression down from a calendrical, cosmic 'Golden Age' – as expected for a Laurasian mythology. Very large 'stellar' numbers scale down to 'smaller' planetary and astrological numbers. These planetary or 'earth centric' numbers scale down again to reigns more in keeping with human lifespans. As the 'Golden Age' became 'our' age, so kingship scaled down from the stars to humans.

Same calendrical system, same source of kingship, same time period. Sitchin's Annunaki did not come from the stars, they are the stars.

Seven Sages

You may have guessed that I suspect the 'seven amphibious sages who came from the East' are the Pleiades. But it is a common pitfall of astrotheological research to assume that just because an event or person can be matched to one asterism or another then that event did not happen or that person did not exist. We need to adopt the more mythic thinking of our ancestors: any purported civilising refugees coming from the direction of the rising of the Pleiades would be associated with that asterism. It is a 'both' form of thinking, rather than an 'either/or.' In fact it may be that if their arrival had coincided with the heliacal rising of the Pleiades then they might have received a better reception and it was this fortunate timing that led to their civilising efforts being so successful.

For whatever it is worth, many scholars of Mesopotamia are surprisingly open to the idea this was an actual event, presumably without fully thinking through the implications of it: if the sages were real, where did they come from? Stephanie Dalley, in her *Myths from Mesopotamia: Creation, The Flood, Gilgamesh and Others*, notes that the god Ea, whose first temple resided in Eridu, was 'credited with bringing in the seven amphibian sages from the East to teach crafts to man.'

SUMMING UP

Reexamination of the similarities between our earliest cultures in light of the presumed cosmology of Sundaland paints a very compelling story of the period between 20,000 BCE, through the end of the Ice Age and up to the appearance of Harappan and Sumerian civilisation.

The case against extending this timeline is flimsy, particularly when the hard genetic and geological data are factored in: three cultures with hugely overlapping mythemes separated in time and space by thousands of years and entire oceans coming up with the same names, calendars and spiritual concepts. These include:

- The prominence of the Pleiades, Taurus and Orion.
- A Lunar calendar that predates a solar one.
- Precision alignment of buildings to particular asterisms, or the creation of 'maps of the sky' here on earth.
- Kingship descending from the stars and the ritual requirement of the king to return to them to secure his own immortality and safeguard the life of the tribe/city.
- The simultaneous appearance of this magical technology, along with other technologies such as irrigation-based agriculture (such as you find in the ancient rice paddies of Southeast Asia).

There is also sufficient overlap in the magic and ritual structures of South America (and China to some considerable extent) to make the case that we can precisely locate the influencing ancestor culture at the last point on earth where these three cultures had the opportunity to diverge.

What you are looking at here might be called Proto-Hermeticism: a magical technology that involves mirroring the sky on the ground for the purposes of achieving union with the universe/immortality. We are thus presented with the amusing situation of proving accidentally correct all those Renaissance magicians who saw the wisdom of Hermes Trismegistus as coming down to mankind from a time before the Flood. In a way, it did.

If you believe that the appearance of the same beliefs, calendars, rituals and names/functions for the stars can emerge simultaneously – immediately following an extreme climate event that would have scattered much of the world's population – in an unrelated or coincidental manner then I have a large, pointy tomb beside a river to sell you. Only one previous owner.

Perhaps less.

VIII THE MIRROR OF HEAVEN

When it came to the stars, the Egyptians were not fucking around. In order to explore this crucial pivot point in the development of western astrotheology, I have to assume the reader has a reasonable knowledge of Ancient Egypt history and topography, because there simply is not the space for hand-holding. In terms of the latter, a quick image search on your phone will suffice to locate any cities or sites you may be unfamiliar with. In terms of the former, there are any number of worthwhile books to choose from.

I mention this because there is a persistent tendency among occultists to treat the entire length of Ancient Egyptian civilisation as broadly the same. But the Isis of the Late Period is not the Isis of the Old Kingdom. An analogy with Jesus, who has been a god for a lot less time than the Mother of Horus, is illustrative. Early depictions of Jesus show him as a peacock or a fish, then a glowing, Apollonian child, then the actual sun. Sometimes he has a beard and sometimes he doesn't. In the east he shows up in icons with the sort of creepy stare you associate with escaped mental patients riding on the same bus as you. He's black in a few places but not all that many. During the Renaissance he becomes a pin-up for some profoundly homoerotic, hyperreal sadomasochism. By the time we get to the megachurches of regional America he is an unadorned stick in an enormous room, standing behind a man who is loudly asking a bank of television cameras for more money. He has had a busy 1,800 years, especially for someone who never physically existed.

We see a similar thing in Egypt over a much longer time frame, with gradual changes to cosmology matching the changes in society and the shifting of centres of power up and down the Nile as priesthoods rise and fall, before finally reaching a dizzying hybridity in the Late and Graeco-Roman Period as the Egyptians adopted the same 'Lego block' approach to divinities as the Greeks. That final hybrid phase is the fertile swamp from which a largely recognisable modern western magic grows.

Endlessly fascinating as the full sweep of Ancient Egyptian history is, our principal focus is on the parts leading up to the First Intermediate Period in the following table.

Predynastic Egypt	N/A	Before 3,100 BCE
Early Dynastic Period	1st – 2nd Dynasties	3,100 – 2,686 BCE
Old Kingdom	3rd – 6th Dynasties	2,686 – 2,181 BCE
First Intermediate Period	7th – 10th Dynasties	2,181 – 2,055 BCE
Middle Kingdom	11th – 12th Dynasties	2,055 – 1,650 BCE
Second Intermediate Period	13th – 17th Dynasties	1,650 – 1,550 BCE
New Kingdom	18th – 20th Dynasties	1,550 – 1,069 BCE
Third Intermediate Period	21st – 25th Dynasties	1,069 – 664 BCE
Late Period	26th – 31st Dynasties	664 – 332 BCE
Ptolemaic Period	N/A	332 – 30 BCE

The official narrative goes something like this. The Predynastic Period was a time of scattered villages up and down the Nile, building things out of mud bricks. The Dynastic Period begins in earnest with a king from Upper Egypt unifying the country by force. Thereupon he and his descendants start building pointy tombs of increasing complexity, then decreasing complexity but this time with writing inside them, and then Egypt is invaded and collapses (the First Intermediate Period). Things get slightly better again, access to the afterlife is democratised and commoners start painting gods and judgement on the inside of their coffins, some new priests are in charge and then the whole place collapses through invasion again. The New Kingdom is where all the telegenic stuff you see in documentaries happens: Ramses, Tutankhamun, that pointy headed one with the lady hips on the History Channel who worships UFOs or something. Then there's another collapse from which the country never really recovers. It proceeds through a succession of largely foreign rulers until Alexander the Great invades the place, installs the Ptolemies on the throne and that period ends with Cleopatra committing suicide with a snake to the boob.

But if you look back up at the first row in the table, you will see that 'before 3,100 BCE' has so far been where all the action in the book has been. To get a clearer picture, we must erase some of these artificial horizons and look at the whole spectrum.

THE (GRAND) ROGUES' GALLERY

Though we went to some trouble to shine a light on the highly dysfunctional culture of academia in a previous chapter, Egyptology certainly deserves to be singled out before we go any further, as it has been filled with thieves, vandals, hate-mongers and lunatics for centuries.

Nowhere is the need for reorienting of our understanding of the past around hard data more critical. Doing so tends to make 'expert consensus' opinion melt away like cake in the rain, which may explain why they are so loudly hostile to its introduction into the discourse. Egyptological gate-keeping is probably the most shrill among all the humanities subjects masquerading as hard sciences.

Speaking of gatekeeping, a story told by an independent researcher is metaphorically and literally illustrative. During research trips for his two latest books, *Egyptian Dawn* and *The Sphinx Mystery*, Robert Temple had to get authorities to smash rusted locks with hammers because the keys had been lost decades ago, granting access to parts of the Valley Temple and Sphinx Temple, where he found entirely undocumented chambers and described them for the first time. These are sites that, even with the calamitous drop-off in tourist numbers in recent times, millions of people walk past each year and can often peer into, as they are open to the air. Some of the temple areas he 'discovered' actually had cables running through them that were laid down by staging technicians for the evening light show! That is how poorly the official narrative actually matches the facts on the ground. It was not a lack of funds that prevented bringing these 'discoveries' to the public – borrowing a hammer to break a lock is free – anymore than a lack of funds would prevent the discovery of a second Magic Mountain at Disneyland. It was systemic ineptitude and cronyism on the part of Egyptology. Given Giza's importance to Egyptian history – and probably the esoteric history of much of mankind – this is outrageous.

Outrage, inevitably, is a common emotion among Egyptology watchers. You will no doubt be familiar with Zahi Hawass and his ubiquitous hat from the last two decades of largely content-free cable history programmes. (And the subsequent Department of Justice investigation into *National Geographic* and Zahi Hawass for allegations of bribery. By their own admission, they are paying him $200,000 a year for life. His government salary was approximately £10,000.) From humble beginnings in the Egyptian Delta, Hawass was plucked from his minor Giza inspector role by the direct intervention of the son of Edgar Cayce, Hugh Lynn; who arranged a full scholarship at the University of Pennsylvania thanks to a member of the scholarship board also happening to be a member of Cayce's Association for Research and Enlightenment. (This was part of the ARE's multi-decade attempts to get special access to sites on the Giza Plateau, specifically the structures underneath the Sphinx where Cayce believed the Atlantean hall of records was to be found.)

Hawass's curious associations do not end there. In *Breaking the Mirror of Heaven*, Robert Bauval and Ahmed Osman recount the tale of a 'surprise' visit to the Giza Plateau by none other than NATO-deposed Libyan dictator Muammar Gaddafi. Hawass had set up a small table between the paws of the Sphinx to display some recently discovered statues dating back to the Fifth Dynasty. One in particular was exceedingly rare as it still retained some of its original paintwork. The then-head of the Egyptian Antiquities Organisation, the job Hawass was gunning for and got, heard about the visit on the radio as he had not been informed. He raced over there in a taxi only to find Hawass declaring that one of the statues was 'missing.' This was the very same statue Hawass used in a magazine photoshoot with Omar Sharif only three months prior.

The man solely responsible for worldwide archaeological access within Egypt certain kept some unusual company but we can be sure of one thing. Very few of them were Jews, as Hawass is fiercely antisemitic. He has repeatedly declared that anyone who disagrees with him is part of a Zionist conspiracy, held press conferences in which he announces the Jews did not build the pyramids and that Israel is trying to steal the pyramids and Egyptian civilisation. Antisemitism inevitably plays well to the crowd in Arab countries, but Hawass takes even this to exciting, conspiracy-laden levels. In a 2009 interview on Egypt's Memri TV, he said that Jews control the entire world: 'For 18 centuries, they were dispersed throughout the world. They went to America and took control of its economy. They have a plan. Although they are few in number, they control the entire world.'

How did the global archaeological community deal with Hawass's terrifying reign? Uneasily, and with stony, cowardly silence. From a 2005 *New York Times* article by Sharon Waxman:

But there are those who say Dr. Hawass does not merely impose rules, he hogs the field. Last year two French researchers accused Dr. Hawass of treating Egypt as 'his private hunting ground' after they were denied permission to insert a camera lens through the floor of the Great Pyramid at Giza in search of a secret chamber. Dr. Hawass denounced the men as amateurs, though they have successfully made other discoveries with the technique.

Dr. Hawass also denounced as 'nuts' an English archaeologist, Joann Fletcher, who announced a theory in 2003 that a previously discovered mummy was in fact Queen Nefertiti. British press accounts say that Dr. Hawass was more upset that she had revealed her findings on the Discovery Channel, which financed her work, rather than bringing the results to him to announce. She was banned from further work in Egypt.

Egyptology in action, right there. Where is the global outrage from the likes of the British Museum or the Smithsonian? In the May 22 2005 issue of the *Sunday Times Magazine*, Richard Girling wrote:

'They call him the Pharaoh, the keeper of the pyramids. He rules Egyptology with an iron fist and a censorious tongue. Nobody crosses Zahi Hawass and gets away with it ... nobody of any standing in Egyptology will come out to help you,' said one well-known Egyptologist of his colleagues, 'because they'd lose their jobs.' ... Hawass ... holds the keys to the pyramids, the Valley of the Kings, the Sphinx, Abu Simbel, everything. No Egyptologist gets in without his permission, and few will chance his anger. [...]

'There are people digging out there,' says another UK specialist, 'who are praying they won't find anything significant. If they do, they know the dig will be shut down until a certain individual arrives to take over. There are artefacts that have been excavated, only to be put back until the certain personage gets round to visiting the site so that he can "discover" them for himself.'

Another Cayce angle comes by way of Mark Lehner, described as the world's foremost authority on the Sphinx and the Pyramids. The son of ARE members, it was Hugh Lynn, once again, who arranged the funding for Lehner to study at the American University in Cairo. (In fact it was Lehner who made the introduction between Hawass and Hugh Lynn.) To give credit where it is due, the Association for Research and Enlightenment has played a very successful long game. In his previously mentioned book and *The Secret Chamber*, Bauval notes that he has video and photographic proof of ARE excavations and photometric research in and around the Sphinx and the Pyramid enclosures.

But this is, in fact, the heart of the matter. The Hawass regime was a time of 'multiple Egyptologies,' with tightly controlled paid access made available to various private organisations combined with a simultaneous doubling-down on an 'official narrative' that, as we shall see, is positively Discworldian in its absurdity. If you did not stump up the money or toe the line, you were branded a pyramidiot and a Jew. Even as this chapter was being written, Zahi Hawass stormed out of a planned debate with Graham Hancock when he saw an image of Robert Bauval on one of the slides, declared him 'a thief,' claimed he had never heard of Göbekli Tepe, and then would only deign to return to the room if the debate was cancelled. *National Geographic* has certainly had better behaved, better informed (if not better paid) 'Explorers in Residence.'

Very occasionally, this clown show has resulted in exasperation in the wider, more scientifically inclined corners of Egyptology, such as in the following from the *Proceedings of the Ninth International Congress of Egyptologists* in 2004, by the delightfully passionate Alfredo Gennaro.

> Nevertheless we think it is worthy to give credit to some of the figures we had to face in the preliminary study [on hypothetical construction methods and size of workforce]. At the light of these figures, the current hypotheses on how the Giza Pyramids were built appear to be inconsistent, sometimes completely impracticable. [...]
>
> Figures! We need figures, not the generalities we can read in the 'accepted' literature.
>
> Take the ramp theory. A ramp one km long to get the top of the Cheops Pyramid would have a slope not comfortable but possible, with a volume of 5,600,000 cubic meters, the double than the pyramid itself (sic): with the difference that the volume, divided in personal loads of 25 litres (50 kg at a time) would require 224,000,000 travels to be accumulated and as many to be dismantled, namely 90 years of a continuous one thousand person process.

The ramp theory Gennaro refers to is one of the 'explanations' offered by people with evidently no experience in construction for how the Great Pyramid in particular was ever managed to be built as a tomb in two and half decades during the reign of a single king. The 'generalities' he mentions are the Egyptological tendency to breeze past this physical impossibility with a casual backwards comment: 'they probably used a ramp and I am sure we will find evidence of it one day.'

Let me be clear. On available evidence, it is currently *more* likely that the pyramids were built by little green men in flying saucers than by a few thousand men, living in workers' villages we have never been able to find, using a ramp with twice the volume of the structure it was used to build. Nevertheless, the ramp not only refuses to die, but resurfaces in the latest theory by the world's foremost authority on the Sphinx and the pyramids, Mark Lehner, who combines two nonexistent objects into one in a bewildering 'super solve.' From a January 28, 2014 *Live Science* article by Owen Jarus:

> The recent discoveries [that the 'workers' villages' were actually barracks for high-born visitors] at Giza leave a mystery in their wake: Where were the dwellings of the pyramid builders, the regular workers, located?

> The answer may be on the pyramids themselves. 'We could probably be correct imagining workers staying on the immense ramps, on the unfinished pyramid as it rose,' said Lehner in an email to *Live Science*, adding that they could also have been living in the quarries in simple dwellings akin to 'lean-to's.'

Even my truck-and-train obsessed nephew would find logistically dubious the idea of a workforce of up to a hundred thousand living on the construction site they were conscripted to for a period of two decades, having their sleeping quarters in the way of a ramp that would need to place a multi-tonne block in situ every ninety seconds. He is four years old. But we have very little need of my nephew's expertise because the independent Egyptological world – Hawass's Jews and pyramidiots – is, in fact, awash with specialist experts in topics that actually describe reality. These include engineers, nuclear physicists, geologists, desert construction experts – fields where, if they get their numbers wrong, buildings collapse and planes fall out of the sky. And the good news is they appear to be winning the mind war. Not that Lehner's Rampopolis is not a particularly threatening opponent, of course. One may as well say the pyramid workers lived in Narnia and journeyed back through the wardrobe at the end of each day. (We will return to the ramp below, with a potential solve provided, inevitably, by an architect and a chemist rather than an Egyptologist.)

All of this is to emphasise that, when it comes to the story of Egypt's beginnings, the 'home team' does not have a lot going for it, at least not in the past thirty or so years. The Egyptologists of a century ago displayed much greater willingness to follow where the evidence led them and would likely have relished the input of engineers, physicists and geologists, rather than dismissing their facts as irrelevant because 'they are not Egyptologists.' This is akin to declaring crime does not exist because one does not happen to be a court sketch artist.

As ever, we will highlight the physical data and offer an interpretation that covers it rather than ignores it, as well as one that falls into broad alignment with the wider genetic, morphological, mythological and climatic data we have already examined. For magicians it is well remembered that, when it comes to data interpretation, out of anywhere on earth, here we are not playing in the Egyptologists' sandpit. They are playing in ours.

PREDYNASTIC EGYPT

Another artificial horizon is in need of erasure. The Pharaohs themselves did not think in dynasties. It was the third century BCE priest, Manetho, writing in Greek, who first categorised Egypt's ancient kings in this way. The idea is actually quite alien to Egyptian royalty, who focused on continuity, eternal cycles and Maat. In an important sense they each became the preceding ruler, meaning they would make terrible guests on *Who Do You Think You Are*. (Although the episodes themselves would be mercifully brief.)

Once freed of the dynastic concept, it becomes much easier to get a sense of quite how far back the Pharaohs thought their civilisation went. The unification of Upper and Lower Egypt under Menes – where Manetho begins his dynasties – was by no means the beginning of the story, just as the unification of Italy in the nineteenth century is not the beginning of Italian history. In fact, unsurprisingly given their common Laurasian origin, Egyptian kings – just as their Sumerian counterparts did – trace back beyond human kings to an era of semidivine rulers, to a time when Egypt was ruled by the gods themselves. The astronomical numbers used to describe their reigns indicate they saw these beings as the stars, too. In Seti I's Abydos temple – a temple to the ancestors as described below – he is depicted with his young son, Ramses II, petitioning Ptah-Seker-Osiris on behalf of their '72 ancestors.' Seventy two is the precessional number *par excellence*.

Manetho's dynasty-based king list is about as incomplete as the rest of them and, like our other sources for Egypt's rulers, they get messier the further back you go. From Robert Temple's *Egyptian Dawn*:

The chronology of ancient Egyptian history is ... firmly established as far back as 2,000 BCE. Prior to that, there was something called the First Intermediate Period, which was a period of total social and political collapse. It is thought this period was marked by floods, droughts, plagues and lawlessness. No one knows exactly how long this period lasted, but ... many think it was about 150 years. [...]
Before this, there were the Fifth and Sixth Dynasties of the Old Kingdom. They

were a kind of tepid afterflow of the glory of the true Old Kingdom, which consisted of the Third and Fourth Dynasties. It used to be thought that the First and Second Dynasties should be considered part of the Old Kingdom, but now it has become fashionable to speak of those as the 'Archaic Period.' One reason for that is we know so little about them. (However, it must be said that we know even less about the Third Dynasty, but people often overlook that fact.)

The unsettling thing is that prior to – let us say – 2200 BCE, the chronology of Egyptian history essentially falls apart. Everything before that date is more or less lost in a kind of chronological chaos. There are many Egyptologists who do not think this. But that is because they simply comfort themselves with chronological assertions. They simply decide certain dates.

The net effect of this is that no one has any idea how many kings there were in the Fourth Dynasty, the alleged period of Giza pyramid construction, or even how long it lasted. Only three royal funerary monuments from the Third Dynasty have been found. None of the historical sources agree on the number of kings or their names, but they all mention kings in between Khufu, Khafre and Menkaure; so where are their 'pointy tombs'? Second Dynasty kings such as Teti share the same name with Sixth Dynasty kings – they all had multiple names to start with – and several sources used to compile the royal lineage of Egypt list names going back tens of millennia. (A Second Dynasty king's name was excavated in a Giza Valley Temple, purported to have been built in the Fourth Dynasty.)

'Unification'

Emphasising the messiness of Egyptian chronology at the beginning of the so-called Dynastic Period is not another jab at the Ankh-Morpork college of global Egyptology – I have already scratched that itch. It is simply to lengthen out the timelines that we need to work to. As with Sumerologists and Assyriologists insisting that everything be sandwiched into their arbitrary dates, the Egyptological refusal to kick out their timings has given rise to engineering impossibilities like building the Great Pyramid in a couple of decades using logs and dolerite pounders. And this refusal has attracted flying saucers just as surely as garbage attracts flies. It is amazing how much a little humility regarding what we do and do not currently understand about Predynastic Egypt can do to pack the saucers back off to Zeta Reticuli.

As the evidence of missing kings and overlapping dynasties is reexamined, it becomes clear that the story of the Nile valley and delta is anything but neat. Clearly cultures of differing levels of complexity existed simultaneously and side-by-side;

this is the cleanest, indeed the *only*, solve for having simultaneous reigns for Archaic and Predynastic kings. The Nile is a very long river, after all. It is largely our modern belief in national borders that prevents us from thinking about the place as a home to multiple kings and warlords.

There is a growing academic consensus that Menes, the king who unified Upper and Lower Egypt, is probably part of the same mythological 'law-giver' type we find in other Laurasian cultures. Other examples would be 'Manu' or 'Moses.' If he did have an historical existence, then it appears his claim to have unified the country is the 3,100 BCE equivalent of descending from a helicopter onto the deck of an aircraft carrier and unfurling a 'mission accomplished' banner. We may have been too credulous in expecting the politicians of the ancient world to be any different from our own. Otherwise, why do so many kings after Menes exclaim how they have also unified Egypt? One suspects the peasants have been revolting for a very long time.

The African Fertile Crescent

Along the coast of North Africa, between the Egyptian Delta and the Atlantic, there are hundreds and hundreds of megalithic sites, some bearing a startling resemblance to Stonehenge, thanks to the presence of trilithons weighing in at dozens of tonnes. Most often, these are explained away as Roman olive presses, but the explanation does not hold up to very much scrutiny. Certainly, some of the sites may have been *repurposed* as such by the Romans, but we are left with the fact that First Dynasty jars that once contained olive oil are marked as being from Libya or 'Olive Land'/*Ta Tehenu*. Ancient Egyptian conceptions of Libya, or any other foreign land, were far from precise. It is generally accepted that 'Libya/Olive Land,' since predynastic times, referred to the western delta of Egypt proper, all of coastal North Africa and potentially even parts of Southern Spain.

The scale of the agrarian society appears to have been substantial, based on the boasts of livestock volumes having been 'captured' from 'Libya' by kings right up to the Fourth Dynasty numbering in the hundreds of thousands, potentially millions. For those very early kings of Upper Egypt, the tattooed Libyans of the western delta and their vast herds would have looked very appealing.

One of the questions Robert Temple sought to answer in the previously mentioned *Egyptian Dawn* was which cultures that preceded the Old Kingdom had the capacity to move stones weighing well over 100 tonnes and, based on the size and weight of some of these 'Libyan' megaliths, he thinks he has found it. There is certainly good evidence for there being more than one game in town.

Nabta Playa

As a result of the changing climate that followed the end of the Ice Age, around 9,000 BCE, the Monsoon rains of Central Africa moved north and began to fall over southwestern Egypt, turning an arid landscape into one of savannah-style grassland and thousands of shallow pools or 'playas' that would dry and refill again with each rainy season. The monsoonal pattern ended abruptly around 3,500 BCE – and by abruptly I mean potentially in a single lifetime – at which point this part of the Sahara became desert once more. You will note that 3,500 BCE is the 'accepted date' for the emergence of civilisation in the nearby Nile Valley. Funny how these dates keep lining up.

Nabta Playa is the location of several dozen remarkable calendrical circles and other astronomically aligned megaliths in what is now hyper-arid desert. The earliest radiocarbon dates (from firepits, etc.) date back to around 10,000 BCE and end just before 3,000 BCE, with the majority of dates clustering around 6,000 BCE. (You will remember this is the same time as the first appearance of the sheep, an Indian creature, in northeast Africa.) These remains would have been left by nomadic herdspeople bringing their livestock to the area once the rains had led to the grass's return.

In *The Origin Map*, Dr Thomas Brophy undertook a meticulous examination of the astronomical alignments of some of the most prominent stones on the playa. Meticulous may be an understatement. Dr Brophy received his PhD in Physics, worked on NASA's Voyager project, the Japanese Space Program, worked with the Laboratory for Atmospheric and Space Physics and has been published by *IEEE Journal* and *Science*.

The majority of the astronomically aligned stones lie on top of, or are embedded in, playa sediment layers dating from between 6,050 BCE and 5,300 BCE. Complicating this picture is that, underneath the main complex known as the Calendar Circle, the bedrock underneath all the playa sedimentation has been deliberately shaped by human hands. The earliest layers of sedimentation were laid down around 10,000 BCE. (Recall that Göbekli Tepe's bedrock floor was also deliberately shaped, and at around the same time.) Inserted in between the shaped bedrock and the surface Calendar Circle, a large boulder carved in a bovine shape was discovered, buried so as to appear that it was 'standing up.' In an article, 'The Mystery of Nabta Playa,' contributed to special issue vol. 8, no. 6 of *New Dawn* magazine, Dr Brophy writes:

> Nabta Playa ... was filled with shallow water part of the year and the megaliths would have emerged out of the still water that may well have reflected star light along the sight lines to the observer – that would have made the alignments easily apparent for an observer situated at the central megalithic construction.

166   fig. 14   *Reconstruction of the stone circle at Nabta Playa*

Such a phenomenon would also reflect the night sky down on earth, as in a mirror (of heaven). As you probably expect, the stellar alignments of the Calendar Circle are precisely associated with the stars that make up Orion, Sirius and the circumpolar stars. The site displays evidence of being 'calendrically adjusted' over the millennia of its use as the positions of the stars in the sky inevitably changed. Here we have a frankly astonishing example of the continuity of the association between Orion/Shepherd/Bull/Taurus being used as the principal clock of a herding culture as well as – to my eyes – very good evidence for how this cultural clock is folded into conceptions of a stellar afterlife. The 'clock' that indicates the return of the rains is cosmic, after all. It keeps the beat for all of creation. If these ideas sound 'too sophisticated for a herding culture' to your mind, it is worth remembering that, although 10,000 BCE is a very long time ago, it is still a further 10,000 years removed from Dr Witzel's proposed dating for the emergence of the Laurasian storyline, which this certainly falls into. We will return to some of Dr Brophy's more astonishing findings in a later chapter because they speak of the potential consciousness effects that can arise from ritually focusing on specific parts of the night sky. I highly recommend sourcing a copy of his book.

In the mean time, Nabta Playa is important for our story because it provides evidence for the local significance of Osiris/Orion before the advent of agriculture, with which he would later become associated. Here, I suspect he was still seen as 'the shepherd,' the role he moved into after leaving his previous job as 'the hunter.' By definition the teacher must predate the class, and it was believed that Osiris did indeed bring farming to mankind. Perhaps the seed-harvest-seed cycle reminded these early peoples of the actions of their resurrecting god.

The 'Dynastic Race'

As with Sumeria, there is a tendency to overlook the morphological and skeletal research of the past because it often carried racial implications that have not been borne out by the subsequent century of scientific research. Early Egyptologists such as Flinders Petrie discovered dramatically different skeletons in high and low-born graves at around the time the Dynastic Period was kicking off.

Essentially, there are marked differences in morphology between the Predynastic burials and those found in the tombs around Saqqara, Abydos and Giza from 3,500 BCE to 3,000 BCE, and even on into the Fourth Dynasty when compared to those found from the same time in Upper Egypt which are, unsurprisingly, more 'African.' If we leave aside the scientifically useless term 'race,' we are still left with further physical evidence that the era that gave rise to the Old Kingdom building projects was a polyglot one of domestic and international influences upon cultures moving at different speeds; cultures which – just to make it even less clear – seemed to invade one another regularly and declare their own sovereignty over all.

In their report prepared for a controversial 1974 UNESCO symposium as part of the *General History of Africa* project (controversial because the African academics were denied access to Egyptian skin samples held in museums for pigment analysis), Diop, Obenga, Leclant and Vercoutier make the following wise observation:

> A distinction should be drawn between race and culture. In its language, writing and mentality, there is no doubt that Egyptian civilization is first and foremost African, even if, over the millenniums, it borrowed certain cultural elements from its eastern neighbours. Its population, on the other hand, is clearly a product of the Nile valley's position in the north-east corner of the African continent. As a corridor between central Africa and the Mediterranean, for thousands of years a crossroads between the Africa of the Atlantic and East Africa, the Africa of the Red Sea, and between Ethiopia and the Indian Ocean, it was the melting pot in which, from predynastic times, if not earlier, the various prehistoric African types, and the occasional representative of the races of the eastern marches, met and mingled. It would be a vain and useless task to look here for a pure, primitive 'race,' or homogenous population.

A good example of this would be mysterious Badari Culture, dating back to around 5,000 BCE and located about halfway down the Nile. Badarians provide the earliest evidence of agriculture in the Nile Valley, they also fished, farmed – including (Asian) sheep – and evidently traded widely with the Near East, South Asia and Africa: shells from the Red Sea are found in abundance, ivory jewellery and figurines from greater Africa, basalt vessels from the Nile Delta and glazed soapstone beads from southern Iran. Here is how Robert Temple describes them in *Egyptian Dawn*:

> One of the things I like about the Badarians is that they were great dog lovers. They buried their dogs with reverence, which makes them just the sort of chaps I approve of. A lot of people would have us believe that these Badarians were very primitive folk, but there is one problem: their pottery. The amazing thing is that their pottery was so brilliant that it was never really equalled or surpassed in the whole of later Egyptian history. Now, what do you make of that? What happens to the idea of 'progress'?

Within the Badarian sphere of influence, at Nekhen – better known as Hierakonpolis

– was found the famous Narmer Palette. Dating from 3,100 BCE or so, it describes the unification of Upper and Lower Egypt. The monstrous imagery on the palette shows a clear Sumerian influence. Nekhen itself was the pre-eminent cult centre for Horus. By 3,400 BCE there may have been up to 10,000 people living in the city. All of this is to show that when we come to the re-dating of supposedly 'Old Kingdom' sites and objects much early than the Third or Fourth Dynasty, we actually have a lot of room to 'back the truck into' without resorting to alien or Atlantean descriptions. Sophisticated cultures had been living at scale in the area, and participating in the wider ancient world, for millennia prior to 'unification.'

In a scenario redolent of the losing and accidental discovery of century-old anthropological research on Rapa Nui, the earliest depictions of 'unified royal power' in Egypt are older than the Narmer Palette and were discovered before it, in 1890. Archibald Sayce discovered and sketched some rock drawings from Nag el-Hamdulab – up river from Nekhen but before Elephantine – that appear to date from 3,200 BCE – Dynasty 0 – but, based on the shape of the boats, could go back to 3,600 BCE. Sayce's sketches languished with some unpublished reports from the early twentieth century in the archive of Chicago House in Luxor until their examination in 2009. (I only accidentally found the report in the British Library while looking for something else.)

The inscriptions themselves are a series of six discrete vignettes depicting common royal activities such hunting, warfare and riverine or nautical processions. An unnamed king wearing the White Crown appears in three of them. He is accompanied by a dog which could suggest a Badarian influence. Unlike most rock art, which tends to begin in the centre of the available space, these vignettes start at the far right of the available flat surface and proceed to the left – just as one finds with scribes working with papyrus. According to the authors of the report, 'The earliest representation of royal power in Egypt: the rock drawings of Nag el-Hamdulab (Aswan),' this probably indicates the artists were used to working in other, potentially more official media. It could suggest the presence of a royal infrastructural bureaucracy – scribes, papyri, etc. – at a much earlier date than we currently believe.

Depictions of the royal boats are very compelling. In one, we see bowmen and prisoners next to a boat that has two cabins, each with a figure holding a large stick on it. The two boats in the royal nautical procession have many oars and oarsmen, are sickle-shaped, with the lower one depicting a bull standard on its prow. The lower boat has an exaggerated sickle shape with a single cabin on which stands a king wearing the White Crown. The standard on the royal barge depicts Wepwawet, the 'Opener of the Ways.' From the same article we read:

The first tableau is the largest at Nag el-Hamdulab, and is already for that reason of primary importance. The scene is organised around five boats, four of which are grouped in a row, slanting slightly upwards to the right, while the fifth is placed at a higher position. Despite the size and importance of the boats, the focal element of the tableau is the representation of the ruler, followed by a fan-bearer, and preceded by a dog and two standard bearers, situated above the only boat with an elaborately decorated cabin. The king wears the White Crown and holds a prototypical heqa-sceptre. Four of the five boats are of the regular, 'sickle-shaped' type. On the most elaborately drawn, not by coincidence below the king, a falcon standard can be seen, while three of the boats have a standard with bull horns. Both the falcon and the bull are royal symbols, emphasising the royal character of the boats ... In front of the royal boats are four bearded persons, their arms beside their bodies, holding a horizontal line representing a rope. Although the rope does not touch the boat, the men most likely represent people towing the boat, a theme that occurs regularly in rock art.

Not only is the bull a royal symbol, it is also an astronomical one with resonances west toward Nabta Playa and, of course, east into Eurasia. The presence of the royal hawk is highly suggestive of Nekhen, as are the dogs. These depictions conjure in the mind a highly compelling spectacle of a victorious king, his barge pulled along from the shore by his enemies, as part of the early dynastic, biennial ritual event known as the 'Following of Horus,' where the king would travel up and down the land, collecting taxes and generally demonstrating his kingliness. Other depictions of brewing and drinking beer, or women dancing with cattle, add to the impression of a Royal Progress throughout the land. It actually sounds quite enjoyable, assuming you were on the boat rather than pulling it.

The 'Following of Horus' should be familiar to those of you with even a casual understanding of 'alternative Egyptology.' It is very close to 'Followers of Horus' or *shemsu hor*. The four-hieroglyph inscription at Nag el-Hamdulab can be read either way. In the now-received 'lore' of alternative Egyptology, the shemsu hor were wisdom teachers who arrived in the land and imparted magical, legal and architectural knowledge to the indigenous population. The long length of the reign of the shemsu hor – 23,200 years, 31,400 years – makes it considerably more likely these are a reflection of the Laurasian 'era of the demigod rulers' mytheme. But it is nevertheless interesting that we have unknown, vastly ancient rulers with an explicit astrotheology and clear influences from points east running the country at a time so removed from the Pharaohs of later dynasties that they may as well be mythological. I suspect that, at least in part, the shemsu hor story reflects a cultural memory of an era prior to unification when the people of the city of Horus ran the show.

Digging in the right place

We can back the 'story truck' up much, much further than Manetho's arbitrary dynasties, but it is still generally believed that predynastic cultures such as the Badarians – who made world-beating pottery and traded globally – lived, for some reason, in wooden or mud houses that have no longer survived. Thus, there still remains the matter of the otherwise-instantly-appearing megalithic building projects.

I suspect, just as we find in India, these priceless ancient sites are unfortunately located underneath other priceless ancient sites. In 1997, Hungarian archaeologists undertook an examination of a temple on Thoth Hill, outside Thebes. Underneath the Middle Kingdom site were the remains of an Archaic Period temple aligned to Sirius. The intervening millennia meant that, thanks to the effects of precession, the two layers are slightly out of alignment with each other. Evidence of similar rebuilding has been found at Dendera and on Elephantine. We are probably looking at some regular and widely distributed repurposing of earlier sites. By the time of the Middle Kingdom, there were 'laws' against reusing older temples. Specifically, the dead king would announce that he had not reused old temple stones while his heart was being weighed in the Court of Osiris.

In 2008, Juan Antonio Belmonte – whose Göbekli Tepe alignments were referenced in an earlier chapter – participated in a satellite survey of 400 sites in Egypt and the Sudan, the majority of which were astronomically aligned. Given the definitive break provided by the First Intermediate Period, the destruction it would have wrought, and the subsequent Middle Kingdom rebuilding or repurposing of earlier sacred sites, we will likely never know just when large scale megalithic projects began. We do know that mudbrick pyramids were being built in one part of the country while the magnificent Step Pyramid at Saqqara was being built in another, so again, we are dealing with different speeds of technological innovation.

Dating to at least the First Dynasty and presumably earlier – not that anyone has really looked – is the ancient 'city' of Letopolis or 'Khem' in Egyptian. Now buried under a decidedly unlovely Cairo suburb, it was originally sacred to Horus the Elder. Based on the research of Georges Goyon, King Farouk's private archaeologist and a senior fellow at the French National Centre for Scientific Research, Robert Bauval believes Letopolis was once the home of an astronomical observatory tower. Roman geographer, Strabo, specifically mentions that it was from this site, 'Eudoxus' in the Letopolite Nome, that sightings and observations of celestial bodies was recorded.

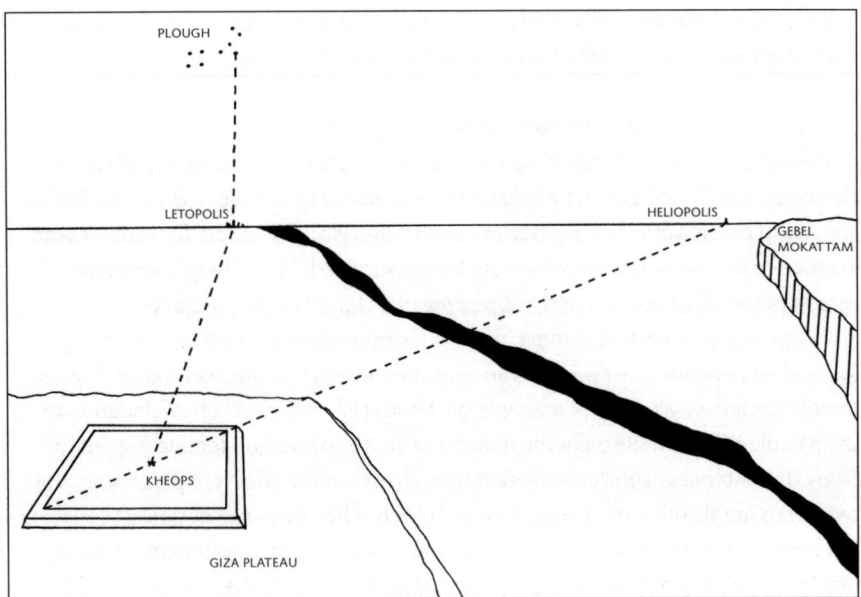

PLOUGH

LETOPOLIS   HELIOPOLIS

GEBEL
MOKATTAM

KHEOPS

GIZA PLATEAU

fig. 15   *Isometric view of Giza Plateau, Letopolis and Heliopolis*

Significantly, the emblem of the Letopolite Nome was the 'Bull's Thigh' or Ursa Major. Bauval also points out that 'Horus of Letopolis' was the traditional keeper of the *adze* – shaped like the Plough – that was used in the 'Opening of the Mouth' ceremony.

These sky/ground alignments and indications of a multi-site building project across Egypt right at the very start of the dynastic period are highly suggestive of a predynastic origin for the wider cosmology that they express. Indeed, that is the entire premise of this book. Returning to Belmonte's archaeoastronomical survey of Egypt and the Sudan, here is what he had to say about *Meskhetyu*, the Egyptian term for Ursa Major, and its ability to confer immortality in Ancient Egyptian belief.

> The archaeoastronomy mission fieldwork in the country, particularly in the fields of pyramids, seem to confirm this fact, provided Meskhetyu could also be the principal celestial object used to align these imposing monuments as well as many other imposing temples along the Nile Valley, such as Dandara or Edfu. Consequently, the architectural arrangement of the pyramids could be a transfer on Earth of the cosmic order prevailing in the sky.

UNAVOIDABLE HARD SCIENCE

Too often when Egyptologists are rejecting scientifically verified dates for objects or artefacts that appear earlier than their dynastic guesswork, their response requires us to believe that there was very little going on in Egypt prior to unification. We have seen this is a patent misread of their own evidence, as well as a misread of how the Egyptians themselves saw their own history. Sandwiching enormous, interconnected building projects such as those found on the Giza Plateau into a century or less, and then refusing to budge, is a recipe for attracting *Ancient Aliens* film crews. Honestly admitting that there was significantly more cultural complexity in predynastic Egypt, and an equally significant cultural *continuity* prior to unification and the first few centuries that followed it, makes the appearance of the Old Kingdom less grotesquely aberrant, but no less inspirational.

The following hard scientific data (a small selection) fall outside the arbitrarily defined dynastic chronology of modern Egyptology but, owning to their status as facts rather than opinions, they must be incorporated into a proposed model of Egyptian history, lest it become entirely dysfunctional.

Dating of the Pyramids

The fact that the Giza pyramids have actually been scientifically dated is not commonly known. In the 1980s, the University of Washington's Robert Wenke, working out of the American Research Center in Cairo, carbon dated some mortar – containing charcoal, wood and reed – from between the exterior stones of the pyramids for testing at the Southern Methodist University in Dallas and the Federal Technical University in Zurich. The dates yielded were an average of 374 years *older* than the presumed dates of the Fourth Dynasty, averaging around 3,101 BCE with some dates from the upper courses of the Great Pyramid yielding a date of almost 4,000 BCE (margin of error: 160 years).

More recently, Robert Temple dated the Great Pyramid to around or slightly before 3,000 BCE, using a dating method invented by nuclear physicist Ioannis Liritzis known as 'optical thermoluminescence.' Whilst this cannot date the age of a stone structure – nothing can – it does date the last exposure to sunlight of two stones that have been pressed together which, in the case of a pyramid, is probably quite useful.

All of these dates cluster around the 3,100 BCE to 3,000 BCE area, centuries too old for the Fourth Dynasty and straddling that curious 'between space' of predynasty and dynasty. As an aside, in the final years of his reign, Hawass banned all scientific dating outside of Egypt.

Constraint Analysis

Constraint analysis is an engineering technique to determine where the bottlenecks lie in a building project. That is, which steps in a construction cannot be made to go faster and/or also hold up the rest of the project.

In the case of extracting an obelisk from a quarry using only dolerite pounders, the bottleneck is in the original 'dig down' phase, which cannot be made to go faster than a single worker's fastest speed. Aerospace machinist, Christopher Dunn, has calculated that it would take just under 50 years to remove and shape a large, New Kingdom obelisk from a quarry using only dolerite pounders. Hatshepsut boasted of getting them out in six months.

With specific reference to the Great Pyramid, the descending passage, carved out of the Giza plateau's limestone bedrock, is only 42 inches square, meaning that only one worker at any one time could be carving it out. This provides a neat and measurable example of constraint analysis: it would have taken almost twice Khufu's reign for a single person to carve out this passageway using a dolerite pounder, and that is working twenty four hours a day. Not only is the pyramid too old to be a tomb, its construction cannot fit into the twenty-something year reign of Khufu.

The Osiris Shaft

The famous 'Osiris Shaft' beside and under the Khafre Causeway was clearly constructed in different stages across several millennia – with the deepest layer, somewhat confusingly, being the youngest. However, in *Egyptian Dawn*, Robert Temple and Ioannis Liritzis dated the 25 tonne dacite sarcophagus in the middle chamber to the predynastic era.

Perhaps more interestingly, there is not a dacite vein anywhere in the continent of Africa large enough to have had a single, 25 tonne sarcophagus carved out of it, meaning this predynastic object is also an international import. Due to the properties of the stone, it is also slightly radioactive, which meant any biological material placed inside would have benefited from a mild increase in preservation, as the environment inside the sarcophagus would have been antimicrobial.

All of this speaks of a substantial awareness of the properties of various stones and minerals, at an extremely early date, across ancient borders. Surprising though it is on first read, it is less surprising when put into the context of the prior ten millennia or so of Laurasian megalithic spirituality.

Further evidence in stone

Tens of thousands of pots, a great many of which date from the First Dynasty, were discovered under the Step Pyramid at Saqqara, believed to date from the Third Dynasty. Much of this pottery is made from supremely hard stone that is physically impossible to be shaped with copper.

Similarly, the famous and stunning statue of Khafre in the Egyptian Museum in Cairo is made of diorite, which is harder than steel. It has no tool marks.

Lastly, if any of the few dozen alleged new pyramids discovered via satellite and Google Earth in the western desert over the last few years turn out to be verified, then we are clearly playing an entirely different, and much older, game. As is commonly known now, the limestone of the Sphinx and its enclosure displays significant water damage over a very long period of time.

OSIRIS

A common criticism levelled at Robert Bauval's Orion Correlation theory in its early days was that Osiris is not mentioned by name anywhere in the Old Kingdom before the Fifth Dynasty. How could the three main Giza pyramids represent his belt stars, then, much less the stones of Nabta Playa?

However, this is a misread of the available evidence. In her classic *The Death of Gods in Ancient Egypt*, Jane B. Sellers points out that not only were most, if not all, the other main characters of the Osiris myth – Set, Isis, Horus, Anubis and Thoth – attested to from predynastic times, but a complete telling of the story was not written down *anywhere* in all of dynastic Egypt, so its exclusion prior to the Fifth Dynasty is not all that unusual. She suggests that perhaps the story was so widely known that it was taken as given by most Egyptians. Most sources cite Plutarch for renditions of the myth, which was penned thousands of years after the end of the Old Kingdom. Here is Sellers's encapsulation of the story:

> Osiris was ruler of Egypt. Isis was his sister-wife, and Seth his evil brother. Seth killed his brother, Osiris, and cast his body enclosed in a coffer into the Nile. Isis rescued the coffer and hid it: Seth found it, cut up the body into fourteen pieces and scattered them about Egypt. The grieving Isis wandered all over the countryside, gathering up the parts of her husband's body and then, with the help of Nephthys, her sister; Anubis, the jackal-headed god of embalming; and Thoth, god of wisdom and words, put together the dismembered body, wrapping it in linen bandages and uttering sacred words, or magical spells. Then Isis fanned the body of Osiris with her wings and revived him long enough to conceive the child Horus.

Further supporting the antiquity of the Osiris story are the numerous Laurasian motifs such as the duelling brothers and separation of their earth/sky parents. There are also some viscerally shamanic and probably Gondwanan layers we shall return to as well, such as the ritual dismemberment and being stored/hidden in a tree trunk. That said, by the time we reach the Pyramid Texts of the Fifth Dynasty, the legend is decidedly astrotheological, not only in the identification of Isis with Sirius and Osiris with Orion, but also Osiris's fourteen parts corresponding to the fourteen days of the waning moon.

It is certainly true that, beginning in the Middle Kingdom, Osiris took on a much more obvious role as Lord of the Underworld and Judge of Souls and Hearts. But this would be in keeping with my thesis that the newly 'democratised' religion of the Middle Kingdom was an 'incomplete rebuild,' following the First Intermediate Period, of a previous – and vastly older – elite Mystery process with very obvious shamanic roots discussed below. The analogy to Christianity is apt: it can be described as a confused assemblage of disparate Classical Mystery traditions built for a wider audience.

Prior to this change, Osiris's role was not exclusively post-mortem. The king did not merely become Osiris when he died but, as described in the Pyramid Texts, was ritually identified with him in life. This may actually reflect a shamanic need to 'claim' the unseen world as well as the seen world as part of one's 'total' realm. It was only from the Middle Kingdom onwards that he was depicted as a mummified god; a religious innovation and, I contend, an over-simplification.

Osiris the Foreigner

Most Egyptologists would agree that that Osirian myth cycle is likely an agglomeration of mythemes: Horus/Set, Osiris/Horus and Osiris/Isis. However this awareness is less often used in an examination of the pre-Fifth Dynasty origins of Osiris.

Much of this is down to nomenclature. The first written example of Osiris's *later* name is found in the Pyramid Texts: the hieroglyphs are those of a seat and an eye. But in J. Gwyn Griffiths's *The Origins of Osiris and his Cult*, he notes that the earliest appearance of Osiris's name has three elements: the seat, the eye and, a classifier, *the seated bearded man*. The beard is a signifier of foreignness and the sitting posture one of status, so 'seated, bearded figure' was, and remained, a signifier for 'non-slave foreigner.' In addition, in the vast majority of cases when a toponym is mentioned in an epithet of Osiris, 'Busiris' is mentioned, rather than his generally accepted 'home' of Abydos. Busiris is an area of Egypt that extends north from Giza to Saqqara and encompasses several vast Old Kingdom and predynastic necropoli.

Given the skeletal evidence of additional cultures appearing at the beginning of the dynastic period, genetic and trade contacts tracing back millennia aross the Near East, Southern and Southeast Asia, the appearance of the constellation Orion in stone and mythological form going back tens of millennia and the belief that it was Osiris who taught mankind agriculture, just as the same constellation did in the Pacific (the same theme I believe is demonstrated at Göbekli Tepe) I put it to you that this little hieroglyphic qualifier may well be the proverbial finger in the dyke.

At this juncture, I suggest you mark a different break point in your internal chronology. Rather than starting off the story of Egypt at the First Dynasty and have it grow in complexity from there, start it with the climate events that accompanied the end of the last Ice Age, which brought new agragian species and new cultures to the Nile Valley, see it grow in cultural and technological complexity to peak around 3,100 BCE to 2,800 BCE and then have it 'decline' for the last couple of Dynasties into the First Intermediate Period. (Consider this: a culture that only recently built the Great Pyramid would presumably be difficult to invade. A culture that had built it centuries before and was now rattling around the edges of its previously impressive monuments would be far easier to invade. Modern Britain is a good go-to example.)

Put the break point at the First Intermediate Period and have the 'reset' and climb back into cultural complexity occur at the beginning of the Middle Kingdom – with the bewildered descendants attempting to piece together a culture they had only ever heard about after one and a half centuries of violence and destruction – and it starts to make a bit more sense.

PYRAMID8

So far, only two undisturbed 'burial chambers' from the Old Kingdom pyramids have been found. The earliest and most impressive is that of Sekhemkhet, beneath his unfinished step pyramid at Saqqara. When the room was excavated in 1950, a beautiful, translucent alabaster tomb was discovered, still sealed. When opened, the sarcophagus was revealed to be empty. Atop it were the remains of plant material, suggestive of rejuvenation, and pottery discovered elsewhere in the complex referred to his Heb Sed festival.

The second comes from another unfinished pyramid at Zawiyet el-Aryan, near Giza, believed to 'belong' to the Fourth Dynasty Nebka. Again, the undisturbed 'burial chamber' contained a sarcophagus with a lid sealed with mortar and covered in clay. It was also empty.

Sekhemkhet was a king of the Third Dynasty, at the beginning of the Old Kingdom. The only (presumably) contemporaneous remains inside a pyramid come from the end of the Old Kingdom, in the pyramid of Djedkare Isesi. A destroyed, granite sarcophagus and the remains of a human male of approximately fifty years were discovered inside the pyramid known as 'Beautiful is Djedkare.' Confusingly, the age of the corpse does not align with any of the known reigns of Djedkare from the various king lists, and his wife and children are known to have been buried elsewhere, at Abusir and Giza rather than Saqqara. Other remains inside Djedkare's pyramid also reference his Heb Sed festival, including an alabaster vase now on display in the Musée du Louvre. That said, several of the other Sixth Dynasty pyramids near that of Djedkare Isesi have been found to contain canopic jars, suggesting that – at least by the very end of the Old Kingdom prior to its complete collapse – humans, and possibly royal ones, were interred in pyramids. This does not preclude the structures having some other ritual function during the life of the king, rather it suggests a cultural change that could have accompanied the general decline of society.

En masse, Egyptologists will insist that pyramids are the looted tombs of Old Kingdom rulers. Interrogate them individually, however – something I have made a habit of doing in London – and they will admit that this is really a 'best guess' as to their function. Not only have no satisfactory remains been uncovered in any of these structures, even in cases such as those of Sekhemkhet, where the objects have remained unmolested for millennia, but we are also faced with the problem that individual kings built multiple pyramids. This is explained away as a ruse to confound tomb robbers, but the logic behind that does not stack up. Firstly, it's an absurd waste of resources better spent simply maintaining guards at the actual tomb. Secondly, prior to the building of pyramids, and in every era after it, there are no examples of pharaohs building 'false tombs' in, for example, the Valley of the Kings. If this 'anti-burglary' method was official policy, why does it only apply to pyramids?

In addition, we also have numerous unfinished pyramids. These are explained away by saying that the king died before his pyramid was completed. Again, this fails logical analysis. Surely the completion of a tomb is more important once a king has died? There is simply no way the next ruler, in all likelihood a relative, would have risked unbalancing Maat and attracting the ire of the gods by failing to complete construction of the tomb of his ancestor. I would go so far as to say their coronation would be illegitimate if they had behaved in such a fashion. Even in secular times, if your parents were weird enough to begin work on their tombstone prior to their death – and then died suddenly – you would not abandon their tombstone, you would complete it.

A non-funerary or at least a non-*exclusively*-funerary interpretation of the role of pyramids necessarily leads us to a re-examination of the so-called 'mortuary temples' attached to many of these structures. A better and now more appropriate name for

fig. 16   *The pyramid at Saqqara*   179

them would be 'royal temples' or 'temples of the royal cult.' Calling them such probably gets us closer to an improved understanding of their function.

Firstly, many of them appear to have been in use *during* the reign of the king, which would be unusual for a mortuary temple. Secondly, many kings built more than one. Sneferu built at least four, including one at the so-called Bent Pyramid which clearly never had a funerary function. It does make reference to the Heb Sed festival, however, and this points us in a better direction.

Heb Sed

You are never more conscious of the paucity of magical or ritual knowledge among mainstream historians than when reading their interpretations of the Heb Sed festival. This is described as a sort of ritualised running race performed by the king in the thirtieth year of his reign and then every three or four years after that. During the Old Kingdom he would attach a tail to his garment and be presided over by priests in leopard skins, which it is reasonable to suggest are vestiges of an earlier shamanic tradition. Clearly there is something else going on besides renewing the vitality of an ageing king, especially as the festival could be held at what appear to be arbitrary times in addition to the classic thirty year interval. In his *Shamanic Wisdom in the Pyramid Texts*, Dr Jeremy Naydler puts it like so:

> A major part of the festival consisted in the king visiting the shrines of the assembled gods of Egypt. These gods, made present in their statues, were brought ceremonially to the festival site from all over Egypt. They represented the spiritual energies of the landscape, which were embodied in the human and semihuman forms of their divine statues. The king was thus engaged in a ritual communion with the spirits of the land of Egypt. The underlying purpose of this was to reach across to the more subtle spiritual world that upholds and vitalizes the physical world, in order to ensure a beneficent connection with it and an unhampered flow of energies from it to the physical.

When you consider that the king was the divine mediator between the spirit world and the physical world for the entire country – the state-appointed shaman, if you will – much of the symbolism and architecture of pyramid complexes becomes clearer. The Heb Sed's main ritual was designed to bring the king into conscious alignment with the various forces of the spirit world and 'renew' their terrestrial connection. Thus the final running race or 'Sed dance' is not an assessment of an ageing king's cardiovascular capacity. As he crosses a courtyard laid out with symbolic waymarkers of his kingdom this is actually a ritual revitalisation of the whole land. He crosses over all Egypt, as do the stars with which he has just been magically identified. Here is Jane B. Sellers's description of the Heb Sed:

Perhaps held on the first day of the first month of the 'Season of Coming Forth' and preceded by five days dedicated to the Osirian Mysteries, these particular rituals appear to be a renewal of the king's ancient right to rule both Upper and Lower Egypt...

From almost the very beginning of Egypt's written history we have what appears to be renderings of Sed rituals. A simple, schematic representation of First-Dynasty King Den depicts the king apparently involved in the running ceremony of 'The Dedication of the Field,' or 'Circuit of the Wall.' King Zoser is represented in a Third-Dynasty rendering of this same ritual, and from the Fifth Dynasty we have inscriptions from the walls of Niuserre's sun temple at Abu Gurob showing the king performing the same rites.

A mace head of Narmer is an even earlier indication of the antiquity of the 'Heb-sed' (or Sed Festival).

At the conclusion of the Heb Sed, the king received a ritual coronation on a specially constructed dais, designed to represent the Primordial Mound. It was stepped, like a stairway leading up to the stars. Like a pyramid. Returning to Dr Naydler:

The crowning itself was a cosmic event that was regarded as accomplishing the union of the Above with the Below, thereby infusing the earth with the fructifying energies of the spirit realm. This union of heaven and earth during the coronation ceremonies was accompanied by these words, spoken by an attendant priest:

Horus appears resting on his southern throne,
and there occurs a uniting of the sky to the earth.

The same formula was repeated once for each of the four cardinal directions toward which the king duly turned.

When you consider the antiquity of the Heb Sed, its obvious astronomical and directional alignments and the association of the 'right to rule' as well as the reordering of the cosmos with its successful completion, you see the clear parallels to Vedic and Polynesian rituals designed to accomplish precisely the same thing. (Influxes of foreign overlords are unsurprisingly rigorous in providing themselves with magical and ceremonial legitimacy.) These parallels will only become more obvious.

A revised architectural chronology

De-emphasising the 'funerary hypothesis' of the purpose of pyramids invites us to consider a new chronology. Without it, we are left with:

- Predynastic Egypt: Kings buried in tombs.
- Early Dynastic Egypt: Mudbrick pyramids appear. Kings remain buried in tombs.
- Old Kingdom Egypt: Some kings buried in stepped pyramids, others buried near pyramids, away from the rest of their family. Tombs get larger, then much smaller, but are still only for some kings. Others continue to be buried in tombs. In the final two dynasties, writing appears inside the 'pyramid tombs' for the first time, even though writing is attested to from actual tombs in earlier dynasties. The 'pyramid tombs' from the final dynasty are a poor echo of some of the earlier masterpieces.
- The rest of Egyptian history: Kings buried in tombs.

If we allow that the pyramids had some ritual magical function during the life of the king, then we also have a better fit for what Robert Temple calls 'a logic of decline.' The dating of the Great Pyramid puts much of it at or just before the dynastic era, after which the astrotheological, megalithic building project appears to get less physically ambitious; ending with some frankly underwhelming sites in the Sixth Dynasty, at which point the country was invaded and collapsed. Clearly a ritual change – a change in the magic – occurred in the final two dynasties with the appearance of writing, the Pyramid Texts, for the first time inside these structures, which could be interpreted as a further 'falling away' from the original ritual function. (Think of the liturgical changes associated with various translations of the Bible.) A revised chronology beckons.

One final observation that may be significant before we examine these texts: if their primary purpose was not funerary, then the Egyptian pyramids would be brought back into alignment with every other Laurasian culture – such as Sumeria and Mesoamerica – that built them instead as calendrical 'World Mountains' or places of ascension and descent between the upper and earthly realm. Such a realignment would be in keeping with the discovery of a proto-stepped-pyramid, Gunung Padang, in Indonesia.

A similar approach is called for when it comes to the Egyptian gods. As Dr Witzel observes, there were four main variants of Egyptian myth, determined at various stages in the culture's history by the respective priesthoods of Heliopolis, Memphis,

Hermopolis and Thebes. This resulted in specific gods assuming the 'lead actor' role in the story. Historians and magicians are often tripped up by this, assuming there is some form of linear progression or evolution. A comparison of the four main variations quickly throws the earlier, underlying 'pan-Egyptian' myth cycle into sharp relief.

THE PYRAMID TEXTS

Is the Bible a funerary text? It is read at funerals. But it is also read at weddings, baptisms, state occasions, white power rallies, sporting events, during Eucharist, before procreative intercourse and – strange as it may seem – even just for fun.

Beginning with the pyramid of Unas in the Fifth Dynasty, we find carved throughout the interior of several of the final few Old Kingdom pyramids the so-called 'Pyramid Texts,' considered among the world's oldest religious writings. Undoubtedly, many of the spells and incantations that comprise the Pyramid Texts have a funerary function. Our best evidence for this is the fact that a goodly number of them survive into the 'Books of the Dead' in the New Kingdom, which is inarguably an exclusively funerary or post-mortem spell book. There is also the fact that the king is regularly referred to as 'Osiris' in the Pyramid Texts. What is less widely known is that he is referred to as 'Horus' equally as often, suggesting the king's magical identification with the divine is not exclusively related to his afterlife state.

Based on his PhD thesis, Dr Naydler's *Shamanic Wisdom in the Pyramid Texts* presents a hugely compelling argument that what we call the Pyramid Texts (PT) are related to the same spiritual function that underpins the Heb Sed; namely that the king, while living, passes into the afterlife and returns; the classic shamanic journey. Consider the following PT utterance:

I am Horus, my father's heir.
I am the one who went and came back ...

From Dr Naydler's book:

Elsewhere it is as Horus that the king 'rests in life in the West (i.e., the Underworld)' and then, like the sun, 'shines anew in the East.' In both these passages, a nonfunerary interpretation in which the king mystically 'dies' by entering into and then returning from the realm of the dead is just as plausible as a funerary interpretation. But however we interpret them, their existence is incontrovertible evidence that the 'dead' king is not always an Osiris.

In many respects, the suggestion that the PT are exclusively funereal is stranger than suggesting their principal function was a Mystery one. Dr Naydler keenly observes that there are similar Mystery ritual practices occurring in contemporaneous cultures to the Middle and New Kingdoms, such as those of the Minoans, Hittites, and Ugarites. Given the prominence afforded to Egypt by the rest of the ancient world as the home of deep magical wisdom and power, the absence of what would become known in the Classical Age as a Mystery initiation should be more surprising than its presence.

In this analysis, the shamanic motifs of the PT, and indeed the majority of the pyramids themselves, are thrown into stark relief. Just as the antiquity of the Heb Sed is suggested by the therianthropic ritual garments of the king and the priests, PT descriptions suggest a 'classic' shamanic experience. From utterance 373:

Oho! Oho! Raise yourself up, O King; receive your head,
Collect your bones, gather your limbs together,
Throw off the earth from your flesh.
...
[H]e sets you at the head of the spirits, the Imperishable Stars.
Those whose seats are hidden worship you,
The Great Ones care for you, the Watchers wait upon you.
Barley is threshed for you, emmer is reaped for you,
And offering thereof is made at your monthly festivals,
Offering thereof is made at your half-monthly festivals,
Being what was commanded to be done for you by your father, Geb.
Rise up, O King, for you have not died!

Ritual dismemberment remains a dominant motif in many initiatory traditions to this day and may ultimately date back to the very beginning of the formation of the Laurasian storyline (and perhaps earlier) where the universe is created from the dismembered parts of a giant monster or ancient god. It is quite possibly a very early conceptualisation of the microcosm/macrocosm connection of the 'unified human' with all of Creation. The most potent visual is, of course, the removal and then return of the head, a seat of power recognised in magic and sorcery for tens of millennia, which is – I posit – reflected in the faceless (headless) T-shaped pillars of Göbekli Tepe and, of course, the 'headless hunter' that is Orion itself. From an Egyptian ritual perspective, when Osiris is headless, he is in the Underworld. The restoration of his head corresponds with his restoration to the Living world thanks to the magic of Isis/Sirius.

The king is repeatedly exhorted to 'claim the throne' of Osiris. Returning to Dr Naydler:

Underlying the whole question of the king acquiring the throne, whether as Osiris or Horus, is the significant fact that several of the Pyramid Texts are clearly linked to, derived from, or are versions of coronation texts. Utterance 213 is illustrative:

O King, you have not departed dead,
You have departed alive.
Sit upon the throne of Osiris, your sceptre in your hand,
That you may give orders to the living;
Your lotus-bud sceptre in your hand, that you may give orders
To those whose seats are hidden.
Your arms are Atum, your shoulders are Atum, your belly is Atum,
Your back is Atum, your hind-parts are Atum, your legs are Atum,
Your face is Anubis.
The Mounds of Horus serve you,
The Mounds of Set serve you.

Here, the king not only 'departs alive,' but he does so in order to claim the throne of Osiris and 'give orders to the living.' His dismembered body is reformed as Atum – meaning 'complete one' – with the face of the god who presides over the comings and goings between the realms. As a result, the assembled forces and settlements of creation and destruction now serve him.

Perhaps significantly, Horus was ruler of the fertile lands and Set was ruler of the desert. Hence the utterance would not look out of place in a Heb Sed ritual where the king 'claims' his territories. Leaving that aside, the utterance looks for all the world like the archetypal journey of the shaman into the Otherworld, his recognition there, and then his return and subsequent installation as tribal mediator between the realms. According to the early twentieth century Egyptologist, Alexandre Moret, the living king became divine precisely because he had been magically identified with Osiris; his accession to the throne required him to be 'redeemed' as Osiris had been. The complete lack of royal mummies in the pyramids begins to make more sense in this light. Yes, the king probably got in the sarcophagus. But he also probably got back out.

With a particular emphasis on the Pyramid of Unas, Dr Naydler not only examines the content of the utterances, but their specific location carved onto the walls and ceilings of the various chambers of the structure. From a ritual magic perspective, this interpretation is hugely useful, especially as it seems much more likely that the vast majority of Old Kingdom pyramids had a ritual rather than funereal role. What emerges from this analysis is a ritual space designed to accomplish the hugely important magical task of enabling the king to claim his sovereignty over the immaterial realm by a process of stellar identification, literally going up into the stars and back again, so that cosmic balance, prosperity and wellbeing are restored to Egypt. Such a goal is almost identical to the goal of the Heb Sed, which is the likely explanation for why there are so many Heb Sed motifs, depictions and ritual objects found in and around so many pyramids. And also why a king would need more than one.

The magical acts, in particular the identification with Orion and the intercession of Sirius (Isis), mean the king also has the 'right' and 'magical ability' to take his place among the Imperishable Stars upon his death. This is similar – although much cooler, obviously – to the way baptism ensures right of access to heaven.

Naydler's analysis of the location of utterances within Unas's pyramid begins with the location of the structure itself. The nine pyramids so far discovered that contain Pyramid Texts are clustered fairly close to each other at Saqqara, itself the necropolis of the Old Kingdom capital of Memphis. Since the predynastic era, Saqqara was associated with Sokar, considered by many to be an early manifestation of Osiris as well as the presiding deity of Memphis, Ptah. He writes:

> As a manifestation of Osiris, Sokar represented his power of rebirth, and was depicted as a falcon resting on, or breaking out of, a mound of earth, placed on a boat. The whole area then was as much to do with rebirth as it was to do with death.

Significantly, Sokar combines a number of the more widespread Laurasian motifs found in Sumeria, India and the Pacific. The bird/earth/ship motif, and the implied Flood/Cosmic Waters motif, is found in the Noah story, Atrahasis and (sometimes in the form of a box of earth rather than a ship) Hindu mythology. This very likely attests to an ultimate origin sometime in the Palaeolithic, appearing in predynastic Egypt in the form of Sokar.

Like all Ancient Egyptian sacred structures, the choice of construction material was deliberate and fulfilled a magical purpose. The sarcophagus is carved from a single block of black basalt (the same stone used at Gunung Padang). The walls of the 'burial chamber' are of polished alabaster, upon which many of the PT utterances are carved. Alabaster is almost translucent, and would have appeared quite evocative in the torchlight of whatever ceremonies happened in the chamber. It would also contrast with the deep black of the sarcophagus. Alabaster was referred to as *ankh*, meaning 'life.' Ankh was 'sap of life,' one of the terms for milk; the 'milk of heaven' or the 'milk of the Imperishable Stars' is mentioned numerous times in the PT.

The complex would have been approached by boat across an artificial lake, arriving at the 'Valley Temple,' before ascending the causeway into the 'Mortuary Temple' and then into the (Hed Sed?) courtyard and around to the entrance which points north, toward the circumpolar stars.

The Utterances of Unas

There are 228 utterances within the pyramid itself. Three are repeated several times, bringing the total number to 234. Only two straddle more than one wall. It is unlikely the number of utterances has any significance as this particular way of grouping them dates back to their first publication in 1910. Indeed, most researchers suspect a good amount of them 'run together' rather than operate as discrete 'spells' such as those found in the New Kingdom Books of the Dead. However, the wall positioning, especially in such a precision-aligned structure, is clearly very important. The utterances are found in the burial chamber, the antechamber, in the passage between the two, and at the end of the entrance corridor that leads down to the antechamber from outside.

Here is Dr Naydler's grouping, beginning in the sarcophagus/burial chamber and working its way out, interspersed with my commentary:

'BURIAL' OR SARCOPHAGUS CHAMBER
West Gable
1 Eighteen snake spells: Utts. 226 – 43

The gable is above the sarcophagus. These spells are apotropaic but any entheogenic psychonaut will also tell you that serpentine imagery is associated with the onset of an hallucinogenic journey. (Perhaps one in the black/nighttime basalt 'sleeping' sarcophagus?)

North Wall
1 Purification: Utts. 23, 25, 32, 34, 35, 36
2 Opening of the Mouth: Utts. 37 – 42
3 Preliminary Presentation of Offerings: Utts. 32, 43 – 57
4 Anointing with the Seven Holy Oils: Utts. 72 – 78, 79, 81
5 The Feast: Utts. 25, 32, 82 – 96, 108 – 71

North is the direction of the Imperishable Stars, commonly associated with the number 7. In later dynasties, the Big Dipper/Ursa Major, called 'Mesekhtiu,' was depicted as a bull's thigh or foreleg containing seven stars. Seven is the number of steps in the Step Pyramid of Djoser (right next door to Unas).

South and East Walls
1 Departing Alive: Utt. 213
2 Becoming a Falcon: Utt. 214
3 Healing Horus and Set, Embraced by Atum: Utt. 215
4 In the Night Bark of the Sun: Utt. 216
5 Solarisation: Utt. 217
6 Empowerment: Utt. 218
7 A Living Osiris: Utt. 219
8 Coronation as Horus; Approaching the Crown: Utt. 220
9 Coronation as Horus; the Royal Rebirth: Utt. 221
10 Joining the Cosmic Circuit of Ra: Utt. 222
11 Awakening: Utt. 223
12 Return: Utt. 224

This is the world's most confusing funeral.

SMALL PASSAGE LEADING TO THE ANTECHAMBER
South Surface
1 Smashing the Red Jars: Utt. 244
2 Flying up to Nuit: Utt. 245
3 Merging with Min at the Doors of the Akhet: Utt. 246

North Surface
1 Reversion of Offerings: Utt. 199
2 Purificatory Libation: Utt. 32
3 Protective Libation: Utt. 23
4 Unas going with his Ka: Utt. 25
5 Hymn to Incense: Utt. 200

East Gable
1 The Nourishment Provided by Osiris: Utt. 204
2 The King is Transformed into a Bull: Utt. 205

3 Two Food Texts: Utts. 207, 209
4 Negotiating the Inverted World: Utt: 210
5 Unas is Born as a Star: Utt. 211
6 The Divine Nourishment of the King: Utt. 212

Facing north in the passage we find the same offering/food/libation refrain as we do in the 'burial chamber' when facing the same direction. This makes perfect ritual sense if the initiate/king had been lifted from the sarcophagus and was perambulated about the rooms on his way out, as this is the direction of the Imperishable Stars – stars he would ascend to in his Ka. When facing east, the direction of both the sunrise and his 'mortuary' temple, the king is then born as a star, perhaps with the sunrise.

fig. 17   *Pyramid of Unas, Antechamber, West Wall*

ANTECHAMBER

West Gable

1 The Awakening of the Initiate King: Utt. 247
2 The Fiery Rebirth of Unas: Utt. 248
3 The Sun Child: Utt. 249
4 Uniting with Sia: Utt. 250
5 Becoming the Strong Horns of Ra: Utt. 251
6 Union with Ra: Utt. 252
7 Lifted up by Shu: Utt. 253

West and South Walls

1 The Death and Rebirth of the Horus King: Utt. 254
2 Overcoming the Ugly One: Utt. 255
3 The Throne of Horus: Utt. 256
4 Bursting through the Sky: Utt. 257
5 A Living Osiris: Utt. 258
6 The One who Went and Came Back: Utt. 260
7 The Lightning Ascent: Utt. 261
8 The Regenerative Journey: Utt. 262
9 Crossing the Reed Floats, Meeting the Dead: Utt. 263
10 Re-memberment and Ascent to the Sky: Utt. 267
11 Uniting with the Ka: Utt. 268
12 Ascent to the Sky, Suckled by Ipy: Utt. 269
13 Awakening the Ferryman: Utt. 270
14 Pulling Papyrus, Raising the Djed: Utt. 271
15 The Gate of Nun: Utt. 272

Being suckled by the hippopotamus goddess, Ipy, has an important astrotheologi-cal component. Our constellation Draco was known to be a hippopotamus in Ancient Egypt. Thus once Unas has drunk from the divine milk of the northern stars, he 'will neither thirst nor hunger [in yonder land] for ever.' Dr Naydler believes the point of Ipy's breast represented the North Pole. Unas was imbibing the immortality of the Imperishable Stars.

The dramatically named 'Cannibal Hymn' requires some explanation. One of the most remarkable texts of the ancient world, it is worth reading in its entirety. The utterances begin with a description of the sky and the stars going dark as Unas claims power 'mightier' than Atum. He is then declared the 'Bull of the Sky,' having been reborn via the cosmic cow goddess's Otherworld womb (Utt. 254). It continues:

His gods are upon him,
His uraei are on the crown of his head,
The King's guiding serpent is on his brow,
Even that which sees the soul, efficient for burning.
The King's neck is on his trunk.
The King is the Bull of the Sky, who conquers at will,
Who lives on the essence of every god,
Who eats their entrails,
Even those who come with their bodies full of magic, from the Island of Fire.
The King is one equipped,
Who assembles his spirits.

Unas devours his fathers and mothers, he eats the magic of the gods and 'summons his helpers' in order to do so, in order to achieve the initiatory goal of becoming 'A Great Power who has Power over the Powers.' And if that isn't a vestigial initiation from a much earlier time resulting in the acquisition of spirit allies from them Otherworld then I don't know what is.

East Wall
1 Twenty three Snake Spells: Utts. 277 – 299
2 Acquiring a Ferryboat, Becoming Sokar: Utt. 300
3 Crossing to the Father God: Utt. 301

Again we see a broad directionality of increasing divinity and increasing 'Horusness' or 'aliveness' as we move further out of the pyramid and back toward the wider world. If this were a journey intended for the soul of the deceased king to undertake once he had been interred, then surely it would get more 'Osirisish'?

Of particular significance is the up/down-ness of the utterances facing north, as the king goes up to the Imperishable Stars and returns. Food/offerings are also mentioned.

THE ENTRANCE CORRIDOR
West Wall
1 The Encounter with Babi: Utt. 313
2 Ox-Calming Spell: Utt. 314
3 The Voluntary Death: Utt. 315
4 Calling the Celestial Ferryman: Utt. 316
5 Becoming Sobek: Utt. 317

East Wall
1 Becoming the Nau Snake: Utt. 318
2 The Bull-King: Utt. 319
3 Babi, Lord of the Night: Utt. 320
4 The Faithful Companion of Ra: Utt. 321

Four thousand years later, we will never be able to reconstruct the precise ritual intention or design of any of the pyramids or their texts. Nevertheless, in light of the complete absence of interred bodies, the Heb Sed imagery found in the majority of pyramid complexes, the explicit astrotheological journey of ascending to the stars *and returning*, it is hard to argue against Dr Naydler's assertion that a broad ritual shape emerges when you read the PT going from the sarcophagus out, rather than the entrance in. The balance of living/dead imagery also becomes much clearer.

Just as we see in the Vedas, in Sumeria and Polynesia, there is a celestial ascent, a presentation to or union with the stellar gods and then a return to earth.

It is quite clear that the PT is older than their first appearance on the walls of Unas's pyramid. Some of the grammar has even been described as archaic when compared to hieroglyphs that appear in secular use half a century before Unas. Probably the twentieth century's preeminent authority on the Pyramid Age, I. E. S. Edwards, believed that the stellar spells in the Pyramid Texts had an entirely separate origin to the solar spells, and that they eventually merged over time into what we call the Heliopolitan cosmology.

Over the course of the final few reigns of the Old Kingdom, some of the PT motifs change and later pyramids begin to incorporate more contemporaneous language. This happens at the same time as we start to see canopic jars appearing in the pyramids, suggesting they were eventually used for burial. Depending on your point of view, this is further evidence of either an inevitable mutation of cosmologies over time or 'falling away from a purer spiritual practice.' If, as seems likely, the main purpose of the pyramids was as Heb Sed ritual zones, then we may speculate that interring the country's 'conduit' between the physical and spirit realms in these 'magical window areas' could have been triggered by the increasing unrest and invasion Egypt was no doubt experiencing as the Old Kingdom drew to a close. Perhaps it was increasing desperation that required the dead kings to become 'permanent' intermediaries?

In the final dynasties, we begin to see the appearance of a few scattered PT spells appearing in non-royal tombs. These non-royal spells are the ancestors of the so-called Coffin Texts that appear in the First Intermediate Period and Middle Kingdom alongside a democratised 'afterlife for everyone' where Osiris now sits in the Hall of Judgement and determines your posthumous fate. But it is the earlier, slightly more savage magic that is of the most interest to us, as it sheds the best light on the pyramids and rituals that preceded the Pyramid Texts.

SAQQARA

Staying in the same area – indeed it is right next door to Unas – we have the famous Step Pyramid of Djoser, believed to be the earliest one built in stone. Although that sequence is contraindicated by the scientific dating performed at Giza – suggesting that Khufu's pyramid may be the older – the Step Pyramid's association with Djoser and thus the Third Dynasty is not in doubt.

Strange as it may seem to say so, the seven-levelled step pyramid is perhaps the least impressive part of Djoser's complex. The remarkable boundary wall, looking centuries old rather than millennia, is a true wonder of the ancient world. Encircling the boundary wall itself is something perhaps more impressive still.

The 'Dry' Moat

Called a dry moat because there are compartments and other structures within it, a three kilometre long channel encircles (or en-rectangles) Djoser's complex and was only discovered in 1985 by Egyptian archaeologist Nabil Swelim, while examining aerial photography taken during the 1920s. When in use, it would have been forty metres wide and 25 metres deep at its deepest point. Three million tonnes would have been excavated to construct the moat, which is greater than the volume of the Step Pyramid. Parts of it appear to date from the First Dynasty, which is not only astounding in and of itself, but says something important about the sanctity and *longevity* of sanctity for the land within it. One does not pick these locations on a whim. Dr Nabil Swelim observed that the moat does not connect the whole way around, but instead resembles the hieroglyph for 'battlemented enclosure,' and that it resembles other, much smaller, moats around royal tombs from the First Dynasty. You will no doubt observe that it also pulls up right in front of the complex, meaning the king could still ritually arrive by boat. Consensus Egyptology calls this 'the Great Trench' and 'its function seems to have been to make entry into the complex more difficult.' Except of course that it clearly doesn't, and seems rather a lot of work to go toward a moat that is defensively useless. As with the rest of the complex, it is aligned 4.35 degrees off true north. There is no evidence the moat was ever filled with water, but there is not much evidence of anything, as it has never been fully excavated.

The Boundary Wall

When considering Djoser's complex, it needs to be remembered that, according to accepted Egyptological chronology, this is the first instance of large-scale, monumental stone building in the country, and perhaps anywhere on earth. This is like jumping straight from the horse and buggy to Tesla Motors with no intervening steps. The boundary wall is the proverbial space ship the History Channel has been looking for.

Because it is not just its perfectly straight angles, corners and precision masonry, it is also that the boundary wall is a calendar calculating both the observed and actual Sothic cycle. These data have been calculated by the previously referenced astrophysicist, Thomas Brophy, and his co-author, Robert Bauval, in what is assuredly their best book, *Imhotep the African: Architect of the Cosmos*.

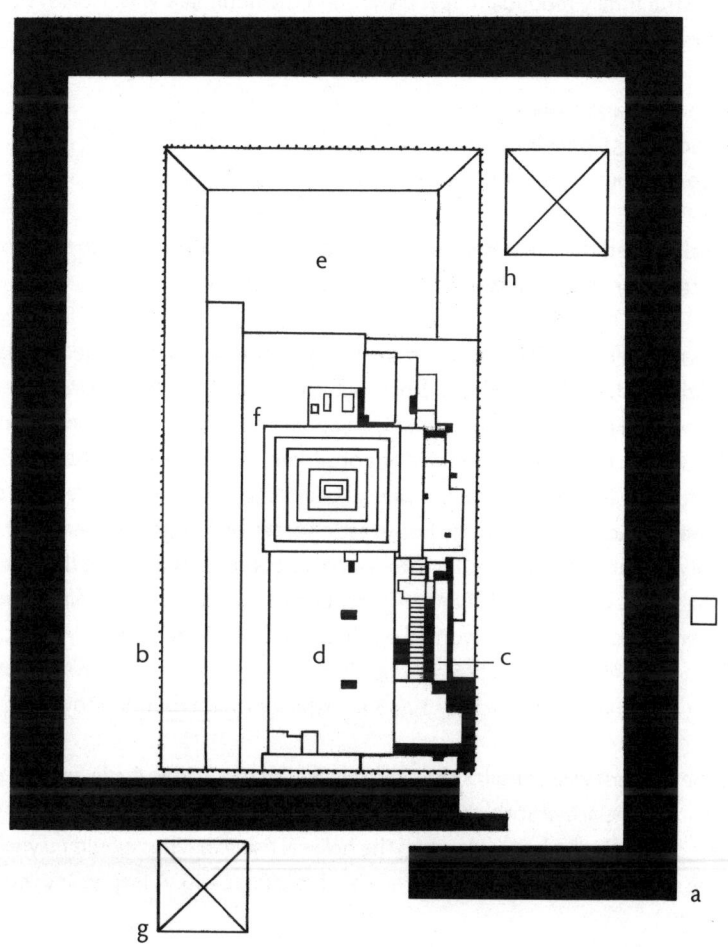

a   Dry moat
b   Boundary wall
c   Heb Sed court
d   Great court
e   North court
f   Pyramid of Djoser
g   Pyramid of Unas
h   Pyramid of Userkaf

fig. 18   Djoser complex

In between the 14 false doors – to which we shall return – there are 4,383 perfectly vertical, structurally redundant, 'panels' around the boundary wall. However, these are not evenly distributed.

- West side: 1,461 panels
- East side: 1,458 panels
- North and south sides: 732 panels each (366 x 2)

Bauval noticed these numbers relate to the Sothic Cycle, which is the number of years it takes for Sirius to return to a heliacal rising position:

[T]his number [1,461] represented the return of the New Year in the 365-day calendar to the heliacal rising of Sirius. But this number was arrived at by assuming an exact ¼ day to add to the 365-day calendar and simply multiplying by four. In other words, this Sothic Cycle was not observed, but calculated. The true or actual length of the Sothic Cycle for the period beginning c. 4226 BCE and ending c. 2767 BCE was, in fact, worked out by British astronomer M. F. Ingham, a fellow of the Royal Astronomical Society. Ingham, who was of course well aware that the length of the Sothic Cycle would change slightly due to the precession of Sirius and the Proper Motion of the star, worked out that the 'Sothic year' (the days it took between two heliacal risings of Sirius) would have been 365.25025 days in that epoch, giving an actual Sothic Cycle of 1,458.5 ... which Ingham rounded to 1,458.

So the western wall contains the civic calculation of a Sothic Cycle and the eastern wall contains the *actual* Sothic Cycle. As for the north and south walls, 366 was the number of days in the leap year when the heliacal rising of Sirius would resynchronise with the solar year. And, of course, there are four times 366. A leap year occurs every four years.

The 1,461:732 ratio of the boundary wall comes close to 2:1 and also creates an angle of 26°30′ which is the same angle used in the descending passage of the Step Pyramid itself, as well as some nearby mastabas. Bauval continues:

If a rectangle is drawn within a circle representing the horizon, such that the corners of the rectangle denote the azimuths of the rising and setting sun at the solstices, then it will have the same nearly 2:1 ratio. From a metaphoric viewpoint, the rectangle would represent the domain of the sun.

As for those 14 false doors? One immediately thinks of the wax/wane moon phases but also the number of pieces that Osiris was split into. It was Isis, encoded everywhere in the rest of the wall, that restored him to wholeness; a cosmic event that was no doubt re-enacted *within* her very boundary.

Not bad for the earliest stone structure in all of Ancient Egypt? It is at Saqqara that the inevitable fixation on the physical looks the most absurd. Just as the construction skills need to come from somewhere, so too must the story the Egyptians were telling in stone. We see here at the beginning of Egypt the lunisolar calendar we find in Egypt and Harappa, with the addition of some exciting local flavour.

Inside the Boundary Walls

The pyramid, the boundary wall and the dry moat are all aligned 4.35 degrees off true north for reasons that will become clear. However the Saqqara site is itself evidently part of the wider Early Dynastic building project only now emerging into view. It is situated at the apex of an isosceles triangle with its base points at Letopolis – described above as home to astronomer priests – and Heliopolis, home of the ancient sun cult. The apex angle bisects at 16.5 degrees, which is also the angle of the sides of the Step Pyramid itself. Giza, Letopolis and Heliopolis also form a 'perfect' right-angled triangle in this same system.

'Sun cult' only tells part of the story of Heliopolis, as the high priest was known as the 'Chief of the Astronomers' and is depicted wearing a mantle covered in stars. In Egyptian cosmology the stars are rarely more important than during their heliacal rising, which is a solar action, obviously. Thus it seems likely that the Victorian antiquarian obsession with assuming everything is a solar cult underemphasises how interconnected these spiritual systems really are. (It is also worth remembering that our sun is, of course, a star.) The site for Djoser's complex was selected by Imhotep, one of the few sages of antiquity we can be reasonably certain actually existed. According to Christian Jacq, Imhotep was very likely an initiate of the Heliopolis school. Pieces of a wider plan beyond a hypothesised burial of an absolute monarch creep into view.

The enclosed space within the boundary walls continues their precision astrotheology. The space inside is unquestionably the site of Djoser's Heb Sed festival. Once again, we find no evidence of a burial anywhere, and all the depictions in the complex and pyramid relate instead to the festival. The site contains robing chambers, chapels for the various regional gods that would 'visit' for the festival, it houses a coronation dais and the large open courtyard for the king's ritual running race.

There are two parallel rows of 24 columns inside the complex, running for 54 metres. 24 was the number of hours in an Egyptian day. The rows of columns also form

18 niches each side, for a total of 36. This is the number of decans in the sky calendar. Whilst it is commonly assumed that the decans first appeared in the Middle Kingdom, the presence of the number 36 in what Bauval refers to as 'Cape Canaveral in stone,' right at the very beginning of the Dynastic Project suggests otherwise. We return to Jane B. Sellers:

> By 2100 BCE, thirty-six star gods had been set in relation to this civil calendar and these gods of the heaven appeared on coffin lids, each god occupying a specific position on the chart or sky clock for 10-day intervals, or one tenth of the sky. It has been determined that the stars chosen for this purpose occupied the zone roughly parallel to, but south of, the path of the sun, and that of these 36 decans, the star god Sahu-Orion, along with Sothis (our Sirius), was the most important.

Putting some further context around the implications of the antiquity of the decans is Jake Stratton-Kent in his splendid *The Testament of Cyprian the Mage*:

> It is still impossible to improve on the succinct comments of Frances Yates: Into the Hellenic astrology which is the background of the philosophical Hermetica an Egyptian element had been absorbed, namely the thirty-six decans ... [which] were really Egyptian sidereal gods of time who had become absorbed in the Chaldean astrology and affiliated to the zodiac. Thus the decans originate with the ancient Egyptians, whose year began with the heliacal rising of the star Sothis (Sirius) in Cancer. The corresponding decan was attributed to Sothis, who 'looked back' at the decans to come.[...]
>   Initially independent of the zodiac, in the Ptolemaic era these decans were assimilated to the Greco-Babylonian system: they have been a feature of Western astrology ever since.

We will return to the idea in the chapters to follow, but if we find the decans, still a feature of western magic to this day, at the very beginning of the Dynastic project, then their ultimate origins are, in fact, far older than the remains of King Djoser, wherever he was buried.

Djoser's Step Pyramid

If it turns out that the pyramid is much older than the boundary wall I would not be the least bit surprised. The condition of the structure is positively ruinous. My suspicion is some of its subterranean components and bottom layers are probably predynastic and date to the time of the construction of the dry moat. First Dynasty pottery has been found in abundance inside the complex and in the pyramid itself.

The base of the Step Pyramid is almost square but not quite, and is slightly offset from the exact centre of the enclosure. Its subterranean features are quite impressive, dominated by a large vertical shaft and a veritable warren of corridors and niches. (Hawass estimated the total length of the corridors to be over five kilometres.) At the base of the large shaft is a granite room called the 'burial chamber,' although there are no remains to make this case. It appears that this room had a ceiling or at least part of a ceiling of limestone blocks decorated with stars. These were removed or destroyed during one of the structure's ill-advised 'reconstructions.'

In a more complete state, the Step Pyramid would have had seven tiers, very likely corresponding to the seven stars of Ursa Major. There is a good chance the pyramid was built in several different stages, which would be in keeping with a non-funerary interpretation, and would explain the various dimensional offsets.

As previously mentioned, its sides are at an angle of 16.5 degrees. Looking to the north, this means that the curious room known as the Serdab, appended to the side of the pyramid, is also at 16.5 degrees. The north-facing wall of the Serdab has two eyeholes, behind which peeped out a statue of Djoser, staring for eternity at a point in the northern sky 4.35 degrees off from truth north at a height of 16.5 degrees – right at Alkaid, reaching its 16.5 degree azimuth just as Sirius was rising in the east.

Alkaid

Thinking in cosmic terms, the 'Pole Star' is more of a job title than an actual star. Due to precessional effects, the star closest to the pole changes over the millennia. During the Old Kingdom, the Pole Star was Alkaid. Curiously, it gets its name from the Arabic *qāʾid bināt naʿsh*, meaning 'Leader of the Daughters of the Bier.' There is an enigmatic suggestion of a survival of the esoteric function of Alkaid given the bier's association with royal funerals in Ancient Egypt.

GIZA

Little commented upon, but probably quite important, is the geology of the Giza Plateau. It is comprised mostly of limestone, gently sloping southeast toward the Nile. The limestone itself is the remains of a reef that grew in the area when it was covered by the ocean around 50 million years ago. Rainfall or underground tributaries, when combined with carbon dioxide, erode limestone and tend to create large tunnel and cave systems when left alone for a few hundred millennia or so.

Tunnel and cave systems at Giza are attested to from the age of Herodotus, through the first Victorian Egyptologists, down to seismic surveys in the late twentieth century, until the age of Hawass, who had a tendency to build padlocked metal gates over their entrances and even, in one instance, allegedly concreted entirely over one. It seems to me that the best answer to why, and potentially when, Giza became a sacred site associated with the Dead is to be found in its geology. A tunnel and cave system on the side of the river where the sun sets becomes both a map of the Underworld and the literal underworld. In fact, one of the original names for the Giza area, Rostau, means 'Mouth of the Passages,' which is highly suggestive of subterraneity. I expect that a rational, sober analysis of subsurface Giza would show ritual use stretching back perhaps tens of millennia, as its association with the afterlife is attested to right back to the Predynastic Era. This may go some way to explaining the dramatically different dates for objects and structures found on the plateau: yes, it was a hugely important site in the Old Kingdom's Fourth Dynasty, but its cultic significance is vastly older still. It may even be that we could find the progression from tunnel/cave use, to *shaped* tunnels/caves, to *built* tunnels/rooms that would provide a more coherent chronology. As to how they managed to select a sacred site that sits at the cross-section of the most land anywhere on earth, thousands of years in the past, that will keep for a subsequent chapter.

Giza's spiritual significance was not just a domestic affair. We have already seen that the twenty tonne Predynastic sarcophagus in the so-called Osiris Shaft would have had to have been cut and transported from somewhere outside of Africa, but it also appears Giza was high on the ancient world's spiritual tourism map. What were previously called 'workers' villages' are now believed to have been accommodation for highborn – and in some cases *foreign* – visitors. Travel was perilous during the Old Kingdom and it is unlikely to have been motivated by the desire to rubberneck some distant tyrant's pointy tomb. A magical motive, such as the conferring of immortality in life as promised by the later Mystery traditions, is more likely. The evidence of foreign dignitaries is a better match for the idea that the Giza Plateau was known as a sacred site for a very long time. These new findings also mean Egyptologists are now, once again, missing a Fourth Dynasty workforce of tens of thousands.

Understanding that the wider site, rather than individual structures, had some sort of ritual significance allows us to begin to make sense of some of the dozens and dozens of mathematical interrelationships between the various pyramids, temples, and so on, because these are certainly in evidence. From the ratios of different side lengths, to the shadows cast on certain days, to 'invisible' lines connecting various points on the pyramid, the golden angle is everywhere found. In *The Sphinx Mystery*, Robert Temple writes:

The mysterious plan of the Plateau of Giza ... is one of the most fantastic survivals of ancient Egypt, in some ways more remarkable than the pyramids themselves, since it actually embodies them within a larger scheme so complex and ingenious that it reminds me of a modern computer program run amok. And it is a plan not only in two dimensions, but three as well ... [T]he Sphinx and the Giza pyramids have a precise and direct relation with one another, a relation so specific that the monuments mutually determine one another's position on the plateau. They form a unified complex.

Just some of the several dozen golden angles connecting the largest Giza structures are as follows. Temple again:

- Great Pyramid: all four corners, the top and three midpoints
- Pyramid of Chephren: all four corners, the top and two midpoints
- Pyramid of Mycerinus: two corners, the top, and one midpoint
  The decrease in number of the salient midpoints in the progression 3, 2, 1 matches the degree of hierarchical size of each pyramid in the group.
  We must not forget that the Great Pyramid itself is full of golden angles and golden triangles and golden sections... the commencement of the Grand Gallery inside the Great Pyramid is, for instance, determined by a golden triangle. The Ascending Passage and the Descending Passage inside the Great Pyramid are both golden slopes, each at the golden angle of 26° 33′ 54″ to the horizontal plane ... The King's Chamber has multiple golden angles determining its size and shape.

Those familiar with R. A. Schwaller de Lubicz's Symbolist interpretation of Egyptian thought, based principally on the angles and measurements of New Kingdom temples, should not be surprised to see these same numbers and ratios appearing in the much earlier Old Kingdom. The extremity of their expression at Giza, however, is unsurpassed elsewhere and is particularly significant given how long the plateau has been a sacred site. These are old mathematics indeed. Or, as Temple writes:

Golden angles, golden sections, golden triangles, and the Fibonacci series of numbers generated from the golden section permeated Egyptian culture for millennia and were a full-fledged priestly obsession for all those thousands of years.

To a magician's eye, the ritual purpose is clear: 'resurrection mathematics' combined with an earthly map of the stars associated with achieving posthumous immortality, specifically Orion, built into a landscape that is simultaneously a map of the afterlife and the *actual* afterlife. That is certainly something to undertake treacherous foreign travel to experience!

Beyond the pyramids and the Sphinx, Giza is an archaeologically rich location. There are the three Valley temples and the so-called Sphinx Temple beside what would have been the Nile shoreline during the Old Kingdom. There are the ruined 'mortuary' temples at the bases of the three pyramids. There are also hundreds and hundreds of Predynastic, Early Dynastic and Old Kingdom tombs, as well as many more burials from much later on in Egyptian history, right up until the Classical Age. Given the area's astounding antiquity and its potent magical ability to ensure one's survival beyond physical death, it is not hard to understand Giza's enduring appeal as the necropolis of choice for the discerning Egyptian.

The Great Pyramid

The Great Pyramid was the tallest structure on earth for over four thousand years, until the building of Lincoln Cathedral in 1311. For most of recorded history it was known that Khufu was not buried inside it. This is because Herodotus, the 'father of history,' explicitly told us so in the fifth century BCE:

> The pharaohs Cheops and Chephren were not buried in the pyramids that bear their names, but were rather buried elsewhere on the Giza Plateau, in their vicinity.

This is from a man who is often the only source of information for events that happened in the Classical World in the two centuries prior to his life. As nineteenth century Egyptology began to bear out some of his previously dismissed claims about New Kingdom Egypt, we hold out hope that one day this shoe – or Grecian sandal – will also drop.

North to south and east to west, the Great Pyramid sits at the cross section of the most land above sea level anywhere on earth. Its perfectly flat base covers an area greater than 6 football pitches and it points north to within 500th of a degree, an architectural feat unmatched for millennia.

It is composed of more than two million stones, all of different shapes and sizes, some of them over 70 tonnes in weight. Over the course of Khufu's twenty year reign, workers operating in 12 hour shifts, 365 days a year, would have to quarry, carve and fit one block every two and a half minutes. By comparison, Teotihuacan, built thousands of years later, is half the size of the Great Pyramid and took 150 years to complete. In all of history, there was nothing like it and there has been nothing like it since.

As previously mentioned, it is impossible for this 'tomb' to have been completed in Khufu's lifetime, and the scientific dating suggests it is centuries too early to have landed in his approximate reign. Nevertheless, and however much this may disappoint some readers, it shows clear evidence of having been built by humans. To my eyes, the tremendous attention to astronomic and geographic detail, as well as the resonant properties discussed below, entirely rule out the 'pyramid as tomb' theory and the earlier dating gives us a more satisfying solve for the lack of evidence for a large, onsite workers village; a structure built over several centuries needs fewer workers at any one time, and if they were building at an even earlier date than expected then it becomes less likely that such evidence would have survived.

Inevitably it is a retired civil engineer, Henri Houdin, and not an Egyptologist, who has perhaps come closest to a satisfactory solve for how the Great Pyramid was constructed. In 1999, he encountered the preposterous ramp theory and quickly realised it was absurd. Houdin proposed a modified spiral ramp theory that had multiple 'chambers' on the corners of the Great Pyramid that allowed for some of the very large stones to be turned. Although not perfect – some of the larger stones would struggle to be turned even with the corner 'chambers' – the theory has some hard scientific data to support it. A 1980 thermal image of the Great Pyramid shows some low density areas that broadly match Houdin's 'internal ramp' layout.

Houdin's theory has some compelling implications for the existence of additional rooms or chambers within the Great Pyramid. Firstly, there are the obvious 'corner chambers' that would have been covered with outer stones. Secondly, according to Houdin's architect son, Jean-Pierre – who built extensive 3D models supporting the theory and expounded it in *The Secret of the Great Pyramid* – there is a secondary entrance into the King's Chamber at the opposite end of the wall which houses the 'main' entrance. For the rest of the chamber, you cannot fit a razor blade between the stones. At the western end of the north wall, however, it is possible to fit 'a credit card' between one large block and the adjacent blocks, implying this particular stone can freely move. This theoretical hidden chamber would align exactly north, in keeping with the architectural style of 'earlier' pyramids. It may also have provided a means for getting the sarcophagus into the King's Chamber, as it is too large to have made it through the existing entranceway.

Built by humans though it was, the Great Pyramid remains truly wyrd, and the King's Chamber is especially so. In his provocative *The Giza Power Plant: Technologies of Ancient Egypt*, master craftsmen and aeronautics engineer Christopher Dunn suggests that the structure was a chemical and microwave-based power generator at the centre of some ancient national grid. While the hypothesis is entirely lacking in supporting evidence, Dunn nevertheless presents some compelling scientific data that are a better match for an 'immortality ritual centre' hypothesis, particularly when the astrotheology and golden angles are taken into account. Principally, these are the obvious harmonic and resonant qualities of the Grand Gallery and King's Chamber. On his website, gizapower.com, Dunn writes:

> The details of the Grand Gallery are extremely important and have no parallel in any other structure on Earth. Its geometric design predicts that sound originating within its space is focused through a passageway past the Antechamber and into the granite complex known as the King's Chamber. This phenomena (sic) has been noted by musicians, acoustical engineers, military scientist and laypeople alike.

The King's Chamber continues this resonant theme. Firstly, it is effectively free-standing within the larger pyramid structure, with a five inch support gap between its granite walls and the surrounding limestone, as well as a floor – which unsurprisingly 'rings' when you walk on it – built atop a 'corrugated' limestone base. Returning to Christopher Dunn, again from his website:

> The acoustic qualities of the design of the upper chambers of the Great Pyramid have been referenced and confirmed by numerous visitors since the time of Napoleon, whose men discharged their pistols at the top of the Grand Gallery and noted that the explosion reverberated into the distance like rolling thunder.
>
> Striking the coffer inside the King's Chamber results in a deep bell-like sound of incredible and eerie beauty, and it has been a practice over the years for the Arab guides to demonstrate this resonating sound to the tourists they guide through the pyramid. This sound was included on Paul Horn's album, (*Inside The Great Pyramid*, Mushroom Record, Inc., L.A., CA) After being advised of the significant pitch produced by the coffer when it has been struck, and the response of the chamber to this pitch, Horn brought along a device which would give him the exact pitch and frequency. Horn tuned his flute to this tone which was emitted, which turned out to be 'A' 438 cycles per second. In a fascinating booklet about his experiences at the Great Pyramid, Horn describes phenomena concerning the acoustic qualities of the inner chambers.
>
> 'The moment had arrived. It was time to play my flute. I thought of Ben Peitcsh from Santa Rose, California (a man who had told Mr. Horn about the pitch of the coffer) and his suggestions to strike the coffer. I leaned over and hit the inside with the fleshy part of the side of my fist. A beautiful round tone was immediately

produced. What a resonance! I remember him also saying when you hear that tone you will be 'poised in history that is ever present.' I took the electronic tuning device I had brought along in one hand and struck the coffer again with the other and there is was - 'A' 438, just as Ben predicted. I tuned up to this pitch and was ready to begin. (The album opens with these events so that you can hear all of these things for yourselves.)'

And, indeed, the sound, which Paul Horn brought to my living room, was most fascinating. One can understand why many people develop feelings of reverence when exposed to this sound, for it has a most soothing effect on the nerves. For this alone, the record was worth the price.

'Sitting on the floor in front of the coffer with the stereo mike in the centre of the room, I began to plan, choosing the alto flute to begin with. The echo was wonderful, about eight seconds. The chamber responded to every note equally. I waited for the echo to decay and then played again. Groups of notes would suspend and all come back as a chord. Sometimes certain notes would stick out more than others. It was always changing. I just listened and responded as if I were playing with another musician. I hadn't prepared anything specific to play. I was just opening myself to the moment and improvising. All of the music that evening was this way - totally improvised. Therefore, it is a true expression of the feelings that transpired.' After noting the eerie qualities of the King's and Queen's Chambers, Paul Horn went out onto the Great Step at the top of the Grand Gallery to continue his sound test. The Grand Gallery, he reported, sounded rather flat compared with the other Chambers. He heard something remarkable at this time. He heard the music he was playing coming back to him clearly and distinctly from the King's Chamber. The sound was going out into the Grand Gallery and was being reflected through the passageway and reverberating inside the King's Chamber!

It is likely that the sarcophagus in the King's Chamber had even more potent resonant effects compared to those that are observed today. According to Robert Temple, up until the middle of the nineteenth century, a small hammer was attached by a rope to the sarcophagus, allowing visiting Victorian tourists to gently strike it and experience the reverberations. This ended one evening when a disgruntled local broke in and smashed one of its corners, feeling its vibratory effects were decidedly 'un-Muslim.'

Above the King's Chamber are the so-called 'relief chambers,' described as such because their speculative purpose was to relieve the weight of the stones above the King's Chamber. However, they are structurally redundant and only relieve their own weight, as the cantilever roof of the King's Chamber does all the actual relieving. These 70 tonne granite slabs must have had another purpose. Given the hundreds of miles these slabs travelled from their quarry, granite's resonant properties and the spaces between each slab, we may speculate these also formed a deliberate part of the auditory/magical ritual space.

That the dimensions of the Great Pyramid reflect the circumference and polar radius of the earth have been known since Napoleon's visit, having been first calculated by Edme-François Jomard in 1798. Dividing its perimeter by twice its height also yields 3.144, remarkably close to π. What looks like redundant complexity in the 'pointy tomb' theory makes complete sense in the context of the wider ritual area: building a microcosm of the earth inside an astronomically aligned, golden numbered, harmonic, sky/ground map.

There is tantalising evidence, discussed below, that the ritual significance of the Giza Plateau – including its planetary dimensions – lasted at least into the New Kingdom in the form of the Book of the Dead, whereupon it just might have influenced the creation of the Hermetica and the Greek Magical Papyri, and thus the western magical tradition. First we must briefly examine the king who gave the structure its current name, Khufu.

Leaving aside some misspelled 'builders' graffiti' of dubious origin found in the 'relief chambers,' there is nothing inside the Great Pyramid that connects it to Khufu. Outside is slightly different. The causeway connecting the Valley Temple to the 'Mortuary Temple' at the base of the Great Pyramid contains a partial depiction of Khufu, dressed in his Heb Sed regalia; a potent indicator as to the function of the pyramid during this particular Fourth Dynasty king's reign. The 'Mortuary Temple' situated at the base of the pyramid contains a large courtyard which Dr Naydler, probably correctly, believes was the site of Khufu's Heb Sed ritual. (Based on the *in situ* evidence of a rope pulley system, Temple believes Khufu is actually interred in a subterranean chamber underneath this courtyard, presenting us with the tantalising possibility that his tomb remains intact.) Given the lack of evidence of a posthumous relationship tying Khufu to the Great Pyramid, and the sole causeway depiction of him in Heb Sed garb, and Herodotus's assertion he was buried not in but near the pyramid, and the open air courtyard as part of his 'Mortuary Temple,' the evidence invites us to assert that this particular king – unquestionably powerful and ruling over an Old Kingdom at the peak of its influence – conducted his Heb Sed ritual at a pre-existing sacred site, but did not actually build the area's most prominent structure. Given the potency of the magic baked into the Giza Plateau, he cannot be faulted for this bold decision.

Returning to the idea that the Great Pyramid was the preeminent structure in an already profoundly magical landscape, we have hints of its ritual significance showing up in the New Kingdom's Book of the Dead, universally acknowledged as a storehouse of at least *some* of the same spells found in the Old Kingdom's Pyramid Texts. In particular, we have references to a 'secret map of the earth' at Rostau (Giza). Referring to the Book of the Dead, Temple writes in *The Sphinx Mystery*:

> There are some portions of the Book of the Dead material that appear to refer to Giza. But the two most important texts about Giza are two sections of the earliest actual 'book' of the underworld, which is now known as The Book of the Am-Duat, or The Book of What Is in the Netherworld. This was not its original title. In the text itself, its original title is given as The Book of the Hidden Chamber. [...]
>
> The Book of the Hidden Chamber ... commences its description of Giza with a picture of a descending passage beside which stands the goddess Neith wearing the Crown of the North ... It seems reasonable to assume, therefore, that this picture refers symbolically to a northern entrance. Because the three main pyramids at Giza all have descending passages with northern entrances, and since the description is meant to be of Giza, it does not seem to be stretching a point to conclude that at least the commencement of the strange illustrations of 'the passages of Rostau' in The Book of the Hidden Chamber begin with that simplest of things, the entrance to a major pyramid. Presumably the Great Pyramid was intended.

From the Middle Kingdom's Twelfth Dynasty, we have a spell from The Book of Two Ways which makes the ritual continuity even more explicit:

> I have passed by the roads of Rostau by water and on land; these roads are those of Osiris; they are in the sky. If a man knows a Spell for going down into them, he will be like a god directed by the followers of Thoth. He will indeed go down to every heaven to which he desires to descend. But if he knows not this Spell for passing on these roads, he will fall prey to the tribunal of the dead [...]

In the same Middle Kingdom text we read that 'the secret figure of the earth' is on the surface at Giza, above the hidden chamber of Sokar. This seems fairly good evidence that not only were the dimensions of the Great Pyramid deliberately built around an understanding of our planet's dimensions, but also that an awareness of this deliberate dimensionality passed into the subsequent Middle and New Kingdoms.

After five thousand years, we may only speculate as to the form of the rituals performed at and within the Great Pyramid, but its astronomical and planetary alignments, its resonant qualities, its deliberate use of stone, its international interest and its precision mathematics all point to them being of huge significance. We may look askance at some of the ritual content via the utterances of the Pyramid Texts. Although they arrived later, their shamanic undertones point to their antiquity and some modified form of them was presumably deployed at Giza. Heading forward in time, we see the fragmentary survival of this 'stellar immortality magic' in the texts of the Middle Kingdom, then the New Kingdom and from there – in an even more fragmentary form – in the Greek Magical Papyri and thus into the western tradition.

Khafre and Menkaure's Pyramids

If the pyramids are tombs, it seems clear that Fourth Dynasty kings did not suffer from penis envy. Remarkable though these structures are, they are quite literally in the shadow of their neighbour and tend to be ignored. From a ritual perspective, a few points are worth noting:

- Khafre's pyramid contains a granite sarcophagus with 90° angles so perfect you would be forgiven for thinking they were machined. They certainly were not constructed with dolerite pounders. (Menkaure's was lost at sea, bound for London.)
- Both pyramids have Valley Temples and 'Mortuary Temples' with open-air courts, suggestive of further Heb Sed activity.
- As Robert Bauval noted in the early 1990s, their comparative size and location matches both the brightness and location of Orion's belt stars.
- There were several kings between Khufu and Menkaure, so it is almost impossible to suggest 'pointy tombs' were a family affair.

The Sphinx

It is now commonly known that, thanks to John Anthony West and Dr Robert Schoch, the erosion patterns on the body of the Sphinx and its enclosure have been subjected to heavy, vertical, water erosion, in addition to the horizontal wind erosion one would expect to find in an area that was desertified by the time of the Old Kingdom. This has led some people to conjecture that the entire Giza complex dates back at least 8,000 or 9,000 years; the last time Egypt was subjected to sustained, heavy rainfall; and that the Sphinx itself – which clearly had its head recarved at least once – was originally a lion, facing the heliacal rising of Leo on the spring equinox. As we have seen, the few pieces of scientific dating performed in the Great Pyramid or the Osiris Shaft do not bear out the suggestion that the entire site is that old.

The necessity to hang so much importance on a single structure has lessened with the discovery of Göbekli Tepe; we now have incontrovertible proof that our Palaeo-lithic ancestors had a sophisticated megalithic cosmology prior to the development of towns or agriculture. In a hypothesis where the Giza Plateau is some sort of long-used, Otherworld 'ritual arena,' it would not be unexpected to find that some of the site's natural features had been shaped during the Palaeolithic, and then successively reshaped in the subsequent millennia before it was eventually covered by the desert sands. Indeed, one proposed 'solve' for Dr Schoch's geological evidence is Robert Temple's suggestion that the Sphinx's original shape was a jackal, Anubis, and not a lion, which is a better match for an Otherworld ritual space given the association of the jackal and the Dead. Temple's explanation for the (vertical) water damage is that the natural erosive properties of dew working on porous limestone – the geological counter-hypothesis to the 'ancient rain' theory – was made worse by the regular dredging of the 'Sphinx Moat.' He is probably correct about the existence of the moat, which we will discuss below, but the vertical water erosion looks to the eyes of hundreds of geologists to be the result of sustained rainfall. I propose the original Sphinx, in whatever form, was originally shaped out of the limestone during a wetter climatic period, and may even have been surrounded by water during the inundation. We know the Nile Valley was inhabited at this time, and we know that contempora-neous rock-shaping and megalithic construction were occurring elsewhere on earth, so the suggestion is not unreasonable. Then, sometime before or during the site's ritu-al use in the Early Dynastic and Old Kingdom periods, the Sphinx was a jackal, sitting in an artificial lake. The evidence for this?

Firstly, as most pet owners will tell you, the body shape and pose is much more canine than leonine. Once you have had this pointed out to you, it is hard to see it any other way. Remember that, over the course of Egyptian civilisation, this culture carved hundreds of thousands, if not millions, of jackals and lions. We are not talking about the first day of art school here.

Secondly, the Sphinx is barely visible from ground level as it has been carved into the bedrock. You will struggle to find other examples of this sort of 'hiding away' of monumental objects. It rather defeats the point. (Doubly so if you still believe that the Fourth Dynasty kings 'picked prominent locations' for their 'tombs' so that every-one who saw them 'would be in awe of their power.') There is also the small matter of the narrow, insalubrious alleyway between the Sphinx Temple and the adjacent Valley Temple of Khafre. There is no other entrance into the Sphinx enclosure, forcing one to picture high priests and kings squeezing down it and scrambling over what Robert Temple suspects is the remains of a sluice gate. The absence of doorways into what we currently call the Sphinx Temple, plus a possible sluice gate, speaks strongly of the sort of enclosure you would need to retain the Nile floodwater that we know made it to the eastern side of the temple during the inundation.

Finally, given the very likely situation that the Giza complex and its magico-spiritual purpose survived in some of the spells of the Middle and New Kingdoms, it is strange that there appears to be no mention of the Sphinx in the Pyramid Texts. Well, there isn't if you are looking for a king-headed lion, or even just a lion. But if you are looking for a 'jackal lake' or Anubis guarding a city of the Dead, or a giant Anubis beside a causeway, then you are in luck. Consider Utterance 268.

> This King washes himself when Ra appears...
> Horus accepts him beside him,
> He purifies this King in the Jackal Lake,
> He cleanses this King's double in the Lake of the Netherworld.

This looks suspiciously like a ritual bathing designed to mirror a nonphysical purification, the cleanings of the king's 'double' in the Netherworld. There is more than a little of the Classical Mystery traditions in it.

In Utterance 301, when the king addresses Horus, the rising sun, as 'O great float-user,' we find:

> Cleanse the King. Make the King bright in this, your Jackal Lake, O Jackal,
> In which you cleanse the gods.
> You have power, you have effectiveness, O Horus, Lord of the Green Stone!
> Four times – Two green falcons.

Again, we are presented with fragmentary glimpses of a wider magical system designed to secure immortality through some combination of ground-based star maps, the stars themselves, the sacred use of stone and the Dead.

Magicians familiar with Eliphas Lévi's Four Powers of the Sphinx are earnestly encouraged to seek out Robert Temple's *The Sphinx Mystery*. I experience a mischievous sense of delight at the very real possibility that, from out behind the overly serious, Neoplatonic silliness of the Four Powers of the Sphinx so beloved of the Victorians, whisper the true voices of wisdom, that of the Dead themselves.

'High' Technology

Suggestions that the Old Kingdom had access to machine tools, electric lighting, microwave energy or any of the other examples of high technology you are likely to see on cable television, as with any other claim in this book, have an obligation of proof. And there is none. Nevertheless, a satisfactory solve is required for:

- The fact that copper tools cannot shape granite at all, let alone to a precision of 1/1000th of an inch.
- The sheer size of some of the stones used in the Old Kingdom, particularly at Giza.
- The structurally redundant curved corners in the Valley Temples.
- The use of 'marshmallow stones,' such as those found in South America, that fit with no gaps between them and seem to 'pillow' out.
- The existence of hundreds of perfectly shaped, Early Dynastic vases and bowls made of gneiss – one of the hardest stones in existence – or the similarly hard statues of Old Kingdom rulers utterly devoid of toolmarks.
- And finally the simple rapidity of the construction projects.

Since the Iron Age, and in particular since the Industrial Revolution, western culture has laboured under a 'metallic bias.' Technology means the precision manipulation of metals. But the Old Kingdom was the inheritor and ultimate exemplar of a reverence for stone that stretched back thousands of years. Mastery of the earth and heavens was achieved and publicly demonstrated through the manipulation of stone, not metal. The evidence for this stone 'technology' abounds:

- The resonant quality of the sarcophagus in the King's Chamber, & the chamber itself.
- The mildly radioactive quality of the dacite sarcophagus (dating to the Predynastic era), important enough to import the mineral from outside Africa. More extreme levels of radioactivity are found elsewhere on the plateau. Ioannis Liritzis, Robert Temple's co-researcher and a nuclear physicist in his own right, observed that the 'magazines' inside Khafre's Valley Temple are so radioactive that, 'any priests working in this temple would certainly have contracted leukaemia within twenty years.' It was access to these 'magazines' that required Robert Temple to have the lock broken on the barred gate as no one had been inside for decades.
- The optical effects of alabaster and other deliberate combinations of granite, limestone, etc within the temples and pyramids. Khafre's causeway and Valley Temple both make extensive use of alternating alabaster and red granite blocks. Temple describes the effect in *Egyptian Dawn*:

Within the Valley Temple, there is a surviving enclosed stairway leading to the roof, which is of course locked and almost never entered by anyone. At first, when I went up and down this stairway I assumed that its walls were of limestone. But then I became suspicious. I pressed my torch against the wall and, sure enough, the stone round the point glowed with a golden light ... [O]riginally this enclosed stairway was a beautiful sparkling white, and if flaming torches were carried up it, a golden effulgence would have followed the bearer on all sides.

- The alabaster used in the Sphinx Temple and Valley Temple does not come from the Hawara Quarry. It is made of stalactite that can only have formed inside limestone caves; caves that one would expect to find under a limestone plateau. The significance of this is often overlooked. As Temple observes, this means that during the Early Dynastic and Old Kingdom periods, the Egyptians were enlarging and shaping caverns and removing alabaster from underneath the earth at some scale, as some of the blocks sitting in the Sphinx Temple are several tonnes in weight.

Just as with the astrotheology of the Pyramid Texts and the resonant qualities of some of the chambers of the Great Pyramid, it is impossible to reconstruct exactly what symbolic/literal effects the various stone types were intended to achieve. I am of the opinion that reconstruction is ahistorical and of limited metaphysical value, anyway. What we can say is the evidence for *a specific, megalithic intentionality is incontrovertible.* This should not surprise us as the Old Kingdom was the apogee of thousands of years of astro-megalithic experimentation, stretching back to the beginnings of Laurasia and potentially before. It is our culture's metallic bias that has prevented us from considering the mastery of stone to be of the same level of technological complexity as the mastery of iron.

This same bias has meant the most compelling 'solve' for the Old Kingdom's mastery of stone has received little traction outside the Francophone world. Dr Joseph Davidovits, a French chemical engineer and world expert in modern and ancient concrete, suggests that much of the stone used at Giza could have been poured *in situ.* This sounds unlikely upon first hearing but the precision use of re-agglomerated stone is attested to from the Roman era, where 'wet-setting' cement was used to build the underwater foundations and abutments for hundreds of bridges, as well as the famous occulus roof of Hadrian's Pantheon – which required the cement to get lighter and lighter toward the aperture – and is still structurally sound to this day. One wonders where the Romans got this technology from in the first place?

Davidovits's process is remarkably simple.

- Wadis beside the Nile were enlarged by breaking off chunks of the limestone walls which were then deposited in carved channels in the bases.
- The flooding of the Nile disaggregated the 'wall chunks' piled in these channels into clay and lime, forming a mud with all the fossil shells (lime) at the bottom.
- Natron salt, found in abundance in Egypt, and extra lime from palm ash was added to this liquid, forming a caustic soda that suspends the lime within it.
- More Nile silt, limestone rubble and fossil shells were added, generating a concrete paste that was carried in baskets and poured into wooden 'block enclosures' onsite.

Again, it sounds strange upon first reading but the Romans did something very similar and Dr Davidovits points out that our 'metallic civilisation' has only been aware of geopolymer processes since the 1960s. A geopolymer process provides a number of critical 'solves':

- There is no longer any need for giant ramps and huge workforces to carry near-hundred-tonne blocks. Baskets of concrete poured in situ are faster, and require a much smaller workforce.
- The inundation that would flood the wadi quarries would occur just as the agrarian workforce had nothing else to do but wait for the floodwaters to recede back from their fields, giving access to a sufficient workforce without putting food production at risk.
- Variants of this geopolymer process likely account for the complete absence of toolmarks on statues made of stone that approach diamond in their hardness. They could have come from moulds. The same would apply for the remarkable gneiss vases and other curved objects our 'metallically biased' culture has assumed can only be constructed using machines.
- Being unable to fit even a cigarette paper between separate stones, of wildly different and often frankly bizarre shape, now makes more sense if they were poured into place and then set.

There is some very compelling scientific evidence that Dr Davidovits has come closest to working this problem out. Firstly, there are the intrusions – hair, detritus, plant matter – found in many of the limestone blocks, just as one finds in modern day concrete. Secondly, and – dare I say – incontrovertibly, is a palaeomagnetic study published in volume 43, number 6 (2012) issue of *Europhysics News*. Quoted on Dr Davidovits's own website, is the introduction to the article:

Our paleomagnetic investigation of the two great Egyptian pyramids, Khufu and Khafre, is based on the assumption that if the blocks were made in situ by the geopolymer concrete technique described above, then their magnetic moments would all have been parallel, oriented approximately in the north-south direction. However, if the pyramids were constructed from blocks transported from the nearby quarries, having been rotated randomly during transport and construction, then the directions of their magnetic moments would be oriented randomly.

A majority of the samples – though not all – did show an alignment of magnetic moments, suggesting that the pyramids were at least partially constructed using this technique, in addition to being augmented with nearby natural limestone. These results are expected when dealing with a culture that did use specific stones for specific magical purposes and was willing to import the correct ones, such as Aswan granite or the dacite sarcophagus inside the Osiris Shaft (from who knows where).

In an interview that opens his book, *Why the Pharaohs Built the Pyramids with Fake Stones*, Dr Davidovits remarks:

> Not only the pyramids but other megaliths from antiquity too often present us with the same puzzles: quarries that are always several dozen kilometres away, for example, posing huge transport problems; the problems of carving these enormous blocks of stone in an age when iron is still unknown. The more I think about it, the more absurd I find the idea.

Dr Davidovits's examination of the Rapa Nui geological reports leads him to conclude that the earliest Moai were made using a similar process – recall that the quarries are 'missing' – and it was only the later ones that were carved from the volcanic rock. We are thus left with the compelling possibility that the 'Laurasian footprint' covers both mythology and technology. In his essay on Davidovits, 'The Pyramid Heretic,' the late, lamented Phil Coppens had this to say:

> Davidovits is also convinced that the method of stone making was at the origin of alchemy. The deity specifically linked with Khufu was Khnum, which means 'to bind,' 'to join,' 'to cement,' 'to unite' and which typifies the process of geopolymerisation.
>   Egypt was seen as the birthplace of alchemy, but for Davidovits, it is also the cradle of chemistry. He argues that certain names, such as *mafkat*, which Egyptologists have been unable to translate or explain, are very much 'invented words' – i.e. technical terms – as they described compounds that ancient chemists had con-

structed. It is therefore not 'white powder gold,' as authors like Laurence Gardner have argued.

Davidovits argues that when Imhotep is credited as 'the inventor of the art of constructing with cut stones,' it is actually a mistranslation of the Greek *xeston lithon*, which does not translate as 'cut stone,' but rather means 'the action to polish stone.' For Davidovits, Imhotep is actually the inventor of working with agglomerates, or geopolymers.

It may be overstating it somewhat to call geopolymerisation the 'origin' of alchemy. Since their translation more than a century ago, it has not escaped the notice of esotericists that there is a distinctly alchemical idiom to the Pyramid Texts with their reference to stones, metals and distinct processes of magical transformation. If geopolymersation was used in the Old Kingdom's grand, astrotheological building project it certainly becomes a part of the legend that grew over the millennia into what we now call alchemy.

From earlier cultures, Egypt inherited much of its star lore as well as the sanctity of stone. The innovations she brought to these beliefs were dramatically improved forms of masonry and a calendrical and mathematical sophistication that went unequalled for thousands of years. The magical efficacy of these developments, their consciousness effects, will be explored in later chapters. We may speculate here that entangling one's consciousness with certain stars led to certain 'inspirations/innovations,' which improved the technology of consciousness entanglement, which led to further 'inspirations/innovations.'

Think of it like a cosmic version of runaway climate change.

EXPLICIT ASTROTHEOLOGY

There are a few pieces of explicit astrotheology that potentially tie together the pyramids, the magical formula for stellar immortality and suggest a revised time depth for their first development. Robert Bauval notes that at least three of the pyramids are named after kings-as-stars: Djedefre is a Star in the Sky, Nebka is a Star and in the case of the Step Pyramid, Horus is the Star at the Head of the Sky. When a 12th dynasty pyramidion was discovered in 1900, the head of the Egyptian Antiquities Organisation described its black granite surface as being 'polished like a mirror.' Its eastern face addresses Horakhti, its southern addresses Anubis, its western addresses Osiris-Sokar-Ptah and the northern addresses Sah-Orion. A mirror reflecting the night sky built atop a stone map of the night sky in a country that esotericists know as 'the mirror of heaven.'

Given the broad consensus that pyramids are typologically similar to obelisks in Ancient Egypt, Bauval then examines the symbolism of the *benben* – the tip of the obelisk – in the context of pyramidions. Obelisks are transparently phallic symbols, and 'benben' is very similar to the Ancient Egyptian word for semen. Geb is regularly depicted with an erect phallus, inseminating the star goddess, Nuit, the mother of Osiris.

The magical formula that suggests itself then, is the insemination of the night sky so that the king or operant can be born as an imperishable star, perhaps the commonest refrain of the Pyramid Texts. Consider Utterance 245, where Nuit speaks to Unas:

> *May you split open a place for yourself in the sky,*
> *Among the stars of the sky.*
> *For you are the Lone Star,*
> *The companion of Hu.*
> *Look down upon Osiris*
> *When he gives orders to the spirits.*
> *You stand far above him,*
> *You are not among them and you shall not be among them.*

The immortality formula specifically associated with Nuit's conference of 'stellarisation' continues into the New Kingdom's Books of the Dead. In the case of spell 177, it is almost word-for-word with the previous Utterance.

> [NAME]: *O Nut, Nut. I have cast my father to the earth, with Horus behind me. My wings have grown into those of a falcon, my soul has brought me and its words have equipped me.*
> NUT: *You have opened up your place among the stars of the sky, for you are the Lone Star of the sky; see O [name], fair are the orders which you give to the spirits, for you are a Power;*
> *You will not go hungry, you are not among them and you will not be among them.*
> *See, upon your head as a soul are horns as of a wild bull, for you are a black ram which a white ewe bore, one who sucked from the four teats. The blue-eyed Horus comes to meet you, the red-eyed Horus, violent of power, waits for you. He meets his soul, his messengers go, his couriers run, they come to him who is supported above the West; this one goes from you of whom it is said: 'The god who speaks to the Field of the Gods.'*
> *Your name is vindicated in the presence of the gods, the Ennead raise you up with their hands, the god speaks to the Field of the Gods. Be strong at the door of the kas of the horizon dwellers, for their doors shall be open to you, they shall praise you and you shall have power over them ... they go forth and lift up their faces, so that they see you before the Great God. Min ...*

Your head. Someone stands behind you and you have power; you shall neither perish nor be destroyed, but you shall act among men and gods.

The hypothesis that the pyramid represents the king as a star as well as being the technology that turns him into one would bring the Egyptian pyramids back into alignments with those found in other Laurasian cultures. From Dr Schoch's *Voyage of the Pyramid Builders*:

> The Sumerians celebrated the power of the world mountain to heal the division of earth and sky with rites that rejoined the male and female in a sacred marriage. The temple at the top of the ziggurat housed a bed where priest and priestess made ritual love. Their physical union reconnected the elements separated at the creation of the world and restored the universe's right order.

The graphically sexual nature of some of the utterances of the Pyramid Texts, as well as the inclusion of Egypt's version of the 'separated divine parents' motif, the 'going up and joining' magical journey and the spiritual function of the Heb Sed festival restoring order to the cosmos, mark the Old Kingdom building project out as a distinctively Egyptian variant of a much older motif.

There is a final component of the Early Dynastic/Old Kingdom stellar immortality formula worth examining for its probable early antiquity, and that is the star goddess herself. For such a critical figure in early Egyptian cosmology, there are comparatively few temples to Nuit. One possible reason for this is she is 'too far up' the creation story and is thus more of a 'universal force' than a goddess. There is probably something to this analysis but it is an insufficient explanation on its own. Firstly, she is actively involved in the Pyramid Text formula and there are other divine forces, such as Maat, that had temples.

Further evidence of her antiquity comes from an examination of her role as one part of the 'separation of earth and sky parents' motif. At first glance, the gender reversal of the pairing – having a female sky and male earth – appears to be an outlier in the motif; 'earth mothers' and 'sky fathers' are seemingly more common. Dr Witzel accounts for the variation below:

> The reversed position may be further elucidated by a comparison with Vedic myth. In daytime, the sky arches over the earth, like Father Heaven, stemmed up by Indra from the prostrate Mother Earth. But at night, the situation is reversed: Earth and the primordial hill or rock, on which she rests, have turned upside down and over-

arch the now prostrate Heaven as the 'stone sky' of Iranian, Hawai'ian and Pueblo myth.

Such an interpretation would explain not only the extremely common depiction of Nuit inside coffins but also the numerous instances of Tefnut, a Mother Earth analogue, painted on the inside of sarcophagi. The deceased is in the Underworld/stars, thus the earth is now his or her sky. Tefnut, in addition to her consort, Shu, are the conjoined couple 'the next level up' from Geb and Nuit, suggesting a 'passing back up through the worlds' for the deceased. Recall also that the ritual timings of the Pyramid Texts and royal mummification rituals rely on asterisms such as Orion and Sirius to rise above the horizon, to 'emerge' from the Underworld/sky, from their Mother, Nuit. The Dead are under the earth and also in the stars.

Stone age carvings from Laussel show the same sexual arrangement, with a woman atop and arching over a bearded, prostrate man. From Laussel we also have the more famous sculpture of the 'goddess' holding the moon. It appears that the Mother of Osiris, like her son, was supremely old by the time she made it to Egypt. If she was not always too old for even the very idea of temples, they would have been elsewhere, and have long since turned to dust or been lost to the waves.

In Egypt's Old Kingdom we thus see the most perfect expression of a supremely ancient idea. The spirits – and by extension, humanity – come from, return to and *are* the stars.

All things fear Time, but Time fears the Pyramids.
Ibn Fadlallah al-'Umari

IX   THE TREE OF MANY BRANCHES

Moving into the historical period, several of the most important vectors of Classical Age thinking and practice, and how they relate to the western magical tradition, have been diligently presented. For such information, I commend to you the work of Jake Stratton-Kent, Owen Davies, Stephen Skinner, Peter Grey and Ronald Hutton.

The possibility of survivals through folklore, especially survivals dating back to the Palaeolithic, has been comparatively underexplored. Dr Witzel refers to such survivals as 'grandmother stories' as opposed to 'grandfather stories'; which would be the continuity of official narratives. One example he offers is the Cental European 'nursery story' of the stork delivering a newborn baby from the 'lake of Heaven.' He considers this a survival of the Gondwana motif of the 'well of souls,' meaning it has been with us for up to 50,000 years.

Western magic veers between considering itself either a 'grandmother' survival or a 'grandfather' survival. Certainly, the continuity of the grimoire tradition owes more to Middle Class/grandfather influences, simply by virtue of the cost of printing and the spread of literacy. However, grandmother survivals – almost by definition – are less likely to appear in the historical record and thus suffer from an 'absence of evidence' problem. Viewed in aggregate over the last two thousand years, it would be hard to argue against the suggestion that, by volume, the majority of magical survivals have been grandmother ones, from simple fortune-telling with roasting chestnuts to tying rags onto trees beside wells. Returning to Wendy Doniger's *The Implied Spider*:

The chameleon quality of myth works in opposition to the more monolithic and dogmatic aspects of religion; where myth encourages a wide range of beliefs, dogma would narrow that range. Martin Buber made this point very well indeed:
All positive religion rests on an enormous simplification of the manifold and wildly engulfing forces that invade us: it is the subduing of the fullness of existence. All myth, in contrast, is the expression of the fullness of existence, its image, its sign; it drinks incessantly from the gushing fountains of life. Hence, religion fights myth where it cannot absorb and incorporate it ... It is strange and wonderful to observe how in this battle religion ever again wins the apparent victory, myth ever again wins the real one.
    What Buber says about religion, I would limit to dogma. With that corrective, I think Buber's statement a marvellous testimony to myth's ability to keep open the doors of imagination within the most constricting dogmatic frameworks. It has been said that a language is a dialect with an army. I would say that dogma is a myth with an army.

Even with the measurability challenge inherent in 'grandmother stories,' now that we are in the historical period we may discern a brilliant whorl of mutating motifs tumbling through time – propelled by unseen motivations – toward us. Much estimable and convincing work has been done in the past decade to demonstrate the continuity of western magic's form and function from the Late Classical World into Europe's grimoire tradition. In *Techniques of Solomonic Magic*, a book based on his PhD thesis on that very subject, Stephen Skinner observes:

It is important to realise that the key nomina magia used in the [Greek Magical Papyri] like Sabaoth, IAO endure from the PGM right through to the 20th century grimoires. Although some of the primarily Egyptian *nomina magia* like Bainchōōōch were dropped, the bulk of those taken from Jews in Alexandria survived. The methods such as threatening one spiritual creature with another, or using a phylactery or lamen or floor circle for protection also endured. Very few new methods were introduced although the exact wording of the conjurations changed over time.

Given the strong Egyptian influences on the admittedly-polyglot Greek Magical Papyri, it is interesting to me that we see the same 'bullying one spirit with another' behaviour in the Pyramid Texts, right at the very beginning of Dynastic Egypt, thousands of years before the creation of the PGM. (And close enough in time to Neolithic shamanism to spy its actual origins on the plains of Africa and Eurasia.) Whether there was a continuous, mouth-to-ear continuity between the pyramid complexes of the Old Kingdom and the era of the PGM may well be irrelevant in just the same way the mouth-to-ear continuity of practice between the PGM and us is irrelevant. Skinner again:

> [I]n Europe ... unrelenting Christian persecution of magic has been in force for at least 1,650 years, and before that, selective Roman persecution (but mainly in cases where magic overlapped with treason). Although it is sometimes possible to identify some of the magicians who owned a specific magician's handbook, it is not often possible to identify the passage of techniques and training from one magician to another. The history of magic in Europe therefore has more often been one of rediscovery, each magician reassembling techniques from the books and manuscripts of previous practitioners, rather than direct oral tradition. Under these circumstances it is remarkable that there is such a degree of commonality.

Remarkable though the continuity of ritual is for the practising magician, there is also some continuity of characters. In *Geosophia*, Jake Stratton-Kent provides solid evidence for the survival of specific spirits into the grimoire tradition that go back as far as Classical times, to Archaic Greece and to points beyond. If we can pin certain spirits that still appear in our grimoires to Archaic Greece – admittedly a long time ago – then that brings them into alignment with the motifs and asterisms we have so far explored in this book, instantly adding a few dozen millennia to their true antiquity. For example, we know Astaroth derives from Astarte. And Astarte from Ishtar. And Ishtar from Inanna. Typically we stop there, but how old do you think Inanna is after reading the Eurasian chapter?

EGYPT

Egypt's reputation as the home of magic is as old as the country itself. Even during the Dynastic Era – and throughout the Greek and Roman periods – Egypt was the undisputed originator and master of the magical arts. Historians of western magic typically begin their story with Alexandria. Whilst, as we have seen, it is definitely not the beginning of the story, Alexandria is certainly a crucial pivot point.

The Rise and Fall of Alexandria

A young city by Egyptian standards, Alexandria was founded in 331 BCE by Alexander the Great. The dynasty he installed, the Ptolemies, filled the city's libraries with books from across the Classical world. Skinner notes that it was in Alexandria that the Old Testament was translated into Greek for the first time. What would come to be known of as the Corpus Hermeticum was composed there and then. Mid-twentieth century historian, Bruno H. Stricker believed the Hermetica got its start with an order from Ptolemy I to write down all the priestly wisdom of Egypt. The Greek Magical Papyri – although the documents themselves are Theban – typify the dizzying hybridity of Egyptian spirituality admixed with Jewish, Greek and Mesopotamian thought.

Over the centuries, this admixture has led scholars to declare wildly variant amounts of 'Egyptianness' in the western magical tradition. Prior to the translation of hieroglyphics in the nineteenth century, 'Egyptianness' was probably overemphasised. Today, it is likely to be underemphasised. As an example, the prominence of astrology in Alexandrian magic has been attributed to Greek and Near Eastern influence. Whilst this is probably the case for planetary astrology, I argue in the previous chapter that the decans and prominence of specific asterisms is not only Egyptian, but was present at the very beginning of Egypt. Much of the confusion lies in the fact that variants of the decans and asterisms are *also* found in the Near East. But this merely argues for an earlier date for their first usage; one old enough to have influenced both cultures before they coalesced once more at the mouth of the Nile thousands of years later.

When examining the western magical diaspora, it is important to realise that Alexandria fell several times and the final two times triggered major departures that would go on to combine and recombine over the next thousand years as magical ideas bounced around the Mediterranean like billiard balls. The first of these falls – Roman Alexandria to the Christian Greeks – in 415 CE saw an influx of hermetic ideas back into the Near East and most notably, to the city of Harran, only a few miles from Göbekli Tepe. Gary Lachman describes this vector in *The Quest for Hermes Trismegistus*:

From its origins in Ptolemaic Alexandria to its rediscovery in Renaissance Florence, the Corpus Hermeticum was secretly shuttled across medieval Egypt, Turkey, and the Middle East. Fleeing the ravages of religious intolerance and wars of conquest, it travelled from Alexandria to the mysterious city of Harran, where it became the prophetic book of a strange community of Hermeticists. From Harran it reached Baghdad, where, in the midst of Islam, it informed the mystical philosophy of the Sufis. And when Islamic fundamentalism came to power, it abandoned Baghdad to find a haven in a Constantinople that would itself soon fall to the Turk.

We will return to Harran later in the chapter and attempt, like Shu separating Geb and Nuit, to split apart the grandmother and grandfather survivals found in the Near East.

The second significant diaspora happened following the fall of Christian Alexandria to Islam in 636 CE, triggering an exodus of Neoplatonists and magicians to Constantinople, under the patronage of Emperor Heraclitus, who sought to revive the glories of the Classical Age. According to Stephen Skinner, it is from Constantinople that the earliest grimoires, those with the clearest Egyptian antecedents, entered Europe, probably by way of Venice.

Grandmother Egypt

Egypt's new masters had a more sophisticated relationship with the magic they inherited than is commonly believed. We see the influence of Alexandrian magic in the libraries of Moorish Spain, an under-examined vector of the Western magical tradition. (Oxford's first library owed much to the books of Moorish Spain, as does the entire troubadour/grail tradition.)

Whilst the practice of ritual magic – the grandfather line – was certainly frowned upon in Muslim Egypt, it seems pretty clear that a high volume of detail about the magic of Dynastic Egypt survived in a folkloric, grandmother capacity. From the beginning of the Arab period, there was a clear association between the pyramids and the stars. More specifically between Hermes Trismegistus, that apocryphal storehouse of Egyptian stellar wisdom; the pyramids; and the belief that they were in some sense 'stone wisdom texts' from before the Flood. The Islamic invaders inherited Alexandria's 'astral folk religion' which bled through into subsequent centuries. This indicates a grandmother transfer among the non-literate classes in Egypt at the time, as there are clear continuities from the Roman and Greek periods into the Arab period.

During the Roman era, Khufu was described as having written an alchemical work and that his pyramid was connected with alchemy. Zosimus (approx. 300 CE) writes that the alchemical process is also known as 'Osirification.' *The Apocryphon of John* retains the Egyptian idea that the decans influence different parts of the human body. The correspondence of the human form to specific asterisms is a clear continuity of the kind of immortality magic found in the Old Kingdom and is retained as the hermetic notion of the microcosm corresponding to the macrocosm. The association between one's fate and the stars, as well as the methods of overcoming it using explicitly astral magic, were regarded as Egyptian in origin and survived into the Arab era. We see a development of prayers to Jesus to remove the bonds of fate as a continuity of some of the PGM spells, such as those to Sarapis in *The Eighth Book of Moses*. Sarapis is entreated to wipe out an unlucky natal chart/astral fate and replace it with a beneficial one. The magician would ascend through various planetary planes – those which inflict fate upon mankind – to the realm of the fixed stars, the Old Kingdom home of 'true immortality.'

By the 900s at the latest, the Arabic tradition considered alchemy to be 'the science of the temples' ('ilm al-barabi) and it was in the temples of Egypt that the secrets of this science, as inscribed by Hermes, were to be found. There were in fact at least three Hermes at this time. According to Zosimus, whose books made it into the famous *Kitab al-Fihrist*, the first lived before the Flood and he, along with the priests of Egypt, carved his wisdom on the walls of these temples using symbolic signs.

The Sabians, those of the Harran exodus, retain yet more explicit associations: Hermes built the pyramids of Egypt before the Flood as a way to transmit and keep safe the sacred mathematical, magical, medicinal and astronomical knowledge of the ancients. In some texts, the pyramids of Khufu and Khafre are the tombs of Hermes Trismegistus and Agathodaimon. Writing in the 13th century and relying on Sabian source material, Al-Halabi suggested that the pyramids were built by a pre-Adamic race of beings, probably making him the world's first Ancient Aliens theorist.

It is worth remembering that the ability to read hieroglyphs had been lost by the beginning of the Arab period. Jan Assmann makes an observation about the understanding of time in non-literate cultures that would apply to semi-literate ones also. There is 'historical time' which is comprised of events in recent tribal or cultural memory. Before this there is 'mythological time' which is a great storehouse of everything else that has happened, more likely arranged by event rather than sequentially. Thus, the Sabians did not retain a direct memory of the end of the Ice Age. However, there are aspects of their culture that were inherited from far earlier times, and the memory of that inheritance is signified by the presence of the Flood. It is a binary, before/after event in 'mythological time.' Failing to recognise these differences has led academics to dismiss any possible transmission wholesale. It has also foundered many an Atlantologist's ship on the rocks of literalism.

Egyptosophy

Prior to the decipherment of hieroglyphs by Champollion in 1822, Europe's understanding of Egypt was parsed through this mythic interpretation of its temples and mysteries. Erik Hornung, Emeritus Professor of Egyptology at the University of Basel, distinguishes this 'Egyptosophy' from the later discipline of Egyptology.

Each era of European history has had its Egyptosophy. Marsilio Ficino's Platonic Academy in fifteenth century Florence saw Egypt through the eyes of the Classical hermeticists. His Egypt bears little relation to the Dynastic era. It was a place of high wisdom, above the petty squabbles of kings, popes and bankers. Hornung writes in *The Secret Lore of Egypt: Its Impact on the West*:

> The founder of this Hermetic religion, whom even Christianity and Islam venerated as a predecessor of their own prophets, became an integrating figure during the early modern period, a bearer of hope and patron of a body of knowledge independent of the Bible and the Quran. Even Copernicus could appeal to him in founding a new system ...

The Egypt of Ficino and Bruno electrified European intellectual life. As the Reformation and Counter Reformation unfolded, the notion of a peaceable, inclusive philosophy held greater and greater appeal. The Rosicrucians, ironically just before the Thirty Years' War, anticipated the renewal of the world via the return of hermetic philosophy.

In later centuries, Egypt exemplified the perfect political model of the Enlightenment: just laws, peace and a cultural Renaissance. French Revolutionaries, Freemasons, everyone saw in an Egyptosophical Egypt a vision of their preferred world: either it was the template for how to live under a benign monarch or it was an example of what happens to the common man when all those dastardly kings and priests are allowed to run the show. That vision of cruelty to the Egyptian workforce at the hands of an evil priesthood – which was used at the time as a metaphor for Catholicism – survived into twentieth century Egyptology.

Catholicism itself vigorously adopted many hermetic trappings in an attempt to align with that 'purer, original' source, as evidenced by the layout and iconography of many Renaissance churches, as well as the face-meltingly obvious hermetic sun temple design of St Peter's itself. With the return to England of Charles II and the foundation of the Royal Society, wizards to a man, people such as Christopher Wren were keen to use hermetic principles to rebuild London as a 'New Jerusalem.'

There is something delightful in the infinite recursion of Egypt – the source of hermetic symbolic magic for all these men – being itself a symbol for each of their perfect world. (Mirror of heaven indeed!) Just as we have the persistence of a ritual form throughout the grimoire period discovered anew, as Skinner notes, with each generation, we similarly have a persistence of *architecture as ritual* from Saqqara to Paris to London to Washington DC, discovered anew by each culture.

Delightful though the recursion is, Egyptosophy is not Egyptology and with the rise of scientific materialist 'Hunger Games academia' in the twentieth century, the two are divided by a Nile of vitriol. Hornung regrets this:

[I]t would be productive for both sides if there were more bridges and less reluctance between the scholarly disciplines and esoteric pursuits. We need think only of the psychological insights won by Carl Gustav Jung from his study of alchemy, and I regret only that he did not have better sources on ancient Egypt at his disposal. In esoteric circles, people are too dependent on the old, outdated works of Budge and ought to take into account more recent literature, which has much to offer of esoteric interest.

Dr Naydler would agree, and goes further:

The interpretation of religion requires not simply a breadth of knowledge of the culture in which that religion flourished ... but also a feeling for, and a personal interest in, the nature of religious experience. Religion – even a so-called dead religion (as ancient Egyptian religion may seem) – is not so much another academic subject to be covered as a universe of human experience to be encountered, engaged with, and affected by ... [T]he deeper understanding arises only when the academic is prepared to allow him- or herself to be existentially challenged by the material that is being studied.

Dr Naydler is certainly correct in this observation. Sadly, that has not been the story of Egyptology's inexorable rise. From the mid-nineteenth century, peaking in the late twentieth century, Egyptology fell into alignment with the materialist, Darwinistic notions of 'progression' from inferior states or cultures to superior ones. This has meant that most of the spiritual material has been translated by 'scholars' who do not believe in the existence of the subject they are studying. It is as if primatologists refused to consider the possible existence of gorillas. Naydler describes the impact of Egyptology's handmaidening of materialism.

The trajectory of history was seen as a steady ascent from the primitive childhood of humanity, dominated by magic and superstition, to our present enlightened maturity, characterized by scientific rationalism ... Egyptology became handmaiden to a much bigger project – that of materialistic science – which was to explain both the outer and inner worlds in terms that excluded all reference to the spiritual as a real and operative dimension of existence.

This denial of any form of indigenous mysticism in Egypt led to the pervasive academic belief that the culture was death-obsessed, a conclusion that is not mentioned even once by ancient writers such as Herodotus, who all praised her wisdom and mystic insight. Leaving the interpretation of Egyptian religion in the hands of scientific handmaidens who do not acknowledge the reality of the subject of their expertise is the principal cause for the persistence of the notion that the pyramids were pointy tombs. To their 'expert' eyes, Egyptian cosmology was primitive and haphazard and the Egyptian mind was 'prephilosophical.' Talk about glass houses!

Denying the Egyptians a form of mysticism led inexorably to the bizarre conclusion that the Egyptians were a practical, materialistic people, caring little for 'The Big Questions' and with no understanding of or interest in any of the laws of forces which governed the universe. Honestly, the mind boggles.

Nevertheless, this was the milieu in which the Victorian magical revival occurred. On the one hand you had a persistent eighteenth century fantasism and London's 'mummy-mania.' On the other you had materialist savages who were too stupid to invent the wheel. Coherence of opinion was in short supply.

NEAR EAST

The mythology of the Near East is a western magical vector in urgent need of re-examination. Many of occultism's 'self-evident truths' were formed at a time when the Hebrew Bible was believed to be an accurate source of history. This presents any number of challenges. We do not know the date of the original composition of most of its books, nor do we know its authors. There is no historical evidence for large kingdoms under David or Solomon, nor the presence of a large Jewish slave force in Egypt and its subsequent Exodus. Successive translations into Hebrew, Latin and English have obfuscated the hybridity of much of Jewish folklore. Ugaritic gods, myths and practices found their way into Hebrew cosmology, Yahweh appears to have had a wife (Asherah) and most of Judaism's plot points – Creation, Eden, the Fall, Noah, the aforementioned 'Golden Age' kingdoms – have antecedents going as far back as Sumeria; an entirely expected outcome for a Laurasian belief system.

Of course, a satisfactory reexamination would not just take entire books, but entire lifetimes to complete. A noble first step in this direction is Peter Grey's *Lucifer: Princeps*, which provides sufficient context for the magical practitioner to begin incorporating these insights into his or her work. Here we need only answer the following question and address its implications: if Sumerian mythology appears in biblical mythology, does Neolithic mythology appear in Sumerian?

The Yeʒidis

We return to the Cult of the Angels which closed out the Göbekli Tepe chapter. You will recall that the bird/totem motif appears to originate in the Palaeolithic. We must be careful with what conclusions we draw from this. In Crowley's day, it was believed that the Yezidis were a Sumerian survival, and that their principal deity was the Devil himself in the form of a fallen angel. Both assertions have long been abandoned as erroneous. Survivals, in *The Lost World* sense of the term, are so rare as to be practically non-existent; continuities are a different matter. They may even turn out to be the norm rather than the exception.

Yezidism could almost form the template belief system for the Eurasian variant of the Laurasian cosmology. It now encompasses several sects showing greater or lesser Islamic influence over the centuries, but the term itself derives from the Kurdish and means 'the angelicans.' In terms of the motifs we are now familiar with:

- It has a distant creator god, followed by seven 'Ages' or 'Emanations' as part of the ongoing act of Creation.
- The universe was built from either a pearl or an egg, out of which the Creator emerged.
- Birds feature prominently, and in some variants the Creation Pearl was placed on the back of a bird for forty thousand years.
- The universe is presided over by seven 'good' angels and seven 'bad' angels, demonstrating the influence of planetary cosmology. This number seven aligns with the seven ages of creation.
- 'God' is closer to a 'universal spirit' and there is a belief in the transmigration of souls, rapid reincarnation and then – at the end of the universe – the 'complete' humans rejoin this universal spirit.

It is Yezidism's propensity for absorption that makes it so worthy of study. One major festival, Jam, occurs at the same time of year as the ancient Eurasian feast of Mithrâkân and appears to be contain continuous motifs from the earlier Mithraic festival. In *The Kurds* Mehrdad Izady writes:

Ancient Mithrâkân celebrated the act of world creation by the sun god Mithras, who killing the bull of heaven, used its dismembered body to create the material world. On the occasion of the feast at Lâlish, riding men pretend to capture a bull, with which they then circumambulate the Lâlish shrine of Shams al-Din (the 'Sun of the Faith'), before sacrificing the bull and distributing its flesh to the pilgrims.

We are now in a position to pull some of these motifs further back in time than Mithraism. The bull of heaven's presence as well as the dismemberment of its corpse speaks to a much earlier layer, and would bring it into alignment – back through Assyria, Babylon and Sumeria – with the bull motifs and horns found at Nevali Çori.

Malak Tâwus, the Peacock Angel himself, also contains much earlier motifs. It is Malak Tâwus, or Lucifer, who creates the material world with the dismembered pieces of the original cosmic egg. Called Azâzil in some tellings, he is depicted as a sculpted bronze bird, often on a pole. We have already seen that the bird 'totem pole' occurs at both Nevali Çori and Göbekli Tepe, but it is the peacock component that requires further analysis.

Firstly, the peacock is a South Asian bird. Secondly, the Dravidic components of Vedic mythology, as we saw in chapter 7, have Karttikeya descend from heaven riding a peacock, with the 'eyes' in its plumage representing the Pleiades. In his form of Murugan, he 'precedes' the other gods just as the constellation Pleiades precedes Orion, Taurus and the rest of the stars – and just as Malak Tâwus is the first of all seven angels – the rest come after him.

Once again, we find ourselves in the same Pleiades / Taurus / Orion corner of the sky, sharing the same motifs. None of these are conscious survivals, but rather continuities stretching back significantly further than it appears on first glance. Yezidi cosmology is a storehouse for the 'blended spirit model' of angels, Nephilim, etc. that tumble down from the plains of Eurasia – moving gods and legends up down and around with each new worldview – and also proof of concept that such a process can carry spirits and practices right through from the Palaeolithic, particularly in marginal, 'grandmotherly' fashions.

Return to the 8tar Temple

Combing through the Bible for muddled Kabbalistic insight will only yield so much magical utility. Treating the Apocrypha as some sort of 'suppressed' or 'hidden' wisdom – standing opposed to the 'orthodox elite' narrative – will yield even less. Instead, what is needed is a realisation that certain groups will prioritise certain stories and motifs for localised, contemporaneous political reasons. To yield maximum insight and utility, the mythology of the Near East must be viewed as an holistic spectrum. Adopting this approach makes it infinitely easier to see the bleed-through from earlier mythological layers and it is these layers that enable us to calibrate potential continuities.

We explored the possibility that the first emergence of large-scale agriculture in the Near East at or around Göbekli Tepe may have survived as a motif in the Cattle and Grain Text (as may have the practice of burying temples when they ceased to function magically/astronomically). It now appears almost certain that some of those Sumerian motifs survived into later Babylonian and then Hebrew mythology. Again, the notion of continuity rather than survival presents itself: by the time of Sumeria, Göbekli Tepe had been lost to memory for thousands of years. Nevertheless, if the site was the preeminent temple in the area where the local cultures first began to learn 'civilisational' skills, then we might expect its impact to be discerned in cosmology: the stone has sunk to the bottom of the creek, but the ripples expand on the surface.

An examination of the many variants of the 'Shemhazai and Azazel' story, best known from the *Book of Enoch*, is particularly useful. Shemhazai and Azazel are known variously as Watchers; Sons of God; angels; giants/Nephilim or the fathers of Nephilim, having produced them by laying with the daughters of man. This assigns them to that permanently liminal category of leftover gods, ancestors and 'other' spirit beings, where we would expect to find them if they are vectors of earlier motifs. The common parts of the Shemhazai and Azazel story involve their descent from heaven, usually with God's permission or as a result of a bet with the Creator; their – typically sexual – interaction with mankind; some sort of instructional role; and then at least one of the two disobeys God's rules or directives to return to heaven.

The astronomical components of the best-known version are particularly compelling. Echoing Babylonian mythology, the generation after the Flood begins to go astray once again and God wonders aloud whether he should have ever created humans in the first place. Shemhazai and Azazel remind him that they were against the idea from the start. Demonstrating the emotional instability that Yahweh is famous for, after initially despairing of mankind, he suddenly leaps to our defence, saying that while they dwell on earth, they are subject to the 'Evil Inclination' which would overpower even Shemhazai and Azazel. The 'Evil Inclination' is likely inspired at least in part by the planetary astrological concept of Fate that can only be overcome by ascending *above* the planetary spheres; everything below these spheres is subject to its inevitable mechanics. (We see this inevitability blended with the decans by the time of the Greek Magical Papyri.) Shemhazai and Azazel descend to prove that they can still 'sanctify the Name' of God whilst on earth and subject to the Evil Inclination.

Predictably, an angelic version of Spring Break unfolds, with the two angels laying with the daughters of man (and the sons of man, and the pets of man), feasting on flesh, drinking and spilling all the divine secrets of metallurgy, astrology, medicine and so on. Shemhazai and Azazel then decide to select brides; Azazel chooses Na'amah of Tubal-Cain and Shemhazai chooses Istahar, 'the last of the virgins.' Istahar – very obviously a continuity of the Mesopotamian Ishtar – refuses, and uses her refusal to trick the secret name of God out of Shemhazai. Isis acquires her magic using similar methods, which may speak to a much earlier origin for this motif (perhaps even Gondwanan, given it is a classic Trickster move). Using the power of the name, Istahar ascends into the sky and becomes its brightest star. When Shemhazai saw Istahar had outwitted him, he recognised it as God's rebuke for his sins, and hung himself upside down between heaven and earth.

In this telling, the 'brightest star in the sky' is actually the planet Venus, which is what Istahar becomes. Again there is a parallel with Ishtar/Inanna here. However, as observed by Howard Schwartz in his excellent *Tree of Souls: The Mythology of Judaism*, 'later' tellings have Istahar become the Pleiades. In both cases, Shemhazai is Orion. Once again we thus have the hunter pursuing his female prey across the sky. This may be a late Grecian influence, but it also may not be, given that the identical motif is found in Australia at a much earlier period.

There are additional elements to this collection of stories that suggest it may 'echo' or 'encode' the development of agriculture at or around Göbekli Tepe. In one version, at God's direction, one of the angels switched to a vegetarian diet while the other refused to give up feasting on flesh, which looks suspiciously like a mythological telling of the coming of agriculture (and its enforcement by the emerging tribal political class). There is also the fact that, most of the time, there are *two* angels, just as there are *two* of Dr Schmidt's 'heavenly beings' formed by the T-pillars in the centre of an astrological temple on the hill. The hunting/Orion/flesh eating component remains, as does the prominence of that same Pleiades/Orion/Taurus/Sirius corner of the sky. And if Belmonte is correct that it was built to mark the appearance of Sirius as a 'companion star' in the sky to the Hunter, then we also have the 'bride-seeking' motif as well. Finally, Göbekli Tepe was the site of beer drinking, flesh eating and, it is reasonably surmised, intertribal wife trading, a practice which continues today during regular religious festivals at sites shared by hunter gatherer groups. When considering these alignments, recall that it would have been in the shadow of these heavenly beings that many of those tribes would have first learned about cultivating wild grasses, first for beer and then for bread, and subsequently taken this information with them.

The Sabians and Harran

Of Harran, the fourth century historian, Libanius, writes:

In Harran there was in the middle of the city a splendid temple considered by many to be equal of the Serapaeum in Alexandria. On this temple was a tower which was used as a military post and watchtower, since from its top one could overlook the entire plain of Harran. There were also powerful images in this temple. But when the praetorian prefect Cynegus ordered the pagan temples in Egypt and Syria to close, at which time most were destroyed, this temple in Harran was partially destroyed, and the idols which were in it also were taken away and in part destroyed.

It seems vanishingly unlikely that the Alexandrian refugees that became the Sabians selected Harran because of its proximity to Göbekli Tepe. At this point in history, the site had been buried and forgotten for many thousands of years. Harran, like Göbekli Tepe before it, was a trading centre – it even derives its name from the Akkadian for 'crossroads' – and, like most trading centres, presumably promised tolerance and access to new ideas from the east and the west. Nevertheless, this coincidence is so unlikely it demands some explanatory model, which may be forthcoming in the next chapter. But first, we need to coincide some more.

Mas'udi, writing during his visit to Harran in 943 CE, gives us the only Muslim eyewitness account of the city itself. Writing in the *Muruj al-dhahab* (*Golden Meadows*) he describes the Harranian Sabians as follows:

The Harranian Sabians have temples according to the names of the intellectual substances and the stars. To these temples belong: the temples of the first cause and of Intelligence, but I do not know whether it is the first or second Intelligence; also, the temple of world order, Necessity. The temple of the soul is round; of Saturn, hexagonal; of Jupiter, triangular; of Mars, long (rectangular): the Sun square; that of Venus, a triangle in a quadrangle; that of Mercury, a triangle inside an elongated quadrangle, and that of the Moon, octagonal. The Sabians have in them symbols and mysteries which they keep hidden.

Sabians are a group of people mentioned in the Koran as one of three 'Peoples of the Book,' the other two being Jews and Christians. Under Islamic law, this meant their practices were permitted to exist in Muslim lands. It is quite clear that the Sabians of Harran are not the Sabians of the Quran. (There is no agreement on who the Quranic Sabians were, or if they even existed as a separate category. Broad consensus appears to be they were likely some kind of Jewish splinter sect.) The Harranian magicians and hermeticists are called Sabians thanks to some frankly brilliant legal advice. When the Abbasid Caliph passed through Harran on his way to make war against the Byzantines, he accused the town of being pagan and demanded to know what religion its people practiced. Unsatisfied with the answer he received, 'we are Harranians' he effectively told them to 'get religion' by the time he came back through or he'd put them to the sword. Luckily for Harran, the Byzantines put him to the sword outside Sardis and he never returned. However, in the interim, they had sought legal counsel from a Muslim jurist who suggested they declare themselves 'Sabians,' who are protected under Islamic law. All they need do was present the 'book' to which they belonged as its 'people,' as well as their 'prophet.' For their book, they chose the Hermetic texts, and for their prophets, they chose Agathodaimon and Hermes, adding that Hermes is also 'Idris,' the Muslim name for Enoch.

It is important to realise that this cartoonish ploy did not fool the majority of Islamic scholars for a second, but nevertheless, the legal protection remained. Mas'udi himself distinguishes several classes of Sabians in another of his texts, the *Kitab al-Tanbih*. Tamara M. Green describes them in her excellent *City of the Moon God*:

1 The kings of Rum who were *al-hanifa* and *al-sabi'un* before they became Christians. The emperor Julian was secretly a Sabian, and when he renounced Christianity, he re-erected the statues which the Sabians put up as images of the highest substances and the celestial bodies, and punished those who did not return to the faith of the hanifs.
2 The Egyptian Sabians, who honour Hermes and the Agathodaimon as their prophets; the remnants of these Sabians are the Harranians. 'They abstain from many foods that the Greek Sabians (i.e. those mentioned above) eat, such as pork, chicken, garlic, beans and other things of this type; they regard as their prophets Agathodaimon, Hermes, Homer, Aratus, Aryasis, Arani, the first and second of his name.'
3 The followers of Zaradrusht (Zoroaster), who formerly had embraced the creed of the hanifs.

Writing in the late 1200s, the medieval Arab geographer Al-Dimashqi exemplifies the arms-length handling of the Harranians. He distinguishes two types of Sabians: those who worship idols and those who recognise the 'cult of the celestial mansions.' The Harranians fall into the latter category but he is under no illusions that these are the Sabians of the Quran, for they travel to the tombs of their prophets (the Giza pyramids) on pilgrimage. Despite their lack of scriptural authority, he considered them a useful source of esoteric information for Islam.

This 'devil you know' relationship persisted from the very beginning of the Islamic period. Umar II, Caliph of Alexandria, even moved the school of medicine to Harran in 717 CE. The Caliphate clearly did not approve of the Harranian methods, but recognised that they needed them – like an early medieval MKULTRA, perhaps.

Harran is steeped in biblical motifs, specifically astrological ones. Although there is no evidence for their physical existence, Harran is believed to have been the home of Abraham, the first of the Three Patriarchs, whose brother was also named Haran. Rather than rejecting it as irrelevant to their astrotheology, the Harranians incorporated this association when it suited them. It formed part of their 'legal justification,' for instance. But they also used Abraham's name antagonistically (and probably unwisely) in theological comparisons with Christianity and Islam. According to the tenth century scholar, al-Biruni, the Harranians claimed Abraham left the city because he was suffering leprosy on his foreskin, and that is why he circumcised himself. The etymology of Abraham is unclear and contentious. There is the obvious phonic similarity to 'Brahman' which could suggest an earlier Eurasian layer. It appears to mean 'exalted,' 'multitude' or 'enlarging,' which would be in keeping with God's covenant with Abraham. Interestingly, God specifically promises that the descendants of Abraham would be 'as numerous as the stars,' another astrological motif layered into the local geography of Harran and Göbekli Tepe.

It is also worth remembering that Jacob had his ladder experience while travelling to the town of Harran, and in some versions of the Shemhazai/Azazel story, they descend to earth via Jacob's Ladder. Plus, as we have seen, Harran was once home to multiple 'towers' with which one could 'ascend' to specific stars. Also recall that most Islamic scholars found a workaround for their unease over the prominence of Hermes in Harran by declaring him Idris, that is Enoch, who also ascended to the stars.

As expected for a city that means 'crossroads,' the continuities were not simply Graeco-Egyptian. Until the 11th century, the southeast gate of Harran's citadel was flanked by carvings of dogs, presumably for apotropaic reasons. This is likely a continuity of Nergal as 'My Lord with His Dogs.' Assyrians would bury dogs under their threshold for similar apotropaic reasons. (The use of cynocephalic, or dog-headed saints, carved on the gates to or bridges into towns continued in Europe right into the Early Modern Period. The patron saint of travellers himself, St Christopher, was initially cynocephalic.)

Remarkably, there are also legends of 'The Head' or head worship at Harran. When an earlier Abbasid Caliph, al-Ma'mun, passed through Harran, he accused the Harranians of being 'Adherents of the Head.' This apparently refers to practices performed on the head of a man who resembled 'Utarid (Mercury). A contemporaneous Arab historian describes what he believed to be the ritual associated with this head cult: the man who resembled Mercury would be placed in a vat of oil and borax until his joints relaxed. Then his head was pulled, stretching his neck. This action was performed each time Mercury was 'at its height.' This head would then prophesy in tongues. We may assume such activity continued posthumously as well, as the *Ghayat al-Hakim*, the *Picatrix*, contains several rituals associated with divination using severed heads, that bear a significant resemblance to these Harranian practices. The *Picatrix* even attributes one of these rituals to 'a philosopher known under the name of Brahma of Brahman, who died in India.' There are certainly Hindu spells that require the use of a head, one even requires it to be set up in opposition to the dragon – suggesting astrological components – but then there is also simply Brahma / Abraham / Harran. Greene keenly observes that none of the accounts of 'head-omancy' can be taken literally as, plainly, the Caliphate would not have allowed such practices to continue. She considers them either religious propaganda – painting 'the savages' as human sacrificers – or symbolising some esoteric doctrine (or both).

> [W]ithin the context of the esoteric traditions surrounding the Harranians, the tale of 'the Head' may be merely a prosaic, if horrific, version of astrological or alchemical symbolism, reminiscent of the language found in Zosimus and other works on the esoteric sciences. It also has affinities with certain aspects of apotropaic magic which found its way into Hermeticism. Proclus, for example, reports that Julianus the theurgist placed on the demarcation line against the barbarians a human head made out of clay and consecrated by him; it was said to have the power of sending down lightning upon the enemy wherever they wished to cross the border of the Empire.

Having mentioned the *Picatrix*, it is important to recognise that, while Skinner is very likely correct in tracing the egress into Europe of the Greek Magical Papyri – in the form of the *Hygromanteia* – from Byzantium and by way of Venice, a significant volume of magical practices also found their way onto the Continent via Moorish Spain, even if their impact on Christian Europe was lesser or, at least, more muddled. And a large amount of this Egypto-stellar wisdom that came through the Arab line actually originated in (or at least passed through) Harran. During Córdoba's height as the capital of Moorish Spain, it had over seventy libraries, some of which had over half a million books. At the same time, France's Royal Library had 900.

The 'measurability challenge' presents itself once again examining this vector. I suspect the impact of Moorish Spain is underemphasised for linguistic and – at least domestically in Spain – prejudicial reasons. We trace the line of the grimoires and then subsequently hermetics through Italy because it is more easily measurable. However, what is important to realise about the figure of Hermes Trismegistus is that he became, particularly in Harran, a 'storehouse' of philosophical/scientific observations of the universe as well as a plethora of 'low' or 'folk' magic practices – grandmother survivals, if you will – pertaining to medicine, drawing down the power of planets and stars, making amulets and charms and facilitating pacts with various astral intelligences. Greene says of him, 'Hermes Trismegistus was the source of all knowledge previously known only to the gods: the explicator of the stars, the sacred healer, the master alchemist.'

Exploring what I suspect are more direct, localised magical continuities from the Arab line in the Iberian Peninsula does not invalidate the North Italian vector. As ever, we must resist singular explanations. Exiled to Brazil as a result of the Inquisition of Lisbon, Antonia Maria describes a folk magic custom that is suggestive of these continuities. She would sit in the doorway to a house and feed pieces of goat's milk cheese to Barabbas, Satanas and Lucifer as offerings (which were followed up by full meals cooked in their honour if/when her objective had been achieved). In Book 3, Chapter 7 of the *Picatrix* – which is described as explicitly Harranian magic in the original Arab version – we find similar ritual activity: in an operation of Mars which requires the use of a young boy as seer, his mother sits in the doorway of the prayer house, holding a rooster, until called. The ritual is clearly derived from PGM-era Alexandria: while his mother is in the doorway, the boy is adorned with animal skins and has fire held under one foot and water held under the other. Eventually, the mother is called into the room and the priest beheads the rooster over the boy. As soon as the boy leaves the house, he puts on his index finger a ring bearing the image of an ape. Baboons were symbols of Thoth in Egypt and the rooster may simply be a domesticated continuity of a 'bird' as symbolic of passage between the physical and spiritual realms, such as we have seen depicted going back to Göbekli Tepe and beyond.

Elsewhere in the *Picatrix*, there are repeated references to Hermes as the teacher of these arts, descriptions of him as the lord of the 'three flowers of things,' as well as specific rules for building cities and structures aligned to the stars and the planets – and warnings for those who build during inauspicious times: 'In founding a city, make use of fixed stars, and in building a house, make use of planets.'

What are we to make of all this? There is, within a day's ride of Göbekli Tepe, a recursion and layering of most of its significant features or motifs. The stars, specifically Orion and his surrounding corner of the sky; calendrical precision; the head, or lack of head, as depicted by the T-shaped pillars; the belief that the area is a conduit for Antediluvian wisdom; dogs and the dog star; the descent of the two angelic teachers via Jacob's Ladder – also in the area; and a stellar covenant with the Creator in the form of the Abraham legend. All this at a crossroads, no less.

How do we account for the recurrence of these motifs over a span of ten thousand years, when 'mouth to ear to mouth' transmissions patently did not occur? At the Inhabited Sky conference in Madrid in May of 2015, Jacques Vallée made the following observation: 'In science, when there is a new phenomenon, you look for patterns that can cut across culture, geography, and so on … The UFO phenomenon … has constant features across time and space.'

In the specific example of the area around Göbekli Tepe and Harran, as well as the Near East more generally, we do indeed see patterns cutting across time. That these patterns are commonly misinterpreted as either direct transmissions or simply not being there at all returns us to the core of the problem Dr Naydler described earlier in the chapter. Academia or materialistic inquiry is permanently ill-suited to examining something it thinks does not exist.

What is clearly needed is a methodology that can at least begin thinking in better directions. This would likely include some sort of unconscious resonance as well as John Keel's notion of 'window areas'; that there are some places in the world more likely to be the scene of extreme paranormal events such as mass UFO sightings or the Mothman of Point Pleasant. This analysis works backwards as well as forwards. Why was Göbekli Tepe built on *this* hill rather than *that* hill? Obviously, we will never know for sure, but the subsequent twelve thousand years of history suggests there very likely was a reason, and given the persistence of explicit star lore in the region, we are justified in proposing some sort of contact event may have taken place at least once. Here is Jacques Vallée again, this time in his classic *UFOs: The Psychic Solution*.

Throughout history the minds of men have been manipulated by sources apparently external to their environment. It has been a common theme in all these communications that the purpose of the message was to show mankind a way to enlightenment, to greater happiness, and to salvation, either from physical disasters or from dangers waiting for us beyond death itself … The historical importance of such communications has generally been trivial but occasionally it has been profound. It has often resulted in the creation of small groups of priests or initiates who claimed direct contact with the higher entities or gods.

THE BOY FROM LEAMINGTON SPA

There is always a risk when examining esoteric history that one marshals the past to support one's preferred worldview, which is certainly not my intention here. (In any case, I am not a Thelemite.) Aleister Crowley sometimes fell into this 'historical worldview' trap and sometimes didn't. More interesting, from our perspective, are the results and insights he received that were a poor match for the understanding of history in his day but, in many respects, have been borne out by subsequent archaeological discovery.

Aiwass

By necessity, we come at this story out of sequence. Crowley spent much of his life, subsequent to encountering the being in Cairo in 1904, trying to work out exactly what or what type of thing Aiwass actually was, in addition to being the author of *The Book of the Law* and his own Holy Guardian Angel.

At the time of his death, he had come to the conclusion that Aiwass was a type of extraterrestrial/extradimensional entity, one of a race of beings intimately involved with the instruction and teaching of mankind. To Crowley, he was 'a messenger from the forces ruling this earth at present.' Kenneth Grant described Aiwass as 'a type of extra-terrestrial Intelligence such as we may expect to come into conscious contact with, as the aeon develops.' Although it forms a surprisingly small component of Thelemic cosmology, Crowley makes it clear that Aiwass is far from alone 'up there.' The universe is filled with extradimensional beings seeking contact with earth. Viewed in light of Dr Vallée's previous comment, we read in *Magick Without Tears*:

> My observation of the Universe convinces me that there are beings of intelligence and power of a far higher quality than anything we can conceive of as human; that they are not necessarily based on the cerebral and nervous structures that we know; and that the one and only chance for mankind to advance as a whole is for individuals to make contact with such Beings.

Aiwass was more than that, though. To his credit, Crowley attempted to keep pace with the archaeological and scientific discoveries of his time. Although both hypotheses were subsequently shown to be inaccurate, in Crowley's day it was believed that the Yezidi were a direct survival of Sumerian spiritual practice – the 'Devil' in Yezidi belief being Sumeria's supreme deity – and that Sumeria itself was the oldest complex culture on earth. Crowley came to associate Aiwass with this hypothetical Sumerian/Yezidi supreme deity.

Further confirmation for this belief arrived while Crowley was living in New York in the form of Samuel Aiwaz Jacobs, an Azerbaijani immigrant who shared his passion for Kabalistic 'word games.' The middle name – which Jacobs himself believed meant Satan – was only the first synchronicity to pique Crowley's interest. Jacobs also provided a Hebrew spelling for Aiwass that gave the number 93 – something that had eluded him.

A combination of Kabalistic 'confirmation,' his personal magical experience and some imprecise historical information led Crowley to write in commentary to his *Book of the Law* that 'Aiwaz is not (as I had supposed) a mere formula, like many angelic names, but is the true most ancient name of the God of the Yezidis, and thus returns to the highest Antiquity. Our work is therefore historically authentic, the rediscovery of the Sumerian Tradition. (Sumer is in lower Mesopotamia, the earliest home of our race).'

It is interesting to observe that while Crowley was wrong about the earliest home of our race and the origins of his particular cosmology in Sumeria, one can almost support his case for 'highest Antiquity,' given the subsequent archaeological discoveries of the last fifty years and the emergence of the Laurasian hypothesis.

Egypt

As already discussed, the Egyptology of Aleister Crowley's day is hugely inaccurate when compared to its modern iteration. This is to be expected as Crowley was born only a few decades after the discovery of the Rosetta Stone: interpreting the writings of the Ancient Egyptians was a new field. The understanding of the pyramids' function was even worse, typically formed by solar-obsessive, Christian antiquarians who saw sun worship everywhere. An intellectual fudge that allowed them to paint historical peoples as primitive while simultaneously aligning their practices with a broadly Judeochristian arc.

I have been unable to find any evidence that Crowley had read the Pyramid Texts prior to receiving *The Book of the Law* in 1904 on his second visit to Egypt. In correspondence with Exeter University's Tobias Churton – author of *Aleister Crowley: The Biography* and *The Beast In Berlin: Art, Sex, and Magick in the Weimar Republic* – he writes that he is nevertheless confident that Crowley was familiar with them, given his long friendship with the Egyptologist (and Theosophist) Battiscombe Gunn. If he had read the Pyramid Texts prior to 1904, these would have been some of Gaston Maspero's sporadically published – but well-translated – articles. A complete version of the Pyramid Texts was only made available after the reception of *The Book of the Law*. This is significant because of the oft-commented-upon similarity between Crowley's remarkable case of automatic writing and its similarity to the Pyramid Texts, as well as many of the spells of the New Kingdom's Books of the Dead. One spell in particular could almost be considered a concise version of *The Book of the Law*. That is Spell 177 – which I've given earlier on pages 116 and 117 – widely regarded as and fairly obviously a clean continuity from the Pyramid Texts. Go back and re-read it.

There are a number of ways, all valid and useful, with which to interpret Crowley's reception of *The Book of the Law*. The first observation is that it clearly demonstrates Crowley's lifelong obsession with what we might uncharitably call the 'Victorian Tantric' worldview. On this particular trip to Egypt, he had arrived after spending time in South Asia. (Including in what may have been part of Sundaland's sphere of influence, which may be synchronistically significant to this book's thesis. Similarly, recall also that Gerald Gardner spent much of his professional life in what was once Sundaland.) The universe as expressed in *The Book of the Law* displays mechanics that are far more 'sexual' than those found in the Pyramid Texts.

The second observation, entirely expected in any case of automatic writing, the mind of the recipient heavily influences the subsequent text. Churton, in his biography of Crowley, sees parallels in his writing as well. Below is an excerpt from Crowley's play, *Tannhäuser*.

> *Isis am I, and from my life are fed*
> *All stars and suns, all moons that wax and wane,*
> *Create and uncreate, living and dead,*
> *The Mystery of Pain.*
> *I am the Mother, I the silent Sea,*
> *The Earth, its travail, its fertility.*
> *Life, death, love, hatred, light, darkness,*
> *Return to me –*
> *To Me!*

Churton observes, correctly to my mind, that this whole sequence is resonant of the words of Nuit he was to receive later in *The Book of the Law*. 'To Me!' in particular. He writes that 'key elements of that revolutionary little book were already coalescing somewhere in Crowley's extraordinary mind.'

Clearly there were certain aspects that Crowley brought with him to the rented apartment during those fateful days in Cairo. There is also the fact that the trinity of gods, although Egyptian, do not form a trinity at any time in Dynastic Egypt, which Crowley would have been aware of. That said, in *The Dark Lord*, Levenda remarks:

Egyptian religion went through many changes over the course of its roughly three thousand – four thousand years of history. Gods and goddesses changed attributes over time, changed rulerships and characteristics, and even parentage ... Thus one could make the argument – perhaps only slightly frivolously – that the *Book of the Law* represents a new iteration of the Egyptian religion and continues the developmental process begun in the pre-Dynastic era.

There was something about this experience that stayed with the master magician his entire life, and yet his diaries are filled with other multi-day, spirit-contact operations, ranging from New York to Paris, from the shores of Loch Ness to the deserts of North Africa. Singular explanations remain unsatisfactory in the case of *The Book of the Law*. Crowley brought his own mind to the experience but, at the same time, there were also some remarkable synchronicities of the type discussed in the previous section, as well as some as yet unexamined alignments with our emerging understanding of Laurasian or Palaeolithic spirituality. Let us consider the sequence of events.

November 22nd, 1903: Aleister and his new wife Rose, honeymooning in Egypt, secured private evening access to the King's Chamber. Crowley performed a modified version of the Headless Rite from the Greek Magical Papyri, discussed in the next section. The chamber filled with a 'brightness as of full moonlight.' From Paris to Marseilles to Naples to Egypt, the honeymoon continued on to Ceylon.

March 16th, 1904: Crowley and Rose moved into a rented Cairo apartment, having arrived in Egypt – their second visit – in February. Crowley performs the same invocation in an attempt to have Rose see the sylphs again. She does not, but she becomes agitated, claiming she is hearing messages.

March 17th, 1904: Rose continues to hear messages for her husband, claiming they are 'all about the child' or 'all about Osiris.' Crowley wrote that Thoth was invoked 'with great success.' An annular eclipse occurred in the sky. Churton writes of it: 'the eclipse was heightened by Venus, the morning star in Aquarius. It faded, reappeared, and caused a stunning ring of fire, bulging toward Venus's silvery glow.' That evening, Rose claimed that their waiter was actually Horus, and that Crowley had offended him.

March 18th, 1904: Crowley, already suspecting he had offended Horus, magically 'cross-examined' his wife. She passed the test and insisted her husband invoke Horus in 'a new way.'

March 19th – 21st, 1904: Exact dates differ, but over this weekend and into the Monday, Crowley invoked Horus unsuccessfully, then successfully, and also took his wife to the Cairo Museum as part of her ongoing testing to she if she recognised any images of Horus. Here, famously, Rose pointed out what Crowley came to call the Stele of Revealing, which carried the catalogue number 666. The stele depicted a leopard-skin-adorned priest, Ankh f-n Khonsu, bowing before an enthroned, falcon-headed Horus, with a winged sundisk above the scene, topped with the arching body of Nuit. Crowley, astounded, insisted on a translation.

March 22nd – April 7th, 1904: The diary entries between the museum incident and the subsequent reception of *The Book of the Law* have some holes in them. (Not uncommon for a man with an appetite for clandestine homosexual behaviour and an interest in younger Arab men.) Crowley appears to have done nothing on March 22nd, and then, before receiving its translation, begun interpreting the stela from the 23rd with an invocation of Thoth. From an historical authenticity perspective, his interpretation was poor. Crowley saw the ritual described as one 'of sex.' He linked Nuit with Sagittarius because her arching body looked like a bow. Because the Sagittarian bow/arrow is associated with genitals, this allowed him to layer on the same 'Victorian tantric' interpretation he slapped over everything. Using tarot cards, he identified the priest Ankh f-n Khonsu with Mercury and Aries; and 'Mars in the house of Venus exciting the jealousy of Saturn or Vulcan.' Saturn, as the tarot trump 'The Universe' was associated with Nuit. What is interesting about this frantic, terrible interpretation is that Crowley knew better. He was a proud Cambridge Classics dropout and a lifelong student of history. When he got like this, when he caught – shall we say – 'acute correspondomania,' it indicates someone attempting to unpack an extreme synchronicity before the term had been coined. Indeed, in his biography of the man, Churton writes, 'Crowley's assertion that it was the stela's discovery that led to the ritual which led to *The Book of the Law*'s dictation suggests the important factor was the stela's *discovery*, not necessarily its *translation*.'

Whilst he would go on to construct a ritual that facilitated contact with Aiwass over the 8th, 9th and 10th of April, it was the encounter with the extremely unlikely – with High Strangeness – that he considered the cornerstone of the experience. Here was the universe noticing him. Here was Contact.

The Headless Rite

Described by Jake Stratton-Kent as 'the single most important ritual in modern magic' is an invocation from the Greek Magical Papyri known as The Headless Rite. Emerging from the Alexandrian chaos that birthed the Western grimoire tradition, *The Stele of Jeu the Hieroglyphist* is one of the more concise and potent invocations found in the entire collection. Crowley did not know it as the Headless Rite. Crowley, or someone in his circle, poorly renamed the ritual. Stratton-Kent describes this unfortunate transliteration in his *The Headless One*:

Either Mathers or Crowley set a fashion for interpreting the phrase 'headless one' – which recurs throughout the original – as meaning 'without beginning' and accordingly altered the phrasing to 'Bornless One.' [...]

Sometime between [the publication of the ritual in English and 1904], some person or persons unknown adapted the ritual and altered the name 'headless' to 'bornless,' on the assumption that since 'Resh' in Hebrew means 'head or beginning' then the term 'headless' might be read as 'thou who art without beginning – unborn and undying.' In other words, the 'translation' relies on Hebrew etymology, which of course need not necessarily connect with a Greco-Egyptian ritual.

Despite the freewheeling approach to the translation, Crowley understood it had definite Osirian notes. The operant describes him or herself as the 'angel of Paphro Osonnophris' or 'pharaoh Osiris.' He used variants of it regularly throughout his life. The two most important times were on these two visits to Egypt. Of the second visit, in which Crowley attempted to use it to create werelights for his wife again and instead ended up with *The Book of the Law*, Stratton-Kent writes:

This is perhaps an indicator of the limitations of the will of the magician, who, producing a ritual for specific purpose, on synthetic lines, overlooks the possibility that what he is adapting has a life of its own. This ritual certainly produced a significant result, but this did not remotely resemble the result intended. This is a point I wish the reader to bear carefully in mind ...

Given Crowley's awareness that it was an incident of High Strangeness rather than his self-proclaimed mastery that was of most significance, it is worth considering the events in that same light, with a renewed understanding of historical veracity.

- *Headlessness:* Even with the name change, Crowley was performing a ritual with a distinctly Laurasian motif, possibly even Gondwanan. Consider the T-shaped, 'headless' pillars uncovered at Göbekli Tepe, a hunters' temple pointing at Orion and Sirius that involves 'heavenly beings' descending to earth. Göbekli Tepe lay undiscovered until almost fifty years after Crowley's death.

- *Osiris/Orion:* Continuing the 'headless' and 'hunting' theme, Crowley performed an invocation to Osiris inside a stone map of Osiris (the Great Pyramid), that contains the same 'up to the sky and back' journey found in the Pyramid Texts; another Laurasian motif, perhaps *the* Laurasian motif. Crowley was unaware of Giza's Orion

Correlation, as well as the headless hunter motif associated with Orion in some of the oldest cultures on earth.

- *Venus and the eclipse:* Crowley began performing the 'Bornless/Headless Rite' the day before and the day of some visually impressive space weather. Atmospheric and stellar events are regularly associated with UFO contact experiences. He would go on to have just such an experience. Possibly related is the continuance of the headless motif into Christianity with St John the Baptist, who, as Venus, 'precedes' the dawn that is Christ. He is headless.

- *Aiwass:* The being that appeared as a result of this 'accidental reactivation of the spaceship' came to be associated in Crowley's mind with the god of the Yezidis, dating back to Sumeria. Whilst it does not date back to Sumeria, the central god of the Yezidis probably came from a Neolithic buzzard cult that is a likely continuance of the 'bird on a stick' stone objects found at places such as Göbekli Tepe and nearby Çatalhöyük. Both sites demonstrate some of the earliest motifs subsequently to turn up in Old Kingdom Egypt. Crowley would eventually consider this evidently-very-ancient-being 'from high antiquity' to be some form of extraterrestial intelligence involved with the teaching of mankind.

- *The Stele of Revealing:* The 25th Dynasty stela pointed out by Rose is neither old nor important by Egyptian standards. Examined under this new light, however, a few things emerge. Firstly, Ankh f-n Khonsu is dressed in a leopard skin, reminiscent of the earliest Heb Sed ritual garb (itself a nod back to its shamanic origins). Secondly, the stela itself is atypical in its inscriptions: it blends Ra-Horakhty (Horus of the Horizon) with Sokar-Osiris; Sokar being the earliest known god of the Giza plateau and an early form of Osiris, and the Giza plateau being where Crowley performed his Osiris ritual, of course, in a stellar-aligned structure 'activated' by Horus of the Horizon. Finally, it is rare for its reverse side containing two spells from the New Kingdom Book of the Dead – a very old set of spells by the 25th Dynasty. They allow the spirit of the deceased to return to the earth at will.

- *Nuit:* Despite his inevitably 'Victorian Tantric' interpretation of it, the fact remains that the principal deity speaking through Crowley's automatic writing encounter was not only a personification of the stars themselves but itself the esoteric version of the crucial piece of the Laurasian Creation story, that is, the separation of heaven and earth. As a female sky, Nuit is 'under the earth,' that is, in the Underworld; the stars being the spirits and achieving a place among them – back home – being our ultimate goal. For tens of thousands of years we have built stellar temples 'for the chance of union' with the stars.

Vectors

Aleister Crowley retains his importance for much of western occultism, but his wider significance needs to be considered alongside such events as the Miracle at Fatima, Andrija Puharich's famous séance in a Maine farmhouse where he contacted the Nine, the Betty and Barney Hill incident and other paranormal events that have outsized cultural impact. Indeed, outsized cultural impact could even be marshalled to support claims of veracity for these events without saying anything about their actual content or implications. In *UFOs: The Psychic Solution*, Jacques Vallée writes:

> We have encountered a multi-faceted phenomenon and we are trying very hard to ignore it, because it does not fit into any neat categories and refuses to be dragged under a microscope to be examined. Instead, it appears to seek confrontation with us on its own terms.

Crowley's outsized cultural impact covers novels, music, comics, secret military programmes such as the Stargate Project and the development of the modern space programme itself. His enigmatic experiences and their impressive influence over the twentieth century point toward the underlying reality of phenomena that have played a part, for whatever reason, in the cultural, spiritual and technological development of mankind. These phenomena have persisted throughout the human journey, they have always been ambivalent, their ultimate motivations opaque and they continue to persist to the present day.

X   CHILDREN OF THE MOTHER OF HEAVEN

Observations are not explanations. It is self-evident that we need a bigger paradigm. In the west, history gave us a monotheism that either denied or ignored the long-lived human experience of spirit encounters. It was this monotheism that gave birth to a materialistic vision of the universe that itself denies the existence of anything nonphysical, reaching the apogee of absurdity with its fiat 'solve' for 'the hard problem of consciousness': no such thing exists! From an interpretive standpoint, this leaves western discourse with not very much room to manoeuvre. Publicly, we have what amounts to two equally unsatisfying vectors of enquiry. Firstly, there are the researchers working within the academic mainstream who are unlikely to find something they do not believe exists. Secondly, there are those working outside the academic mainstream who are fixated on finding something they believe exists – evidence for physical extraterrestrial intervention – but probably doesn't. Or, at least, not in the way it is commonly presented.

The main shortcoming of the extraterrestrial hypothesis is that it remains hamstrung by materialism and undervalues the impact of consciousness and psi effects, which have been scientifically observed for over a century. Its narrative still revolves around physical aliens appearing in physical space ships that subsequently trigger a swathe of cargo cults among physical savages here on earth. The principle of parsimony suggests we should at least begin with a psi or consciousness interpretation, but this isn't to say that both possibilities were not in play at least once in human history. Indeed, none other than Carl Sagan went so far as to estimate the number of times extraterrestrials have visited earth in the human era. He speculated that if some sort of 'Galactic survey ship' had noticed the appearance of Proconsul, a human ancestor, some 25 million years ago, then the rate of sampling or monitoring may have increased from that time, 'perhaps to once every ten thousand years.' Sagan suggested that that contact would have increased even more since the beginning of the post-glacial era as mankind increased in cultural and technological complexity and that if the intervening time between contacts has been reduced down to a few thousand years then 'there is a possibility that contact with an extraterrestrial civilization occurred within historical times.' Sagan's 'possibility' is, to my mind, highly likely. That still leaves us with big question marks hanging over whether such encounters had any impact on human cultural development, 'historical times' being rather recent, after all.

In his unjustly maligned *The Sirius Mystery*, Robert Temple agrees with Sagan's hypothesis and speculates that if a physical extraterrestrial encounter occurred, it would have been between 5,000 BCE and 3,000 BCE – a time he calls the Contact Era – and it was this encounter that triggered the dramatic increase in social complexity we observe in Sumeria and Egypt at the time. While this astonishing increase in social complexity is still lacking a satisfactory explanation or explanations, this book has hopefully shown there are enough observable antecedents to the beliefs, practices, spirits and gods of Sumeria and Egypt to make the singular explanation, 'because aliens,' insufficient. That being said, it is certainly worth observing in passing that the publication of *The Sirius Mystery* attracted constant CIA interference, including the wholesale theft of Temple's only copy of the translation of the original French source material, *The Pale Fox*, by a CIA asset in London in the 1970s as well as attempts to block the book's republication in the 1990s. Quite why the CIA would be interested in an anthropological account of hypothetical psychic contact between the Dogon tribe and beings from the Sirius system that has apparently been 'discredited' has not been adequately explained. We have some ideas.

Despite this intriguing interlude, and the supporting opinions of some very informed experts, we must return to that notion of parsimony by looking first to that which has not only been scientifically observed, but continues to operate on and interact with mankind into the present day; namely, a consciousness- or psi-based, largely nonphysical interaction or experience, rather than an explicitly Extraterrestrial Hypothesis (ETH). The ETH approach matches the available archaeological data less and less with each passing year, as more information regarding the complexity of the Palaeolithic as well as an increasingly precise understanding of hominin population movements comes to light. We should expect that trend to continue.

NON-HUMAN LOGIC

Although sometimes admirably explored in science fiction, the ETH also regularly fails the non-human logic test. Why would an interplanetary species, having travelled across the vast reaches of space, set about insisting we naked apes build them triangular piles of rocks? If they came to teach us, why did they teach us how to scratch and scribble in river-clay tablets and not teach us cold fusion? Palaeolithic brains were actually larger than modern brains. Why did school end halfway through kindergarten? Why – when mankind itself is but a decade away from capturing asteroids made of diamond, orbiting them around the moon and using robots to mine them – did an interplanetary species fly past mineralogically rich, unoccupied planets and planetoids to build squishy chimps to mine gold on this one?

Here is where the practical magical perspective – until quite recently unheard in (public) discussions in the UFO/UAP field – can be particularly useful. Magicians have personal experience of non-human logic; what it feels like, how it manifests in life and culture, and so on. It is characterised by atemporality, high levels of coincidence, repetition of motif and symbol in entirely unrelated contexts and a quasi-fractal capacity to look weirdly resonant at whatever level you observe the phenomenon, from the micro to the macro. We could almost, and probably should, use these experiences as yardsticks to measure the 'non-humanity' of particular signals or collections of experience, based on the reasonable hypothesis that non-human intelligences would communicate in non-human ways.

As an example of this sort of non-human 'cluster' communication, we might use *The Sirius Mystery* and its author. Before writing it, Robert Temple was a friend and student of Arthur M. Young, twentieth century inventor and mystic (and genius, frankly). This gives us a vector running through Young's central American mushroom research – thus touching on one of this book's cornerstone hypotheses – his subsequent involvement with channelling Egyptian/extraterrestrial spirit beings known as the Nine – thus touching another – through to his sharing with Robert Temple the original anthropological work regarding the Dogon that would underpin *The Sirius Mystery*, a book that was encouraged into publication by Temple's friend, Arthur C. Clarke. Prior to striking up this friendship, when Clarke observed the psi abilities of Uri Geller – a Mossad asset whose CIA handler, Andrija Puharich, accompanied Young on his mushroom field trip – he said it was '*Childhood's End* come to life.' Geller was briefly involved with the remote viewers who would go on to accurately psychically view parts of our solar system (and its apparent inhabitants) and also claimed to be in communication with an artificial intelligence communicating with him backwards through time. *Childhood's End* is one of Clarke's many science fiction novels. It describes a postwar earth where aliens that look exactly like medieval demons rule from an orbiting spaceship, institute a soft-fascist regime of global peace, and whose presence begins to trigger psi powers in a growing number of children. (Yes, it's excellent.) This was the book, rather than *2001*, that Stanley Kubrick actually wanted to turn into a film before claiming it was 'too expensive' to shoot, which is patently untrue for someone of his skill and genius. Temple himself visited the set of *2001: A Space Odyssey* in London, thus providing a speculative fiction overlap with the notion of extradimensional/psi/extraterrestrial involvement in the development of the human species (as well as an overlap with problematizing the Apollo missions). After all this, it was reading *The Sirius Mystery* that inspired a young Robert Bauval to go on to investigate and then publish his work on Giza's Orion correlation in *The Orion Mystery*. All of this happened before the discovery of a 12,000 year old star temple, complete with *2001*ish 'monoliths,' pointing at Orion and Sirius. This allows us to close the loop, so to speak, back into the psi/entheogen/ancient astrotheology narrative (and its implications) that is the subject of the book you are holding.

As is the case with most of 'alternate history,' what looks to uncritical minds like conspiratorial knowledge passed down through the generations looks to my eyes like extradimensional agency operating at decidedly non-human timescales and for non-transparent purposes. (Fold the Crowley/Giza stuff from the previous chapter into the same through-line and it gets really interesting.) No one in the above chain of geniuses and remarkable researchers is working for 'the Illuminati.' Instead, we observe a continuum that you can 'step into' at any of the previously described 'nodes' and still end up viewing the same motif or narrative. It is non-sequential communication. Which seems to me to better support an extradimensional/consciousness hypothesis than the ETH.

LITTLE GREEN MEN

The hypothesis that mankind's civilising gods or spirits were, too use a cheekily disparaging term, 'little green men,' relies on taking literally a personally preferred ancient mythology, typically the Sumerian one. However, as we have seen, these are much, much younger variants of older spirits and storylines that, by definition, cannot literally be true, just as the reboot of a film is not the original film. At best, one could argue that there was an original contact event that triggered the emergence of a Laurasian storyline 20,000 to 30,000 years ago but such an argument – like anything else – has the ever present obligation of proof. For example, if 'they' taught us writing, why did we wait so long to use it?

There is also the observation, first described by Jacques Vallée five decades ago, that the phenomena are simply too common to have been the nuclei around which our original religions have formed. 13% of Americans today – more than thirty million people – believe they have been abducted by or otherwise encountered aliens, and these are just the ones that will admit it. Religions rarely form around experiences so common. Instead, there appears to be near continuous, albeit enigmatic, contact or observation with somethings throughout human history. Certainly these encounters or an explanation of them would have been, have been, incorporated into spiritual systems, but one has to be extremely selective with the evidence to suggest these events or beings triggered our first religions.

Finally, the suggestion that 'little green men' are mankind's original teachers fails to account for the varying levels of technological complexity in cultures that supposedly received these teachings, as well as the clear evidence of uneven – sometimes declining, sometimes advancing – levels of technological sophistication. Instead, what we observe is the previously described 'runaway climate change' effect that increased technological sophistication appears coincident with increased astronomical sophistication and declines along the same lines. Whether there is a causal relationship is almost beside the point if there is a 'consciousness entanglement' effect in place. One indicates the other in such a scenario. When the teacher is 'in the classroom,' we learn things. When the teacher is absent we do not. A singular explanation cannot account for this.

A CONSCIOUSNESS EFFECT MODEL

One of the myths most commonly cited by proponents of the 'ancient aliens theory' is the Vedic motif of the *vimanas*. Vimanas are artificial aircraft used by various gods and asuras to fly about the world and occasionally attack other aircraft or ground targets. This would seem to be a startlingly precise description of 'alien' spacecraft were it not for the fact that, just like Ezekiel's vision and other 'mythological descriptions' of supposed UFOs, calling these craft 'aerodynamically ambitious' would be a kindness. And so there is an element of 'burying the lead' here because there are some compelling data to be extracted from these stories once one lets go of one's preferred interpretation. For instance, when the asura, King Salva, attacked Krishna's city of Dwarka, his vimana was observed to split apart, bounce along the surface of the ocean, and reabsorb its various split parts back into a whole, all while Krishna was firing projectiles at him from the city. Viewed dispassionately, this is remarkably reminiscent of Norway's 'Hessdalen Lights'; an aerial phenomenon observed with surprising regularity. They also appear to behave as if consciously controlled and regularly split apart from each other before reforming, often moving around or through the mountains around the Hessdalen valley at tremendous speeds. The story of King Salva and the Hessdalen Lights offers some compelling parallels to the 9th century Lyon story of Magonia that gave Jacques Vallée the title to his masterwork, *Passport to Magonia*. Bishop Agobard of Lyon observed a sky battle between competing wizards from the cloud realm of Magonia. Several occupants of one of the downed craft were even captured and kept for days. There is nothing in the good bishop's account that suggests these 'wizards' had descended from the clouds to teach us about genetics or quantum computing. Mostly it is just complaints about the damage the Magonians caused to the local crops.

What this suggests is that there is a continuity of observation that can be used to calibrate ancient anomalous encounters that all-too-many of us hastily throw onto the 'proof of aliens' bonfire. To say these beings 'aren't' aliens is not to rob the myths of their potency. This very book rests on the proven hypothesis that local mythology can be a container for recognisable astronomical, climatic and consciousness-based experiences. The 'container assumption' is required to interrogate what I believe to be the circumstantial mapping of the human journey out of Africa and the subsequent uneven rise of cultural and spiritual complexity. Such a mapping better incorporates 'complexity pivot points' including:

- Encountering entheogens in the food supply and their resulting cultural impact.
- The rise of precision astronomy in cultures where it is technologically redundant.
- The notion that it was the (often enthegeonically-contacted) spirits that gave mankind astronomical and navigational skills, as well as conferring kingship.

Using a wider model accounts for the capricious nature or presentation of these phenomena. If they are our 'teachers' then they are crack-addicted relief teachers who only show up to steal the lightbulbs from the faculty lounge. The universe owes us nothing and it is only our deep-seated psychological need for structure that attributes such nobility to the motives of phenomena that have *never* demonstrated a coherent awareness of human morality, whatever and however useful that may be. Caveat emptor.

A 'capricious, sporadic spirit contact' model not only leaves the door open for the perfectly reasonable – although currently, materially irrelevant – suggestion that earth has been visited by physical extraterrestrials at some stage in human history, it also provides a least worst set of assumptions with which we may explore these so-called teachings.

'TEACHING MACHINE' EXPERIENCES

Perhaps one of the only genuinely global spiritual beliefs – found in both Laurasian and Gondwanan cultures and thus suggesting it is Pan-Gaean – is the notion that mankind was instructed in the ways of magic, culture, language, law and technology by the spirits. We invented very little. We were *shown* most of it.

An example from historical times, wellknown to western magicians, may be useful in 'backcasting' certain scenarios; that is the creation of the Enochian alphabet and magical system by John Dee and Edward Kelley. The Enochian phase of Dee's fascinating life began in 1582 when Kelley saw an angel, 'the hythe of a little chylde,' who profers them a shewstone. Dee would subsequently employ Edward Kelley as a seer and the two of them would go on to receive/create an alphabet and hundreds of words that are 'wrong' in the sense that they do not exist but are remarkably consistent on an internal basis. This would be comparable to the experiences of Andrija Puharich and Uri Geller when the later began to receive tensor equations that were also 'wrong' but internally consistent, and certainly well beyond the mathematical skills of a stage magician. Incidentally, Enochian words also appear sporadically in the 'channelled' UFO literature of the mid-twentieth century.

Both Sumerian and Egyptian writing have observed pictographic antecedents but, especially in the case of Egyptian hieroglyphs, this is sort of like calling the wheel the direct antecedent of the stealth bomber. A strictly materialist, evolutionary hypothesis looks inadequate, especially when the Egyptians flatly stated that Thoth – who lives on the moon, by the way – taught them writing and when we have a number of similar experiences observed in the historical era. Jacques Vallée opens *UFOs: The Psychic Solution* with five statements that will be useful in cohering these phenomena with an expanded view of human history as provided by genetics, linguistics and geology.

1 The things we call unidentified flying objects are neither objects nor flying. They can dematerialize, as some recent photographs show, and they violate the laws of motion as we know them.

2 UFOs have been seen throughout history and have consistently received (or provided) their own explanation within the framework of each culture. In antiquity their occupants were regarded as gods; in medieval times, as magicians; in the nineteenth century, as scientific geniuses. And finally, in our own time, as interplanetary travellers. (Statements made by occupants of the 1897 airship included such declarations as 'We are from Kansas' and even 'We are from ANYWHERE ... but we'll be in Cuba tomorrow.')

3 UFO reports are not necessarily caused by visits from space travellers. The phenomenon could be a manifestation of a much more complex technology. If time and space are not as simple in structure as physicists have assumed until now, then the question 'where do they come from?' may be meaningless: they could come from a place in time. If consciousness can be manifested outside the body, then the range of hypotheses can be even wider.

4 The key to an understanding of the phenomenon lies in the psychic effects it produces (or psychic awareness it makes possible) in its observers. Their lives are often deeply changed, and they develop unusual talents with which they may find it difficult to cope.

5 Contact between human percipients and the UFO phenomenon occurs under conditions controlled by the latter. Its characteristic feature is a constant factor of absurdity that leads to a rejection of the story by the upper layers of the target society and an absorption at a deep unconscious level of the symbols conveyed in the encounter.

In the light of these five statements, as well as the experiences of Dee and Geller, it is useful to consider a story told to Vallée in the early 1970s by an engineer who encountered anomalous phenomena during an archaeological field trip when he was still a student. This engineer wandered away from the group, came to a clearing behind some trees and encountered a twenty-foot-wide disc with a translucent elevator that transported him aboard. 'As in a dream or a movie,' the vehicle instantly transported him to a desolate area and deposited him on a hilltop beside a five-by-twenty-foot computer. (The encounter happened in the early 60s). He spent what he thought was three hours with the computer, reading row after row of 'recordings' that transmitted 'advanced information' directly into his mind, before the disc returned and flew him back to the same spot. What he thought was three hours turned out to be 18 days. His father, a government official (which may or may not be relevant), had had the military out looking for him. The engineer still had impeccable clothing, the flower in his lapel had not decayed and he did not need a shave. In the following six months, the man required an abnormal amount of sleep, 13 hours a night, after which he needed less and less. At the time of his encounter with Dr Vallée, over a decade later, he said he still only needed a few hours a night, and had not had, or at least recalled, a single dream since the incident. His experiences at university changed as well: he instantly understood and recalled with perfect clarity everything he was taught. He also believed he had psychokinetic powers as well as the ability to astral project at will.

If you swap the giant, 1960s computer with the classic shamanic 'Otherworld,' then this is a story as old as time. But even the presence of the computer is quite illustrative. These phenomena appear in the most technologically advanced way possible for each individual culture, which is why over the last 150 years the aerial components have gone from airships in the late 1800s, to flying saucers in the mid twentieth century to triangles or chevrons in a post-stealth-bomber world. As a thought experiment, let us replace this engineer with, for example, Imhotep, and keep the story the same. Imhotep vanishes for days and then returns with stories of encountering the gods wherein they showed him how to liquefy and pour rock 'in honour of Them.' The complete design for Djoser's Heb Sed temple, right down to the exact number of false doors and pylons, is recalled with perfect clarity. This temple reliably replicates the spirit contact experience Imhotep himself went through. He remains in psychic contact with his tutelary gods, Ptah and Thoth, for the rest of his life and often sleep-journeys back to visit them for further tuition.

Let us try another thought experiment, and jump back 10,000 years from Imhotep to a Eurasian shaman. He is not overly interested in improvements to stoneworking technology, but he is interested in knowing which valleys the deer will run down upon their return from the north. Unlike Imhotep, his spirits do not transport him to a gleaming stone city but to an open plain under a warm, clear night sky, where great fires have been lit and masked revellers feast and dance under constellations both familiar and unfamiliar. Nevertheless, he returns with a precise map of the valleys and rivers where the deer will run and the men of his tribe have a successful hunting season that year. He begins to sing to the constellations he recognises from his night journey. They ask for stones to be erected in their honour.

This sort of sustained, culture-specific form of contact is what Dr Vallée refers to as a 'control system.'

If the hypothesis is true, then what the witnesses have seen were manifestations of a process not unlike that of a thermostat in a house. The thermostat is a mechanism that stabilises the relationship between our body temperature requirements and the changing weather outside. Similarly, UFOs may serve to stabilize the relationship between man's consciousness needs and the evolving complexities of the world which he must understand.

Let us return, then, to Robert Temple's notion of a 'Contact Era' between 5,000 BCE and 3,000 BCE. Viewed without the automatically-appended context of physical alien visitation, there is much to recommend a modified version of the concept. Specifically, that would be an improved and improving capacity for experiencing or even deliberately triggering whatever the phenomena we have just explored actually 'are.' Such a 'modified Contact Era' model would go a considerable way to providing an improved explanation/interpretation for the similarities between the 'original civilisations' of Indus, Sumer and Egypt that cannot be accounted for via trade and genetic contact: we could go so far as to suggest they may have been having similar 'teaching machine' experiences viewed through the lenses of their respective cultures.

COUNTER-CHECKING THE HYPOTHESIS

On the surface, it may seem an entirely reasonable objection to say that we simply do not know the contents of the ancient mind, thus any attempt to do so is pure conjecture. Such a sentiment typically emerges out of academia's post-traumatic, postmodernist response to the cosy universalism of an earlier age. Any form of comparative analysis is largely so woefully out of fashion that it has been relegated to the cupboard behind the shoulder pads and perming rods. But in rejecting the flawed notion that 'everything is the one thing,' it need not follow that 'nothing is the same as any other thing.' Particularly thanks to advances in biology, morphology and consciousness studies, there are some opportunities to compare modern experiences to ancient in pursuit of a hypothesis, without suggesting that our ancestors conceptualised the world in exactly the same way.

The first two potential similarities are instructive on at least a personal level, and the latter two on a wider cultural one.

Entheogenic Experiences

Here in the opening act of the twenty first century, we are in a position to observe with a high degree of confidence that the human brain has remained almost entirely unchanged for hundreds of millennia. We also have a large number of clinical studies documenting the effects of psychoactive substances such as DMT and psilocybin on the modern brain – and thus the modern mind. This provides us with a valuable vector of enquiry in hypothesising about the minds of ancient men in cultures that we know overlapped with the presence of these substances in the local environment.

Such data facilitate both positive and negative hypotheses. On the positive side, it allows us to 'match' physical and cultural artefacts to the images and visions seen by modern minds under the influence of psychoactive substances. Some of these results are particularly compelling. As Dr Sheldrake observes, there is no acceptable materialist reason why a born and bred Londoner would experience jungle imagery such as panthers, pythons and dense greenery under the influence of ayahuasca taken in, say, Chiswick. Nevertheless, a high volume of urban, western experiencers report such imagery and encounters. This suggests that either the imagery is somehow inherent in the molecule itself – which would still allow us to undertake comparative analysis – or, more likely, the molecule provides access to an independently existent, nonphysical reality – which would certainly allow us to undertake comparative analysis.

On the negative side, we can also anthropologically observe the contemporary use of entheogens in cultures that have 'declined' away from its ritual use. As Gastón Guzmán noted in his twentieth century ethnomycological study of Papua New Guinea, many of the tribes no longer use the locally-occurring psilocybin and boletus mushrooms in ceremonies. Much of this appears to be due to the impact of deforestation reducing encounter rates among the hunter-gatherer tribes. On the rare occasions when these mushrooms are consumed, presumably accidentally, they can lead to violence and murder.

Examining the contemporary experience of psychoactives in cultures that have 'fallen away' from their ritual use is an essential counterpoint to the universalist tendency to sort of 'spread' the Mesoamerican experience of psilocybin into any culture where the molecule is naturally occurring. That is a tactic straight out of the Choronzon School of Anthropology.

Contemporary Magical Experience

Contentious, supremely personal and near-impossible to draw quantifiable conclusions from, the contemporary magical experience nevertheless seems a legitimate source of counter-checking for the wider hypothesis. It is not so much the *content* of contemporary magical experience – that overused phrase, 'personal gnosis' – so much as it is its *context*. Recall, for instance, the experience of the reception of *The Book of the Law* from the previous chapter.

Contemporary magical experience can be marshalled to countercheck the hypothesis not in terms of 'the spirits told me this is what happened' (for they are ever-unreliable narrators) but in the wider synchronicitous context in which it occurs: what kind of 'non-human logic' was discerned in its aftereffects?

A Modern 'Contact Era'?

We move toward ever more speculative means of counter-checking. If the hypothesis holds that increases in technological complexity are associated with increasingly sophisticated astronomy and astrotheology, and that both are associated with an increase in what we still call UFO phenomena, then perhaps we need look no further than the twentieth century itself for a counter-check?

Consider the fact that it was in this century, particularly in the decades after World War II, that mankind achieved the greatest ever increases in technological complexity in our entire two million year history. While many of the UFO phenomena observed during this period – perhaps even most – were Cold War cover stories, these years could still be characterised as a flap of UFO flaps.

What else were we doing during this era? Building precision space platforms that physically took humans off the earth for the first time, installing telescopes in orbit and sending robots to planets named after ancient gods.

Ancient NDEs

Many readers will no doubt already be aware of my particular interest in the Near Death Experience. Since the installation of defibrillators in ambulances in the 1960s, we have had a reliable way of bringing people back from the leading cause of death in the world. Thus we have accrued a dataset that is vast in both number and implications, often actual clinical conditions. There is simply no better source from which to draw upon in determining which parts of the human consciousness experience: leaving the body, visiting geographically distant locations on earth, the continuity of one's ancestors and the 'shape' of any potential afterlife.

In his book, *Conception of the Afterlife in Early Civilizations*, Gregory Shushan admirably attempts to map many of these experiences to mythological descriptions of afterlife journeys, magical night flights, the achievement of immortality, and so on. In doing so, he wades through some of the crudest academic dismissal of in-your-face evidence seen this side of Egyptology.

> [T]he issue of universality is controversial in NDE studies, with some researchers promoting cross-cultural difference at the expense of similarity. For example, in his assessment of perhaps the earliest western NDE account which explicitly claims to be factual (related by the Greek philosopher Clearchus of Soli, c.310 BCE), Bremmer ... states that the only similarity between the account and the modern NDE is a 'feeling of drifting away.' This, despite clear references to typical NDE elements such as OBE, meeting deceased relatives, moral evaluation assisted by mystical/divine beings, and clairvoyance. In a study of Chinese NDEs, the researchers (Zhi-ying and

Jian-xun 1992) seem to have interpreted cultural/individual expressions of typical NDE elements as dissimilarities. Sensations of weightlessness and 'feeling estranged from the body,' for example, must surely be equated with the OBE. 'Unusually vivid thoughts,' a feeling that thought has sped up, a sense of peace and euphoria, and a life review are all standard NDE elements reported by their subjects. Murphy (2001) states that there is no being of light in Thai NDEs – despite reports of the Buddha appearing as a star, and an encounter with 'spiritual lights.' (ibid.) He also states that Thai NDErs do not report feelings of bliss, ecstasy, peace and the like, but rather 'pleasantness, comfort, a sense of beauty and happiness.' Rather than seeing these as analogous emotional states, he sees discontinuity. Encounters with deceased friends and relatives are similarly classified as dissimilarities because they do not specifically greet the NDEr, but rather instruct him/her. Murphy's conclusion that 'accounts of Western NDEs would seem to be useless in helping Thais know what to expect at their deaths' is not supported by Thai references to OBE, travelling in spiritual form to another realm, life review with moral evaluation, encounters with divine/mystical presences, positive emotions, transcendent feelings and an impression of knowing 'all the truths of the universe,' visions of the future, deceased relatives, and being instructed to return.

Cross-cultural comparison is obviously not identical to cross-temporal comparison, but hopefully we have demonstrated that not everything needs to be the same thing for comparative examination to still have some use. Especially when you consider the academics just described are pitching nothing but deliberately misinterpreted balderdash in support of a dominant, anti-comparative agenda.

It seems likely that a comparative analysis can also provide insight into the *personal esoteric experiences* at the heart of the Laurasian storyline. For any initiatory ritual to 'work,' be it a Heb Sed or the installation of a new tribal chieftain or shaman, it must necessarily be experienced as consciousness effects.

Beginning with Vedic India, Shushan interprets the symbolism of the solar/underworld journey. Each day, the sun emerges from the stone of Varuna, which is equated with Yamaloka, the underrealm of the god of Death. Shushan writes:

> The deceased thus journeys with the sun through the netherworld on its way
> to the dawn. This is done via sailing a boat on the primeval ocean. The soul is a
> microcosm of the sun, an inner light hidden in the heart, just as the sun hides under
> the earth. Birds are symbolic of both the sun and this inner light. The celestial and
> subterranean worlds are associated with each other when the visionary in the text

equates the face of Agni (god of fire, light and the sun) with that of Varuna; and with the father-son relationship of sun-god and netherworld god. Elsewhere it is stated that Soma enables one to see the light of heaven and to find the sun.

An underworld that is also the night sky, a boat journey on a primeval ocean, the heart as home of the soul that is also equated with the sun and solar birds. So far so 'Egyptian royal burial.'

Let us now consider Gilgamesh. Although it appears that the Sumerian gods denied mankind immortality, Shushan observes that the fact they installed Gilgamesh as a divine judge suggests that it was *physical immortality* that was denied to us, as opposed to a posthumous continuity of existence. There are further elements to the Gilgamesh story that not only map a hypothetical Laurasian esoteric experience, but also the classic NDE experience.

In seeking Utnapishtim, Gilgamesh travels along 'the hidden road where the sun rises,' around 'mountains.' Shushan notes that the word for mountain, *kur*, also means Netherworld. Gilgamesh encounters the Scorpion People – likely asterisms – who guard the sun's gate at both horizons. This is very suggestive of the Vedic journey, especially when you factor in the boat journey across the underworld waters of Ea that he must undertake to find Utnapishtim.

In one of the earliest versions of his epic, Gilgamesh asks the sun god, Shamash, if the netherworld is a place of rest because he has been asleep 'all these years.' He continues by saying 'but now let my eyes look on the sun so I am sated with light. The darkness is hidden. How much light is there? When may a dead man see the rays of the sun?' Shushan cautions that these should not be considered rhetorical questions. Gilgamesh, especially given his preoccupation with immortality, is clearly on a quest to achieve it. Shushan observes, '[t]hat he addresses these questions to the sun-god before entering the mountain further demonstrates that he is indeed embarking on a solar/underworld journey.'

Again we have the sun journey/primeval ocean/stellar underworld component with an additional explicit reference to the face of the sun and its role in achieving immortality – as in Vedic India and Egypt. There are further descriptions in the Gilgamesh story that would be extremely familiar to someone who has had an NDE. As we have learned, Dilmun eventually lent its name to a trading partner of the Sumerian/Babylonian cultures, but it was also the name of a 'pristine' land of peace, silence, abundant grain fields, clear fresh water and light; a realm where animals do not attack humans or steal their food, and where sickness and death is unknown. This may as well be a description of the Egyptian afterlife straight out of the New Kingdom

Books of the Dead as a perfectly serviceable description of heaven from modern NDE encounters.

Perhaps making the NDE association even more explicit, after entering the mountain (netherworld), Gilgamesh outruns the sun and emerges into the 'bright light of a jewelled garden.' The garden is the commonest setting for an NDE encounter with deceased relatives and wisdom teachers. It is here that Utnapishtim confers his magical secrets to Gilgamesh, who is washed and given new clothes – a clear symbol of his subsequent transformation. Gilgamesh finds his plant of immortality – a Soma analogue – but it is stolen by a snake, which is not only the earliest god of man available in the archaeological record, but also among the commonest visions described by those under the influence of entheogens (particularly DMT). There is thus a highly compelling match between the motifs associated with the more 'esoteric' Laurasian storylines and contemporary experiences of both NDEs and entheogens. And so, inevitably, to Egypt.

Emerging with the Middle Kingdom as part of the general democratisation of the afterlife, we have the classic 'weighing of the heart in the court of Osiris' motif, which would persist until the fall of Alexandria, thousands of years later. Shushan asks the question, what is this but a life review? The Egyptians delighted in their magical capacity to contact or visit the otherworld; their famous board game, Senet, is built around the shamanic capacity to visit the land of the dead and return. To be proficient in the game was to demonstrate your mastery over such a treacherous, albeit essential, journey.

The same motifs of solar faces, night journeys with the sun through a stellar underworld, boats, solar birds and the individual securing of immortality through magic that we see in the Old Kingdom rituals of the pyramids and Heb Sed festivals recur in the other 'high Laurasian' civilisations of Vedic India and Sumeria. It is to be expected that, as Egypt picked up the pieces of the collapse of the Old Kingdom, many of these experiences and motifs would recur in a more distributed fashion. Here is Shushan's summation of his mapping of the Egyptian afterlife experience with NDEs:

> [D]espite some uncertainties of language and meaning, it is clear that multiple yet unified experiences are being described. In addition to encounters with/transformations into divine beings, the Egyptian afterlife includes leaving the body in spiritual form and journeying to realms which are considered the 'home' or origin state, an encounter with one's own corpse leading to the realization of one's spiritual immortality, entering darkness and emerging into light via descent into and ascent from the Duat, water crossings and ferrymen, interrogations with a stress

on the knowledge of the deceased, meeting one's deceased relatives, judgement or self-judgement based on one's earthly moral conduct, a panoramic life review, obstacles/barriers and perils with the threat of annihilation, and a cyclical existence of continual rebirth and renewal.

Clearly there are some very specific corollaries between the ancient encounters with the sacred and modern consciousness experiences. Any possibility of learning from or being inspired by not only our ancient but also our Palaeolithic ancestors relies on such an observation.

FURTHER HISTORICAL SURVIVALS

In addition to discernable consciousness effects in the mythology of the ancient world, the historical period also presents us with hundreds of anomalous encounters – some of which have shaped the course of empires – that suggest further continuities of contact, experience and 'thermostat manipulation.' Many of these are described in religious terms but are clearly extradimensional encounters. These include the Miracle at Fatima and the story of the Virgin of Guadalupe, complete with its own light show in the sky and radiation effects on plant life. In fact the extradimensional Mary stories are so numerous that Jacques Vallée refers to them in their own separate category as 'the technology of the BVM.'

Below are a few examples, drawn largely from Vallée and Chris Aubeck's highly recommended *Wonders in the Sky*, that are representative of the range of encounters we have every reason to suspect happened during the distant Palaeolithic era.

- *Apulia,* 216 BCE: During Rome's largest defeat at the hands of Hannibal, 'in the sky above Apulia, round objects in the shape of ships were seen. The prodigies carried on all night long. On the edge of such objects were seen men dressed in white, like clergymen around a plough.'
- *Constantinople,* 438 CE: As the citizens were fleeing an earthquake that levelled much of the city, a child was suddenly lifted into the sky 'by a strong force,' so high that he vanished from the view of the people. Upon his slow return to earth, he told the emperor that he had 'attended a great concert of the Angels hailing the Lord in their sacred canticles.'
- *Syburg, Germany,* 776 CE: Saxons rebelling against Charlemagne witnessed 'two shields red with flame wheeling over the church.' They were so frightened they fled the siege they had laid upon the castle and were defeated.
- *Florence,* 1347 CE: During an outbreak of the Plague, residents witnessed 'strange

cigar-shaped objects slowly crossing the sky, sometimes at low altitude, dispersing in their passage a disturbing mist.' Epidemics followed their appearance.

- *Milan, 1491 CE:* Seven mysterious men dressed in togas and 'wearing shining shoes' appeared one night in the study of the local philosopher and friend of Da Vinci, Fazio Cardano. They confessed to being creatures of air who died just as men did, although they could live for up to three centuries. When Cardano asked them to show him treasures they said they were forbidden from doing so 'by a peculiar law.' They stayed with him for over three hours during which he interrogated them about God and the universe, and there was no unity in their answers. One suggested that, contrary to the Bible, God created the universe 'moment to moment' and that if he stopped, 'the world would perish.'

- *Bahamas, 1492 CE:* From his ship, Christopher Columbus witnesses a light 'like the light of a wax candle moving up and down' in the night sky. Although some believed it to come from land, it was deemed too small. No land was sighted.

- *Waldstadt, Germany, 1551 CE:* A woman who got drunk and uttered blasphemies at a party was taken up into the air by the Devil 'in the presence of everyone.' She was lifted up and hovered over the edge of the village, as the revellers followed after her on the ground, whereupon she was dropped to her death with the whole town watching.

- *Wiltshire, 1634 CE:* A curate at a local school, while walking over the Downs, encountered a group of dancing elves in a fairy ring. He was paralysed on the spot and fell to the ground. The elves surrounded him and 'pinch'd him all over, and made a sorte of quick humming noyse all the time.' He awoke to find himself in the centre of a freshly-pressed fairy ring in the grass.

- *London, 1670 CE:* From her teenage years, Jane Lead (née Ward) of Norfolk confessed to hearing divine voices. In 1670 she described encountering a cloud with a brilliant woman inside it, 'her Face as the terrible Crystal for brightness, but her Countenance sweet and mild.' She would go on to write about her repeated abductions at the hands of beings who were neither devils nor angels. She called these abductions 'Transports.'

Clearly there are patterns worth exploring here, and it is only the 'absence of evidence' challenge that restricts our interpretation of both our earliest available mythologies as well as the implications of Palaeolithic architecture. We must move past the binary of 'physical evidence as described by materialist archaeologists' and the 'anything goes' world of personal spiritual gnosis. Much is to be gained from a more coherent analysis.

AN INCOMPLETE LIST OF CHILDREN

Given the persistence of ritual 'shape' down through the centuries, surprisingly few grimoire spirits are directly connectable on a nominal basis to the gods of the ancient world. It seems to me there are a number of important reasons for this.

- I believe the impact of local mythology is underemphasised in the grimoires. If you think about the gods and beasties of the classical world, they all had names. By the time we get to the Golden Legend, they are largely nameless. In at least some cases, I suspect local monster legends provided the names to would-be transcribers.
- Although there is a high degree of conservatism in the *nomina magica*, we are nevertheless dealing with spirit lists that were originally written down phonetically so as to ensure correct pronunciation, and then parsed through multiple languages, depending on their route into Europe: Greek, Latin, Arabic, German, Italian, Hebrew. They then bounce around internally for centuries.
- The sheer lack of textual evidence. Honestly, it cannot be overemphasised just how few written texts pertaining to magic survived from the end of the Classical Age. If secondary titles for spirits, decans or asterisms were used, then it becomes doubly difficult.

Not that it matters much. As we have seen through the development of Gondwana motifs into the Laurasian storyline and then on into the historical period, it is the form or shape, rather than the title, which is conserved across language and time. The purpose of this book is to suggest that some aspects of the western tradition that have tumbled down to us along grimoire lines have evidently been tumbling for a very, very long time and not – perish the very thought – that the grimoire tradition has its origins in the deepest Palaeolithic. Some of these magical motifs that can be traced to the Classical World invite a practical reappraisal in light of their apparently dramatically lengthened timescales. For me, it is comforting to ponder upon the fact that the crane, the peacock, the bull, the seven sisters, the serpent or dragon, Cerberus/Naberus and even the very Devil himself in the form of the Pan-Gaean Trickster have not only been our spirit companions since the fall of Alexandria, but for much of – and in some cases the entire – human journey. It is doubly comforting to look up and still see them in the sky, and know that the our distant ancestors were telling bull stories about *those* very stars, or bear stories about *those* ones, or ship stories about *that* one.

As with all aspects of western magic, the race to reconstruction is heartily discouraged. In fact, if your takeaway from reading this far is an urgent need to recreate a Palaeolithic spirituality based on the implications of the partially excavated site of Göbekli Tepe, I will find you and personally knock this book out of your hands on a crowded train. Instead, *recontextualisation* of existing practices as they have arrived down through the centuries to us is encouraged. I would even say mandatory.

Astaroth

Because I promised her I would, I am singling out Astaroth as the example of mankind's long-lived spirit companion par excellence. Have Jake Stratton-Kent catch you up to speed. From *The True Grimoire*:

> The history of Astaroth in the Middle East and Egypt is long and complex. It involves millennia of time, a vast swathe of geography and several language groups, besides a multiplicity of roles. Just one of her oldest forms, the Sumerian Inanna, has been called the many-faceted goddess.[...]
>
> [T]he lion is – as with other storm deities – a key attribute. She drives a chariot drawn by lions, rides a lion, or is herself a lion.[..]
>
> Another key role of Inanna is as goddess of Venus as both the Morning and Evening Star ... As Evening Star ... she judges the just and the unjust. As the Morning Star represented productive work, so the Evening Star represented rest and recreation, and another key role of Inanna follows from this; Inanna as harlot, goddess of music and dance, the protector of prostitutes and of ale houses. The Morning Star ... was also associated with her as goddess of war, a symbolism of surprisingly wide distribution among people of Asiatic descent.

Inevitably, Jake is correct regarding the widespread distribution of the association between Venus as the Morning Star and goddess of war. And, as Dr Witzel teaches us, where we find widespread distribution we are likely looking at a significantly earlier origin for the motif. This is to be expected given Inanna's prominence in Sumerian mythology which, as discussed, sprung 'fully-formed' as a quintessential Laurasian storyline around 3,500 BCE, thus implying significantly earlier antecedents.

You will recall that Sarasvati was originally a river goddess, likely originating before the end of the Ice Age given that her river – described in full flow in the oldest Vedic texts – had long since dried up by the time they were apparently written down. In these same early texts, she is also a goddess of war and victory, then later adding patroness of music and fine arts to her portfolio. Through her identification with the goddess Vac in Brahmanic texts, she is also addressed as a lioness and goddess of victory. Asko Parpola believes he has traced the etymology of *vac* to the Proto-Dravidic word meaning 'voice, sound, song, war-cry, shout of excitement or joy,' which as a verb means to 'roar (like a lion or a river), summon, make known or reveal' (as in daybreak). The term is even a homonym for 'daybreak,' 'lamp' and 'Venus'; all concepts clearly associated with Inanna in her guise as goddess of victory. Parpola writes:

> Thus the lighted lamp (*vilakku*/*vilakkam* in Tamil and Malayalam) is a central cultic symbol for the goddess of victory, who as Light annihilates the dark forces of night and death. In Mesopotamia, the planet Venus, the brightest morning and evening star, is a symbol of Inanna-Ištar, the Goddess of War and Sex, and in the Hindu tradition, Friday, connected with the planet Venus, is associated with women and the goddess.

What this means is that if the Laurasian model holds, the being we have come to know as Astaroth, currently enshrined on my humble little altar in west London, 'whose DNA,' in the words of Peter Grey in *Lucifer: Princeps*, 'luminesces in the vision of Revelation as the Whore of Babylon,' was once summoned by the banks of a long-dead, roaring glacial river to bring victory in battle over neighbouring Ice Age tribes.

Approach with newfound caution and humility.

The Headless Rite

In a compelling example of the sort of non-human logic described at the opening of this chapter, we have the Headless Rite. Straddling the modern and supremely ancient world, it is an invocation of an asterism that led tribes across the globe for tens of millennia, that had 'headless' star temples raised in honour of it and its consort where hunters would feast, take drugs and learn the skills of grain cultivation, that became associated with stellar immortality (and still grain) to such an extent that great stone maps of it were built upon the earth. In a transparently shamanic survival, alignment with this asterism conferred kingship over the realm of the spirits. So potent was the initiatory power of headlessness – to have one's head in another realm – that it has survived into two of the three great religions of the Near East in the form of John the Baptist, who 'initiates' Christ and thus brings that same promise of victory over death back down to earth.

How or why could you possibly improve on that? There is no need to toddle off to Devon for a 'shamanic initiation' weekend. The blood spilled at Göbekli Tepe still stains the Headless Rite's words of power. Speak them.

Everything under creation [...] is represented in the ground and in the sky.
David Bungal Mowaljarlai, Ngarinyin elder

CANOPY OF STARS

How would you describe a hologram to a Neanderthal shaman? As our under-standing of space and the wider universe out beyond our gravity well – and our explo-rations of inner space – continue to deepen, it becomes clearer and clearer that we are playing in a bigger game than we had hitherto presumed.

Has something tried to describe a hologram to a Neanderthal? What if the Nean-derthal had asked perfectly reasonable questions like 'what is this place?' or 'what is it made of?' or 'how does it work?' How would such answers be reflected in the culture that asked them? Let us not pretend for a moment that these questions did not pass through the minds of early humans. Mircea Eliade believed that all creation myths were an attempt to explain how consciousness, how self-awareness, first arose. Inter-esting then, in the context of just who would be answering, that Dr Witzel's research suggests it is the Trickster, at a time depth of more than 70,000 years, who is our first culture hero and civilising god, and that providing us with answers may have violated some sort of cosmic taboo.

I believe Dr Witzel is probably correct in his findings that the Trickster sits at the very bottom of our global tree of gods. 'Trickster' is the best mythic description of the capricious, unreliable, sometimes truthful, sometimes deliberately manipulative nature of whatever the UFO/extradimensional/spirit phenomenon actually is. We appear to be dealing with – and have been dealing with for a very long time – a range of phenomena with at least one subset interested in 'teaching' us or otherwise transmitting knowledge in an oblique fashion. This knowledge appears designed to impress us with its slight superiority and 'inspire' us in specific directions. Consider how its presentation has changed over the millennia, from therianthropic gods to demons to angels to flying chariots to elves and fairies to the Virgin Mary to airships to flying saucers to cigar-shaped craft to flying triangles. In 1997, what are now known as the Phoenix Lights were witnessed by thousands of modern Americans, including air force pilots who were scrambled to intercept the phenomenon. It was described as a giant, silent, triangular craft with a wingspan the size of several football fields. Would a family group living on the plains of Southern Africa 70,000 years ago have the cultural context to interpret that phenomenon? Would they even be able to see it?

Since leaving Africa, the human story appears to be one of colonising and exploring a physical world that is deeply and intrinsically interrelated with at least one other higher or extradimensional realm. From the scant but nevertheless compelling evidence of the ritual activity of other hominins, particularly Neanderthals, we were not alone in attracting the interest or attention of this other realm. Each year, more and more archaeological and genetic evidence paints a picture of a Palaeolithic world rich in culture, nuance and star lore. It must be remembered that the vast majority of human existence was lived in this state – in a hunter-gatherer world, free of light pollution and populated with near-genetic neighbours (and at least one hobbit) that we occasionally interbred with. Perhaps we have fallen away from this state of awareness? Perhaps 'they' have fallen away from us?

Just how far one wishes to follow this line of reasoning is entirely personal. Famously, Princeton psychology professor Julian Jaynes suggested in the 1970s that, prior to 1250 BC, the entire human race literally heard voices in their head which they considered to be from their gods, spirits and ancestors. It is really more of a thought experiment than an actual theory owing to its complete unfalsifiability, but it is instructive nonetheless. Firstly, most textual sources state explicitly that the gods spoke to Gilgamesh or Achilles or Ramses, and Jaynes used the more recent example of Joan of Arc by way of comparison.

The hearing of literal voices was Jaynes's frankly quite reasonable explanation for some bizarre burial practices, including live internment of servants and the provision of loaves of bread: 'This practice has no clear explanation except that their voices were still being heard and perhaps demanding such accommodation.' More interestingly, he – correctly, to my mind – dismissed the fertility explanation for the explosion of figurines and life-size images in the closing years of the Neolithic given that fertility did not appear to be a problem among the people who fashioned them. Instead he suggested that these figures actually spoke and were heard by the tribespeople. (It certainly throws Old Kingdom royal cults into new light.) Precedent for such behaviour includes the biblical description of the King of Babylon 'consulting with images' or the Aztecs' story to the Spanish that their civilisation began when a statue in an ancient, ruined temple began instructing their leaders.

Inevitably for a psychological theory that is almost forty years old, it relies on some wildly outdated speculation regarding brain function and falls into the modern trap of assuming our ancestors were dumb or savage. The point, nevertheless, is well made: if we consider Jaynes's theory to be '100% spirit contact' and the contemporary western world to be around '6% spirit contact,' there is simply no way to know quite how literally these consciousness effects were experienced, or where the people of the Palaeolithic fell on the 'spirit scale.'

COMPLEXITY OF RECEIVED INFORMATION

Another reason why Jaynes's theory is not well-loved in magical circles is the implications that the voices heard in one's head were 'made up' rather than issuing from some external source of agency. This, at least, is a testable hypothesis, and the evidence points, in some instances, to transmission from external sources. If you do not like this idea, you can simply expand the concept of consciousness to the unconscious to the collective unconscious and achieve the same result.

Returning to the Dogon, the notion that they 'tricked' their French anthropologists with their knowledge of the invisible-to-the-naked-eye Sirius B, or that the anthropologists made it up, is nonsense. The tribe also managed to describe its elliptical orbit, the fact that it was significantly smaller than Sirius A, but that it weighed much, much, more and also the presence of a third star, Sirius C, which was confirmed by astronomers in 1995. According to Laird Scranton, their Nommo iconography also shows a surprisingly sophisticated understanding of the operation of chromosomes inside a cell. It is indeed unlikely that physical extraterrestrials would land in West Africa, pointlessly explain some information about the mass of their home star system, impart some information about biology the Dogon couldn't possibly use and then fly back home.

A psychic contact scenario is a better match for the presence of redundant complexity in the Dogon stories of Sirius. Any magician worth her salt has experienced the phenomenon of receiving more information than required from the spirit world. It is interesting, yes. But ultimately pointless.

This same mechanism of action provides more parsimonious explanations for any number of anomalous data points, such as the famous Piri Reis map. Whilst the map does appear to show a superficial resemblance to the coastline of Antarctica without ice, which do you think is more likely: an accurate description of a coastline surviving down more than a million years or some sort of early navigational variant of remote viewing? (You don't think the best ancient navigators were clairvoyant? I put it to you that someone either saw or was shown that coastline.) Further examples, relevant to some of the areas covered in this book, appear to bear out the 'redundant complexity as evidence of contact with an external agency' scenario.

Nabta Playa

The pastoral tribes of Neolithic East Africa are not currently known to have been an intergalactic people. When Thomas Brophy – who, I remind you, is an actual rocket scientist – was examining the outlying stones around the calendar circle, he noted that their distance from the circle scale to represent the actual distance of the stars away from earth. Even more impressively, those aligned to Vega – used as a marker star to corroborate the various alignments – scale to represent the radial velocity of the stars they represent.

Brophy notes, in regards to the carved bedrock underneath the calendar circle, which had the cow stone buried between it and the surface, '[a]stonishing as it may be, the bedrock sculpture underneath Complex Structure A' at Nabta Playa appears to be an accurate depiction of our Milky Way galaxy, as it was oriented astronomically at a specific time: vernal equinox heliacal rising of the Galactic Center in 17,700 BC.' The cow stone itself was located above the location of our sun on the 'galaxy map' beneath it.

The Nabta Playa results are probably the most interesting on a personal level as they strike me as the best match for an hypothesised Laurasian 'stellar immortality technology' or a sort of 'stone age hermetics.' Not only was Complex Structure A a ground map of Orion, calibrated to both Sirius and the Imperishable Stars, it demonstrates a scaling of the 'as above, so below' concept to a genuinely galactic level that is simply quite beyond the skills of Neolithic cowherds. One wonders who gave them the idea.

The Vedas

As with Nabta Playa, we have explored some of the Vedic mathematics that, while hugely impressive, are not quite beyond the astronomical skills of the people who sung them. There are other elements which suggest someone was on the other end of the line, so to speak:

- Not only do the Vedas state that the sun does not move, it is also described as an ordinary star 'in the daytime.'
- The Vedas demonstrate an awareness that not all the stars are the same distance from earth.
- The Vishnu Purana describes earth's tidal action: 'in all the oceans the water remains at all times the same in quantity and never increases or diminishes; but like the water in a cauldron, which in consequence of its combination with heat, expands, so the waters of the ocean swell with the increase of the moon. The waters, although really neither more nor less, dilate or contract as the moon increases or wanes in the light and dark fortnights.'
- Both the Rig Veda and the Yajur Veda describe sun spots.

THE NUIT FORMULA

Why Nuit? Yes, she appears on the Stele of Revealing so Crowley should probably have expected her to show up, but as answers go it still seems faintly unsatisfying. Nuit is an odd goddess. She has very few temples but is commonly depicted in others, particularly those of her children, Osiris and Isis. She is also regularly depicted inside coffins and tombs. With the rise of Horus she becomes, not the mother of the gods, but the grandmother of the gods – a further step removed from agency in the day-to-day lives of Egyptians, but, like a true grandmother, still, affectionately 'there.'

In many ways she is only half goddess and half 'cosmic formula.' She is a perhaps a step too far 'up' the cosmological description of the universe to be quite as approachable to humans as are her children. Nuit is the personification of the entire underworld that is also the night sky, a place we must pass through to become immortal. She – as the sum total of all the stars – is our origin and our home. Nuit is the last vestiges of the cosmos's personality before it dissolves into a benign, undifferentiated pantheism. Mankind's emergence into full consciousness is intimately related to the stars, and recognising and reactivating that awareness is what the stellar goddess represents. When you speak of her you are speaking of the entire range of cosmic and spirit phenomena.

Nuit is how you explain a hologram to a Neanderthal.

WHO OWNS THESE STORIES?

How outrageous of me to get so far into a book of this nature without checking my privilege. To speak of New Guineans without having brown skin, to speak of biology without having a diploma and just simply to speak about more than one thing. Surely the world has seen enough universalisms issuing from London to last the rest of the Kali Yuga?

Well, comparison is not the same thing as universalism. Indeed, Wendy Doniger says that 'eclecticism is essential to the comparatist's methodology.' When it comes to magic, I would go even further. Magicians are not simply opportunistic comparativists, magicians are thieves. In *The Dark Lord*, Peter Levenda echoes the sentiment.

> Modern western magic is a refusal to accept the position of post-modernism that each culture is unique and owes nothing to other cultures, even when similar ideas, symbols and rituals are involved ... [T]he symbol systems of different cultures may reveal superficial differences as a result of geography, history and even religion, but the states of consciousness represented by these symbols are identical or nearly so. There would be no syncretic religions if this were not the case ...

Not only is it self-evident from the perspective of personal magical experiences, there is also good scientific evidence demonstrating commonalities of consciousness experiences across time and space. The occultist is aware that the world's storehouse of magic techniques is a great soup of runes. His kleptomania arises from his understanding that there is probably always a better spoonful on the other side of the bowl and he is perfectly prepared to risk death by poisoning to find out if it is so. It is thanks to this fear of missing out that we have the Greek Magical Papyri.

So who owns these individual stories? If one is not retelling them, they belong to the world. If one is retelling them, they belong to the culture in which one finds them. But your microscope and your telescope always belong to you.

As for western magic's wider story? In light of the last few decades of scientific and archaeological advancement it is safe to say we are at the very beginning of a new retelling. This is no time for solipsism. You don't drink the water if you don't dig the well. The restoration of context is the goal, not the acquisition of the next shiny new thing.

What do we do with this restored context? What we have always done. Go, burn a little incense, out under the Stars.

Welcome to the neighbourhood.

BIBLIOGRAPHY

Abi-Rached, Laurent. 'The Shaping of Modern Human Immune Systems by Multiregional Admixture with Archaic Humans.' *Science* Vol 334, No 6052. http://www.sciencemag.org/content/334/6052/89.short. Last accessed Sep 5, 2015.

Achenback, Joel. 'Scientists: Mysterious Kennewick Man looked Polynesian and came from far away.' http://www.washingtonpost.com/national/health-science/scientists-mysterious-kennewick-man-looked-polynesian-and-came-from-far-away/2014/08/25/45411b2a-27b3-11e4-86ca-6f03cbd15c1a_story.html. Last accessed Sep 5, 2015.

Afonso, Alexandre. 'How Academia Resembles a Drug Gang.' http://alexandreafonso.me/2013/11/21/how-academia-resembles-a-drug-gang/. Last accessed Sep 5, 2015.

Aldhouse-Green, Miranda & Stephen Aldhouse-Green. *The Quest for the Shaman*. Thames & Hudson. London. 2005.

Alfonso-Goldfarb, A.M. & Jubran, S.A.C. 'Listening to the Whispers of Matter Through Arabic Hermeticism: New Studies on the Book of the Treasure of Alexander.' *Ambix* Vol. 55; No. 2. 2008. Black Bear Press Ltd. Cambridge. 2008.

Allen, Thomas George. *Occurrences of Pyramid Texts with Cross Indexes of these and other Egyptian Mortuary Texts*. University of Chicago Press. Chicago. 1950.

Ananthaswamy, Anil. 'World's Oldest Temple Built to Worship the Dog Star.' https://www.newscientist.com/article/mg21929303.400-worlds-oldest-temple-built-to-worship-the-dog-star/. Last accessed Sep 5, 2015.

Araus, José L. et al. 'Agronomic conditions and crop evolution in ancient Near East agriculture.' Nature Communications, 2014; 5 DOI: 10.1038/ncomms4953. http://www.sciencedaily.com/releases/2014/05/140528104026.htm. Last accessed Sep 5, 2015.

Assmann, Jan. *Cultural Memory and Early Civilization*. Cambridge University Press. New York. 2011.

Banning, E.B. 'So Fair a House: Gobekli Tepe and the Identification of Temples in the Pre-Pottery Neolithic of the Near East.' *Current Anthropology*. Vol. 52; No. 5, 2011. University of Chicago Press.

Bartlett, Xavier. 'The Concept of Civilisation.' *New Dawn* Special Issue Vol. 8, No. 1. 2014.

Bauval, Robert & Ahmed Osman. *Breaking the Mirror of Heaven*. Bear & Co. Rochester. 2012.

Bauval, Robert & Thomas Brophy PhD. *Black Genesis: The Prehistoric Origins of Ancient Egypt*. Bear & Co. Rochester. 2011.

Bauval, Robert & Thomas Brophy PhD. *Imhotep the African: Architect of the Cosmos*. Disinformation Books. San Francisco. 2013.

Bauval, Robert. *Secret Chamber Revisited*. Bear & Co. Rochester. 2014.

Bauval, Robert. *The Egypt Code*. Century Books. London. 2006.

Bauval, Robert. 'The Great Pyramid's Missing Capstone: What Happened to it?' *New Dawn* Special Issue Vol 8, No 6. 2014.

Bawaya, Michael. 'Migration mystery: Who were the first Americans?' https://www.newscientist.com/article/mg21729102.100-migration-mystery-who-were-the-first-americans/. Last accessed Sep 5, 2015.

Belmonte, Juan Antonio and Mosalam Shaltout, foreword by Zahi Hawass. *In Search of Cosmic Order: Selected Essays on Egyptian Archaeoastronomy*. Supreme Council of Antiquities Press. Cairo. 2009.

Belmonte, Juan Antonio et al. 'Light and Shadows over Petra: Astronomy and Landscape in Nabataean Lands.' *Nexus Network Journal* 15 (3): 487-501, Dec 2013. http://link.springer.com/article/10.1007%2Fs00004-013-0164-6. Last accessed Sep 5, 2015.

Belmonte, Juan Antonio et al. 'On the Orientation of Ancient Egyptian Temples: (5) Testing the Theory in Middle Egypt and Sudan.' http://digital.csic.es/bitstream/10261/80000/1/2010-Belmonte%20et%20al.%20-%202010%20-%20On%20the%20orientation%20of%20ancient%20Egyptian%20temples%20(5)%20testing%20the%20theory%20in%20Middle%20Egypt%20and%20Sudan.pdf. Last accessed Sep 5, 2015.

Belmonte, Juan Antonio. 'Archaeoastronomy: Archaeology, Topography and Celestial Landscape – from the Nile to Rapa Nui.' http://www.sea-astronomia.es/drupal/sites/default/files/archivos/proceedings9/DIVULGACION/INVITADAS/belmontej/F-belmonteja.pdf. Last accessed Sep 5, 2015.

Best, Elsdon. 'Maori Personifications: Anthropogeny, Solar Myths and Phallic Symbolism: As Exemplified in the Demiurgic Concepts of Tane and Tiki.' *The Journal of the Polynesian Society*. http://www.jps.auckland.ac.nz/document/?wid=1219. Last accessed Sep 5, 2015.

Best, Elsdon. 'Maori Religion and Mythology: The Poutiriao, or Tutelary Beings.' http://nzetc.victoria.ac.nz/tm/scholarly/tei-Bes01Reli-t1-body-d3-d11.html. Last accessed Sep 5, 2015.

Betz, Hans Dieter. *The Greek Magical Papyri in Translation*. University of Chicago Press. London. 1996.

Biagi, Paolo. 'The shell-middens of the Arabian Sea and Gulf: Maritime connections in the seventh millennium BP?' http://a.harappa.com/sites/g/files/g65461/f/shell-middens-arabian-sea.pdf. Last accessed Sep 5, 2015.

Billing, N. & Hawass, Z. *Text and Tomb: Some Spatial Properties of Nut in the Pyramid Texts*. International Congress of Egyptologists: Egyptology at the Dawn of the Twenty-First Century; Cairo, 2000. American University in Cairo Press. Cairo. 2003.

Blaszczak-Boxe, Agata. 'Prehistoric High Times: Early Humans Used Magic Mushrooms, Opium.'

http://www.livescience.com/49666-prehistoric-humans-psychoactive-drugs.html. Last accessed Sep 5, 2015.

Brahic, Catherine. 'Human exodus may have reached China 100,000 years ago.' https://www.newscientist.com/article/mg22329813.000-human-exodus-may-have-reached-china-100000-years-ago. Last accessed Sep 5, 2015.

Brennan, J. H. *Whisperers: The Secret History of the World*. Overlook Duckworth. London. 2013.

Brier, Bob and Jean-Pierre Houdin. *The Secret of the Great Pyramid*. Collins. London. 2008.

Brophy PhD, Thomas G. *The Origin Map: Discovery of a Prehistoric, Megalithic, Astrophysical Map and Sculpture of the Universe*. Writers Club Press. London. 2002.

Brophy PhD, Thomas. 'Imhotep the African: Architect of the Cosmos.' *New Dawn* Special Issue Vol. 8, No. 1. 2014.

Burnham, D. 'Explorations into the Alchemical Idiom of the Pyramid Texts.' *Discussions in Egyptology*. NUM 60, 2004. DE Publications. Oxford. 2004

Carter, Tristan. 'The Contribution of Obsidian Characterization Studies to Early Prehistoric Archaeology.' http://maxlab.ca/Carter-%20contribution%20of%20obsidian%20characterization.pdf. Last accessed Sep 5, 2015.

Carville, D. J. 'Schwaller de Lubicz and the Symbolist Key to Egypt.' *New Dawn* Special Issue Vol. 8, No. 6. 2014.

Casey, Michael. 'When did dogs become man's best friend?' http://www.cbsnews.com/news/when-did-dogs-become-mans-best-friend/. Last accessed Sep 5, 2015.

Çelik, Bahattin. 'Karahan Tepe: A New Cultural Centre in the Urfa area in Turkey.' *Documenta Praehistorica* XXXVIII. 2011. http://arheologija.ff.uni-lj.si/documenta/pdf38/38_19.pdf. Last accessed Sep 5, 2015.

Cervicek, P. 'Rock art and the Ancient Egyptian Pyramid Texts.' Sahara / Centro studi Luigi Negro. Issue 10, 1998, 110–111. PYRAMIDS SNC. 1998.

Chang, Chun-Hsiang et al. 'The first archaic homo from Taiwan.' http://www.nature.com/ncomms/2015/150127/ncomms7037/pdf/ncomms7037.pdf. Last accessed Sep 5, 2015.

Chen, Stephen. 'Made in China – 3,700 years ago: scientists reveal "hi-tech" celadon pottery production site.' http://www.scmp.com/news/china/article/1651923/made-china-3700-years-ago-scientists-reveal-hi-tech-celadon-pottery. Last accessed Sep 5, 2015.

Choi, Charles Q. 'Ancient Human Fossil Could Be New Primitive Species.' http://www.livescience.com/49588-ancient-human-fossil-primitive-species.html. Last accessed Sep 5, 2015.

Churton, Tobias. *Aleister Crowley: The Biography*. Watkins Publishing. London. 2011.

Clark, Laura. 'Did Fishermen Find Evidence of an Unknown Group of Primitive Humans?' http://www.smithsonianmag.com/smart-news/did-fishermen-find-evidence-unknown-group-primitive-humans-180954054. Last accessed Sep 5, 2015.

Clarke, Ardy Sixkiller. *Sky People: Untold Stories of Alien Encounters in Mesoamerica*. New Page Books. Pompton Plains. 2015.

Coghlan, Andy. 'Island-hopping odyssey brought civilisation to Europe.' https://www.newscientist. com/article/dn25695-island-hopping-odyssey-brought-civilisation-to-europe/. Last accessed Sep 5, 2015.

Cohen, Julie. 'Study examines 13,000-year-old nanodiamonds from multiple locations across three continents.' http://phys.org/news/2014-08-year-old-nanodiamonds-multiple-continents.html. Last accessed Sep 5, 2015.

Conman, Joanne. *Ancient Egyptian Sky Lore*. Decan Wisdom Books. 2013.

Copenhaver, Brian P. *Hermetica*. Cambridge University Press. New York. 1992.

Coppens, Philip. *The Canopus Revelation*. Frontier Publishing. Enkhuizen. 2004.

Counts, Derek B. & Bettina Arnold (editors). *The Master of Animals in Old World Iconography*. Archaeo-lingua Foundation. Budapest. 2010.

Craig, Oliver. 'Earliest Evidence for the Use of Pottery.' *Nature*. 2013.

Cremo, Michael A. *The Forbidden Archaeologist*. Torchlight Publishing Inc. 2011. (Kindle edition.)

Cronin, Frances. 'Egyptian pyramids found by infra-red satellite images.' http://www.bbc.co.uk/news/world-13522957. Last accessed Sep 5, 2015.

Croucher, Karina. *Death and Dying in the Neolithic Near East*. Oxford University Press. Oxford. 2012.

Crowley, Aleister. *The Law is for All*. (editors: Louis Wilkinson & Hymenaeus Beta.) New Falcon. Tempe. 1996.

Dalley, Stephanie. *Myths from Mesopotamia: Creation, the Flood, Gilgamesh, and Others*. Oxford University Press. Oxford. 2008.

Davidovits, Joseph. 'Paleomagnetism study supports Pyramid man-made stone.' http://www.davidovits.info/paleomagnetism-study-supports-pyramid-man-made-stone/. Last accessed Sep 5, 2015.

Davidovits, Joseph. *Why the Pharaohs Built the Pyramids with Fake Stones*. Institut Géopolymère. Saint-Quentin. 2009.

Davidson, Iain and David Andrew Roberts. '14,000 BC: On being alone – the isolation of the Tasmanians.' https://www.academia.edu/273234/14_000._On_being_alone_the_isolation_of_the_Tasmanian. Last accessed Sep 5, 2015.

De Trafford, A. Goyon, J.C. Cardin, C. 'The Pyramid Texts: A Contextual Approach.' *ORIENTALIA LOVANIENSIA ANALECTA*. International congress of Egyptologists; Grenoble, France, 2004; Sep, 2007. Peeters. Louvain. 2006 – 2007.

Denham, Tim. 'Early Agriculture and Plant Domestication in New Guinea and Island Southeast Asia.' *Current Anthropology*. Vol 52, No S4. University of Chicago Press. http://www.jstor.org/stable/10.1086/658682. Last accessed Sep 5, 2015.

Devereux, Paul. Acoustic Archaeology: Presented to Scientific & Medical Network, London, 2008. http://www.uwhg.org.uk/reports/other_meetings/acustic_arch/acustic_arch.html Last accessed Sep 5, 2015.

Dietrich, Oliver et al. 'The role of cult and feasting in the emergence of Neolithic communities. New evidence from Gobekli Tepe, south-eastern Turkey.' *Antiquity* Vol. 86; No. 333. 2012.

Dietrich, Oliver. 'Göbekli Tepe: A Stone Age Ritual Center in Southeastern Turkey.' *Actual Archaeology Magazine*. Summer 2012 Issue 02. 2012.

Dietrich, Oliver. 'Göbekli Tepe: Agriculture and Domestication.' https://www.academia.edu/6100898/G%C3%B6bekli_Tepe_Agriculture_and_Domestication. Last accessed Sep 5, 2015.

Dietrich, Oliver. 'Göbekli Tepe. Preliminary Report on the 2012 and 2013 Seasons.' *Neo-Lithics* 1/14: The Newsletter of Southwest Asian Neolithic Research. 2014.

Ding, Qiliang et al. 'Neanderthal Introgression at Chromosome 3p21.31 Was Under Positive Natural Selection in East Asians.' *Oxford Journal of Molecular Biology and Evolution*. Vol. 31, Issue 3.

Diop, Cheikh Anta et al. *The Peopling of Ancient Egypt*. Karnak House. London. 1997.

Donegan, John. 'Explainer: Who were the first Australians?' http://www.abc.net.au/news/2015-06-29/explainer-who-were-the-first-australians/6576364. Last accessed Sep 5, 2015.

Doniger, Wendy. *The Implied Spider: Politics & Theology in Myth*. Columbia University Press. New York. 1998.

Ducheyne, S. 'The Secret History of Hermes: Hermeticism from Ancient Times to Modern Times.' *Annals of Science: a quarterly review of the history of science since the Renaissance*. Vol. 66; No. 2, 2009. Taylor & Francis. London. 2009

Ducklau, Heinz. 'Modern Humans More Neanderthal than Once Thought, Studies Suggest.' http://www.cbsnews.com/news/modern-humans-more-neanderthal-than-once-thought-studies-suggest/. Last accessed Sep 5, 2015.

Edwards, Edmundo & Alexandra Edwards. 'Flag 83 Expedition Report.' *Rapanui Archaeoastronomy & Ethnoastronomy*. http://www.pacificislandsresearchinstitute.org/Flag_83_Report.pdf. Last accessed Sep 5, 2015.

Edwards, Edmundo. 'Megalithic Astronomy of Easter Island: A Reassessment.' *Journal for the History of Astronomy*. Vol. 35, Part 4, No 121. 2004.

Edwards, I. E. S. *The Pyramids of Egypt*. Penguin Books. London. 1961. (Revised edition.)

Eliade, Mircea. *The Sacred and the Profane: The Nature of Religion*. Harvest Books. New York. 1959.

Engelking, Carl. '4,600-Year-Old Pyramid Uncovered in Southern Egypt.'

Erdal, Yilmaz Selim. 'Bone or Flesh: Defleshing and post-depositional treatments at Körtik Tepe (Southeastern Anatolia, PPNA Period).' https://www.academia.edu/8530779/Bone_or_Flesh_Defleshing_and_Post-Depositional_Treatments_at_K%C3%B6rtik_Tepe_Southeastern_Anatolia_PPNA_Period_. Last accessed Sep 5, 2015.

Faulkner, R. O. *The Ancient Egyptian Pyramid Texts*. Digireads Publishing. Stilwell. 2007.

Finkel, Irving. *The Ark Before Noah: Decoding the Story of the Flood*. Hodder & Stoughton. London. 2014.

Fox, R.L. et al. 'Harran, the Sabians and the late Platonist "Movers."' *Conference in honour of Peter Brown; The Philosopher and Society in late antiquity: Essays in honour of Peter Brown*. 2005. Classical Press of Wales. Swansea. 2005.

Garfinkel, Yosef. *Dancing at the Dawn of Agriculture*. University of Texas Press. Austin. 2003.

Gatti, Hilary. *Essays on Giordano Bruno*. Princeton University Press. Princeton. 2011.

Gennaro, Alfredo. 'Giza Pyramids Today. Figures Against Assumptions.' *ORIENTALIA LOVANIENSIA ANALECTA*. International congress of Egyptologists; Grenoble, France, 2004; Sep, 2007. Peeters. Louvain. 2006 – 2007.

Gigal, Antoine. 'How Did This Civilisation Begin? Egypt Before the Pharaohs.' *New Dawn* Special Issue Vol. 8, No. 6. 2014.

Girling, Richard. 'King Tut tut tut.' http://www.thesundaytimes.co.uk/sto/style/article133853.ece. Last accessed Sep 5, 2015.

Glucklich, Ariel. *The Strides of Vishnu*. Oxford University Press. Oxford. 2008.

Gough, Myles. 'Aboriginal legends reveal ancient secrets to science.' http://www.bbc.co.uk/news/world-australia-32701311. Last accessed Sep 5, 2015.

Greene, Tamara M. *The City of the Moon God: Religious Traditions of Harran*. Brill. Leiden. 1992.

Greer, John Michael and Christopher Warnock. *The Picatrix*. Adocentyn Press. 2010.

Griffiths, John Gwyn. *The Origins of Osiris and His Cult*. Brill. Leiden. 1980.

Grof, Stanislav. *When the Impossible Happens*. Sounds True Inc. Boulder. 2006.

Guerra-Doce, Elisa. 'The Origins of Inebriation: Archaeological Evidence of the Consumption of Fermented Beverages and Drugs in Prehistoric Eurasia.' *Journal of Archaeological Method and Theory*. http://link.springer.com/article/10.1007%2Fs10816-014-9205-z#. Last accessed Sep 5, 2015.

Gunduz, Sinasi. *The origins and early history of the Mandaeans and their relation to the Sabians of the Qur'an and to the Harranians*. (Thesis.) University of Manchester. 1991.

Guzmán, Gastón. 'A Worldwide Geographical Distribution of the Neurotropic Fungi: An Analysis and Discussion.' http://www.museocivico.rovereto.tn.it/UploadDocs/104_art09-Guzman%20. Last accessed Sep 5, 2015.

Győző Vörös. 'Preliminary Report of the Excavations at Thoth Hill, Thebes. The Temple of Montuhotep Sankhkara (Season 1995 – 1996).' *Mitteilungen des Deutschen Archäologischen Instituts*, Abteilung Kairo. Vol. 53, 1997. Philipp von Zabern. Mainz. 1997.

Győző Vörös & Hawass, Z. 'The Ancient Nest of Horus above Thebes: Hungarian Excavations on Thoth Hill at the Temple of King Sankhkare Montuhotep (1995 – 1998).' *International Congress of Egyptologists; Egyptology at the Dawn of the Twenty-first Century*; Cairo, 2000. American University in Cairo Press. Cairo. 2003.

Győző Vörös (trans. David Robert Evans). *Egyptian Temple Architecture: 100 Years of Hungarian Excavations in Egypt, 1907-2007*. Kairosz Press. Budapest. 2007.

Hamacher, Duane. 'A shark in the stars: astronomy and culture in the Torres Strait.' https://www.academia.edu/9325566/A_shark_in_the_stars_astronomy_and_culture_in_the_Torres_Strait. Last accessed Sep 5, 2015.

Hamacher, Duane. 'Aboriginal Astronomical traditions from Ooldea, South Australia, Part 1: Nyeeruna and the "Orion Story."' https://www.academia.edu/6774066/Aboriginal_Astronomical_traditions_from_Ooldea_South_Australia_Part_1_Nyeeruna_and_the_Orion_Story_. Last accessed Sep 5, 2015.

Hamacher, Duane. 'On the Astronomical Knowledge and Traditions of Aboriginal Australians.' https://www.academia.edu/1905624/On_the_Astronomical_Knowledge_and_Traditions_of_Aboriginal_Australians. Last accessed Sep 5, 2015.

Hamacher, Duane. 'Stories from the Sky: Astronomy in Indigenous Knowledge.' http://aboriginal-astronomy.blogspot.co.uk/2014/12/stories-from-sky-astronomy-in.html. Last accessed Sep 5, 2015.

Hamacher, Duane. 'Stories from the Sky: Astronomy in Indigenous Knowledge.' https://www.academia.edu/9621614/Stories_from_the_Sky_Astronomy_in_Indigenous_Knowledge. Last accessed Sep 5, 2015.

Hancock, Graham. *Supernatural*. Century. London. 2005.

Hancock, Graham. *Underworld: Flooded Kingdoms of the Ice Age*. Penguin Books. London. 2003.

Hanegraaff, Wouter J. and Roelof van den Broek (editors). *Gnosis and Hermeticism from Antiquity to Modern Times*. University of New York Press. Albany. 1998.

Hays, Brooks. 'Does the peer review process stifle scientific innovation?' http://www.upi.com/Science_News/2014/12/23/Does-the-peer-review-process-stifle-scientific-innovation/5521419367701/. Last accessed Sep 5, 2015.

Hays, Harold M. *The Organization of the Pyramid Texts: Typology and Disposition*. Brill. Leiden. 2012.

Hellum, J. Knoblauch, C.M. Gill, J.C. 'The Use of Myth in the Pyramid Texts.' BAR international series. Australasian Conference for Young Egyptologists; Egyptology in Australia and New Zealand 2009; Melbourne, Vic, 2009, 2012. Archaeopress. Oxford. 2012.

Hendrickx, Stan et al. 'The Earliest Representations of Royal Power in Egypt: The Rock Drawings of Nag el-Hamdulab (Aswan).' *Antiquity 86*. Antiquity Publications Ltd. 2012.

Heritage Daily. 'Evidence of Domestic Cereal Grains in Sudan as Early as 7,000 Years Ago.' http://www.heritagedaily.com/2014/11/evidence-of-domestic-cereals-in-sudan-as-early-as-7000-years-ago/105714. Last accessed Sep 5, 2015.

Holloway, April. 'Entire Neanderthal genome finally mapped – with amazing results.' http://www.ancient-origins.net/news-evolution-human-origins/entire-neanderthal-genome-finally-mapped-amazing-results-001138. Last accessed Sep 5, 2015.

http://blogs.discovermagazine.com/d-brief/2014/02/04/4600-year-old-pyramid-uncovered-in-southern-egypt. Last accessed Sep 5, 2015.

http://mbe.oxfordjournals.org/content/31/3/683. Last accessed Sep 5, 2015.

http://pvs.kcc.hawaii.edu/ike/hookele/hawaiian_star_lines.html. Last accessed Sep 5, 2015.

http://www.nature.com/nature/journal/v496/n7445/full/nature12109.html. Last accessed Sep 5, 2015.

Hynek, J. Allen. *The UFO Experience: A Scientific Enquiry*. Corgi Books. London. 1974.

Izady, Mehrdad R. *The Kurds: A Concise Handbook*. Crane Russak. London. 1992.

Jakarta Post Travel. 'A new archaeological discovery in Gunung Padang may redefine what we know about Indonesia.' https://sg.news.yahoo.com/archaeological-discovery-gunung-pa-dang-may-redefine-know-indonesia-170000648.html. Last accessed Sep 5, 2015.

Jarus, Owen. '"World's Oldest Temple" May Have Been Cosmopolitan Center.' http://www.livescience.com/19085-world-oldest-temple-tools-pilgrimage.html. Last accessed Sep 5, 2015.

Jarus, Owen. '6,000-Year-Old Temple with Possible Sacrificial Altars Discovered.' http://www.livescience.com/48352-prehistoric-ukraine-temple-discovered.html. Last accessed Sep 5, 2015.

Jarus, Owen. 'Ruins of Bustling Port Unearthed at Egypt's Giza Pyramids.' http://www.livescience.com/42902-giza-pyramids-port-discovered.html. Last accessed Sep 5, 2015.

Keel, John A. *Our Haunted Planet*. Bounty Books. London. 2005.

Knappert, Jan. *Pacific Mythology: An Encyclopedia of Myth and Legend*. Aquarian Press. London. 1992.

Knight, Christopher & Alan Butler. *Before the Pyramids*. Watkins Publishing. London. 2009.

Kurth, Dieter. *The Temple of Edfu*. American University in Cairo Press. Cairo. 2004.

Lachman, Gary. *The Quest for Hermes Trismegistus*. Floris Books. 2011. (Kindle edition.)

Leeming, David. *The Oxford Companion to World Mythology*. Oxford University Press. Oxford. 2005.

Levenda, Peter. *The Dark Lord*. Ibis Press. Lake Worth. 2013.

Lewis-Williams, David & Sam Challis. *Deciphering Ancient Minds*. Thames & Hudson. London. 2011.

Lieff-Benderly, Beryl. 'An Academic Cartel?' http://sciencecareers.sciencemag.org/career_magazine/previous_issues/articles/2013_11_26/caredit.a1300260. Last accessed Sep 5, 2015.

Luckert, Karl W. *Stone Age Religion at Göbekli Tepe*. Triplehood. 2013.

Lutz, Diana. 'Genetic study tackles mystery of slow plant domestications.' https://news.wustl.edu/news/Pages/26750.aspx. Last accessed Sep 5, 2015.

Lutz, Diana. 'More questions than answers as mystery of domestication deepens.' https://news.wustl.edu/news/Pages/26815.aspx. Last accessed Sep 5, 2015.

Lutz, Diana. 'The story of animal domestication retold.' https://news.wustl.edu/news/Pages/26781.aspx. Last accessed Sep 5, 2015.

Magli, Giulo. 'On the Possible Discovery of Precessional Effects in Ancient Astronomy.' http://arxiv.org/pdf/physics/0407108.pdf. Last accessed Sep 5, 2015.

Mahadevan, Iravatham. 'A Notes on the Muruku Sign of the Indus Script in light of the Mayiladu-thurai Stone Axe Discovery.' http://a.harappa.com/content/arrow/stone_celt_indus_signs.html. Last accessed Sept 5, 2015.

Malville, J.M. et al. *Astronomy of Nabta Playa*. Ghana Eclipse Conference; African cultural astronomy: current archaeoastronomy and ethnoastronomy research in Africa; Cape Coast, Ghana. Springer. Berlin. 2006.

Manansala, Paul Kekai. *Sailing the Black Current*. Self-published. 2007.

Mann, Charles C. 'The Birth of Religion.' *National Geographic Magazine*. http://ngm.nationalgeographic.com/print/2011/06/gobekli-tepe/mann-text. Last accessed Sep 5, 2015.

Maraqten, M. & Abdallah, Y. 'A Recently Discovered Inscribed Sabean Bronze Plaque from Mahram

Bilqis near Marib, Yemen.' *Journal of Near Eastern Studies*. Vol. 61, Part 1. 2002. University of Chicago Press. Chicago. 2002.

Marlar, M.; Goyon, J.C.; Cardin, C. 'Excavations of the Temple of Osiris at Abydos Reported on behalf of the University of Pennsylvania Museum – Yale University – Institute of Fine Arts, New York University Expedition to Abydos.' *ORIENTALIA LOVANIENSIA ANALECTA*. International congress of Egyptologists; Grenoble, France, 2004; Sep, 2007. Peeters. Louvain. 2006 – 2007.

McEvoy, Maria. 'Cold War satellites find lost cities in Middle East.' http://www.telegraph.co.uk/news/worldnews/middleeast/10793066/Cold-War-satellites-find-lost-cities-in-Middle-East.html. Last accessed Sep 5, 2015.

Milic, Marina. 'The Consumption of Obsidian at Neolithic Çatalhöyük: A Long-Term Perspective.' https://www.academia.edu/5389781/The_consumption_of_obsidian_at_Neolithic_%C3%87atalh%C3%B6y%C3%BCk_A_long-term_perspective. Last accessed Sep 5, 2015.

Morgan, Mogg. *Tankhem: Seth & Egyptian Magick*. Mandrake of Oxford. Oxford. 2005.

Morgan, Stephen. '40,000-year-old bracelet made by extinct human species found.' http://www.digitaljournal.com/science/40-000-year-old-bracelet-from-extinct-human-species-discovered/article/432798#ixzz3ZeTMp6YA. Last accessed Sep 5, 2015.

Murgano, R.; Goyon, J.C.; Cardin, C. 'The Sun and Stars Double Cult in the Old Kingdom.' *ORIENTALIA LOVANIENSIA ANALECTA*. International congress of Egyptologists; Grenoble, France, 2004; Sep, 2007. Peeters. Louvain. 2006 – 2007.

Naydler, Jeremy. *Shamanic Wisdom in the Pyramid Texts*. Inner Traditions. Rochester. 2005.

Nichols, Joanna. *Linguistic Diversity in Space and Time*. University of Chicago Press. London. 1992.

Ogdon, J. R. 'Studies in Ancient Egyptian Magical Thought, VII. Pyramid Texts-Pepi 1, Passage A-S, South Wall, Line 9.' *Discussions in Egyptology*. ISSU 50, 2001, 55–62. 2001.

Oppenheimer, Stephen. *Eden in the East: The Drowned Continent of Southeast Asia*. Phoenix. London. 1998.

Orriols i Llonch, M. Goyon, J.C. Cardin, C. 'Divine Copulation in the Pyramid Texts. A Lexical and Cultural Approach.' *ORIENTALIA LOVANIENSIA ANALECTA*. International congress of Egyptologists; Grenoble, France, 2004; Sep, 2007. Peeters. Louvain. 2006 – 2007.

Owen, Sri. *The Rice Book*. Frances Lincoln. London. 1993.

PAP – Science and Scholarship in Poland. '70,000 year-old African settlement unearthed.' *Past Horizons*. http://www.pasthorizonspr.com/index.php/archives/07/2014/70000-year-old-african-settlement-unearthed. Last accessed Sep 5, 2015.

Parpola, Asko. 'Beginnings of Indian Astronomy with Reference to a Parallel Development in China.' *History of Science in South Asia* Vol. 1. 2013.

Parsell, Diana. 'Monumental Shift.' http://www.smithsonianmag.com/science-nature/monumental-shift-160227897. Last accessed Sep 5, 2015.

Perkins, Sid. 'DNA study links indigenous Brazilians to Polynesians.' http://www.nature.com/news/dna-study-links-indigenous-brazilians-to-polynesians-1.12710. Last accessed Sep 5, 2015.

Peters, J. et al. 'Birds in the megalithic art of Pre-Pottery Neolithic Gobekli Tepe, Southeast Turkey.' *DOCUMENTA ARCHÆOBIOLOGIÆ*. International Council for Archaeozoology. Feathers, grit and symbolism: birds and humans in the ancient old and new worlds. Munich. 2004.

Pingree, D. 'The Sabians of Harran and the Classical Tradition.' *International Journal of the Classical Tradition*. Vol 9, Part 1, 2002. Transaction Publishers. Piscataway. 2002.

Polynesian Voyaging Society. *Hawaiian Star Lines and Names for Stars*.

Powell, Alvin. 'The Surprising Origins of Europeans.' http://news.harvard.edu/gazette/story/2014/12/the-surprising-origins-of-europeans/. Last accessed Sep 5, 2015.

Priyadarshi, Premendra. *In Quest of the Dates of the Vedas*. Partridge Publishing. 2014. Gurgaon. 2014.

Pustovoytov, K. 'Soils and Soil Sediments at Göbekli Tepe, Southeastern Turkey: A Preliminary Report.' *Geoarchaeology: An International Journal*. Vol. 21; No. 7. John Wiley & Sons, Ltd. London. 2006.

Rajaram, N. S. 'The Harappan Civilization and Myth of Aryan "Invasion."' http://archaeologyonline.net/artifacts/aryan-harappan-myth. Last accessed Sep 5, 2015.

Reader, C. D. 'A Geomorphological Study of the Giza Necropolis, with Implications for the Development of the Site.' *Archaeometry*. Vol. 43; Part 1, 2001. Research Laboratory For Archaeology and the History of Art. Oxford. 2001.

Reich, David et al. 'Denisova Admixture and the First Modern Human Dispersals into Southeast Asia and Oceania.' http://www.sciencedirect.com/science/article/pii/S0002929711003958

Reid, N. 'Indigenous Australian stories and sea-level change.' 18th Conference of the Foundation for Endangered Languages (FEL): Indigenous Languages: Value to the Community, Okinawa, Japan 17-20 September 2014. http://research.usc.edu.au/vital/access/manager/Repository/usc:14264?queryType=vitalDismax. Last accessed Sep 5, 2015.

Renfrew, Colin et al. 'Religion in the Emergence of Civilization: Catalhoyuk as a Case Study.' *Current Anthropology*. Vol. 52; No. 6, 2011. University of Chicago Press. Chicago. 2011.

Reyes, Raphael. 'The Austronesians, the Nusantao and the Lapita Cultural Complex: A Review of Neolithic migration in SEA and Oceania.' https://www.academia.edu/10134524/The_Austronesians_the_Nusantao_and_the_Lapita_Cultural_Complex_A_Review_of_Neolithic_migration_in_SEA_and_Oceania. Last accessed Sep 5, 2015.

Richards, Zoe et al. 'New precise dates for the ancient and sacred coral pyramidal tombs of Leluh (Kosrae, Micronesia).' http://advances.sciencemag.org/content/1/2/e1400060. Last accessed Sep 5, 2015.

Roberts, Alison. *My Heart My Mother: Death and Rebirth in Ancient Egypt*. Northgate Publishers. Rottingdean. 2000.

Romero, Simon. 'Discoveries Challenge Beliefs on Humans' Arrival in the Americas.' http://www.nytimes.com/2014/03/28/world/americas/discoveries-challenge-beliefs-on-humans-arrival-in-the-americas.html. Last accessed Sep 5, 2015.

Rootsi, S. et al. 'Distinguishing the co-ancestries of haplogroup G Y-chromosomes in the populations of Europe and the Caucasus.' *EJHG: European Journal of Human Genetics, the official journal of the*

European Society of Human Genetics. Vol. 20, No. 12, 2012. Nature Publishing Group. London. 2012

Roullier, Caroline et al. 'Historical collections reveal patterns of diffusion of sweet potato in Oceania obscured by modern plant movements and recombination.' *Proceedings of the National Academy of Sciences of the United States of America.* http://www.pnas.org/content/110/6/2205. Last accessed Sep 5, 2015.

Rower, Lutz et al. 'Continent-Wide Decoupling of Y-Chromosomal Genetic Variation from Language and Geography in Native South Americans.' http://journals.plos.org/plosgenetics/article?id=10.1371/journal.pgen.1003460. Last accessed Sep 5, 2015.

Rush, John A. (editor). *Entheogens and the Development of Culture.* North Atlantic Books. Berkeley. 2013.

Schillereff, Daniel. 'From mud to moai statue: lake sediments reveal new insights into Easter Island colonization.' http://blogs.egu.eu/network/geojenga/2013/12/17/frommudtomoaistatue/. Last accessed Sep 5, 2015.

Schmidt, Klaus. *Göbekli Tepe: A Stone Age Sanctuary in South-Eastern Anatolia.* Exoriente. Berlin. 2012.

Schmidt, Klaus. 'When Humanity Began to Settle Down.' *Reports of the Deutsche Forschungsgemeinschaft.* Vol. 30; No. 1. John Wiley & Sons, Ltd. London. 2008.

Schoch, Robert M. *Forgotten Civilization: The Role of Solar Outbursts in Our Past and Future.* Inner Traditions. Rochester. 2012. (Kindle edition.)

Schoch, Robert M. 'Personal Refections on the Mystery of the Great Sphinx.' *New Dawn* Special Issue Vol' 8, No' 6. 2014.

Schoch, Robert M. 'Sundaland Rising: Gunung Padang – Indonesia's Mysterious Lost Civilisation?' *New Dawn* Special Issue Vol' 8, No. 1. 2014.

Schoch, Robert M. *Voyages of the Pyramid Builders.* Tarcher Penguin. New York. 2004.

Schoch, Robert. 'Journey to Gunung Padang: The Case for a Lost Civilization in Indonesia.' http://atlantisrisingmagazine.com/2014/03/01/journey-to-gunung-padang/. Last accessed Sep 5, 2015.

Schoch, Robert. 'The Mysteries of Easter Island: A Proposal to Investigate and Possibly Uncover Significant New Evidence.' http://www.robertschoch.com/articles/schochbaddeleyeasterislandproposal.pdf. Last accessed Sep 5, 2015.

Schultz, Collin. 'Archaeologists Just Found a 5,600-Year-Old Pre-Dynastic Egyptian Tomb.' http://www.smithsonianmag.com/smart-news/archaeologists-just-found-5600-year-old-pre-dynastic-egyptian-tomb-180951389/. Last accessed Sep 5, 2015.

Schwaller de Lubicz, R. A. *Symbol and the Symbolic.* Inner Traditions. Rochester. 1978. (Reprint.)

Schwartz, Howard. *Tree of Souls: The Mythology of Judaism.* Oxford University Press. Oxford. 2004.

Science Daily. '"Immune gene" in humans inherited from Neanderthals, study suggests.' http://www.sciencedaily.com/releases/2013/11/131122084405.htm. Last accessed Sep 5, 2015.

Sellers, Jane B. *The Death of Gods in Ancient Egypt.* Penguin Books. London. 1992.

Shalomi-Hen, R.; Goyon, J.C.; Cardin, C. 'The Earliest Pictorial Representation of Osiris.' *ORIENTALIA LOVANIENSIA ANALECTA.* International congress of Egyptologists; Grenoble, France, 2004; Sep, 2007. Peeters. Louvain. 2006 – 2007.

Shushan, Gregory. *Conceptions of the Afterlife in Early Civilizations*. Continuum International Publishing Group. London. 2009.

Sidharth, B. G. *The Celestial Key to the Vedas*. Inner Traditions. Rochester. 1999.

Skinner, Stephen. *Techniques of Graeco-Egyptian Magic*. Golden Hoard Press. Singapore. 2014.

Skinner, Stephen. *Techniques of Solomonic Magic*. Golden Hoard Press. Singapore. 2015.

Slav, Irina. 'Written Communication May Be 40,000 Years Old.' http://www.newhistorian.com/written-communication-may-be-40000-years-old/3851/. Last accessed Sep 5, 2015.

Smith, Michael E. 'V. Gordon Childe and the Urban Revolution.' http://www.public.asu.edu/~me-smith9/1-CompleteSet/MES-09-Childe-TPR.pdf. Last accessed Sep 5, 2015.

Smith, Sylvia. 'Bahrain Digs Unveil One of the Oldest Civilisations.' http://www.bbc.co.uk/news/science-environment-22596270. Last accessed Sep 5, 2015.

SMU Research. 'Comet theory false; doesn't explain cold snap at the end of the Ice Age, Clovis changes or mass animal extinction.' http://blog.smu.edu/research/2014/05/12/dating-of-supposed-extraterrestrial-impact-indicators-unreliable-fails-to-prove-comet-sparked-climate-change-at-the-end-of-the-ice-age-or-killed-clovis-people/. Last accessed Sep 5, 2015.

Soja, E. W. 'Cities and States in Geohistory.' *Theory and Society*. Vol. 39; No. 3 – 4. 2010. Springer Science & Business Media. New York. 2010

Solheim, Wilhelm G. *Archaeology and Culture in Southeast Asia: Unraveling the Nusantao*. University of Philippines Press. Manila. 2007.

Soltysiak, Arkadiusz. 'Physical anthropology and the "Sumerian problem."' http://www.antropologia.uw.edu.pl/SHA/sha-04-07.pdf. Last accessed Sep 5, 2015.

Spencer, Jeffrey. *Aspects of Early Egypt*. British Museum Press. London. 1996.

Srivastava, Vanita. 'Harappan-era Seal Found in Rajasthan.' http://www.hindustantimes.com/science/harappan-era-seal-found-in-rajasthan/article1-1178990.aspx. Last accessed Sep 5, 2015.

Staff Writers, *Archaeology Magazine*. 'Genetic Study Links Amazonians and Australasians.' http://www.archaeology.org/news/3502-150721-amazonian-australasian-link. Last accessed Sep 5, 2015.

Staff Writers, *Archaeology Magazine*. 'Stone Bracelet May Have Been Made by Denisovans.' http://www.archaeology.org/news/3270-150507-siberia-denisovan-bracelet. Last accessed Sep 5, 2015.

Steiner, Richard C. 'Early Northwest Semitic Serpent Spells in the Pyramid Texts.' *Journal of Semitic Studies*. Vol. 57, No. 2, 2012. Oxford University Press. Oxford. 2012.

Stevenson, Alice. 'Cultural convergence in the Nile valley Neolithic: a prehistoric perspective on Egypt's place in Africa.' https://www.academia.edu/6411856/_co-authored_Cultural_convergence_in_the_Nile_valley_Neolithic_a_prehistoric_perspective_on_Egypt_s_place_in_Africa. Last accessed Sep 5, 2015.

Stoddart, Simon & Caroline Malone. 'Editorial.' *Antiquity* 75. Antiquity Publications Ltd. 2001.

Stoneking, Mark et al. 'Denisova admixture and the first modern human dispersals into southeast

Asia and Oceania.' *American Journal of Human Genetics*, 22 September 2011. http://www.mpg. de/4438282/denisova_asia?page=1 Last accessed Sep 5, 2015.

Stratton-Kent, Jake. *Geosophia: The Argo of Magic*. Scarlet Imprint. Dover. 2010.

Swain, Tony & Garry Trompf. *The Religions of Oceania*. Routledge. London. 1995.

Swelim, Nabil. 'The Great Dry Moat Surrounding the Step Pyramid Complex of Horus Netjerykhet.' http://www.nabilswelim.com/downloads/DM_ab.pdf.pdf. Last accessed Sep 5, 2015.

Symmes, Patrick. 'Turkey: Archaeological Dig Reshaping Human History.' http://www.newsweek. com/turkey-archeological-dig-reshaping-human-history-75101. Last accessed Sep 5, 2015.

Temple, Robert & Olivia Temple. *The Sphinx Mystery*. Inner Traditions. Rochester. 2009.

Temple, Robert. *Egyptian Dawn*. Arrow Books. London. 2011.

Temple, Robert. *The Sirius Mystery*. Century. London. 1998.

Tindale, N. B. et al. *Celestial Lore of some Australian Tribes*. International conference on ethnoastron-omy; Songs from the sky indigenous astronomical and cosmological traditions of the world; Washington D.C, 1983. Ocarino Books. Bognor Regis. 1983.

Upton, John. 'Ancient Sea Rise Tale Told Accurately for 10,000 Years.' http://www.scientificamer-ican.com/article/ancient-sea-rise-tale-told-accurately-for-10-000-years/. Last accessed Sep 5, 2015.

Usborne, David. 'US investigates National Geographic over "corrupt payments" to Egypt's keeper of antiquities.' http://www.independent.co.uk/news/world/americas/us-investigates-national-ge-ographic-over-corrupt-payments-to-egypts-keeper-of-antiquities-8909454.html. Last accessed Sep 5, 2015.

Vallée, Jacques & Chris Aubeck. *Wonders in the Sky*. Tarcher Penguin. London. 2009.

Vallée, Jacques. *Revelations: Alien Contact and Human Deception*. Ballatine Books. New York. 1991.

Vallée, Jacques. *The Invisible College*. Anomalist Books. San Francisco. 2014. (Reprint.)

Vallée, Jacques. *UFOs: The Psychic Solution*. Panther. St Albans. 1977.

Van De Mieroop, Marc. *A History of the Ancient Near East*. Blackwell Publishing. Malden. 2007.

Vergano, Dan. 'Cave Paintings in Indonesia Redraw Picture of Earliest Art.' http://news.nationalgeo-graphic.com/news/2014/10/141008-cave-art-sulawesi-hand-science/. Last accessed September 5, 2015.

Vogt, Yngve. 'World's oldest ritual discovered. Worshipped the python 70,000 years ago.' http://www.apollon.uio.no/english/articles/2006/python-english.html. Last accessed Sep 5, 2015.

Wade, Lizzie. 'Drones and satellites spot lost civilizations in unlikely places.' http://news.science-mag.org/archaeology/2015/02/drones-and-satellites-spot-lost-civilizations-unlikely-places. Last accessed Sep 5, 2015.

Waxman, Sharon. 'The Show-Biz Pharaoh of Egypt's Antiquities.' http://www.nytimes. com/2005/06/13/arts/design/the-showbiz-pharaoh-of-egypts-antiquities.html. Las accessed Sep 5, 2015.

West, John Anthony. *Serpent in the Sky*. Quest Books. Wheaton. 1993.

Western Daily Press. 'The "Singing" Stones of Stonehenge.' http://www.bathchronicle.co.uk/sing-ing-stones-Stonehenge/story-20750831-detail/story.html. Sep 5, 2015.

White, Gavin. *Babylonian Star-Lore*. Solaria Publications. London. 2008.

Williams, Mike. *Prehistoric Belief: Shamans, Trance and the Afterlife*. History Press. Stroud. 2010.

Winter, Olaf et al. 'Austronesian Sailing to the Northern Marianas, a comment on Hung et al.' *Antiquity* 86. Antiquity Publications Ltd. 2012.

Witzel, E. J. Michael. *The Origins of the World's Mythologies*. Oxford University Press. Oxford. 2012.

Yirka, Bob. 'Sweet potato DNA indicates early Polynesians traveled to South America.' http://phys.org/news/2013-01-sweet-potato-dna-early-polynesians.html. Last accessed Sep 5, 2015.

Young, Susan. 'Canoodling with Cavemen gave Healthy Boost to Human Genome, study finds.' http://med.stanford.edu/news/all-news/2011/08/canoodling-with-cavemen-gave-healthy-boost-to-human-genome-study-finds.html. Last accessed Sep 5, 2015.

Zapp, Ivar & George Erikson. *Atlantis in America*. Adventures Unlimited Press. Kempton. 1998.

Zimmer, Carl. 'A New Theory on How Neanderthal DNA Spread in Asia.' http://www.nytimes.com/2015/02/20/science/a-new-theory-on-how-neanderthal-dna-spread-in-asia.html?_r=0. Last accessed Sep 5, 2015.

INDEX

Doniger, Wendy xiv, 3, 13, 30, 44, 108, 220, 272

Dragon 30, 48, 50, 52, 55, 92, 235, 263

Dravidian culture 2, 129, 131, 132, 136, 140, 141, 150

Dunn, Christopher 174, 203, 204

E

Egypt xii, xv, 7, 27, 29, 47, 48, 50, 52, 60, 61, 63, 77, 85, 91, 92, 94, 106, 107, 108, 126, 131, 137, 146, 149, 155, 156, 158, 159, 161 – 167, 169, 171, 172, 173, 175, 176, 177, 180, 181, 182, 184, 186, 190, 193, 197, 199, 201, 202, 203, 208, 213 – 218, 221 – 227, 232, 236, 239 – 244, 247, 255, 259, 260, 264

Elamo-Dravidian 131

Elephantine 169, 171

Eliade, Mircea 10, 57, 267

Enki 39, 119

Enlil 39, 121

Enoch 60, 233, 234

Enoch, Book of 52, 60, 230

Entheogens 80, 251, 256, 260

Eridu 115, 116, 117, 149, 150, 151, 152, 153

Eurasia 9, 47, 48, 57, 71, 72, 73, 74, 75, 108, 132, 135, 136, 140, 170, 221, 229

excarnation 36

extraterrestrial 52, 61, 238, 246, 247

Extraterrestrial Hypothesis 248, 249

F

Ficino, Marsilio xv, 225

Finkel, Dr Irving 120, 147, 148
   The Ark Before Noah 120, 147

Flandrian Transgression 115, 116, 149, 152

Flood 12, 42, 48, 51 – 54, 56, 57, 60, 61, 64, 65, 73, 76, 83, 108, 111, 112, 114, 115, 116, 119 – 123, 132, 148, 152, 153, 154, 186, 213, 223, 224, 230

Followers of Horus 170

G

Gardner, Gerald 215, 240

Geller, Uri 249, 252, 253

Gilgamesh 117, 153, 259, 260, 268

Giza 9, 18, 157, 158, 159, 160, 161, 163, 167, 172, 173, 174, 175, 176, 177, 178, 193, 197, 199, 200, 201, 202, 203, 206, 207, 208, 209, 210, 211, 212, 233, 243, 244, 249

Gnomons 145

Göbekli Tepe 9, 9, 17, 18, 19, 20, 21, 22, 23, 24, 25, 26, 27, 28, 29, 30, 31, 32, 33, 34, 35, 36, 37, 38, 39, 41, 42, 49, 58, 59, 63, 73, 76, 100, 105, 107, 122, 139, 160, 165, 171, 177, 184, 209, 222, 228, 229, 230, 231, 232, 234, 236, 237, 243, 244, 264, 265
   T - pillars 21, 25, 26, 27, 29, 30, 31, 33, 34, 35, 36, 184, 231, 237

Golden Age 48, 51, 52, 60, 61, 153, 227

Golden Dawn 14

Gondwana 48, 51, 53, 54, 55, 56, 57, 58, 59, 62, 67, 69, 87, 89, 90, 94, 107, 132, 219, 263

Grandfather stories 62, 219

Grandmother stories 62, 219, 220, 236

Grant, Kenneth xv, 238

Great Pyramid 18, 126, 159, 160, 163, 173, 174, 177, 182, 201, 202, 203, 204, 206, 207, 208, 212, 243

Greece 49, 50, 52, 62, 122, 221

Greek Magical Papyri (PGM) 206, 208, 220, 221, 222, 224, 230, 235, 236, 241, 242, 272

Greene, Tamara M. 235, 236
   City of the Moon God 233

Grey, Peter 219, 228, 265
   Lucifer: Princeps 228, 265

Grimoires 220, 221, 226, 242, 263

Gunung Padang 9, 56, 78, 79, 83, 98, 100, 182, 186

Guzmán, Gastón 59, 256

H

Hamacher, Duane 87, 88

Hancock, Graham 5, 27, 160

Harappa 3, 4, 107, 130, 135, 136, 137, 141,
145, 147, 148, 197

Harappan culture/civilisation 2, 3, 90, 115, 128,
129, 131, 132, 135, 136, 139, 140, 141,
142, 143, 144, 145, 146, 147, 154

Harpur, Patrick xiv

Harran 21, 222, 223, 224, 232, 233, 234, 235,
236, 237

Hathor 27, 44

Hawass, Zahi 158, 159, 160, 161, 173, 199, 200

Headless Rite 241, 242, 244, 265

Head cult/worship 234

Heb Sed 177, 178, 180, 181, 183, 184, 185,
186, 192, 193, 195, 197, 206, 208, 217,
244, 254, 258, 260

Heliopolis 172, 182, 191, 197

Hermes 154, 223, 224, 233, 234, 236

Herodotus 4, 40, 199, 202, 206, 227

Heuman, Linda 8

High God 48, 54, 55

Holocene 135

Homo erectus 46

Homo floresiensis xi, 67, 101

Hornung, Erik 225, 226

Horus 93, 155, 169, 170, 171, 172, 175, 176,
181, 183, 185, 188, 190, 191, 210, 215,
216, 241, 242, 244, 271

Houdin, Henri 203

Houdin, Jean-Pierre 203

Hunter-gatherers 22

Hygromanteia 235

I

Ice Age 31, 34, 46, 53, 56, 60, 61, 65, 66, 67,
70, 72, 73, 75, 78, 80, 83, 85, 86, 87, 89,
90, 107, 108, 110, 111, 112, 113, 115,
117, 118, 120, 123, 124, 127, 128, 131,
133, 134, 137, 144, 147, 148, 150, 152,
154, 165, 177, 224, 264, 265

Immortality 27, 59, 60, 90, 92, 94, 108, 123,
146, 154, 172, 190, 200, 201, 204, 208,
210, 215, 216, 217, 224, 257, 259, 260,
265, 270

Imperishable Stars 184, 186, 187, 188, 189,
190, 192, 270

India xiv, 2, 3, 4, 27, 30, 46, 54, 58, 67, 70, 72,
73, 77, 85, 92, 100, 106, 114, 128, 129,
131, 132, 133, 134, 135, 136, 137, 138,
139, 147, 150, 171, 186, 235, 258, 259,
260

Indo-Aryan mythology 48

Indus Valley 9, 76, 130, 131, 147

Io 95

Ishtar 221, 231

Isis 44, 155, 175, 176, 184, 186, 197, 231, 240,
271

Islam 223, 225, 234

Island Southeast Asia 2, 57, 65, 70, 75, 77, 86,
128, 140

Israel 2

Izady, Merhdad 40, 41, 228

J

Jaynes, Julian 268, 269

Jerf el Ahmar 37

John the Baptist 244, 265

Jōmon 70, 76

K

Kalevala 72

Kalibangan 143, 145

Karahan Tepe 18, 19, 21

Kelley, Edward 252

Khafre 163, 174, 175, 208, 209, 211, 214, 224

Khufu 163, 174, 193, 202, 203, 206, 208, 214,
223, 224

King's Chamber 201, 203, 204, 205, 206, 211,
241

Kingship 85, 97, 108, 146, 152, 153, 251, 265

Kish 150, 152, 153

Knight, Christopher 125, 126, 127

COLOPHON

Star.Ships: A Prehistory of the Spirits was published in the United Kingdom by Scarlet Imprint, Bucknell, SY7 0AH.
Copyright © Gordon White, 2016. Designed by Alkistis Dimech; text set in Magma Pro, and titling in Anacharsis.
The standard hardback and paperback editions were printed and bound by Gomer Press and the fine edition was
bound by Ludlow Bookbinders.

Image credits: Cover) 'Rocky Shore And Sea Against Sky At Night' by Rahmat Ahmadi / EyeEm.1) Author's collection; 2)
copyright © Teomancimit / Wikimedia Commons / CC BY-SA 3.0; 12) Photograph of Seal H-9 *(115, ASI 80.2.4) courtesy*
of the Archaeological Institute of India; 13) Photograph of Seal M-304 *(DK 5175, NMI 143) courtesy of the National*
Museum of India; 14) copyright © Raymbetz / Wikimedia Commons / CC BY-SA 3.0; *16) William Henry Goodyear,*
*Brooklyn Museum Archives (*S10.08 *Sakkara, image 99); 17) Brooklyn Museum Archives (*S10-08 *Sakkara, image 9643).*
Maps etc. redrawn for this publication. All other images public domain / copyright free.